THE LAW CAN WORK FOR YOU
IN PROTECTING THE ENVIRONMENT

The many ways in which the law has been used and can be used should not be a mystery to the individual citizen. Norman Landau and Paul Rheingold have set out to show exactly what can be done and how, in terms easily understood by laymen.

THE ENVIRONMENTAL LAW HANDBOOK is designed to go to work immediately in the hands of lawyer and citizen alike.

Survival in the 70s
Depends Upon Your Being Informed

THE ENVIRONMENTAL LAW HANDBOOK

Norman J. Landau
and
Paul D. Rheingold

A FRIENDS OF THE EARTH/BALLANTINE BOOK
An Intext Publisher
NEW YORK

SBN 345-01995-4-125

First Printing: June, 1971

Printed in the United States of America

FRIENDS OF THE EARTH
30 East 42 Street, New York, N.Y. 10017
451 Pacific Avenue, San Francisco, California 94133
917 15th Street, N.W., Washington, D.C. 20005

BALLANTINE BOOKS, INC.
101 Fifth Avenue, New York, N.Y. 10003

"Environmental Degradation and Legal Action" by An-
thony A. D'Amato, from THE BULLETIN OF THE
ATOMIC SCIENTISTS (March 1970). Copyright ©
1970 by the Educational Foundation for Nuclear Science.
Reprinted by permission of Science and Public Affairs
(Bulletin of the Atomic Scientists).

"Civil Cause of Action for Lung Damage Due to Pollution of Urban Atmosphere" by Paul D. Rheingold, from
33 BROOKLYN LAW REVIEW. Copyright © 1966 by
Brooklyn Law School. Reprinted by permission.

"Pollution, Law, Science, and Damage Awards" by
Thomas M. Schmitz, from 18 CLEVELAND STATE
LAW REVIEW (January 1969). Copyright © 1969 by
Cleveland-Marshall Law School. Reprinted by permis-
sion.

"Air and Water Pollution: What To Do While Waiting
for Washington" by John C. Esposito, from HARVARD
CIVIL RIGHTS-CIVIL LIBERTIES LAW REVIEW
Vol. V (January 1970). Copyright © 1970 by the Harvard Civil Rights-Civil Liberties Law Review. Reprinted
by permission.

"What Can The Citizen Do About Air Pollution" by
Richard T. Marshall and Larry H. Schwartz. Prepared
for the El Paso League of Women Voters. Reprinted by
permission of the authors.

"DDT: After The Sound And Fury" by William H.
Rodgers, Jr. Reprinted by permission of the University
of Washington.

We are indebted to many lawyers who have provided us with copies of legal papers and information about lawsuits in which they have been involved.

We dedicate this book to our wives, Marjorie and Joyce, and to our children, who will inherit this planet in the condition we leave it.

Contents

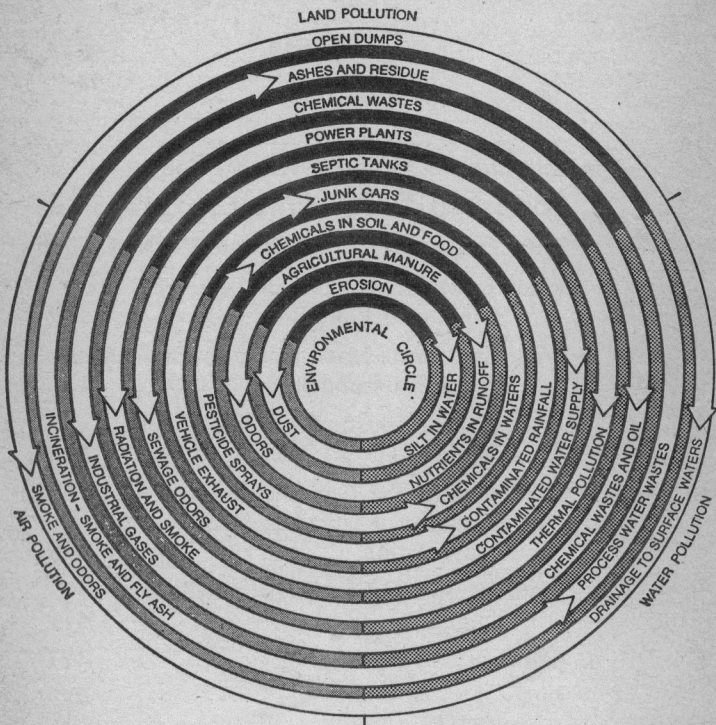

ENVIRONMENTAL CIRCLE

Showing Many Kinds of Pollution and the Effect on the Total Environment

LAND POLLUTION
OPEN DUMPS
ASHES AND RESIDUE
CHEMICAL WASTES
POWER PLANTS
SEPTIC TANKS
JUNK CARS
CHEMICALS IN SOIL AND FOOD
AGRICULTURAL MANURE
EROSION
ENVIRONMENTAL CIRCLE

SILT IN WATER
NUTRIENTS IN RUNOFF
CHEMICALS IN WATERS
CONTAMINATED RAINFALL
CONTAMINATED WATER SUPPLY
THERMAL POLLUTION
CHEMICAL WASTES AND OIL
PROCESS WATER WASTES
DRAINAGE TO SURFACE WATERS
WATER POLLUTION

DUST
ODORS
PESTICIDE SPRAYS
VEHICLE EXHAUST
SEWAGE ODORS
RADIATION AND SMOKE
INDUSTRIAL GASES
INCINERATION – SMOKE AND FLY ASH
SMOKE AND ODORS
AIR POLLUTION

NEW YORK STATE DEPARTMENT OF HEALTH

Nelson A. Rockefeller, Governor

Hollis S. Ingraham, M.D., Commissioner

THE
ENVIRONMENTAL
LAW HANDBOOK

Introduction

For decades the rampant contamination of air, water and soil by factories, mines and vehicles was treated by the law as a problem of "balance the equities." What this meant was simply that in the few cases that judges allowed to be tried, the equity of economic activity was balanced against the equity of human beings enjoying and using the natural environment and their property free from such pollutions. Almost invariably the industrial activity won against the right of citizens to be free from the environmental outrage wreaked upon their property and bodies. In the few cases where the industrial activity was enjoined, it was usually because of the foul smell of the emission, not the emphysema or cancer-producing characteristics of the gas or particulate matter. A reason for this anomaly is that there was no private or governmental institution that was researching and documenting these periods of pollution in ways that lawyers could use on behalf of aggrieved clients. "Out of the fact comes the law," goes the old Roman adage, and for generations the facts were either suppressed or not developed.

The times have changed. Environmental actions is a phrase which no longer puzzles listeners. Such action deals with the physical recovery of the earth and man from a technology whose imbalanced development is poisoning the natural habitat. Public awareness that pollution is more than something smelly and ugly that it is a silent, lethal, long range form of violence, is on the increase. The stage is set for creative legal action, which means more than relying on lawyers. Lawyers are a most cautious breed. This is particularly the case when the retainers are slim or nonexistent. Several conditions can help change the stagnant, unimaginative posture of lawyers in the pollution area. First is the emergence of citizen outrage and action oriented concern. Second is the understanding by citizens that lawyers do not always level with them about the possibilities of legal action against entrenched economic interest. Lawyers are very often part of this establishment or they do not like to take new kinds of cases with which the law is not familiar or they do not like to take cases where the fee is speculative or the labor is long. Two lawyers, Paul Rheingold and Norman Landau, who have brought together the materials in this book, do and think otherwise. They adhere to the view that non-lawyers have read about the potential range of legal rights which exist or can be developed to protect the environment and reduce the serious hazards of pollution. They have dared, moreover, to produce a book directed to both lawyers and non-lawyers in order to show to all both the potential of the law and its grossly underdeveloped state as far as environmental pollution is concerned. Finally, they display the tools that need to be used and the legal imagination and obligation that are required to discipline the polluter. This book may proliferate hundreds of deserved law suits to curb this industrial and individual violence to our environment. The more quickly it becomes obsolete, the more signal its success. Let the readers make it obsolete fast.

—RALPH NADER

CHAPTER 1

HOW TO MAKE THIS BOOK WORK FOR YOU

3

HOW TO MAKE THIS BOOK WORK FOR YOU

1.1 The Power of The Private Law Suit

This book is about environmental law and specifically about how the citizen can use the legal process to improve the environment.

We believe that the major fight against pollution today is going on in the courtroom. We, the authors, believe that it is through the legal process that the primary attack on the pollution problems of this country will be made and solved. Hence, for you, the citizen, to participate fully in this process, it is essential that you understand the operation of the law.

To illustrate the power of the environmental suit by the citizen or industry, we set forth a few examples, taken from events of the past year:

• Filling in by a state of a portion of the Hudson River to create an ill-placed highway was stopped by a suit of conservation groups. (See §6.6. We have numbered every section of this book to increase ease of making cross references. Thus "§6.6" means Chapter 6, Part 6.)

• The government was forced by a private suit instituted by conservationists to take action prohibiting the sale of DDT—action it had long been procrastinating in taking (see §4.10).

• A road through Alaskan wilderness was stopped dead by a citizens' suit as a violation of national environmental policies [see §1.11(a)].

• A smeltery was forced to terminate all air pollution as a result of a suit by a professor of law (see §5.4).

7

In assigning to the legal process a major if not the predominant role in the eradication of pollution, we do not mean to denigrate the other significant forces at work in this country: governmental pressures, efforts of citizens' groups, technological advances, and the like. At the same time, we feel quite strongly that the private lawsuit by a citizen presents a solution to the ecological problems of this nation that is unique.

One of the few experts in ecological law, Victor J. Yannacone, jr., has had this to say: "The courtroom is the last arena where the individual citizen can meet mighty government or big business and hope to survive. Thomas Becket and Thomas More are only two of the many that have died so that you the citizen can have your day in court. The environment—the very breath of life—needs the protection of those courts now."

When we speak of the legal process, we mean the whole concatenation of the law: civil lawsuits in court; criminal actions by the people; statutes passed by legislatures; administrative regulations and actions; and even the political process itself. Each of these can represent paths to environmental control. Some can work against it, however. This is especially true of the actions of the administrative branch, which not only may fail to stop pollution by others but may itself contribute to it.

You may ask if it would not be better for you to leave lawsuits to the lawyers and for the citizenry to concentrate on the many "around-the-house" steps which can be taken to eradicate environmental degradation. Certainly, we do not advocate abandonment of all of the self-help methods nor of the political process. But we do say that it is the private suit that will scour the environment as virtually no other method will.

This book is intended for the layman as well as the lawyer. You will find it, for the most part, as readable as any book for the layman. And even the out-and-out law sections with concentration are no more difficult to understand than is, say, a good scientific piece on pollution. The primary purpose of the chapter you are now reading is to introduce you to the legal concepts involved in environmental law so that you will be able to understand the following chapters in the book.

The private suit can seek damages for injury and can seek an injunction to prevent further pollution (see §1.9). It can be against a private polluter or against the government (§§1.11, 1.12). It can be on a whole range of legal theories including negligence, nuisance, trespass, and strict liability (see §1.7). And it can be maintained by an individual, by a group of persons—such as an established conservation group or an ad hoc citizens' group—or by a class of persons—a device allowing one person to sue for all persons similarly affected (see §1.10).

The private suit to vindicate public rights is not a development merely in ecology cases. It has already been put to good use in civil rights cases, where one student suing on his right to attend an integrated school is going to integrate the whole school system. It has been used in consumer cases, where the reforming of one unconscionable installment sales contract will change a whole industry's practices. Wide use and success has been made of the private suit in the products liability cases, where showing that one person was injured by the carelessness of a pill manufacturer opens the way for a national change in practice.

The courts have rightly described the person bringing the private lawsuit on account of a public interest as acting as a "private attorney general." And so you will be. In fact, you may have started such a good suit that the state will appoint you deputy attorney general to continue the suit on behalf of the public, as actually occurred last year when Milton Kelner, a dedicated Miami lawyer, sued factories, power companies and towns located on or near Biscayne Bay for water pollution.

When an administrative body becomes interested in exercising its power to clean up the air or water, it is often met with staggering political pressures. The local legislator gives it a call. The industry involved puts in a behind-the-scenes appearance. If the administrative body has been around a while, it listens more to those it is supposed to regulate than to those for whom it has been entrusted to act. These political and commercial pressures are largely absent in the private lawsuit. It is just for you, your lawyer, your opponent, and the judge. What higher use can be made of the courthouse?

We have provided in this book almost all of the basic information needed to understand environmental law and to bring a lawsuit. In our opinion this calls for the following:

(a) an analysis of the written laws, especially federal statutes (Chapter 3);

(b) an analysis of the leading cases (precedents) in the area (Chapter 4);

(c) a selection from leading articles on the law (Chapter 2);

(d) comments and papers on the cases going on right now in the courts (Chapters 5 and 6);

(e) an explanation of how you prove a pollution case in court (Chapter 7).

A word about legal citations. Do not be concerned about the numbers you see when we discuss law cases. These are the legal abbreviations for the books in which cases appear. (If you are curious, however, it works this way: by example, "360 U.S. 570 (1970)" means that the case in question is in the 360th book of United States Supreme Court decisions at page 570 and that the case was decided in 1970.)

Even though you need to understand the legal process in order to make it work for you, the layman cannot handle his own lawsuit. Hence, we include a section (§1.5) on dealing with lawyers. But you will get more out of your lawyer, and will be better able to understand and direct his activities if you master what is in this book. After all, he never had a course on environmental law either.

1.2 The Scope of the Problem

As to what the problems are which threaten the environment, we do not intend to catalog and discuss them here in this book—merely to suggest what the law can do about them. There are many sources giving information as to what problems are posed today. (See the list of suggested reading at the end of this chapter.)

It is important, however, for us to indicate the type of environmental problems with which the private lawsuit can deal effectively. This is indicated as follows:

1. Air pollution—from one or many sources
2. Water pollution—from one or many sources
3. Thermal and radiation pollution from power plants
4. Radiation pollution—as from machinery and television sets
5. Pesticide hazards—as they affect food, water, and persons
6. Conservation of resources—land and wasting assets
7. Solid waste disposal problems
8. Noise pollution—as from SSTs
9. Fish and wildlife preservation
10. Protection of waterways
11. Public land use control
12. Billboards and other esthetic issues
13. Strip mining
14. Highway routing
15. Continental shelf and underseas exploitation
16. Population management

There is another, major significance to the sort of division which has just been drawn. Numbers 1–6 represent the area of private litigation and the area where persons have been directly injured in their person or property. We concede, of course, that other authors might well stress the conservation concern as compared to the injury concern, and the role of government as compared to the role of the private lawsuit. While we have covered all of these bases, including most of the topics in 7–16, we prefer to believe in the power of the lawsuit.

Occupational hazards to health is a special area that we give only indirect attention to in this book. Almost all states have written rules (statutes and regulations) which deal with injuries which arise on the job due to occupational hazards. Examples of such hazards are the lung dust diseases (pneumoconiosis), asbestosis, beryllium poisoning, lead poisoning, benzine poisoning, radiation hazards. The risks to the worker in modern commerce are almost endless, really.

These occupational disease laws work as part of the workmen's compensation laws of the states: they make money awards to workers for their injuries. These awards are a payment of their medical expenses and their lost wages (the latter being measured by rather complicated formulas). These are not so much private suits as they are administrative actions. Thus, we do not discuss them generally here, but their importance should not be overlooked, if only because a succession of such suits may have a lot to do directly with environmental quality improvement. What manufacturer is going to go on exposing all of his workers to some sort of toxicity unnecessarily when he realizes the penalties he will have to pay?

1.3 The Development of Environmental Law

It is only within the last year or two that the term "environmental law" has come into common usage, even though in that brief time it has grown to be an important part of our jurisprudence. At the same time there is actually very little *new* law in the field of environmental law. It is more a conglomeration of legal doctrines which had their start in other fields of law and have existed for a long time. However, in the process of being applied to the pollution and conservation problems at hand, these old doctrines have been greatly modified, once again proving the ability of law to adapt itself to new legal challenges. A good example of the law's ability to adapt is in the law of standing —the question of "who may sue" has been answered by the inclusion of new citizens' groups and conservation groups which never before had any standing in court [see §1.11 (a)].

The sources of the explosion of environmental law are basically two: the conservation suits and the pollution suits. The conservation type of suit is exemplified by the one brought by the Sierra Club to prevent the filling in of the Hudson River to create a new highway (see §6.6). In this area, a citizens' group or conservationist organization seeks to stop the government from taking a step which would degrade the environment. The suit is not to recover damages for property loss or personal injury, but to enjoin conduct which, if it ever came to pass, would cause irreparable harm to the environment. Many of the groups active in this area are listed in §1.4, along with an indication of the type of suits they have been bringing. It has been the willingness of these organizations to go to court —and their belligerence once they have gotten to court— that has led to many important decisions in environmental law.

The second source of present-day environmental law may be illustrated by the suit of a person living near a beryllium factory who develops lung damage, or by a farmer whose cattle die due to upstream water pollution. This is the area of nuisance, negligence and trespass law, which is covered in detail in §1.7. This law is of very early origin—in fact, it was adopted by the colonies from England. Lawsuits in this area generally involve claims for money damages, as well as an injunction to prevent the commission of future pollution. The emphasis is upon eradication of what has been done, not on the prevention of damages to as yet unspoiled lands.

Law modifies itself to meet social needs. In the past decade litigation in the courts has centered on civil rights issues. We believe that in the 1970s the leading challenge in the courts will be environmental considerations. And the leading concern of our federal and state legislatures in this decade will be to turn out laws responsive to the social drive for protection of the environment.

1.4 Conservation Groups and Lawyers Active in Environmental Litigation

The following discussion of lawyers and groups active in the new field of environmental law is both a suggestion of persons who may assist the citizen in bringing an environmental suit and a review of the type of litigation currently pending in the courts.

(a) The Sierra Club

This organization was involved quite early in environmental litigation. The cases in which it has been a party include the Hudson Highway case (§6.6), the action against the government for allowing the Disney organization to build a road to a proposed alpine village in a national park [§1.11(a)], and the action against Secretary of the Army Resor for threatened destruction of the Gila River in Arizona [§1.11(a)]. An instance of testimony by a Sierra Club witness at a conservation trial is set forth in §7.1.

(b) Friends of the Earth

FOE was one of the parties bringing suit against former Secretary of the Interior Hickel for the wrongful issuance of a permit for the construction of a road over Alaska's tundra which would serve oil company interests [§1.11(a)].

(c) The National Audubon Society

One of the parties in the action against two departments of the government for their failure to take DDT off the market promptly was the Audubon Society (§6.2). Through the end-pages of its magazine, *Audubon*, it recounts the legal battles in the environmental field.

(d) The Wilderness Society

This group was another of the parties suing the government because of the proposed Alaskan road.

(e) The National Parks and Recreation Association

A witness from the organization testified in the Storm King case (see §7.1).

(f) The Izaak Walton League

The League was one of the plaintiffs in the Florida Power and Light case (see §5.1) and in the Washington DDT action (§4.10).

(g) The Environmental Defense Fund

The Fund differs from the preceding groups in that it was founded especially to bring lawsuits in this area. Located at 162 Old Town Rd., E. Setauket, N. Y., its motto is, "EDF takes environmental offenders to court to get results." That it has done, in such cases as the Washington DDT action, the Cross Florida Barge Canal case [see §1.11(a)], and the Alaska road case. Executive director is Roderick A. Cameron, a lawyer; general counsel is Edward Lee Rogers.

(h) Natural Resources Defense Council

A new legal organization dedicated to protection of natural resources, defense of the environment, and service as a clearinghouse on environmental law is Natural Resources Defense Council, Inc., 36 West 44th Street, New York, New York. This group was organized in 1970 and is headed by Stephen P. Duggan, a Wall Street lawyer. Its board of directors reads like a who's who in conservation. Executive director and counsel is John H. Adams, formerly Assistant U.S. Attorney in New York.

(i) National Pollution Control Foundation

This newly-formed New York organization aims to work with industry in controlling pollution through the creation of a world legal data bank listing all state, national, international, and even local pollution laws, along with the establishment of a research center at the University of Texas Law School.

(j) David Sive

Mr. Sive is one of the leading lawyers in the field of conservation cases. His offices are in Manhattan. He has been involved in many cases including the Storm King case, the Hudson Highway case, and the Hilton Head case. The latter was a successful suit by residents of a wild spot in South Carolina to prevent construction of a factory by a German manufacturer, Badische Anilin und Soda Fabrik, A.G.

(k) Victor J. Yannacone, jr.

This Patchogue, N.Y., lawyer became involved in environment suits in the early 1960s. Much of his early work was with EDF. He has had important victories in the DDT cases (see §6.2), the Florida Everglades Airport action (see §6.5), and in the Florissant fossil beds case, where he saved an important record of Colorado's natural history from destruction.

(l) Other Lawyers

In this book we have had occasion to refer to legal writings and lawsuits by such leading practitioners as Bernard S. Cohen of Alexandria, Va. (see §5.7); Richard Marshall of El Paso, Texas (§2.5); Berlin, Roisman & Kessler of the District of Columbia; Roger J. Diamond of Los Angeles (§5.6); Professor Joseph L. Sax of the University of Michigan [§1.10(b)]; Professor Eva Hanks of Rutgers Law School [§1.11(a)]; John C. Esposito, on Ralph Nader's staff [§1.6(a)]; and James Moorman of the Center for Law and Social Policy (§4.10). Reference should also be made to Professor David Currie of the University of Chicago Law School, and Malcolm Baldwin, lawyer for the Conservation Fund, Washington, D.C.

In addition to the names above, one in search of a lawyer may want to consult the nearest law school, which is likely to have a professor active in the area and a student environmental law organization. The American Civil Liberties Union has also shown great interest in the area.

1.5 See Your Local Attorney

When we speak, as we do throughout this book, of the power of the private suit and the right of the citizen to go to court to sue some polluter, we don't mean it literally. We envision that the suit will be handled by a lawyer, one who is knowledgeable about environmental litigation. It is true, of course, that there is no requirement that a suit be commenced by a lawyer—it can be commenced, per se, by the citizen in person. Such suits have a disastrous history in the courts, however, because there are many procedural requirements to maintaining a lawsuit—requirements which even the lawyer generally has to look up in his lawbooks.

When you consult your local lawyer, you can tell him

what the pollution problem is and what you have gleaned from reading herein that supports your viewpoint that a suit should be brought. Your family lawyer may be knowledgeable in this area, or he may feel that the best thing is to refer you to a specialist.

If a group of persons are interested in suing, one thing your lawyer can do before he commences suit for you is to give your group some organizational character. Most likely he will want to incorporate the group into something like "Citizens for Clear Air, Inc." or "Committee to Preserve the Raritan." There are many benefits to corporate status, one of which is enhanced standing in the eyes of the court. Information may be found in the handbook, "Corporate and Tax Problems of Conservation Organizations", published by the Conservation Foundation, 1717 Connecticut Ave., N.W., Washington, D.C.

(a) Selecting a Lawyer

How do you select a lawyer in the first place? Our primary advice is to see your family lawyer—the man who you have confidence in by virtue of some other things he has done for you—written a will, represented you at a real estate closing, whatever it may have been. Or ask your friends. Or call the local legal aid or bar association service or your town's attorney. Or watch the papers for names of lawyers who have been bringing suits or speaking out against pollution. Or note who is the lawyer who is speaking at the next meeting on pollution.

(b) Paying the Lawyer

Most attorneys handle cases on a fee basis. That is, they are used to either being paid on an hourly rate or receiving an agreed upon amount at the end of the job (plus a retainer). In personal injury cases, most attorneys are used to working on the contingent fee basis whereby they take a percentage (frequently one third) of whatever is recovered for the persons. If nothing is recovered, they receive no legal fee.

If the pollution action you are taking to your attorney involves a claim for damages and not just an injunction, and if the damages are more than a nominal amount—if they are intended as compensation for real injuries [see §1.9(a)]—then the promise to pay the lawyer by a contingent fee may be an adequate (if not more than an adequate) inducement to him to handle the case. If for example you have developed a lung condition due to pollution, the typical arrangement you would enter into is to give the lawyer a percentage—and most lawyers would enter into such an agreement.

On the other hand, what if the lawyer is not going to be recovering any money for you at all? What if the relief you desire is merely to stop pollution—by abatement or injunction. In this instance, it would be nice to be able to pay the lawyer his hourly rate (often $25 to $50 an hour), or to agree to pay him a set sum upon completion of the task (a sum which would somehow reflect the anticipated hours of his time). But it will often happen that you cannot afford to pay this sum of money or any sum that is substantial. This is true, often, because the very people most concerned about pollution are those who can least afford to pay for legal services.

One solution is to find a fund which will pay him, or to interest a group, such as a conservation group, to join in with you. Conservation groups may have lawyers on retainers. There are a number of legal groups which are available, on a very selective case basis, either to bring an environmental suit or to assist local lawyers in doing so. Some of these groups are discussed in §1.4.

If the protection of lands is at stake, you can find support from those who may gain financially by the protection of the land. If the pollution of a stream is going to lower property values (or, to put it more realistically, if the purification of the waters by abatement of prior pollution is going to upgrade the value of surrounding property), then all of those property owners stand to gain financially from the suit—and may be willing to fund the lawsuit.

Another solution is to find the lawyer—rare as he may be—who is committed personally to combatting pollution, and who will donate his services to the cause. Many such lawyers do exist, especially younger ones, who will take on such a challenge. Of course, the actual costs of the litigation—filing fees, taking depositions, copying documents, and the like—could be paid by the client; it is the legal services which are performed for free.

A number of lawyers well versed in environmental suits are listed in §1.4 (*j-l*). And, as James Reston of *The New York Times* (April 26, 1970) recently observed:

> In every community, there are young lawyers eager to use all legal methods to enforce the new anti-pollution laws, and young men and women willing to work in the 1970 elections for candidates who will commit themselves to a cleaner and quieter environment.

In a later section we discuss punitive damages [§1.9 (*b*)], a sort of punishment which the court awards, not related to the injuries but to the conduct of the defendant. It may happen that you are going to sue for damages, but they are nominal. However, if the conduct complained of is wanton or gross enough, there may be a realistic claim and chance for recovery of a large punitive damages sum. To offer to the attorney a contingent fee in these damages may be the inducement needed to get him going. Or an action may lie in recovering a reward for information as to polluters [§1.10 (*f*)]—creating another fund to use for payments.

Another solution is the class action, a procedural device, discussed in §1.10 (*d*), that allows a great number of persons to sue at once. Each of their claims, taken separately, may be very slim. That is, each may have suffered only slight damages due to the inhalation of vapors from some nearby factory. But if the lawyer is suing for 10,000 persons, each with his "minimal" $1000 suit, he is now suing for $10,000,000, and a contingent share of a recovery of that magnitude will hold great interest. Hence it is another benefit of the class suit for the environment that it allows the filing of suits for which no attorney could otherwise be found.

1.6 The Statutory Framework—Laws on Pollution

The rules of law that govern any sort of an environmental suit come from two basic sources. (1) written laws:

—constitutions (the highest law of the land), statutes (passed by federal and state legislatures), ordinances (passed by cities and towns), and rules and regulations (promulgated by administrative bodies in filling out and defining statutes and ordinances); (2) decisions of a court. Court decisions do two things primarily. They explain and interpret the written laws just mentioned and they create new rules themselves. It is this latter function that had caused the expansion of the law over hundreds of years, creating a body of precedents known as the "common law." The common law is regarded as unwritten law in that it is not codified in any one place—it is in all of the cases taken together. Its particular genius is that it can expand to meet the changing needs of a changing world.

In this section we are interested in what the written laws are relating to pollution; in §1.7 we consider what the judge-fashioned common law actions are. For one contemplating a citizen's suit against pollution, the common law gives most of the legal remedies today.

It is nonetheless important to study the statutory framework. First, a written law may well be the basis for a private pollution suit [see (c) below]. Second, knowing the powers a government has against polluters is some indication of what may be expected from that government in itself eradicating pollution, even if the government may be somewhat lethargic (see §1.4). Third, where the government has a statutory power but is failing to exercise it fully, a private suit may lie against the government to compel it to act (see §1.11). And, fourth, the statutes and regulations may be useful in a private civil suit to establish standards of care which it can be said the polluter failed to meet (see Chapter 7).

The statutes and ordinances which give federal, state, and local governments power to act against those who defile the environment are partly penal and partly administrative. Without plunging into a whole law course, we should at least point out that this means that some of these governmental rules are part of the criminal law which provides a penal sanction, by action for fine or imprisonment. See, for example, The *Harbors and Rivers Act,* §3.1 (*e*): up to a year in jail for water pollution for violation of the law. Other parts of the law are considered as administrative, in which the government's remedy is by way of civil action and may be the power to prevent the pollution (such as a "cease and desist order") or to fine the polluter. Or, it may be the administrative power to conserve land or protect wildlife. A good example of administrative action is the recent ruling by the Federal Water Quality Administration banning thermal pollution of Lake Michigan. The ruling prevented the discharge of water into the lake that was even 1°F more than the lake's temperature at that point.

(a) Federal Laws

An extensive set of powers and interests have been given to the administrative branches of our federal government in the environmental area by Congress, especially by legislation passed in the last decade. There is at present such an interest in passing laws in the ecology area, as a matter of fact, that many of the laws which we discuss in this book are presently pending revision in Congress. Because of the paramount importance of the federal laws on the environment, we have set forth the various acts in Chapter 3 of this book, along with quotations from some of the sections which explain the purpose and aims of Congress in passing the laws.

The typical federal act first sets forth its policy. It assigns responsibilities to an agency. It states what acts are to be prohibited, but only in broadest category, looking to administrative regulations to spell this out. And it sets forth the penalties for violation of either this general provision or any regulations promulgated pursuant to the law. It often sets up commissions to study and research the problems.

The agency granted responsibilities under the new law then formulates regulations, which spell out and give detail to the aims of the law. These regulations are often more important in daily practice than the act because they describe in minute detail what the standards are to be, such as the desired purity of the air or water. They also explain what means are required to achieve these ends.

Standing as a sort of national declaration on the environment is the recently passed National Environmental Policy Act of 1969 [discussed in §3.1(a)]. This law has been described as a "Bill of Rights" for the environment, and is in effect paramount among the federal laws. It instructs all federal agencies to consider the ecological ramifications of their acts. And it sets up the Council on Environmental Quality to oversee the nation's efforts on pollution.

The organization of the federal government in the attack against pollution has undergone frequent revision in the past few years. At the present time, the majority of the environmental efforts are grouped under the Environmental Protection Agency (EPA). The following are its consolidated departments:

- *water pollution:* Federal Water Quality Administration, transferred from the Department of Interior
- *air pollution:* National Air Pollution Control Administration, transferred from the Department of Health, Education and Welfare
- *pesticides:* programs transferred from the Departments of Interior, Agriculture and HEW
- *radiation:* Functions transferred from Atomic Energy Commission, Federal Radiation Council, and Bureau of Radiological Health of HEW
- *solid waste:* Bureau of Solid Waste Management, transferred from HEW
- *ecological systems study:* transferred from Council of Environmental Quality

By the same reorganization plan (created by President Nixon with Congressional approval), there was established a National Oceanic and Atmospheric Administration within the Department of Commerce. The functions of the previous Environmental Science Services Administration were merged into NOAA. At the time of this general reorganization, President Nixon explained that the role of the Council of Environmental Quality was to function at the White House level to make recommendations for programs.

The new Environmental Protection Agency has been highly active since birth. Pursuant to the mandates of the Clean Air Act [see § 3.1(c)], it has proposed national air quality standards. These standards are applicable to automobile exhaust. In 1971, EPA sought a delay in the construction of the Alaskan pipeline for hot oil because of its possible adverse environmental effects. However, also in 1971, it deferred immediate suspension of all uses of DDT and 2,4,5-T, on the basis that these pesticides were not imminent human hazards.

A recently released study by Nader's Raiders is must reading on the issue of the operation and reorganization of our efforts at a national level on air pollution. A Task Force Report on Air Pollution was issued in 1970 by the Center for Study of Responsive Law, with John C. Esposito as task force director. The report centers on the activities of the National Air Pollution Control Administration and points out many of its inadequacies in dealing with the pollution problem. The pressures of industry and of politics are documented, and criticism is made of the role of Senator Edmund Muskie in antipollution legislation. This study has been released as a book by John C. Esposito, *Vanishing Air*. (New York, Viking Press, 1970.)

(b) State and Local Laws

Every state and many counties, cities, towns, and villages have laws on their books on environmental protection. To even attempt to list by names or legal citation all of these laws—or even the chief ones at the state level— would be foolhardy. What we believe we can do is to inform the reader about the types of laws in general, as a guideline. And, as further aid, we set forth a model law on air pollution which can be used by a community (§3.4), and discuss a modern approach by a state to pollution (§3.3).

When we said before that your lawyer can sue for you, we didn't mean that your favorite lawyer will not have to look beyond this book for information. He is going to have to search out what the state and local laws and regulations are, and how they may affect a potential suit. If you work along with him, you will see that he will have considerable trouble finding out what the applicable local ordinances are. Unlike federal and state laws, which are all codified according to some logical system in a few books, local ordinances and rules tend to be a hodgepodge of rules, not printed in any one place nor produced in any logical order.

Another booby trap for the lawyer searching local laws —and often even state laws—is the old law which was never erased from the books even though it has been unused for decades. Every viewer of late-night TV movies recalls the brilliant young criminal lawyer who goes up on a ladder to the dustiest books at the top of the bookcase to discover some long-forgotten law which will free his client. This is really not a filmatic cliché because in the area of pollution there may be pay dirt among the dust. Your energetic lawyer may find some law, passed a century ago, which prohibits the placing of any substance into the waters within your state or local community. And that rule may open the way to a suit.

A number of states have comprehensive laws on pollution control, sometimes more extensive than the federal laws themselves. These include California (which leads the way in a number of areas, including air pollution), New York (known for its sanitation laws), New Jersey, and Michigan (a leader in conservation). New York recently reorganized from the ground up its environmental activities, constituting a valuable reference for other states (outlined in §3.3). A glimpse of California's extensive scheme is set forth in the legal papers in the famous Diamond action in §5.6. (Often a good pleading in a lawsuit will set forth the actual provisions of the law, rather than assuming that the judge and other persons who will be reading the papers are familiar with the many applicable laws.)

It should be noted that generally nothing prevents a state from passing laws more stringent on pollution than the federal government, and nothing stops a locality from being even stricter than the state or federal law [see Huron Cement case, §4.5 (c)]. In only rare instances is the federal law deemed to "preempt" the field so as to forbid state or local rules which are tougher on polluters [see discussion in D'Amato article, §2.1 (b)].

In some instances, a state's constitution may be helpful. The constitution is the fundamental set of rules of the state, passed by the people at a constitutional assembly. It has a higher status than any law passed by the state legislature; hence such laws are to be within the powers and purposes of the constitution. New York, for instance, has an interesting set of provisions in its constitution dealing with conservation (see quotation in §3.3). This also contains the famous "forever wild" provision—that lands held by the state shall be forever wild, and "wild" means without roads, structures, and the like. In fact, if use of the land is contemplated, such as for skiing or other purpose, the constitution will have to be amended by the cumbersome provisions applicable to constitutional amendments.

Researchers should check carefully what county and townships have done in the pollution area, generally by rules set forth by a Board or Department of Health. With the growing interest in environmental protection, many cities, towns, and villages have put ordinances on the books in this area. To take a "for instance," the home town of one of the authors, Mamaroneck, New York, has a village ordinance which deals with its harbor, a noted community asset on Long Island Sound. Chapter 9, §8, of the laws prohibits the discharge into the water by any means of any litter or anything else (itemizing such things as soapy water, noxious liquids, junk, and garbage).

One purpose for giving the attention we do here to laws and regulations is that the reader may be in a position to improve the rules of his own state or locality. If there is in some other state a law which would be desirable in his state, he can present a copy of it or a citation to it to his local elected representative for consideration. Indeed, the reader may be a member of the state legislature or of some county or town board.

(c) Rights to Bring a Suit Granted by Statute

Most of the causes of action which will be brought for pollution effects are based upon the common law, as we have previously described. A few exist because a statute or some other written law creates or allows the suit. One good example of a suit created by statute is the antitrust action [discussed in §1.7(*f*)] which arises by virtue of the Clayton Antitrust Act. Another is the environmental action law passed in 1970 in Michigan [see §1.10(*c*)].

If the courts do not fashion an adequate legal remedy for suit by consumers and those who want to protect the environment generally, then there will be pressure upon state legislatures to pass special laws authorizing suits against pollution and for conservation purposes. On the whole, the flexibility of a court-fashioned remedy is preferable to rigidities of a law.

1.7 What Are the Legal Theories Available for Suing Polluters?

Every lawsuit needs a legal theory, and an environmental suit is no exception. If anything, such a suit involves a more complicated search for a sufficient legal foundation than the more prosaic type of suit usually being brought in courts today.

The first place to look for a possible basis for a pollution suit is the statutory law itself. We have already discussed statutes in the environmental area and have compared that source of law to the judge-made common law (see §1.6). The suit in this area actually authorized by the terms of a statute is a *rara avis*. In fact, we discuss here but one such instance: the antitrust action brought pursuant to the terms of the Clayton Antitrust Act [see (*f*) below]. Statutes also have relevance in defining who has standing to sue (see §1.10).

If a statute does not create a right to sue in so many words, then lawyers inquire if there is nonetheless some statute which has language related to the wrong to be righted. This is because in some instances the violation of a statute, even though it empowers only a governmental unit to enforce its provisions, may constitute the basis for a "negligence per se" cause of action. Such a cause of action is deemed to be one at common law for negligence, but its basis is the violation of the provisions of the statute. As a rule the only type of statute the violation of which can give rise to this negligence per se action is one which (a) is directed against the type of conduct which the defendant has committed and (b) was passed to protect persons in the same class that the plaintiff is in.

With all of the technicalities surrounding the founding of a common lawsuit on the violation of an environmental statute, it is not surprising that there are few examples today of such an action in the environmental area. There are many new laws going on the books in the pollution area, however, and it is predictable that this type of suit will become more common in the future. And it should be noted that any type of law on the books can be of value to a plaintiff bringing a private suit: it may help to set the standard by which the defendant is to be judged. That is, even though the suit is not based upon the violation of the terms of the statute, the fact of violation is some evidence of want of due care in a common lawsuit. On the use of statutes in this fashion, see Chapter 7.

Almost all of the pollution suits we consider in this book are simply actions at common law based upon the legal theories developed over the years. It is this source that will continue to give direction and shape to the citizen's private environmental suit for many years to come. At the same time, many changes are called for in the present attitude of the courts because many of the precedental decisions on the books do not favor the private suit. Says James B. Coulter, designer of the State of Maryland's comprehensive plan for resource management: "Our whole system of common law and water control is based on protecting the rights of polluters."

We begin this section with a discussion of three legal theories which have been well-developed in the courts for many decades and have been frequently applied to pollution cases: negligence, trespass, and nuisance. We then consider the newly emerging areas: ultrahazardous liability, product liability, antitrust actions, maritime suits, shareholder suits, and inverse condemnation. The two newest theories—with perhaps the most promise for the successful pollution suit—are considered in the next section (§1.8): the constitutional right to a clear environment and the "trust" action.

(a) Negligence

Negligence is the most ample legal theory available for use. Simply stated, the concept of negligence is the concept of carelessness: that the person or persons being sued deviated from the standard of care the law declares that they owed the plaintiff (person suing), and therefore are responsible for the injuries sustained by virtue of that deviation.

There is ample precedence in the law for the application of the negligence, or carelessness, theory of liability to the polluter. In the simplest sort of case, one who lives next door to a polluter, and who has thereby suffered property damage, personal injury, or both, has traditionally been allowed to sue the adjoining polluter on this theory. To win, he must bear the burden of proving that the polluter—let us say a factory—was careless in causing noxious emissions. Put in a more technical way, he must bear the burden of proof that the conduct of the polluter, by virtue of acts or omissions (it makes no difference generally) failed to come up to that standard of care which the reasonable person in his position would have, under all of the circumstances.

Of course, as we point out continually, allegation is one thing, proof is another. Thus, if one is not going to be able to come up with proof of carelessness in his case, then he should look further for a theory, other than negligence, upon which to sue. And, in every case, he must be prepared to show that his injuries are due to the conduct of the one sued.

Since a duty to use due care is at the heart of a negligence action, one of the pressing issues today is the duty of a manufacturer or other polluter to use the latest devices to arrest pollution. For example, must he adopt the latest emission precipitation devices on his smokestack, or does he meet his duty of care by using only that sort of devices which others around him are using? While this is a much debated question, without clear answers, the trend of the law is in favor of requiring the use of the best devices available. [See further discussion in (c) below; and see *Boomer* case, §5.5.]

Several of the articles in Chapter 2 discuss the primary negligence action (see, for example, Rheingold, §2.2). Many of the leading decided cases were founded in negligence [see, for example, *Yturbide,* §4.8(d); *Hagy,* §4.8(a); *Heck,* §4.8(b); and *Kelly,* §4.2(a)]. And, a number of the recently filed major pollution cases have also involved allegations of negligence, generally combined with other legal theories as well (see Chapters 5 and 6).

The point should be made that generally in the law there is no ban on joining a number of legal bases for recovery in one suit (complaint). This is so even if they are inconsistent, in the sense that the proof necessary to show one of these theories may actually undermine the other. As a rule, lawyers plead the whole world and then prove just what is going to work best at trial.

(b) Trespass

A cause of action for injury due to trespass is one of the ancient rights of action in the law. In simplest terms, it creates liability for damages following the entrance onto the land of another. It is not necessary that a person enter upon the land; a thing may. This legal theory differs from negligence in two essential ways: it is not necessary that one prove carelessness to win a trespass action, but there is, as a sort of counterbalance, a requirement in a trespass action that intent be proved. It must be shown that the defendant (person being sued) deliberately or intentionally caused the entry onto the plaintiff's land. The concept of "land" is not just literally one's earth, but all of his property, including his person, and including the air space over his land (up to a point).

The trespass theory has been used in pollution cases.

Most of the courts have had no trouble with what might be called visible, particulate trespass, that is, actual pieces of matter coming onto the plaintiff's land—rocks, ash, and so on. What had at one time given the courts problems is where it is gas, visible or invisible, toxic or merely odorous, which came onto another's land. Today the trespass action will clearly lie for this conduct. And the concept has been extended generally by the courts to what might be called an indirect trespass, as where vibrations from blasting enter the property through the earth.

The legal cause of action for trespass is discussed in the Rheingold article (§2.2) and was the basis of such key cases as *Renken* [§4.1(*b*)], *Martin* [§4.6(*d*)], and the Diamond Los Angeles case (§5.6).

(c) Nuisance

The law of nuisance is one that no lawyer in his right mind would want to discuss for his fellow lawyers let alone the layman. It has been called the most confusing of all of the tort areas of the law and defies simplification. Even after we have finished with the attempt at an analysis given below, we believe that it is just as easy to think of this legal theory in the everyday meaning of the word "nuisance."

Nevertheless, it is important to try to understand the concept of "nuisance" because it has immediate application to environmental actions. Indeed, it is the most widely relied upon theory today. One meaning for the concept of "nuisance" is unreasonable interference with the interest a person has in the enjoyment of property. This interference may be of the intentional variety, making the action similar to a trespass action [(*b*) above] except that the doing of substantial harm generally must be proved in the nuisance action. Or the interference may be of the negligent variety, making it similar to the negligence action [(*a*) above].

The law also makes a distinction between a "public" nuisance and a "private" nuisance. The discussion above is primarily about a private nuisance. There, generally only the person whose property rights have been interfered with may sue, as is true also in the trespass action. In the area of public nuisance, a defendant has, by act or omission, created damage to the public generally. Thus it is up to the public (the city or whatever) to abate the nuisance. A private person may sue for the commission of a public nuisance only if he suffers special damage, that is, more than suffered by the public generally.

The significance of a court branding a certain activity a nuisance is broader than merely the right it gives to one for damages. After all, damages may be awarded under the trespass or negligence theories [(a) and (b) above]. A determination that a nuisance exists also gives to the court the right to enjoin (stop) the conduct complained of. Relief by way of injunction is discussed in detail in §1.9(d). When a nuisance is enjoined, it is frequently referred to as an "abatement." How the nuisance is characterized may determine whether damages are to be awarded, as compared to an injunction, and what type of damages are to be awarded. For example, if it is a "permanent nuisance," then damages will be awarded for all of the injury done and to be done—damages for all future pollution [see §1.9(d)].

All types of polluting sources have been declared nuisances, as is brought out in the articles by Schmitz [§2.3(b)] and Rheingold (§2.2). The cause of action is an ideal one to counter pollution of water or air since that precisely is the sort of conduct for which the nuisance action was created by the courts. One of the limits of the action, however, is who may sue. In the private nuisance area, it is only the one owning or in possession of the property who may sue. In the public area, it is only when, as previously noted, a person or group of people have suffered a particular injury greater than that of the public which is exposed generally to the nuisance that a private suit can be maintained, and often this is held to require an injury of a different type, not one merely to a greater degree.

Intertwined in the concept of nuisance is the concept of reasonable use, which again distinguishes it from the trespass action [(b) above] or from the ultrahazardous action [(d) below]. The law recognizes that any use of land by one person may in some way interfere with the other's use of his land, and it attempts to balance conflicting interests. Thus, if the proposed defendant is making a reasonable use of his land, he will not be liable (for damages or injunction) under the nuisance theory where he injures the other to a not unreasonable amount. The two interests have to be balanced.

Factors to be considered in making a balance are the social utility of the defendant's conduct (including the public's interest in his business), the degree of injury to the plaintiff, and the reasonable means available to the defendant to avoid the damage. Thus, a gas works, needed by a city for its power, in an industrial area might not be a "nuisance," whereas a factory located in a predominantly residential area, putting out the same air pollutants in the production of parts for TV sets, might be a "nuisance."

Many of the precedent cases digested in Chapter 4 deal with nuisances [see, for example, *Whalen,* §4.1(a), *Renken,* §4.1(b); *Kelly,* §4.2(a); *Martin,* §4.6(d); and *Eastern Airlines,* §4.8 (c)]. Permanent nuisances are discussed in *Harrisonville* [§4.4(d)]. Instances where the government has brought the nuisance action are *Nourse* [§4.5(b)], and *Huron* [§4.5(d)]. And governments have been sued for committing a nuisance themselves, as in *Costas* [§4.4(a)], *Steiffer* [§4.4(b)], and the *Harrisonville* case.

Likewise, many of the presently pending pollution cases have been framed, at least in part, on the traditional nuisance theory (see, for example, the El Paso Asarco action, §5.2). Another good example of a successful nuisance action is Heine v. The Budd Company, No. 56172, Circuit Court for the County of Wayne, Michigan (1969). There, a Detroit lawyer, Donnelly W. Hadden, won compensation of $53,613 in 1969 for air pollution by the Budd Company in a suit brought by a citizens' group. The trial judge found that a nuisance, as defined by nineteenth century Michigan cases, was being committed. Shortly after the decision, the

Budd Company installed modern pollution abatement equipment (communication to authors by Mr. Hadden).

(d) Strict Liability—Ultrahazardous Activities

After the law had pretty well rounded out liability in the three areas of trespass, negligence, and nuisance, it expanded itself to meet the modern hazardous type of conduct which the twentieth century has evolved, by creating another theory of liability, often known as strict liability. This concept means that the defendant should pay for the damage he has done, under certain circumstances, even where he was not at fault.

Under this concept, where one carries on that type of activity which may be characterized as "extrahazardous" or "ultrahazardous" or "abnormally dangerous," he is made to pay for all the damages which follow even though he was not being careless and did not do the act intentionally. The point is that while he is allowed to engage in the conduct, because of its presumed social utility (and he cannot be enjoined from carrying it on), he must pay his way.

There is a decided trend of extension of the concept of strict liability to those who endanger the environment. In the earliest cases such liability was imposed for storing water on one's land (which flowed onto another's), or for blasting or setting fires. A most important precedent, the Luthringer case, is digested in §4.7(a). In that case, one who used pesticides was liable for their spread even if he didn't know it could occur and could not have prevented it.

Another case in which ultrahazardous liability was applied, this one involving a drifting crop spray, is *Chapman Chemical Co. v. Taylor,* 215 Ark. 630, 222 S.W. 2d 820 (1949).

(e) Product Liability

The law recognizes a special class of defendants who are sued because a product with which they have had connection causes injury to another. Common examples are the manufacturer of an automobile which has defective brakes, or the store which sells spoiled food. We need not concern ourselves here with the various legal theories which can be used, except to note that they may be negligence [(a) above], strict liability (also called warranty) [(d) above], or, rarely, fraud.

The product suit that has been suggested most commonly by a number of commentators in the environmental area is for air pollution from the internal combustion engine in automobiles. The defendants in these suits could be either (or both) the automobile manufacturers or the gasoline manufacturers. The most simple suit would be by one person against the manufacturer for a vehicle with a defective muffler (see Rheingold, §2.2).

A sophisticated pollution suit today would be against all of the automobile manufacturers, for mass pollution, brought by one injured person (let us say he has developed emphysema), or brought by a class of persons (such as all the residents of a city). Another sophisticated suit would be against all of the manufacturers of gasoline, let us say for the inclusion of tetraethyl lead in the gas or for other pollutants. [See general discussions of these types of suits in Rheingold, §2.2(b), and Esposito, §2.4(b)]. For suits brought under these theories, see the Diamond action, against all polluters in Los Angeles, §5.6, and the antitrust action against the "Big Four" automobile manufacturers for delaying pollution control, §4.7(b).

(f) Antitrust Actions

In one instance there is a statute which empowers a private cause of action in the environmental area, the *Clayton Antitrust Act*. Section 4 of that action (15 U.S.C. §15) states:

> Any person who shall be damaged in his business or property by reason of anything forbidden in the antitrust laws may sue therefor . . . and shall recover threefold the damages by him sustained, and the cost of suit, including a reasonable attorney's fee.

The type of activity in which one or more defendants might engage which would give rise to the suit in the pollution area is typified by the various antitrust actions brought because of the conspiracy of the Big Four automobile manufacturers to delay the use of pollution devices for automobile emissions. While the action originated with a Department of Justice suit on administrative aspects of federal antitrust laws, there have subsequently been filed many private suits for treble damages under the Clayton Act provision quoted above [see discussion of this case in §4.7(*b*) and discussion of treble damages in §1.9(*c*)].

(g) Maritime Suits

There is a whole body of law which we need but briefly describe which is known as admiralty or maritime law—special acts and court decisions which govern conduct on navigable water and the high seas. It is in these waters that the foul tort of polluting the water with oil has become so topical today.

At least one court has recently held that allowing the escape of oil into navigable waters gives rise to an action in admiralty for a new maritime tort. It allowed the State of California under the *Federal Maritime Act to* sue a ship which had committed the pollution, and it allowed an action against the ship itself, without requiring special service of papers, a great facilitation [see *California v. S.S. Bournamouth,* California Federal Court, 1970; also Mendelsohn, "Maritime Liability for Oil Pollution," 38 *George Washington Law Review* 1 (1969)]. Other actions may be based upon the 1966 amendments to the 1924 Oil Pollution Act.

(h) Shareholder Suits and Proxy Fights

In a thoughtful article which we present in Chapter 2, a lawyer on the staff of Ralph Nader's Raiders suggests that perhaps stockholders might have suits against corporations in which they hold shares to stop polluting activities by those companies [see §2.4(*c*)]. Mr. Esposito points out that minority groups of shareholders have always had the right to sue the management of their companies where their actions, or inactions, were injurious to the value of the stock.

The stockholder who is a public-spirited citizen might also seek to have certain resolutions put before the voting shareholders at the annual meeting of the corporation in question, as Mr. Esposito points out. That suggestion was put into practice in the action by Nader and others of submitting to the stockholders of General Motors for the 1970 annual meeting a resolution dealing with the protection of environmental quality.

An excellent example of a shareholder's suit against a corporation which is irresponsibly causing pollution is the Florida action brought in 1970 by Mrs. Abigail Starr Avery against Florida Power and Light Company and its officers. Mrs. Avery alleges mismanagement by the company because of its polluting of lower Biscayne Bay by operating power plants. She also alleges, by her attorney, Dan Paul of Miami, that the company is violating SEC law, is proceeding illegally in not obtaining permits, and is taking illegal steps in creating a canal which will spread the pollutants. She further accuses the management of misappropriating millions of dollars annually in attempting to convince the public that it is not polluting, rather than spending this same money in preventing pollution. For the state's suit against Florida Power and Light for the same water polluting, see §5.1.

(i) Inverse Condemnation

By its power of eminent domain the government may take your land from you, but it has to pay you fair compensation for it, of course. But what if, instead of an outright condemnation of your land, the government merely carries on near or over your land some type of activity which interferes with the usefulness of the land as it formerly was? For example, it builds an airport near your property and flies planes noisily over your land, ruining your health or cracking up your house.

The courts have developed the doctrine of "inverse condemnation" to make recompense for the deprival ("taking") of property interests created by a governmental activity which does not amount to the actual condemnation of land by eminent domain (as well as for any action by a person who has not been paid for the taking of his land). Under this power, persons have sued and collected damages for such acts as invasion of air space by airplanes, creating a nuisance such as a city power plant which emits smoke or odors, vibration injury due to blasting operations, or covering land with water (see 26 Am. Jur. 2d Eminent Domain §157 *et seq*).

1.8 The Constitutional Right to Clean Air and Water; The Trust Theory

In addition to those theories of liability discussed just above, there are a number of theories which revolve around "higher law"—provisions in the constitution and basic bills of rights. We have already explained that the constitution is supreme over the statutes and the decisions of courts, and this holds true nationally for the United States Constitution (with the Bill of Rights and other amendments), and the state constitutions.

(a) Constitutional Rights

Perhaps the freshest idea in a decade for actions against pollution is that there exists in the United States Constitution a right to have clean air and water and to protect our natural resources. Such a right, if it can be found in the Constitution, would readily form the basis for a suit against one who was threatening to deprive a citizen of any aspect of that right.

Concededly, there is nowhere in the Bill of Rights, or elsewhere in the Constitution, a statement that there is an inalienable right to clean air and water. However, some solid legal thinkers feel that a court can readily "find" the guarantee in the Bill of Rights, by reading between the lines if need be (see, for example, the Esposito article, §2.4). These lawyers point to two sources. One is the Ninth Amendment to the Constitution, the so-called "forgotten amendment." This recognizes that just because certain rights are listed in the Bill of Rights does not deny the fact that others did not exist and were always held by the people.

A strong argument can also be made that in the First Amendment (freedom of speech, religion, etc.) and the Bill of Rights generally, the right to an untrammeled environment exists—that, in effect, this is one of the fundamental, inherent rights that the people have always had.

An excellent analogy is the right to privacy, which the Supreme Court recently "found" in the Bill of Rights even though there is no reference to it therein. This was in *Griswold v. Connecticut,* 381 U.S. 479 (1965), which was a case involving the right of a married couple to receive birth control advice, notwithstanding a state law to the contrary.

The Fourteenth Amendment might also be looked to by a lawyer bringing a private suit against a state. It prohibits a state from depriving a person of life, liberty, or property without due process of law, denying him equal protection of the law, or abridging his privileges and immunities. (And a citizen of the United States enjoys protection from deprivation of life, liberty, or property without due process of law at the hands of the federal government by virtue of the Fifth Amendment.) While these restraints apply to governments, they may also be applied to individuals where "state action" is involved, as was alleged in a recent action in the federal court in New York against the principal manufacturers of DDT [see §6.6(c)].

One of the most comprehensive analyses of the role of the Bill of Rights in environmental protection is by David Sive [see §1.4(j)] which appears in the April 1970 issue of *Civil Liberties,* an *ACLU* newspaper. Mr. Sive places great emphasis upon the due process clause of the Fifth and Fourteenth Amendments, dwelling upon such cases as *Wolf v. Colorado,* 338 U.S. 25 (1949). He points out that the Ninth Amendment is relied upon in the Cross Florida Barge Canal case [see §6.4(a)] and that violation of the Fifth Amendment is pleaded in the Santa Barbara oil spill case (*Weingland v. Hickel,* No. 69-1317-EC, United States District Court, C.D. Cal.). The pleading refers to "the right to live in, and enjoy, an environment free from improvident destruction or pollution," and "the right to ownership, use, and enjoyment of property, free from improvident invasion or impairment." (See also §6.6.)

(b) An Environmental Bill of Rights

If the United States Constitution (and those of the states) does not give a right to the public in our area, how about adding an "Environmental Bill of Rights" to our laws? This has been seriously proposed by a number of scholars. Of course, this can probably be done by simply passing a new statutory law, without the necessity of the cumbersome process of constitutional amendment. And, of course, we have already pointed out that the National Environmental Policy Act of 1969 [see §1.6(*a*)] may create such a listing of rights, most notably by its statement that "each person should enjoy a healthful environment."

Students at Northwestern University Law School in 1969 proposed an Environmental Bill of Rights, seriously suggesting that it be added to the Constitution by amendment. This would cover the following four points:

1. an inalienable right to a clean environment;
2. power to the legislature to pass laws necessary to buy and preserve land in a wild state;
3. power of redress for a citizen if his environment is adversely affected by the government or any other person; and
4. power of a citizen to challenge any governmental action in which the government could not show that its acts would not adversely affect the environment.

(c) Trust Theory

A concept closely related to the constitutional issues just discussed is the so-called "trust doctrine" which has been advanced by a number of outstanding practicing lawyers, including Bernard Cohen and Victor J. Yannacone, jr. This doctrine builds upon a premise affirmed by the courts more than once: the land in this country is held in trust for the public generally. This applies not only to public land but to private land. Cases previously litigated which have involved the "trust doctrine" have dealt, for example, with rights in lands underwater.

Cohen, Yannacone, and many others believe that an action may lie against the government or against private parties for violation of this trust. Cohen has based his current Virginia suit against those who would take wild lands for the construction of apartments upon the violation-of-trust doctrine (see §6.5). The sale of the land to private interests would constitute a violation of the trust, as well as of the plaintiffs' rights, privileges, and immunities under the Constitution. For an extended discussion by a professor of law from the University of Michigan who has given considerable thought to this area, see Sax, "The Public Trust Doctrine in Natural Resource Law: Effective Judicial Intervention," 86 *Michigan Law Review* 471 (1970). Cohen's views may be found in "The Constitution, Public Trust Doctrine, and the Environment," *Utah Law Review,* June, 1970.

1.9 What Remedies Are Available—Damages and Injunctions

Fundamentally, there are but two sorts of remedies which a court can grant in a private environmental action. One is the payment of money as recompense for what was lost, damaged, or injured, known in the law as "damages." The other is the more drastic remedy—to enjoin the conduct complained of, which is known as "injunction." It should be pointed out that if, instead of a private action, a criminal or administrative action is brought by the state, the remedies are fine, imprisonment, cease and desist orders, and the like (see §1.6).

(a) Compensatory Damages

The usual means of relief in a civil action of any sort is the payment of money. The damages are measured by the amount of demonstrable loss and may be awarded both for property damages and for personal (bodily) injury, the latter including death, of course.

Environmental actions may raise a number of interesting questions in the law of damages. One of these is the way to handle continuing damages, as when a factory commits a continuous trespass to adjoining land by constantly emitting a noxious effluent. As a rule, the litigant gets but one day in court, and at that time he collects whatever it is he is going to get for all wrongs to him past, present, and future. This means that on that day he must prove what his future damages will be—what the harm to him hereafter may be—and he may not come back to court again just because something has changed.

In the situation of continuing trespass, however, some courts have allowed, or compelled, the one suing to sue only for the past trespass damages, and then have allowed, or required him, to bring a fresh suit for continuing trespasses. Others follow the general rule of one suit for all damages. Tactically, a plaintiff might on some occasions prefer numerous suits as a means of pressuring the polluter to pay, but on other occasions continuing suits may be more a legal and financial harassment to the plaintiff than to the polluter [see general discussion in Schmitz article, §2.3(b); *Boomer* case, §4.12].

We have previously referred to the concept of a "permanent nuisance," one which is not going to disappear in the course of time or otherwise be eradicated [§1.7(c)]. The consequence of making a determination that a nuisance is not merely a temporary one is to open the awarding of damages for all injury, past, present, and future. If it is only temporary, then no future damages will be awarded, as the future cannot be told [see, in the chapter on leading cases, *Harrisonville*, §4.4(d)].

Another problem which arises in the law of damages deals with the situation where several polluters are sued because their combined effluents have caused one, inseparable injury. This is especially common in an air pollution case where it will be virtually impossible to distinguish the acts of one polluter from another, and it may also arise in a water pollution case where several factories put the same type of pollutant into a stream. As the reader has already surmised about the law, the courts are divided on how to handle this situation. Some would place the burden upon the plaintiff to show what part each of those sued had with pollution, a requirement which often will be impossible to meet. Others, recognizing the problem, allow the plaintiff to show the overall damage, and are prepared to hold the whole group of polluters liable jointly unless and until one or more of them can establish precisely what his role in the overall mess was (see discussion in Rheingold, §2.2).

In many instances, of course, the court will apportion damages among the various defendants if it can be done.

Thus, if one upstream polluter puts in seventy-five percent of the pollutants and the other twenty-five percent, the total damage done to a downstream owner can be divided on those same proportions. Similarly, if the proof reveals successive injuries, damages may be awarded to the plaintiff separately as against the first, and then the following polluter. Here again, however, it may be that the defendants' acts, though they did not occur at the same time, will produce but one indivisible injury. Here the principles discussed in the preceding paragraph are applicable.

One of the realities of life is insurance, which almost everyone buys to protect himself against damage claims he may have to pay. Another reality is that you may become a little bit more careless in polluting or whatever, if you know you are "covered." Thus, it is good news to report that many insurance companies have been considering whether they ought to cover risks arising out of pollution suits. And one of the major ones, the Insurance Company of North America, decided recently that it would no longer write liability policies protecting its assureds from lawsuits stemming from pollution (*New York Post,* April 13, 1970 p. 72).

(b) Punitive Damages

We have been discussing so far compensatory damages —that type which compensate the plaintiff for the wrong and are intended to make him whole. In addition, the law sometimes allows the awarding of "punitive" or "exemplary" damages (sometimes called "smart money") beyond compensatory damages, for punishment of the defendant who has caused injury by more than mere carelessness— who has through wanton, willful, reckless, or malicious conduct caused injury.

Punitive damages are especially meaningful today where the primary damage done, for which compensatory damages are to be awarded, is very slight, hardly more than righting a technical wrong. Here it is the threat of a possibly large punitive damages award that can deter conduct that the threatened compensatory damages cannot.

There are many instances in pollution suits wherein

punitive damages may be sought. When the polluter acted not only negligently, but willfully or maliciously, in spewing out some sort of effluent, especially after notice to it of severe risks to life it was taking (as, for example, during the time of a known thermal inversion one ejects highly toxic gas into the air), punitive damages could rightly be allowed. In a number of states, even where the allegation is trespass or nuisance, punitive damages could be sought so long as the defendant acted with the requisite state of mind.

Punitive damages are also a threat because of the vague means by which they are measured. In many states they are measured on the degree of the wrong—the more wanton and antisocial the conduct the more the damages which can be sustained. Frequently, too, a "means" test is justified: the damages award can be tailored to the means of the defendant. It would take more to make General Motors smart than it would Jack's Bar and Grill, presumably.

A serious problem for lawyers bringing claims for punitive damages arises when the defendant being sued is a corporation or is an employer of another who is actually guilty of the antienvironmental act. Generally, the courts hold the corporation or employer liable in punitive damages in these situations, but sometimes only upon proof that the company directed, approved, or ratified the conduct complained of.

Examples of cases wherein punitive damages were sought are set forth in *Lampert* [§4.3(*a*)], *McElwain* [§4.3(*b*)], and the Diamond Los Angeles pollution case (§5.7). The topic is also discussed in the Schmitz article [§2.3(*b*)]. On punitive damages in nuisance cases, see 31 A.L.R.2d 1346. The *Lampert* case is an outstanding one. Proof of the existence of the state of mind required for a punitive damages award was shown in part by the statement of the defendant's manager that "it is cheaper to pay claims than to control fluorides." That precisely is why we need the law of punitive damages.

(c) Treble Damages

As with punitive damages, a court and jury may award under certain circumstances treble damages (the lawyer's way of saying *triple damages*). A variety of laws allow the court, as a punishment for socially undesirable conduct, to triple the damages once it has been established that there is responsibility on the part of the defendant. Thus, it is sometimes provided by statute that if one without justification cuts down trees on the land of another treble damages may be awarded.

Treble damages may also be awarded in antitrust actions, a type of suit by statute which has already been discussed [see §1.7(f)]. It is the risk of being subjected to three times the actual damage that one has done that gives long pause for thought to those who would seek to engage in conduct violative of the antitrust laws.

(d) Injunction

Injunction is the power of the court to prevent the continuation of conduct being engaged in by a defendant. This is a remedy which arose in a system of courts that for a while existed separately from the law courts which awarded only money damages. This other system, known as "equity" had the alternate and much more meaningful power to stop wrongful conduct directly. Hence, enjoining is called an "equitable remedy" by lawyers, not because it is any fairer than damages but because it arose in the equity courts.

It should be noted that there are both positive and negative injunctions. The courts have the power under some circumstances to direct that something be done as well as direct that it not be done. Further, it should be noted that the determination is for the court, not a jury— a factor that influences its choice in any particular lawsuit.

The general basis for granting the extreme remedy of injunction is that if the wrongful conduct is allowed to be carried on (with only damages awarded eventually) there will be irreparable harm, or it may be justified on the basis that the law's remedy (damages) is inadequate. It should also be noted that an injunction may be permanent or temporary. We are primarily describing in this section the permanent injunction—the halting of the complained of activity for all time unless and until it can be operated without causing damage. The temporary injunction, often called a temporary restraining order, is issued by a court on the basis that between the time the suit was commenced and the time of trial, irreparable injury may be done. A court may deny a temporary injunction for this interim, and yet, after a full trial, enter a permanent injunction.

Injunction in the pollution area is a remedy most usually associated with nuisance actions [see §1.7(c)]. In fact, it is the usual remedy in nuisance cases, where it is often referred to as "abatement." Rarely would a wrong by negligence or trespass be the subject of injunctive relief, although it is technically available in these and other areas.

Determining whether or not to grant a requested injunction often involves a court in a balancing question. The court has to decide whether the value of continuing the conduct, if any, outweighs the injury which is being done or may be done to the plaintiff. The court may decide, for example, that the conduct is wrongful but that awarding damages alone may be sufficient to solve the problem without necessitating the granting of an injunction. Or it may award both.

Taking a concrete factual situation may help in understanding the distinction between an injunction and damages. In the Boomer case (discussed in §4.12), a cement plant was polluting the air injuring the person and property of a family that lived near it. The plaintiffs asked that the plant be enjoined from operating until it could do so without polluting the atmosphere, and they further sought damages. The highest court in New York, by a majority of its judges, held that an injunction would not be granted because the court would not take it upon itself to clean up the air by edict. All it would do, it was held, was to allow the payment of damages.

One judge dissented from the view, favoring an injunction (see §4.12). The decision, he said, was to allow the cement factory to pollute for a fee. It is obvious that under these circumstances a polluter would rather continue to conduct his business, make profits, and merely pay this fee or fine for operation than have his plant closed down.

To be contrasted with this decision on injunctions is

another one from New York, *Whalen*, §4.1(*a*). There, a pulp mill which cost more than $1 million to build was polluting a stream to the limited extent that a downstream property owner was being injured an estimated $100 per year. The court there enjoined the operation of the plant until it could stop polluting the stream. It is hard for lawyers, laymen aside, to harmonize these two decisions. Fortunately, the trend of the cases nationally is toward the result in the pulp mill case.

Thus, the primary attraction of the injunction in a private environmental suit is that it shuts down the nuisance. Even though only one person has sued, the injunction granted to him benefits everyone. A further decided advantage of the injunction in this field is that it can be on terms. In most courts, the judge is not limited to a mere decision to stop the conduct or not. He may prescribe the terms. He may say, as frequently happens, that the factory is given one year within which to stop the pollution, and it will be shut down only if it does not have its problem under control within that year. Or, he may even prescribe the type of pollution-arresting devices to be installed. If they are not promptly utilized, the injunction will issue. Courts, of course, move most carefully in an area such as this since they do not have all of the research facilities and other necessary information at hand in order to make a scientifically valid order.

Many of the precedent cases digested in Chapter 4 deal with the injunction power of the courts. In *Costas* [§4.4(*a*)], the court went into detail on the means of abating the nuisance. In *Renken* [(§4.1(*b*)], the court ordered an injunction because the damages remedy was inadequate. If only damages were allowed, the plaintiff would be on a "judicial merry-go-round," the court observed, in having continually to sue for damages [see also, §§4.1(*a*), 4.1(*c*), 4.4(*b*)–4.5(*d*), and 4.6(*c*)]. Generally, on the power of injunction, see the article by Schmitz [§2.3(*c*)].

A demand for injunction or abatement has also been the remedy usually sought in the recently filed cases, analyzed in Chapters 5 and 6 (see *Asarco Puget Sound*, where an injunction was granted, §5.4; the *Interstate Sanitation Commission* case, §4.11; the *Florida Power and Light* case, §5.1; and the DDT case, §6.4).

1.10 Who May Sue

Probably the most interesting and challenging question in this chapter is who can sue—who can be a proper plaintiff in an environmental action? The strength and, at times, the very existence of the suit may depend upon who is entitled to bring it. This is said generally regardless of the theory of suit (§§1.7 and 1.8) or the remedy sought (§1.9).

We call this a challenging area because the law is far from clear. It has expanded so rapidly that there are few cases to which lawyers can look as precedents to determine who can sue. At the same time, great flexibility is created by these unknowns, and legal creativity is at its zenith here.

A few comments on why it matters who is suing. First, and most fundamentally, there may be no one who can sue privately. The matter may be one for action by government alone, pursuant to some sort of criminal or administrative proceeding (see §1.6). Second, there may be more or less power, muscle, or leverage behind the suit, depending upon who the parties are. If the suit can be brought in the name of a large number of persons and organizations, as has been done recently (see below), there is more of a threat in it than when merely one person sues.

Indeed, if so many people can be suing that they don't have to be named—a device known to the law as a "class action" [see (*d*) below], tremendous leverage is involved. This is most clearly so when damages are being sought. If fifty thousand people are suing for $100 damage each, the defendant being sued is going to have to become more concerned than if there is only one person at bar.

One special aspect of who may sue is known to lawyers as the question of "standing to sue." And the most crucial question in the area of "standing" is whether a person or group has standing to challenge the conduct of the government or one of its administrative agencies. Standing to sue the government is covered in §1.11 below.

(a) The Government as Suing Party

The first answer to the question, "Who may sue?" is "The government." It has been our point throughout this book that the primary obligation to bring actions to eradicate pollution rests with the government. Hence, it is important to understand what sorts of actions the government can bring, even if, on the whole, the government cannot be counted on to bring all of the suits it may and is empowered to, and even though the power of the private suit in most instances lies as a parallel remedy with the governmental action. It is also important to understand government actions because a private person may be able to intervene in them [see (e) below].

We have already pointed out that governmental action may be either criminal—seeking fine or imprisonment—or administrative (civil)—seeking an injunction or fine. A number of actions in which the government is the suing party are among the cases discussed in detail in Chapters 5 and 6 (note the New Jersey action against the airline using Newark Airport, §5.5; the Interstate Sanitation Commission action against Portchester, New York, §4.11; and the United States action against Florida Power and Light, §5.1). Precedent cases involving the government as plaintiff, in actions to wipe out pollution, are set forth in Chapter 4 [§4.5(a)-(f)].

There are many other examples of suits by the government. One is pending by the State of Florida against Humble Oil & Refining Company for oil pollution of Tampa Bay by the vessel discharging the oil. The state is seeking damages, measured by a five-percent loss of tourist business in the area. There is the 1970 suit by the State of Ohio against various industries for discharging mercury into Lake Erie, thereby causing the fishing industry to be shut down. Damages as well as a permanent injunction are sought by the state there. And in 1970 the federal government brought a criminal action against the Chevron Oil Company under the Outer Continental Shelf

Lands Act of 1953 for the escape of oil from wells in the Gulf of Mexico, because of intentional failure to install safety caps on the wells. Large fines were awarded by the Court.

The government has also been making expanded use in the last year of the Rivers and Harbors Act of 1899, 33 U.S.C. §407, which flatly forbids the dumping of refuse into navigable waters without permission from the United States Army Corps of Engineers. While it is clear that any sort of industrial pollutant is to be deemed "refuse," industry has for years been dumping without permission, and without fear of having to pay a fine. The fine which can be levied is up to $2500 a day, and the act also provides for imprisonment of guilty individuals for a period of not more than a year. (See 33 U.S.C. §441 for pollution of New York Harbor.) An injunction may also be granted by the courts.

Actually, the direction to the government to sue for pollution under the Rivers and Harbors Act has always been there. The act states explicitly that the government shall "vigorously prosecute all offenders." The district attorney is to commence the action on the recommendation of the Corps. Over forty actions have recently been filed. One half of any fine collected shall be paid to the person who gives information leading to a conviction, which should constitute an inducement of the private citizen to report the presence of pollution in navigable waters, harbors, streams, and lakes (in which boats can float) to the government. [See (f) below re suits to collect a reward; generally, see 16 L.ed.2d 1256.]

In July 1970, both the Army Corps of Engineers and the public won a notable victory in the Zabel decision rendered by the Fifth Circuit Court of Appeals. In 1967 the Corps had refused to grant a permit to two Florida landowners to dredge and fill wetlands in Tampa Bay for the construction of a trailer park. Whereas in the past the Corps had routinely given such permission, in this instance the permit was refused as not in the public interest because of the potential adverse effect upon the ecology. The decision of the appellate court upheld the power of the Corps to so refuse the permit. (See discussion of case and quotations, §4.9.)

The government also has powers to act in the area of highway beautification and the banning of signs which might "pollute" the road environment. The federal interest is stated in the Highway Beautification Act of 1965, 23 U.S.C. §131. In a recent case, the power of Dade County, Florida, to prohibit signs near expressways was upheld. The court stated: "The American public has more and more concluded that it has a right to view a natural landscape unobstructed by billboards, whether the view is untouched or ravished by man." [E. B. Elliott Advertising Company v. Metropolitan Dade County, Fifth Circuit Court of Appeals, 1970.]

(b) The Simple Suit

"Ah, for the simple suit!" you might say, after you've plowed through all of the fine legal technicalities which lawyers force themselves to deal with. It turns out that many of the pollution suits—certainly the majority of those brought in the past—are quite simple. They involve one person suing one person for a nice, demonstrable injury. For example, Farmer Brown's cows are dying because the Grubby Machine Works Company upstream is dropping arsenic waste into the local stream. Questions of standing, class actions, the government as a party, constitutional rights, etc., hardly give us pause for concern.

There will continue to be many "simple suits." But what will clean the air and the water for the nation will not be that type of suit as much as the suit involving a large group of citizens versus a large menace, and so we push on again.

(c) Standing to Sue Polluters

In every action brought, the plaintiffs suing must have "standing"—the power or the right of the person to have the court's ear. The "standing" issue is not to be confused with the substantive question of whether the person has a cause of action (*i.e.,* a legal theory—see §1.7), but this is an idealistic statement because frequently if the person has standing then he has a legally protected right to sue [see §1.11(a)].

The question of whether one who is suing has standing arises most frequently in the type of action where the government is being sued. Hence, we have placed our primary discussion of standing in §1.11 (a). As pollution suits proliferate, however, standing issues are bound to be raised in actions brought against industrial polluters.

Let us assume that I am a resident of Rye, New York. Through the city, but not next to my property, flows the Henry River, which the Dracma Corporation is polluting. I can claim "property damage" in only the loosest sense: if the river becomes foul enough to become notorious, property values may fall generally in Rye. Or, I can claim that, since I drive by the river now and then, its color and odor offend me, and hence I have been injured esthetically. And, I might be equally upset about the pollution of the Hudson River, which flows twenty miles away from Rye, New York, and in this concern I might be joined by the Friends of the Earth in New York City and the Sierra Club back in California.

When one of these organizations and I commence suit against the polluter of the Henry River, or the Hudson River, and we have no property damage to show and no bodily injury to claim, the lawyers for the polluter may be expected to raise the standing question—just as the government routinely raises it when it is sued [§1.11(a)]. In the area of suits against the government, standing may be justified on the basis that each citizen has an interest in seeing that his government acts reasonably and is accountable to the will of the public. In the case of a private defendant, the type of public interest which will have to be cited will be the effect of victory—the cleaning of the air and the water by virtue of the suit. Still, the industrial polluter will cite the doctrine of *damnum absque injuria* (a wrong without injury) as a defense: that the basis of standing is actual injury, not just the commission of a wrong.

Many of the key suits presently before the courts have in fact involved as plaintiffs persons and groups without

much direct connection to the subject matter of the suit—
persons who have hardly suffered injury from the wrong
which has been done. See, for example, the Zion suit
(§6.4), where perhaps a hundred thousand persons, members of the United Auto Workers, are suing about thermal
pollution. Few if any of them live on Lake Michigan where
the pollution will occur, and many may go from year to
year without seeing the Great Lakes. Similarly, the conservation group seeking to prevent apartment house construction in Virginia is not being kept off its property; it
is merely seeking to keep the land wild for all (see §6.5).

In July 1970, Michigan became the first state to grant by
statute the right to any citizen to bring a private environmental action in court. The drafter of the bill was Professor
Joseph L. Sax of the University of Michigan. This bill gives
the private person the necessary standing to sue that he
otherwise may lack. Similar bills are pending in other states
and in the Congress (Koch Bill), and we would urge that
they be rapidly passed.

(d) Suits by Groups of Persons; Class Actions

After your lawyer has decided that there has been a
legal wrong which can be righted, and he knows the
remedy and that someone at least has standing to sue,
the question arises as to which groups or classes of people,
if any, may become part of the suit on the plaintiff's side.
As we have pointed out already, there is strength in numbers on the suing side of a law action. The more people
that are suing, especially when damages are being sought,
the more the leverage or power that the suit will have.

There are many instances in which a group or organization can sue as plaintiffs, and this includes established
conservation groups as well as *ad hoc* citizens' clean air
committees and the like. Among the many instances covered in this book, see the Hudson Highway case [§4.6(*b*)]
involving the Sierra Club, towns, a citizens' group, and
others; the Storm King case [§4.6(*a*)], involving conservation groups; and the Zion thermal pollution case (§6.4).

Groups of persons may also be involved in a lawsuit
where a number of individuals have been injured and

they band together to sue. In a simple instance, the Griffith case [§4.6(c)] shows three farmers suing for damage to one pond. An Ohio court recently ruled that 731 residents of Sandusky could sue collectively for damage done by coal dust blowing from a railroad's coal dock (see *Business Insurance,* July 21, 1969, p. 37). Chevron Oil Company has been sued, because of the escaping of oil from its offshore wells in the Gulf of Mexico, by two thousand shrimp fishermen for $70 million damages and by one thousand oyster fishermen for $31.5 million (*Business Insurance,* April 13, 1970, p. 22).

One of the most fascinating questions to lawyers is whether a large number of persons may sue in a "class suit." The class suit is a legal procedure which has been rapidly expanding in the last decade. It allows an exception to the rule that everyone who is aggrieved, and hence is looking for relief, must be named in the lawsuit papers as a suing party. It allows one or more persons to sue as representatives of the whole class of injured persons.

In the usual class suit, the court must first determine if there is a group of persons who have a common interest in some occurrence ("questions of law or fact common to a class"). It must then decide that the class is so numerous that naming and joining all of its members in the legal papers is impracticable. It must find that proceeding by a class action is better than other available means for handling the dispute, and that the persons in whose name the suit is being brought will do a fair and adequate job of protecting the interest of the class. These particular requirements are taken from Rule 23 of the Federal Rules of Civil Procedure. Most states have a similar provision in their laws applying to suits in state courts. But some states do not have liberal class action rules, and many courts are not willing to construe liberally the laws for class actions which are on the books.

Imagine the feeling of power if our lawyer can draw up a paper for you in which the suit is being brought by you "on behalf of all persons similarly situated." If it is for air pollution in San Francisco, then he has joined as a class with you all of the residents of that fair city. If it is for damage due to the manufacturing and distribution of DDT (see the Yannacone pesticide case, §6.6), then he has joined all of the persons in the United States! The only broader class would be that of all the people in the world—and that is going a bit too far because we don't have a world court as such—yet.

On the whole, the courts have been unresponsive to the request for liberalization of the class action concept in environmental or other areas. In New York, for example, although the class action law as written on the books is sweeping enough, the courts would not allow a class to be formed for all those injured by one or a series of acts of pollution. Virtual identity of interest—a common fund being attacked or something like that—would be required. Of course, one plaintiff may be able to achieve in some instances exactly what a class would. If an injunction is granted, the pollution will be stopped, as much for one person as for all.

Newly proposed federal legislation would do much for the class action in the environmental area and for the substance of the pollution suit itself. As proposed by Rep. Seymour Halpern of New York, the bill would allow for class actions in the pollution area, with treble damages in the event of proof of willful violation of antipollution laws.

On class actions, see the articles by Esposito [§2.4(a)] and D'Amato [§2.1(a)]. For class actions presently in use see the Virginia Land case (§5.8); the Diamond case (§5.7) (all persons in Los Angeles—more than seven million people), and the antitrust auto suit [§4.7(b)].

(e) Intervention

One may come into a suit sometimes by intervening into one already going between other parties. This process, known as "intervention," may work to allow conservation or pollution issues to be raised which were otherwise not being injected into the case. In this case, the intervenor is a middle party. Or, it may in effect allow a person or group to join as additional plaintiffs with plaintiffs already suing, adding strength to the suit. On the merits of intervention in a governmental suit, see the article by Marshall (§2.5).

Some of the most interesting cases discussed in this book arose out of an intervention. The leading Storm King case, in which the FPC was told by the courts to reconsider its licensing of a power plant on the Hudson River, involved intervention in an administrative proceeding between the power company and the FPC by a conservation group [see case analyzed, §4.6(a)]. Intervention there worked wonders: the FPC was directed by the courts to reconsider. In the Puget Sound Asarco case (§5.4), a law school professor, on behalf of a citizens' group, intervened in a similar administrative matter, with the result that the smeltery works there was denied a license to pollute large regions through the use of a tall chimney.

(f) The Writ *Qui Tam*—Suing for a Fine

At old common law, still in point today, if a statute provided for a reward for an informer, and a person gave the government information which would lead to apprehension of a law violator against whom a fine could be assessed, then the informer could himself commence the action for a fine against the law violator if, within a reasonable time after being informed, the government failed to prosecute. This was commenced by a writ *qui tam*. It has been pointed out by Wisconsin's Representative Henry S. Reuss, Chairman of the Conservation and Natural Resources Subcommittee of the House Committee on Government Operations, that under such statutes as the Rivers and Harbors Act of 1899 [considered in (a) above], which provides for a fine for pollution, if the government fails to prosecute a polluter, a private citizen who reported the pollution to the government could begin his own action. Representative Reuss has referred to these laws as a "handy kit" for private suits. (*The New York Times*, March 29, 1970). In September 1970, $2000 was paid to the Hudson River Fisherman's Association under the 1899 Act for supplying information about pollution of the Hudson River by the Penn Central Railroad. The right to the writ, however, is in question today.

1.11 Suing the Government

We have placed together here the various legal aspects about suing the government. Part of this, dealing with standing of persons to sue the government [(a) below], could as well have been covered in §1.10: standing to sue. And the remainder, from (b) on below, could as well have been considered in §1.12: who can be sued. The reason we bring these sections together here is to bring home to the reader the fact that the government, especially the federal government, is a key defendant in these pollution suits. In fact, it is probably the prime defendant today. This is especially so because, by intervening in a suit in which the government is suing a private polluter, you may be suing both government and industry.

It is essential to make a careful, initial analysis of what one is going to sue the government for. The main possibilities are:

(1) unauthorized or otherwise improper conduct on the part of some agency—see (a) below, which also discusses generally the standing problem;
(2) pollution created by the government—see (b) below;
(3) failing to enforce laws to stop industrial pollution or failing to pass laws against pollution—see (c) below;
(4) violating the rights of a citizen under color of law—see (d) below;
(5) making unnecessary use of the condemnation powers—see (e) below.

(a) Standing to Challenge Administrative Actions

We have already explained in general the legal concept of "standing": the power a person has to go into a court to raise an issue, here of environmental degradation [§1.10(c)]. Few areas of the law are undergoing as much change today as the law relating to standing to sue the government. It has been the subject of numerous articles by law professors and has been the issue in many recently filed cases discussed below.

The basic question dealing with standing is how minimal the interest a person or group suing may have in the matter of the lawsuit, and yet be allowed to bring action. If, at the one extreme, the action of a governmental body has directly injured a person—in his property, his health, or his employment—one would hardly pause on the question of "standing," it being clear that he is injured and can sue.

On the other hand, what if the right which the group or person asserts has been violated is one where the violation has injured the persons suing no more than anyone else? What if merely a "public right" is involved, in which we all, as citizens of this country, are interested? For example, suppose the government is about to fill in Lake Tahoe or to sell timber rights in Yellowstone Park. A resident of Maine and a conservation group in Texas, while quite upset about the threatened conduct, are not *directly* affected by such an action, at least in the sense of livelihood, health, or property.

The revolution that has been worked in the past few years is that the courts have begun to recognize the standing of almost any member of the general public to seek judicial review for the vindication of any rights, even those which are strictly public rights. They are willing to allow the suit to commence even though the persons suing have not been specifically wronged, so long as some sort of legal right has been violated, and they can be said to be "aggrieved." At this point, the recent cases themselves tell the tale best.

(1) The Hudson Highway Case. We have analyzed this case [see §4.6(*b*); §6.6], and we discuss it only briefly here therefore. Here the Sierra Club, a local conservation group known as Citizens Committee for the Hudson Valley, and a town on the Hudson sued the federal government because the United States Corps of Engineers had granted a permit to New York to build a superhighway on the banks of the Hudson. Part of the project involved building into the river. The groups suing claimed that the Corps did not have authority to grant the permit, since approval of both the United States Congress and the Department of Transportation was needed, and yet had not been obtained.

The prestigious Second Circuit Federal Court of Appeals held that the Sierra Club and others had standing to challenge the conduct of the Corps. These groups were acting as "private attorney generals," the court said, to protect the public interest:

> We hold . . . that the public interest in environmental resources—an interest created by statutes affecting the issuance of this permit—is a legally protected interest affording these plaintiffs, as responsible representatives of the public, standing to obtain judicial review of agency action alleged to be in contravention of the public interest.

The suit was brought under the Administrative Procedure Act, 5 U.S.C. §702, which gives standing to one to gain the review of an administrative action in court if he has "suffered legal wrong" or is "aggrieved by agency action." While this provision is a useful one as a basis for standing, it is not a necessary one for the environmental suit against the government in this book. One may come into the suit by virtue of the National Environmental Policy Act of 1969 [see §§1.6 and 3.1(a)], by intervention (see below), and by many other means.

(2) The Storm King Case. This is another case we have digested [§4.6(a)]. In this case conservation groups were held to have standing to intervene in a matter involving the Federal Power Commission and Consolidated Edison which had applied for a permit to build a power plant on the banks of the Hudson River. The groups claimed failure on the part of the FPC to consider all of the ecological ramifications of the proposed power plant. Again, the Second Circuit held that the groups had standing to intervene in this administrative matter. (And, the court decided the case in favor of the groups, telling the FPC to reconsider its permit.)

Three other cases of interest show how far the courts have gone on the standing issue. In one, a church group was given standing to intervene in a licensing procedure before the Federal Communications Commission, even though the standing of those intervening was merely that of the viewing public, a position that anyone in the area would have, Office of Communication of the United Church of Christ v. Federal Power, 359 F.2d 944 (D.C. Cir. 1966).

And in two decisions by the United States Supreme Court, standing was found for business groups that could show at best that they would only be slightly affected by the government's activities, Barlow v. Collins, 397 U.S. 159 (1970) (tenant farmers challenging Department of Agriculture); Association of Data Processing Service Organizations v. Camp, 397 U.S. 150 (1970) (data-processing service salesmen challenging comptroller of the currency).

So far we have been speaking just of the "private attorney general" suit to enforce public rights. One's standing to challenge governmental activity is immediately enhanced if he is a taxpayer (as most of us are). The standing of taxpayers to seek judicial review (the court's review of the conduct of a governmental agency) is also an area which has recently undergone ferment. In Flast v. Cohen, 392 U.S. 83 (1968), the Supreme Court of the United States held that being a taxpayer gave one standing to challenge certain expenditures of public funds, in this case uses which might be in violation of the Bill of Rights and in particular of the freedom of religion. An example of a taxpayer's action in the pollution area is the case in §4.11.

Will Flast apply to environmental suits? One court so far has held that it does. In Crowther v. Seaborg, D.C. Colo., 1970, Justice Arraj determined that a group of Colorado residents had standing to complain about Project Rulison, an AEC experiment involving the nuclear stimulation of gases, on the argument that the project constituted a threat to their safety. The persons suing, who were landowners and residents, had a direct enough interest in the AEC's activities, and were directly enough connected with any possible ill event, as to give them a concrete interest in the case, and hence standing, the court said. It also held that a public benefit corporation, as the persons were organized, could be the plaintiff. The A.P.A. provision, 5 U.S.C. §702, discussed above in the Hudson Highway case, was utilized in this case, too.

We have already discussed the "trust" theory in detail [§1.8(c)]—the theory that, since the lands of this country are held in trust for all of the people, violation of that trust may give rise to a cause of action. Such an action can be maintained against the government as well if not better than against a private person. The violation of the trust could theoretically arise by agency action, as discussed in this section, or by the governmental acts discussed in the following sections.

As has been so well stated by a professor of law with deep interests in ecology, Eva Hanks, these cases "show a willingness to find a congressional intent to protect broad classes of people and to permit appropriate representatives to participate in the decision-making processes of administrative government," Hanks and Hanks, "An Environmental Bill of Rights: The Citizen Suit and the National Environmental Policy Act of 1969," Rutgers Law Review 230 (1970).

The recent cases tell the tale of the significance of the advances made in the standing of persons to sue the government:

• Three conservation groups recently brought suit in Washington, D. C. against the Department of the Interior to prevent it from issuing a permit to a coalition of oil companies to build a 390-mile highway over the frozen tundra in Alaska as a means of gaining access to a proposed hot oil pipeline from the North Alaska field. The three groups were Friends of the Earth, the Wilderness Society and the Environmental Defense Fund. In April 1970, the federal court held in favor of the groups and issued the injunction. Counsel for the groups was James Moorman of Washington, D.C. He urged upon the court the necessity of evaluating the road in light of the National Environmental Policy Act of 1970, which the court did. The court found that the policy behind that act made the issuance of a road permit illegal.

• The Sierra Club in 1970 commenced suit against the Army Corps of Engineers for proposing action contrary to the provisions of the National Environmental Policy Act. The Corps would have bulldozed large portions of the Gila River in Arizona, killing much of the unique plant life there. The federal court granted a temporary injunction.

(See *Sierra Club* v. *Resor*, S.D.C. Ariz. 1970, Civil No. 70-78 TUC.)

• In Florida, various conservation groups, represented by attorney Victor J. Yannacone, jr., began suit against the Secretary of Transportation and the Dade County Port Authority to prevent the further construction of an airstrip in the Florida Everglades on the basis of irreparable harm to that swamp (see §6.5). Also in Florida, suit was commenced by similar groups to prevent the dredging and widening of a scenic Florida river to form the "Cross Florida Barge Canal" (see §6.4). In that action the Army Corps of Engineers was again the defendant. The conservationists prevailed.

• Minnesota, joined by a number of other states, has found a way to challenge the adequacy of Atomic Energy Commission standards relating to radiation emission for nuclear power plants. Companies constructing and operating such plants have recently been shielding their responsibilities for high emission by citing compliance with the lax AEC standards. (See *Northern States Power Company* v. *Minnesota*.)

When, in 1970, Minnesota sought to impose higher standards than the federal ones upon a power plant, the company sued it. Four states have intervened so far on the side of the state of Minnesota. By this device, a challenge has been made to the AEC view that their standards have preempted the field. However, it was held that the weak AEC standards governed.

• On March 2nd 1971, the United States Supreme Court ordered the Department of Transportation to re-evaluate the proposed 6-lane highway I-40 which would sever the zoo from the remainder of the Overton Park in Tennessee. Justice Marshall instructed the District Court to find feasible and prudent alternatives, and to make all possible plans to minimize harm. (See *Citizens to Preserve Overton Park Inc., et al* v. *Volpe, Secretary of the Department of Transportation, et. al.*, 309 F. Supp. 1189.)

• Among other cases following the leading Scenic Hudson case in granting standing to groups concerned with all types of environmental degradation, are the *Nashville I-40 Steering Comm.* v. *Eillington,* [387 F.2d 179 (6th Cir. 1967), cert. den. 390 U.S. 921 (1968)], in which standing to challenge the construction of highway I-40 through North Nashville was granted to an association of some 30 Negro and white community leaders who were residents of North Nashville. Their committee was unincorporated. Also, in *Road Review League* v. *Boyd* [270 F.Supp. 650 (S.D.N.Y. 1967)], it was held that a similar organization of citizens concerned about the path of a road had a right to sue to question the road.

• In a granddaddy of pollution cases, *Murphy* v. *Butler* [362 U.S. 929], a Long Island, N.Y., resident sought in 1957 to stop DDT spraying. See the enlightening dissenting opinion of Justice William O. Douglas, who was in favor of allowing the suit to come before the Supreme Court.

• The two decisions of the federal court in Washington in 1970 relating to DDT prohibitions gave standing rights to EDF and others to challenge governmental inaction on DDT (see §4.10). These two cases are key ones in the expansion of the standing concept.

• One reversal in the expansion of the standing concept —though it is perhaps only temporary—should be noted. The Sierra Club, in a California federal court, challenged the power of the Department of the Interior to grant to the Walt Disney organization the right to build a road through the Sequoia National Park to service an alpine ski area it was constructing. A power line would have accompanied the road. The plaintiffs claimed that the issuance of a permit for construction was in violation of national environmental interests. After granting a temporary injunction, the court in 1970 refused to permanently stop the department. The Sierra Club has appealed the decision, which was affirmed. Presently the U. S. Supreme Court is considering reversal.

For the lawyer with interest on the standing question, we suggest the following: Hanks and Hanks, "An Environmental Bill of Rights: The Citizen Suit and the National

Environmental Policy Act of 1969" [to appear in Dorsen, ed., *A.C.L.U. Guide to Your Rights* (1970)], *Rutgers Law Review* 230 (1970); Berger "Standing To Sue in Public Actions: Is It a Constitutional Requirement?" 78 *Yale Law Journal* 816 (1969); Jaffe, *Judicial Control of Administrative Actions,* chaps. 12 and 13 (1965); Comment "Standing To Sue and Conservation Values," 38 *Univ. Colorado Law Review* 391 (1966); Jaffe, "The Citizen as Litigant in Public Actions: The Non-Hohfeldian or Ideological Plaintiff," 116 *Univ. Pennsylvania Law Review* 1033 (1968); Davis, "Standing: Taxpayers and Others," 35 *Univ. Chicago Law Review* 601 (1968); Comment, "Of Birds, Bees, and the FPC," 77 *Yale Law Journal* 117 (1967) (on the *Storm King* case); Sax, "Public Rights in Public Resources: The Citizen's Role in Conservation and Development," in Johnson and Lewis, eds., *Contemporary Developments in Water Law,* p. 136 (1970) (on the *Glen Canyon* case).

(b) Suing the Government as a Polluter

The government has been a notorious polluter in its own right. The cities' dumps and public housing developments spew out air pollution. State-operated hospitals may pollute water and state land projects may endanger wildlife. Armed forces installations add to pollution, including air pollution from jet planes. Hence, the government may be the defendant in a contemplated suit—because of its own conduct.

The first hurdle to suing any government is *immunity*. In the old days in England it was believed that "the King can do no wrong," which, translated, meant that a government, on any level, could not be sued. Much of that immunity has been swept away by the passage of laws which allow a governmental body to be sued—but only on its own terms, of course. The federal government, for example, can be sued, pursuant to the *Federal Torts Claims Act,* 31 U.S.C. §240, with many limits (e.g., not for discretionary acts). And in many states the state can be sued, but only in its own special claims court. In many areas, the defense of "sovereign immunity" still holds sway.

The second hurdle is *standing to sue*. Of course, if the pollution has injured you there's no problem here, but if it is a question of enforcing some sort of public right where you have been hurt no more seriously than anyone else in the public generally, the same standing problems as previously reviewed in (*a*) above must be considered.

There are other legal hurdles as well, regarding the environmental suit against the government, all involving concepts which are rather complicated, even for lawyers. First, there is the doctrine of "exhaustion of remedies," which requires following the administrative process to completion before taking to the courts to sue [see §1.13(*c*)]. Next, there is the requirement that the matter being taken into court be "reviewable" by that court—that the court have the power and the right to review the conduct of the government. This work of the court, known as "judicial review," was discussed in the preceding section on "standing." Third, there is the concept of "justiciability"—the requirement that the subject matter of the lawsuit be appropriate for judicial decision. For example, a case which is primarily in the political area would be avoided by the courts, on the theory that it is a matter best left to the legislature. Few problems in the environmental area today, however, would be found not to be justiciable.

The biggest push to stop governmental pollution is to be found in the National Environmental Policy Act of 1969 [see §3.1 (*a*)]. Section 103 thereof places upon every federal agency the burden of reviewing its activities to determine if it is complying with the announced congressional policy of the act: the prevention of pollution. This refers as much to governmental pollution as to government-tolerated private pollution. The President has made it clear that this places a burden on each agency to prevent pollution [Executive Order No. 11,230, 35 Fed. Reg. 4247 (1970)].

For cases dealing with the liability of the government for its own pollution, and on the immunity issue, see Steiffer, §4.4(*b*), and Harrisonville, §4.4(*c*). See general discussion in the Schmitz article, §2.3(*e*). An example of a recent suit is one commenced in 1970 by the State of

California against the United States because of federal pollution resulting from Fort Ord's dumping of raw sewage into Monterey Bay (see *Time*, March 16, 1970).

(c) Suing the Government for Failure to Force Industry to Stop Polluting; The Writ of Mandamus

Let us say that a governmental body has been given the power to act against pollution, but it refuses to act. It could, for example, commence an action against a factory which is dumping effluents into a stream, but it sits back. This bureaucratic lethargy (or worse!) is well-known and indeed, the fact that it is so common has led to the concept of the private suit to eradicate pollution.

How about a suit against the governmental body, then, which is failing to exercise its powers, seeking to compel it to act? There is much legal basis for such a suit [see discussion in the Esposito article, §2.4(*d*), and Schmitz article, §2.3(*e*)]. Sometimes this action against the government seeks a writ of mandamus from the court. By this writ the court directs the governmental body to act. There are, of course, all types of legal fine-points here in governmental immunity, in the discretionary versus ministerial dispute, and in standing, most of which are discussed in the articles just cited.

An even more complex suit would be one arising in the situation in which you feel that the government has not adopted the rules it should—the step before the failure-to-enforce problem discussed above. It may be, for example, that by law the state has authorized local governments to pass certain laws against pollution, but your city has taken no steps. In this event, it is generally held that a court lacks the power to direct a government to pass an ordinance, regulations or whatever may be in point.

(d) Suing under the Civil Rights Act

An old (1871) Civil Rights Act provision creates a responsibility on the part of any person who "under color of" any law or custom subjects any other person to a deprivation of his rights and privileges under the United States Constitution or any law. That responsibility is enforced in terms of a suit by the injured person for damages, injunction, or any other proper redress (42 U.S.C. §1983). It should be noted that the suit is against an official and not against the government itself.

Based upon other sorts of suits which have been brought under this provision of the law, it is fairly clear that failure by a federal, state or local official to enforce the law can amount to a deprivation of a right protected by this provision. Neglect as well as action can be the basis of a suit. It has been predicted, therefore, that this provision of the law will have a future in environmental litigation [see Esposito, §2.4(e); Marshall, (2.5)].

(e) Stopping Abuses of the Condemnation Power

One final aspect of the potential suit against the government should be mentioned. This arises out of the power of a government to take land by condemnation—through the process known as eminent domain. This power can be employed to take lands for any sort of use, and thereby an excellent conservation area can be destroyed. In fact, to rub the wounds with salt, the government might even build a pollution-creating facility on such land.

A recent article has argued against the exercise of condemnation powers by a government which works against conservation. Francis E. P. McCarter, counsel for Wildlife Preserves, Inc., has described his losing battle in keeping two highways and assorted pipe, sewer and electricity lines off a New Jersey preserve. He argues that a broad "public use" defense should be accorded charitable groups such as his to prevent condemnation [see "The Case That Almost Was," 54 *A.B.A.J.* 1076 (1968)].

1.12 Who Are the Persons Who Can Be Sued?

One answer to the question, "Who can be sued because of pollution?" is "Anyone," but that is concededly not very helpful. What is of relevance in a book on environmental suits is whether there are any limits on the persons who may be sued. The nature of suits against the government, one of the key defendants, has already been considered in §1.11.

(a) Suing the Actual Polluter

In the usual pollution suit it is easy to identify who is causing the pollution. He is then made the defendant in the lawsuit, in whatever name and capacity that is proper legally.

(b) Suing Multiple Polluters in One Suit

Very often, the suit is not against one polluter or person affecting the environment but many. It may be all of the automobile manufacturers, as in the antitrust case [see §4.7(b)]. Perhaps the record for defendants in one case is Attorney Diamond's Los Angeles air pollution case—over 200 defendants! (see §5.7).

Generally the problems which have been met with naming a big group of plaintiffs to a lawsuit [see §1.10(e)] have not occurred when a big group of defendants is named. All that is required is (a) the allegation (and later the proof) that each named defendant (or they could be sued as a class—theoretically) in its own way contributed to the pollution; (b) the service of process upon each of them individually. The latter may become a serious problem, however, in that the various polluters may be located in a number of states and cannot, under the laws of jurisdiction, all be sued in any one legal action anywhere. (The alternative here is to commence suits in a number of states, which is quite unwieldy.)

One problem in the area of proof, however, may create difficulties, which reflect upon the question of who, among all potential defendants, may be joined in one suit. This problem arises when each of the parties to be named as wrongdoers in the complaint contributed a certain amount of degradation to the overall pollution damage of which the plaintiff complains. Thus, in suing four factories and power plants for damages for air pollution of a city, it may be virtually impossible to state *which* defendant contributed exactly *what* to the overall pollution complained of. If the courts therefore were to take the viewpoint that the person suing must pinpoint the wrong done to him separately by each of those sued, as a condition of continuing to press his action, it is apparent that the plaintiff would fail in his action.

Many courts fortunately—but far from all—take realities into account and would allow the joint suit here contemplated, even though the specific contribution of each defendant cannot be pinpointed. These courts would say that the burden of proof has shifted to the defendant; any of them can go forward to prove that its particular particulate pollution did *not* cause plaintiff's damages. Of course, this is generally as impossible of proof for the defendant as it was for the plaintiff. Thus, whoever has to bear this burden will lose. A few courts, however, stick to the requirement of proof by the plaintiff [see discussion in Rheingold article, §2.2(c); Esposito, §2.4(a)].

In many pollution cases, of course, even though several polluters contribute to one harm, their roles can be distinguished. If, for example, factory A puts so many pounds of soot into the air in a day and factory B twice that much, the responsibility of factory B for the plaintiff's damages can be set at two thirds, and that of factory A at one third. The same apportionment could be made in the case of a number of polluters of water. It is much easier to make these calculations, of course, when the same sort of pollutant is being released. If factory A puts out SO_2 and factory B CO_2, an expert would be needed to show the relative harmfulness of these substances—if it can be done at all.

1.13 Are There Any Defenses To My Action?

The reader has already seen that there are many pitfalls in handling a pollution suit. One being sued—for anything —can be expected to resist as stoutly as he can. He may assert any of a number of matters already mentioned— such as the fact that the wrong persons are suing him (§1.10), or the wrong theories are being asserted (§1.7), or the relief sought cannot be granted (§1.9).

Beyond these points, we wish to alert the prospective litigant to the existence and status of a flock of defenses available for assertion by the defendant. Every case should be evaluated in advance of suing for a determination of whether the defenses to be asserted are strong ones, ones which may defeat all or a substantial part of the case.

(a) "Balancing of Interests"; "State of the Art"; "I Did All I Could"

One of the most pernicious defenses arises out of a consideration which courts give undue weight to in pollution cases: a supposed "balancing of interests." To be balanced against the potential injury to plaintiffs, some courts say, is the importance of the conduct being carried on by the defendant. Especially when there is any public benefit whatsoever to the activity being carried on (sometimes merely a factory that makes goods for the public), the court may refuse to act on behalf of the invasion asserted by the plaintiff [see the Schmitz article §2.3(e)].

Fortunately, a number of courts have taken the view that a nuisance is a nuisance and is to be abated even if there is a great deal of community benefit in its productivity. This is especially so where risk to health is involved [see, for example, the *Whalen* case, §4.1(e); *Boomer* case, §4.12; *Hilton Head Island* case, §6.6].

A variety of this defense is that there is no way for the defendant to do anything about his effluents (a "state of the art" defense). This may move a court even when there is only the defendant's own say-so as to the absence of a means for him to control his pollution. Some courts, fortunately, refuse to consider this as a defense, and others will listen to proof—if the plaintiff is enterprising enough to come up with it—of new developments which the defendant is not paying attention to. A variety of this defense —that the defendant did all he could to stop pollution— was rejected in a leading case [*Yturbide,* §4.8(d). See discussion in Esposito article, §2.4(a); D'Amato article, §2.1(b)].

The D'Amato article also points out that the plaintiff will be enhancing his case if he can show to the court that there are ways for the public to have its needs satisfied other than through the devices of the defendant. That is, in seeking to enjoin an atomic plant, one may anticipate the defense that the public needs power. If other sources of such power can be shown—or other places to put that power plant which won't affect the environment so badly —then this old canard can be rebutted.

(b) Government Approval or Acquiescence

That the government has approved the act of pollution involved is often a defense asserted. To name examples, it may have issued a permit to a power company to construct an atomic plant, with the awareness that the plant would release tritium into the water. Or it may have taken an action against some polluter, and then have settled the case with it by agreeing to allow it to pollute, but only to a limited extent. As a citizen you feel that the defendant should not have been allowed to pollute even to the limited extent it has. Or you as a citizen believe that the tritium release is dangerous, even if the government does not.

Government approval may be a potent defense. Even if it is not a totally legal defense, it is a pretty good argument for the polluter to use before the judge or jury which is trying its case (a sort of "Good Housekeeping Seal of Approval"). Generally the courts have recognized correctly that the question in the common lawsuit is a different one from what transpired in an administrative proceeding. They say that while the fact that the United States government has specifically approved the conduct is some evidence of reasonableness, the jury can still decide against the polluter on the basis of other testimony from biologists, to the effect that even the level permitted by the government is a dangerous one (see Chapter 7). Even the fact that the government itself has sued—and lost— may not preclude a private suit when the parties are different.

(c) Failure to Exhaust Administrative Remedies

It is one of those law school rules that crops up from time to time that one cannot sue anyone in the courts until the "administrative remedies" are exhausted. "Administrative" here refers to rights of complaint, review, and the like, which are created through departments and agencies of a government (the administrative, as compared to the judicial or legislative).

Local law may provide, for example, that in the event of the creation of a radiation exposure, one should register a complaint with the Board of Health. It may further provide the way the Board of Health is to investigate, report, and act. And it may well provide that in the event that the person making the complaint is unhappy about the way in which the Board has acted (or failed to act), an appeal may be taken to a Board of Appeals. If you tried to sue the radiation polluter in court first, he could be expected to set up the defense of administrative exhaustion.

"Exhaustion" of remedies is a pretty descriptive term here, since it is often exhausting, time-consuming, and unproductive to have to go through the bodies involved. Serious damage may be done while one waits, or the hurdles may be so difficult that one just drops the suit. Fortunately, it has often been held that in the pollution area there is no requirement that remedies in the administrative branch be exhausted before resort to the courts is had [see the *Martin* case, §4.6(*d*); Schmitz article §2.3(*d*); DDT cases, §4.10].

The doctrine of exhaustion of administrative remedies may also be applied when the administrative agency itself is the one which is supposed to act on its motion to abate pollution. Thus, it might seem that one would have to wait for the agency to act and do all it can before going into the courts. The citizen's remedy in this area is to sue the government, to compel it to act (see §1.11).

(d) Contributory Negligence; Assumption of the Risk

The granddaddies of all the defenses are contributory negligence and assumption of the risk. The former concept means that the person suing contributed to his own damages, and hence should not be allowed to sue (or should at least have his damages cut down). The latter concept means that you ought not to be able to sue for injuries arising out of a risk of which you were aware and to which you consented to expose yourself.

In a number of pollution suits these defenses have been asserted. For example, if you know your health or crops are being ruined by pollution from next door, but are doing nothing about it—going on breathing the bad air or watering your cows in the bad water—that may be a defense. Many courts, however, consider what the reasonable alternatives were to the person suing. You can't stop breathing after all, and it is not reasonable for you to go away. Hence, it would have to be a truly volitional situation to be said to give rise to one of these defenses—a sort of foolish continuance of exposure of the self to fully appreciated risks.

(e) Statute of Limitations

For every type of action which may be brought, the law specifies a period of time within which it must be brought ("statute of limitations"), or the suit will be deemed barred. Every state has a different system of times for the various types of actions, and it would be one of the most difficult legal searching problems to attempt to state, for the various types of actions contemplated in this book, what the periods of time are—in the 50-some jurisdictions. The time within which to commence suit after injury has been done, may be as little as one year, although sometimes it can be six or more years. Suits against the government are generally governed by a short period of limitations (two years against the federal government), and beyond that there is often an unfair requirement that *notice* of the claim (as compared to the suit itself) be given in a very short period, such as ninety days! (See also §5.3.)

(f) Aims of National Uniformity

When all of the old defenses have been bypassed in a pollution case, such as have been considered above, a defendant may raise the argument that a court should not decide individual cases in the pollution area. If the issue before the court involves more than merely local pollution —let us say the national distribution of DDT, or some statewide pollution—then the argument goes that individual courts deciding these cases may decide differently. As a result, the argument continues, we may have conflicting decisions among the courts, with a resultant failure to have national uniformity. Such an argument is made in Miller and Borchers, "Private Lawsuits and Air Pollution Control," 56 *A.B.A.J.* 465 (1970). (It should be noted that the authors, both connected with the National Air Pollution Control Administration, have an interest in the national approach.)

We reject this argument flatly, while not disagreeing with the proposition that the government should use every effort to achieve national uniformity through tough new anti-pollution laws. But until that elusive goal is achieved, the courts should be free to go on fashioning their own remedies in the pollution area. The risk of lack of uniformity is hardly indigenous to this type of suit; every lawsuit has that supposed risk, always outweighed by the societal benefits of action.

1.14 A Few Procedural Considerations

(a) Jurisdiction and Venue

As with the filing of any sort of suit, there will be choices and limits for the litigant as to the state and place to commence his suit. Common problems have arisen as follows:

(*i*) *Desire to join many defendants, not all of whom can be sued in any one jurisdiction.* Generally this should not be a problem because the polluters will be in the same geographical region, but this may necessitate maintaining a suit in more than one place, or forgoing one or more parties to the suit.

(*ii*) *Desire to use a class action suit or other procedural device for joining multiple plaintiffs.* Here, if there are choices open as to the place to bring the suit—state versus federal courts or between various states—the place might be selected which is most hospitable to the procedure sought.

(*iii*) *One state has better laws on pollution than others.* Often the same law will apply to the suit no matter where it is brought, but sometimes a decided advantage can be gained by trying the case in one state over another, because of law differences, or perhaps just because of the greater receptivity of the expected judges and juries to the issues in the case.

An interesting example of selecting the forum is in the Asarco suit (§5.5). This suit was originally commenced in

Texas, in the El Paso courts. It involves air pollution by the American Smelting and Refining Company in that city and across the border in Juarez, Mexico. This suit was recommenced in New York City. The basis for taking the suit there was that it was the headquarters of Asarco. The perceived advantage to the plaintiffs in suing in New York was the greater hospitality for this type of suit expected in the courts of that city. Against this was to be balanced, of course, the fact that the suit was now in the bailiwick of the defendant and not of the injured plaintiffs.

(b) Consolidation of Cases, Multidistrict Suits

We have already discussed group and class actions, intervention, and the like (§1.10) as devices to bring plaintiffs together. The parties to suits, and the courts, have additional procedural devices for accomplishing the same thing.

Let us imagine, first, several suits going against the same polluter. A number of persons are individually and independently suing the factory for air pollution, and at the same time there is a large class action pending, plus a suit by a conservation group. Any of those suing, or the polluter himself, may ask the court where all of the suits are pending to consolidate the cases: to join them together for all purposes, trial and pretrial. Often it would be the defendant who would seek this measure, because he could deal more handily and inexpensively with all of the people in one ball than in a lot of separate suits. And unless there was some concerted harassment involved in the multiple suits, the plaintiffs would do better to band together, too. Of course, differences in philosophy or even undesirable competition among various environmental groups might point toward nonconsolidation.

The courts also have the inherent power, in most instances, to order consolidation. Thus even if neither the plaintiffs nor the defendant wanted it, the court could consolidate the cases as a move toward judicial economy. One of the few limits on this practice would be when it would deprive a party of a fair day in court. For example, if the various plaintiffs had different injuries, relating to different polluting acts on the part of the defendant, it might be fairer to allow each to present his own case separately; otherwise a jury could become confused.

The federal courts also have the power to oversee the handling of cases pending in more than one federal court at the same time. While it does not move case A in court A to court B to combine it with the one in court B, a court can order that discovery and preparation be carried on in a joint fashion, pursuant to 28 U.S.C. §1407, the multi-district litigation law, and the rules formulated by the Judicial Panel on Multidistrict Litigation [on this, see Speiser and Rheingold, "Negligence Case Techniques" (1969), p. 69].

(c) Marshaling Proof in an Ecology Case

After your pollution action has survived all of the attacks upon its standing, the time comes to prepare it for trial. This is often the time when the case is won or lost—not at the actual trial itself. What evidence will you be able to gather which will prove the polluting source, the damage done, the reasons for abatement, the absence of alternatives to the relief you seek, and so on? Pertinent to these questions, Chapter 7 discusses the sources of proof, the sources of standards, the sources of scientific data.

Knowledge of standards that exist for the measurement of pollution, in the air or in water, are most useful in pollution cases. This is true whether they are governmentally adopted or industry-created standards. When it can be shown that a factory did not meet the minimum standards applicable to its effluents, there is then some proof of its carelessness. [Of course, proof by the polluter that it complied with the laws is some proof of carefulness, but it can always be shown that these are minimal laws, and that under the circumstances of the case more was called for—see §1.13(b).] One distinct aid to the private suit would be the promulgation at the various levels of government of much more stringent standards by which pollution is to be gauged.

Chapter 7 is also a distillation of the process of presentation of proof at trial. Three sections deal with the use of expert testimony. If you want to see a pollution case at trial in microcosm, read the outline of the Heck v. Beryllium case in §7.3.

1.15 An Afterthought: The Population Question

It is the opinion of many of the scientists concerned with the pollution problem that the most fundamental path to eradication lies with control of population. This process involves conceiving some sort of ideal population for the world, and then using means to stick to it. As lawyers we are involved in this problem, but we present no law review articles, no cases, and no pleading in this area, because the law has not reached here yet.

It is safe to predict, however, that within the very near future there will be litigation, starting slowly and increasing rapidly, in the area of population control. Most of the legal issues will be constitutional ones: does the federal or state government have the constitutional power to take some birth control measures, and in doing so has it violated any of the fundamental guarantees of the United States Constitution including the Bill of Rights?

Typical of the questions which may arise are the following:

(1)—Is it constitutional to stop income tax exemptions after two children?

(2)—Is it constitutional to actually add a surcharge (a "negative exemption") for each child in a family over a certain number, for example, 3?

(3)—Has the government the power to compel the sterilization of persons, after they have had a certain number of children, or even on a random basis before they are married?

(4)—Is there any constitutional right which would prevent the government from limiting the size of a family to two offspring?

It would take a better crystal ball than we have to predict the way in which the courts will rule on such issues as these. Certainly any attempt *today* to limit family size by compulsory sterilization, or having a two-offspring quota system would be declared unconstitutional by the Supreme Court. The Court would find in the Bill of Rights the right to have children, quoting from such cases as *Meyer v. Nebraska,* 262 U.S. 390 (1922) (referring to the "right to marry and establish a home and bring up children"). But what seems so clear today can change radically in a decade or less.

If the courts are confronted at a later time with a world situation of mass starvation and overpopulation, then an overriding matter of national health and security could be deemed by the courts to outweigh any of the constitutional niceties relating to the right to have a large family. There is much precedent for such an invasion into rights previously considered fundamental and sacrosanct, when necessity exists. For example, the courts can order compulsory sterilization of a defective person [*Buck* v. *Bell,* 274 U.S. 200 (1927)]. And they can compel vaccination for diseases that threaten the public [*Jacobson* v. *Massachusetts,* 197 U.S. 11 (1905)].

Actually, we have come farther down the road toward birth control by legislation and judicial decision than many people would like to think. We have just mentioned compulsory sterilization. In the area of abortion, state after state is passing laws which liberalize (if they don't totally do away with) the restrictive conditions under which abortions may be done. Comstock laws which have for decades prohibited the dissemination of information about contraceptive devices are being ignored or held unconstitutional. Indeed, the Supreme Court has upheld the right of a married couple to have contraceptive information made available to them by their doctor, in the leading case of *Griswold* v. *Connecticut,* 381 U.S. 479 (1965) (see §1.8).

If we have to say something about what our legal gazing-ball says, it is that the legal process will shift toward the passing of statutes controlling population, and the courts will shift toward upholding them. It will then be our primary task—the task of lawyers and laymen alike—to preserve the wonderful concepts of the dignity of human life that the world has developed so painfully over so long a battle.

SUGGESTED READING ON ECOLOGY AND ENVIRONMENT

Carson, Rachel. *Silent Spring*. New York: Fawcett World, 1969.

Commoner, Barry. *Science and Survival*. New York: Viking Press, 1967.

De Bell, Garrett, ed. *The Environmental Handbook*. New York: Ballantine Books, 1970.

Ehrlich, Dr. Paul S. *The Population Bomb*. New York: Ballantine Books, 1968.

Fuller, R. Buckminster. *Operating Manual for Spaceship Earth*. New York: Pocketbooks, 1970.

Graham, Frank, jr. *Since Silent Spring*. Boston: Houghton Mifflin Co., 1970.

Laycock, George. *The Diligent Destroyers*. New York: Ballantine Books, 1970.

Leopold, Aldo. *A Sand County Almanac*. New York: Ballantine Books, 1970.

Marx, Wesley. *The Frail Ocean*. New York: Ballantine Books, 1969.

Mitchell, John G. and Stallings, Constance, eds. *Eco-Tactics: The Sierra Club Handbook for Environmental Activists*. New York: Pocketbooks, 1970.

Rienow, Robert and Rienow, Leona Train. *Moment in the Sun*. New York: Ballantine Books, 1969.

Shepard, Paul and McKinley, Daniel, eds. *Subversive Science: Essays Toward an Ecology of Man*. Boston: Houghton Mifflin, 1970.

Shurcliff, William A. *S/S/T and Sonic Boom Handbook*. New York: Ballantine Books, 1970.

Whiteside, Thomas. *Defoliation*. New York: Ballantine Books, 1970.

CHAPTER 2

THE LEGAL FABRIC OF THE PRIVATE LAWSUIT

THE LEGAL FABRIC
OF THE PRIVATE LAWSUIT

Excerpts from five leading articles on the law are set forth in this chapter. Three of these are from articles which appeared for lawyers in law reviews and two were written originally for the layman. All of them hold digestible information, however, for both lawyer and layman.

Of the two articles prepared by lawyers for the public, one was done for the *Bulletin of the Atomic Scientists* (§2.1). In this article, Professor D'Amato of Northwestern University School of Law discusses group efforts and his own experience in the *Zion* case, where a power company is being sued for thermal and radiation pollution. More facts on this suit are given in §5.2. In the other article, two lawyers from El Paso, Texas, have prepared a brief for the League of Women Voters on actions which can be brought by a committee of citizens for clean air (§2.5).

The law review article by Schmitz, who is an engineer as well as a lawyer, takes the position that the courts need a real prodding to make the private suit work. His paper also constitutes a fine review of the present-day state of the law, especially in the nuisance area (§2.3). The article by Esposito, who is a lawyer on the staff of Nader's Raiders in Washington, D.C., expresses reasonable impatience with the ability of government to eradicate pollution (§2.4). He analyzes the problems from an economist's standpoint primarily. Attorney Esposito describes a number of very advanced concepts that should be used in bringing a private pollution suit.

We have also placed a short excerpt in this chapter from a paper done by one of the authors of this book (§2.2). This is one of the earliest articles to appear on pollution.

It stresses the suit for lung damage which can be brought
against the mass polluters of urban air. There is also a
discussion of the problem of the apportionment of damages.

The footnotes to the various articles are given at the
end of the chapter, and they themselves make both interesting reading and excellent reference sources. In addition
to the articles we set forth here, and those cited in the footnotes, we can also suggest the following law review articles
for reading by the person who wants to go more fully into
the legal problems in the pollution suit.

Additional References

Bermingham, "The Federal Government and Air and
Water Pollution," *The Business Lawyer,* Jan. 1968, p.
467 (this is a review of federal legislation).

Edelman, "Air Pollution Control Legislation," in *Air Pollution,* Stern, ed. (2d ed.; 1968), vol. 3, p. 553.

Juergensmeyer, "Control of Air Pollution through the Assertion of Private Rights," 1967 *Duke Law Journal*
1126.

McCarter, "The Case That Almost Was," 54 *American
Bar Association Journal* 1076 (1968) (the author
argues for laws to prevent the taking of conservation
lands by eminent domain power).

Reitze, "Pollution Control: Why Has It Failed?" 55
American Bar Association Journal 923 (1969) (the
author concludes that federal and state attempts at controlling pollution will not work).

Seamans, "Tort Liability for Pollution of Air and Water,"
1 *Natural Resources Lawyer* 146 (1970).

Note, "The Cost-Internalization Case for Class Actions,"
21 *Stanford Law Review* 383 (1970) (a student author,
Gerald A. Wright, discusses the eradication of pollution
in economic terms, and then makes a detailed study of
class actions).

Wilson, "Air Pollution: The Texas Lawyers' Neglected
Responsibility," *Texas Trial Lawyers Forum,* May–June
1969, p. 9.

Muskie, "Environmental Jurisdiction in the Congress and the Executive," 22 *Maine Law Review* 171 (1970).

Edwards, "Legal Control of Thermal Pollution," 2 *Natural Resources Law* 1 (1969).

Allison and Mann, "Trial of a Water Pollution Case," 13 *Baylor Law Review* 199 (1961).

Miller and Borchers, "Private Lawsuits and Air Pollution Control," 56 *American Bar Association Journal* 465 (1970).

Hildebrand, "Noise Pollution: An Introduction to the Problem and an Outline for Future Legal Research," 70 *Colum. L. Rev.* 652 (1970).

Rodgers, "Persistent Problem of Persistent Pesticides: A Lesson in Environmental Law," 70 *Colum. L. Rev.* 567 (1970).

Sive, "Some Thoughts of an Environmental Lawyer in the Wilderness of Administrative Law," 70 *Colum. L. Rev.* 612 (1970).

2.1 Group Actions and the Zion Case

Professor D'Amato illustrates the use of group actions to prevent environmental despoliation, in this instance the construction of a nuclear power plant. The reader will profit from the approach he uses—telling the citizen what steps can be taken on his behalf to head off environmental damage.

ENVIRONMENTAL DEGRADATION AND LEGAL ACTION*

by Anthony A. D'Amato†

There is not much point in discussing public legal action against air or water polluters, for the attorney general and various federal and state agencies are moved to act, if at all, by political considerations. If an aroused citizenry

* Reprinted with permission from the *Bulletin of the Atomic Scientists*, March 1970, p. 24.

†Professor D'Amato, a member of the faculty of the Northwestern University School of Law, has written on the ecological effects of nuclear testing by France in the South Pacific and on the effects of chemical weapons in Vietnam.

brings pressure upon these public bodies, then the bodies will act or make a semblance of acting. But an initial flurry of citizen concern does nothing to insure the integrity of the agency over a period of years. Most regulatory agencies were established in the midst of public scandals, but as time went on they became almost clients of the industries they were supposed to regulate. The process is an understandable one: members of a government agency are in daily contact with the businessmen whom they should watch over, and eventually the regulators adopt the perspectives and attitudes of those businessmen. Fidelity to an earlier enacted statute or to a vague concept of "public trust" is hardly sufficient to keep a regulatory commission on its toes.

I shall address myself instead to private legal initiatives. There is a deep tradition in this country that the courts exist to redress imbalances that may remain after the political branches of the government have had their say and played their part. Surely today the accelerating pace of environmental degradation on all fronts betokens an abiding failure on the part of the political branches of government. Thus citizens naturally feel that they ought to be able to turn to the courts for help. The courts are a penultimate resort; after that only demonstrations and riots can possibly work, but it is unlikely that the majority will ever be aroused to go that far. (Note, however, the demonstrations and activism of the previously staid Santa Barbara citizens after the oil spills.)

The basic difficulty with a lawsuit against an air or water polluter, or a proposed new airport or housing development or ski resort in the midst of a wilderness area, is that such a suit does not fit the accustomed court idea of what a lawsuit should be. Private law in this country, and earlier in England, developed its manifold rules and procedures in cases and controversies where one side had allegedly harmed another. This harm could be redressed by a judicial judgment ordering the defendant to pay a sum of money to the plaintiff. The concept of an injunction grew out of the basically private harm situation. The defendant here would be ordered to do something, or desist from doing something, but whatever he did would redound to the benefit of the plaintiff in a way that the mere payment of money could not. Again, injunctions tended to be private matters, such as ceasing to trespass upon the plaintiff's land or desisting from an unfair method of business competition.

(a) Group Suits

Historically, individual plaintiffs have sued to redress private injuries. The law has known some exceptions, such as limited class actions to abate a public nuisance, or shareholders' derivative suits. But by and large public nuisances, or corporation frauds, have been the province of the attorney general suing in behalf of the public. Legislation making such activities criminal in itself takes effective control out of the hands of the public, since no private person can bring a criminal action against any defendant.

In theory, courts would not have to stretch too far to allow lawsuits brought by a number of people who claim to be affected adversely by the activities of an air or water polluter. There would be some problems inherent in the fact that if the plaintiffs lost, other members of the public later would be barred from suing again on the same grounds. The latter might object to being stopped in this manner. But such problems are inherent in any class action, and can be dealt with by publicity of the lawsuit in newspapers and in legal notices columns.

But in practice courts have been very reluctant to allow what is now becoming fashionable to call "public interest litigation." The doctrine of "standing" is invoked by the courts—prodded, of course, by defendants—to bar the lawsuit before the merits of the case are ever allowed to be heard. Proper "standing" is, in the usual case, an important safeguard for courts. To invoke judicial authority, a litigant must have been hurt in some way. It would make no sense, in the extreme, to allow the reader of a newspaper in New York to sue the Union Oil Company for the oil spill off Santa Barbara simply because the New Yorker's sympathy was engaged for the Santa Barbara citizens and he felt that he should do something about it. In a somewhat less extreme, but still easy example, courts do not allow a citizen to sue the President to cease and desist from engaging in war in Vietnam. Even though the citizen may claim that he is being "hurt" by the taxes extracted from him by a government to support what the citizen claims is an illegal war, courts nevertheless uniformly hold that the citizen lacks "standing to sue." The reason given is that his particular "harm" is suffered equally by everyone else, and thus his "case" is actually a public matter, a political question. In furtherance of this denial of standing, courts often say that the citizen's harm is not distinguishable from that of the public generally, and therefore he lacks standing.

The emphasis upon a distinguishable harm suffered specifically by a given plaintiff has taken a bad twist in cases involving environmental degradation. Many courts have recently held that a group of private citizens suing a company that contributes heavily to community air pollution lacks standing to sue because the harm it is suffering in the form of polluted air is not distinguishable from the harm suffered generally by the public. In other words, the courts have borrowed from the concept of "standing," as enunciated principally by the U.S. Supreme Court in taxpayer cases where one taxpayer is no different from two hundred million other citizens, and applied the jurisdictional bar to a plaintiff or group of plaintiffs complaining about air pollution, when it is obvious that the air pollution does not equally affect two hundred million other citizens in the same manner. To some extent this may be sheer naïveté on the part of courts: assuming that the "air" is "polluted" all over equally, they find no particular group of plaintiffs in any distinguishable position with respect to it. Of course, any scientist would be able to testify that the air is not polluted uniformly and that indeed some citizens may have a distinguishable case. But these lawsuits do not get to the trial stage where there is testimony; they are barred at the outset on the basis simply of the pleadings.

The fact is that rational argument as to what constitutes "standing" is only the top of the iceberg in the game that lawyers play in influencing courts. Clearly the "public interest" type of lawsuit now assuming some prominence in the environment area falls somewhere between a purely private lawsuit by a plaintiff claiming that a defendant has harmed him and a general lawsuit against the government by a taxpayer who does not like a particular policy of that government. In the former case there clearly is standing; in the latter there is not. A judgmental question exists as to the middle ground.

Convincing a court to accept a public-interest lawsuit in the environment area is mostly a matter of strategy and of education. As the public becomes more concerned with the fundamental threat to human existence posed by the continuing degradation of the environment that sustains us, it will follow that judges, reading the same newspapers and magazines, will also begin to want to do something about the problem. Judicial sympathy will go a long way in the determination of whether "standing" is a barrier to a given lawsuit. Public education, therefore, will have a direct effect upon the law as well as upon the public. As for strategy, lawyers must do everything they can to make their case appear to be one that is at the private end of the spectrum between a general taxpayer suit and a traditional "he hit me" tort case.

One type of strategy is to emphasize the threat to property values in a case against an environmental polluter. Courts are more inclined to find that a plaintiff has standing if his land values are threatened than if he complains that his health, physical or mental, is impaired. This tendency may only be slightly due to the fact that courts are more "at home" with questions of wealth rather than questions of well-being. A more important reason for the tendency is that courts have been historically convinced that land is unique (a major exception to the law of damages in contracts in early Anglo-Saxon law was the requirement of "specific performance" of contracts for the sale of real estate, on the basis that money alone cannot make up for a unique parcel of land). The threat to land and property values seems to add an element of specificity to a lawsuit and thus combats the standing barrier. Indeed, in a small but growing number of cases over the past couple of years, courts have allowed standing to litigants alleging a threat to the "scenic values" of their property posed by the intended construction of manufacturing facilities or electric power plants in their vicinity. The "scenic value" of a parcel of land may seem to be a rather intangible thing, but courts are quite alert to it. That they may be less alert to someone dying of emphysema from air pollution is simply a datum that must be taken into account by anyone planning a public-interest lawsuit.

A second strategy is the addition of an established organization to the group of plaintiffs. An organization of citizens has a quasi-public aspect to it and thus would seem to represent part of the public interest. If the "public" theoretically has standing, then part of the public, represented by an organization, does also. It is apparently better to get an organization that preexists the problem; a citizens' group against air pollution (such as GASP) would strike a court as an ad hoc group and thus not representative of the public at large.

(b) The Zion Case

An interesting case in the pleadings stage in the Circuit Court of Cook County, Illinois (*Johnston v. Commonwealth Edison Company,* No. 69 L 13755), joins riparian property owners along Lake Michigan, the United Automobile Workers' Union (UAW), and several residents of communities bordering on Lake Michigan as plaintiffs. They are suing to enjoin the construction of the Zion nuclear power plants north of Chicago by Commonwealth Edison Company, asking the court to require Edison to change the construction so that heated and radioactive waters will not be discharged into the lake. The plaintiffs allege substantial thermal pollution of the lake from the 2.16 billion gallons per day of water heated 20°F higher than lake water. They also allege that radioactive tritium will be discharged into the lake. By the number and types of plaintiffs involved, there is a good chance that the "standing" barrier will be surmounted in this case.

If the standing barrier is surmounted, there are numerous legal obstacles remaining. It would be unproductive to go into the numerous problems here, for different ones exist in different situations. In the Lake Michigan case, just to give an example, there is a substantial question whether one can sue a utility which alleges that it has complied with the standards promulgated by the Atomic Energy Commission. As a federal agency, the AEC might be held by a court to preempt state or local standards, though the statute setting up the AEC is quite unclear about this point (it talks about cooperation between federal and state standards). There are numerous evidentiary difficulties with the case: Is tritiated water harmful to persons in the minute quantities to be injected into the lake? Will there come a point when the amount in the lake is harmful to health? Will such a point depend on how many other nuclear power plants are constructed on the lake? What kinds of lake currents are there that will affect the ecology of the lake with respect to the thermal pollution as well as radioactive pollution? These and many other questions would suggest a long and expensive suit if the case gets to the trial stage.

An expensive trial usually redounds to the benefit of the utility (or other defendant). It has great resources to conduct legal battles, whereas plaintiffs typically are loath to contribute much to a public-interest lawsuit that will benefit the noncontributors as much as it will help themselves. On the other hand, a lengthy trial tends to be in favor of plaintiffs. Here, perhaps, is the final and most important aspect of private legal initiatives in the environment area. Up to now, new industries, airports, and power plants have been eminently welcome to communities which look upon them as a source of jobs, revenue, and growth.

Companies, in turn, like to go into areas in which they are welcome. When a group of people in a given community band together and institute lawsuits against a proposed invader of their environment, the corporate invader looks elsewhere for his location. Of course, he may only look, while remaining to fight the battle in the courts. But as Herman Kahn pointed out in the international context, "legal harassment" is usually quite an effective weapon. Although the plaintiffs might lose, if they can get their day in court, the day may stretch into weeks, months, and years; by then, the defendant may simply get up and go elsewhere.

However, we must not conclude that by chasing the defendant away the problem will be solved. Eventually some defendants must move into a particular area because the public needs them. This is particularly true of electric power plants. Electricity in this country is approaching a critical shortage (although the electric utilities continue to urge the public via advertising to heat their homes electrically and to install air conditioning). The rising resentment against utilities for burning oil and coal, thus contributing to air pollution, will surely be used by the utilities as an argument in favor of going nuclear. The new nuclear power plants will be sold to the public as "clean" with respect to the air. The tremendous hazards of radioactive pollution will be downgraded, particularly because such pollution is not visible. But courts will tend to be persuaded that the public must have electricity and that nuclear power stations should not be blocked by judicial action since there is no reasonable alternative. It thus becomes an important argument for lawyers who want ultimately to be successful in court in this type of case to suggest at some point in the proceedings a reasonable alternative to nuclear electric power. Here they will need great help from scientists and technicians. Ideas such as geothermal steam power, geothermal hot water, and sea-tidal power must be developed, and scientists should testify as to the possibilities of solar-thermal power as well.

Ultimately, judges and juries are very practical; they will hesitate to rule against something the public wants unless there is a reasonable alternative. Law and science can no less be divorced in the development of such alternatives than they can be separated in the laborious course of testimony about the ecological and environmental effects of a given corporate defendant's activities.

2.2 Some Traditional Theories and Some Modern Ones

Here the reader will first receive a basic tour of the types of suits which have been brought for injuries due to pollution. The article then suggests a number of radical legal theories for suit including a suit for emphysema or other lung damage due to pollution, and a suit against the manufacturers of gasoline for producing a product which causes pollution.

CIVIL CAUSE OF ACTION FOR LUNG
DAMAGE DUE TO POLLUTION OF UR-
BAN ATMOSPHERE*

by Paul D. Rheingold†

• • •

(a) Well-Recognized Causes of Action

A number of causes of action for personal injury due to pollution of the air are well recognized in the law. They are reviewed here briefly, primarily to provide support for newer causes of action discussed in (*b*) below.[1]

1. *Occupier Adjacent to Factory.* Recovery for personal injury, as well as for crop damage and other economic loss, has been allowed in numerous cases where a person, generally an occupier of land, lives downwind from a factory or other similar source of pollutants.[2] The most common theory under which these cases have been brought is that based upon commission of a private nuisance: the creation of a substantial interference with the use of another's property.[3]

The nuisance cases are virtually impossible to summarize or even categorize since they differ so greatly from state to state as to the reasonability of the defendant's conduct, the nature of the plaintiff's interest, and the interrelationship with other remedies such as public nuisance.

Ultrahazardous liability has also been used as a basis for recovery for air pollution damage.

* Reprinted with permission from 33 *Brooklyn Law Review* 17 (1966), with some sections omitted. Footnotes renumbered.

† Member of the firm of Speiser, Shumate, Geoghan, Krause, & Rheingold, New York City.

Trespass has also been used as a basis for recovery in these air pollution suits, even where there were only gases and no solid particles involved in the pollution.[4] In addition, an action may be bottomed on negligence—carelessly allowing dangerous gases to be emitted—when that theory can be proven.

2. *Premises Liability*. Invitees, licensees, and others who are injured on the premises when they inhale gases which the occupier or owner of the premises has released have prevailed in a number of suits.[5] Typical actions may involve a tenant injured by the inadequate ventilation of an apartment, or a shopper suddenly gassed in a store. This sort of suit is almost always founded on ordinary negligence principles.

3. *Person Off Premises*. At times, the person "gassed" may have been neither on the premises of the person causing the pollution nor an adjacent owner, which is the primary basis considered in 1 above. A number of cases have allowed recovery for damage done to those passing premises which are emitting pollutants. . . .

4. *Contractors; Maintenance Companies*. Another class of defendants sometimes sued for injuries due to air pollution are builders, contractors, engineers, and those who repair or maintain equipment or premises.[6] For example, a building may be so ill-designed that intended exhaust is not removed from the building, or a machine leaks gas because of improper overhaul. Here again, negligence is the theory generally used.

5. *Gas Dealers*. Persons who deal in gas, or who store it, or who transport it, have frequently been held liable for the harm resulting from the escape of that gas.[7] These suits may be maintained on the negligence theory as under 4 above, or on a nuisance or ultrahazardous liability theory, see 1 above.

6. *Products Liability*. Manufacturers and suppliers of defective equipment have frequently been sued for the escape of gas from their products.[8]

7. *Motor Vehicles*. Numerous cases have involved actions by passengers against bus companies and other carriers for lung damage due to the inhalation of exhaust

gases.[9] Liability is generally predicated upon negligence—
the operation of a bus in a defective condition, a point
often proven through the use of *res ipsa loquitur*.[10]

8. *Occupational Disease and Other Statutes.* Perhaps
the largest class of suits for lung damage and other injuries attributable to air pollution is brought under the
special statutes which protect workers. Occupational disease statutes generally cover common types of lung damage which are incurred on the job, especially when it is
the product of long-term pollution.[11] In addition, more
and more actions are being brought for disability payments under the Social Security Act for lung injuries,
especially emphysema, attributable to air pollution.

(b) Newer Causes of Action

1. *Action by Urban Resident.* A man who has lived
all his life in a heavily polluted urban area develops emphysema at the age of fifty-five. He has never smoked
cigarettes and has no previous history of lung disease.
Investigation shows that sixty percent of the pollutants
in the air, over the years, were released either by the large
power company in the city or by the city through such
varied operations as buses, dumps, and furnaces.[12]

An action under these circumstances against the power
company and the city presents in a simple fashion the main
type of action contemplated by the author in this paper.
It indicates the great problems that are added when one
departs factually from the situation of the local polluter
sued by someone in close proximity to the source. There
are, first of all, certain problems relating to the fact that
not all of the polluters are being sued including: the
permissibility of joint suits, failure to sue all defendants,
the obligation to prove what harm is attributable to each
of the defendants, and an apportionment of damages.

As to the theory of suit, the cause of action sounding
in negligence would be proper if its requirements could
be made out factually. It might be shown, for example,
that the defendants failed to use what reasonable control
devices were available to prevent the release of the gases
into the atmosphere; that there were reasonable alterna-

tives to free atmosphere escape of the contaminants, such as burial of debris; or that the emissions should have been postponed until more favorable weather conditions prevailed.[13]

An action based upon private nuisance would also be a proper theory for action by urban dwellers where the various technical requirements of that action could be met.[14] In addition, liability might be predicated upon trespass,[15] or upon engaging in ultrahazardous activities.[16]

In different cities there may be different *chief* sources of pollution. However, it is believed that generally it would be necessary to join no more than three parties in order to have under suit the agencies contributing the majority of the pollutants in the air.

2. *Action against Government.* A city might be sued not only for its own contributions to the pollution but also for its failure to take reasonable steps to control the pollution being created by others. Negligence might be predicated either upon failure to enforce ordinances or upon failure to promulgate adequate controls for pollution.[17]

Where a government, which has been relied upon by its populace to prognosticate the weather and warn of impending dangerous conditions, fails to so warn and such failure is the product of carelessness, the way is open to a negligence action against the governmental body for injuries due to a fog or smog which may have been avoided by staying inside, or by leaving the area.[18]

3. *Products Liability Action against Automobile Manufacturers.* A products liability action might be contemplated when a person can trace his damage to the inhalation of the exhausts of motor vehicles. As has previously been noted,[19] a direct relationship has been established in a number of studies between auto exhaust and lung damage. In addition, successful products liability suits have been brought by persons who were gassed by fumes negligently released from ill-designed or ill-constructed products.[20]

The negligence alleged here would be the improper design of the motor vehicle which allows the escape of large amounts of exhaust with pollutants and unconsumed fuel.[21] Devices have been in existence for some time which could almost completely eliminate major pollutants from auto exhausts, either by chemically transforming the gases, by passing them through an afterburner, or by recirculating them through the combustion cycle.[22] The fact is that such devices have been required by law to be installed on all new vehicles sold in California since last year and that they must be on all cars in the country beginning with next year's models.[23]

A person, then, suing for lung damage due to auto exhaust, such as a toll taker or a worker in a tunnel, might jointly sue General Motors, Ford, and Chrysler for his injuries. He could be sure that by joining the three major manufacturers he had under suit the majority of the agencies responsible for the emission of the gases which he had inhaled. And, if he were not able to show negligence predicated on failure to install exhaust inhibitors, he might turn to a breach of warranty cause of action wherein the alleged defect was the absence of the special exhaust control device.

(c) Where Various Pollutants Combine: Apportionment of Damages

As noted, atmospheric pollution involves the mixture of numerous pollutants in the air. Even a relatively simple pollution case will involve several sources for the pollutant, and a complex one will undoubtedly involve some unidentifiable sources as well. A suit by a city dweller for general lung damage, such as emphysema, will therefore involve serious problems, not only of multiple defendants but also of unknown or nonliable third parties.

In the situation where there is more than one pollutant but *all* of the offending sources are sued, there is precedent for joint and several liability.[24] The most common precedent involves the pollution of water downstream by the discharge of pollutants into the water upstream by several different factories, not acting in concert. Here, some cases have held that, since one indivisible harm has been done to the downstream owner, he may obtain one judgment against all the polluters and collect full damages against any of them, at least if his was a significant source of the total pollution.[25]

The plaintiff has a much harder road when he can only name some of the polluters, as, for example, when he sues the city and the local power company for lung damage. Under the doctrine that a tort-feasor is any person who has caused substantial injury to the plaintiff, although not the totality of it,[26] the suit could be maintained against the major polluters. Here, however, most courts would place the burden upon the plaintiff to show what harm each defendant did to him.[27] There is precedent, nonetheless, for placing the burden on the tort-feasors sued, to limit their liability by showing only what part of the whole they were responsible for, where by the very nature of the injury the plaintiff has suffered but one disease or injury, the parts of which he cannot segregate.[28] This is the view taken by the Restatement of Torts.[29]

• • •

2.3 Primer on Environmental Pollution Actions

No one could ask for a more systematic review of the legal problems and hurdles connected with a pollution action than is provided in the following article by Schmitz. In itself it is a primer on the law, especially in the nuisance area.

POLLUTION, LAW, SCIENCE, AND
DAMAGE AWARDS*
by Thomas M. Schmitz†

(a) History and Defenses

Man-created environmental pollution is an ancient problem.[30] The first smoke abatement law was passed in 1273, and in 1307 a Royal Proclamation was issued prohibiting the use of coal in furnaces. The following year a violator of the proclamation was executed for that offense. Even then,

* Reprinted with permission from 18 *Cleveland State Law Review* 456 (1969). Some sections have been omitted and section headings changed. Footnotes have been renumbered.

† Member of the Ohio Bar; Chemical Engineer; Registered Professional Engineer.

the seriousness of environmental pollution was firmly established.

Early in the present century, the United States Supreme Court proclaimed that a wrong or injury resulting from pollution, such as that of a stream, is not to be condoned merely because of the importance of such operation to either the public or the operator, and that for such a wrong there is a remedy.[31] In 1933 the same Court declared a municipal sewer treatment plant to be a permanent nuisance, generously granted the complainant $500 damages, and permitted the wrongdoer to pollute a stream undisturbed after paying his debt to society.[32] Yet, the Court commented that $500 damages was cheaper for the wrongdoer than compelling him to install pollution abatement controls. Although this decision was handed down during the Depression, the Court thus had set an extremely dangerous precedent.

Many philosophies aimed at evaluating competing interests have evolved from the voluminous case law related to environmental pollution.[33] A wide variety of circumstances surrounding individual cases and "relevant facts" has been laboriously considered by courts, to the extent that many of these factors have acquired the status of pseudo-defenses.[34] The "doctrine of convenience," for example, is a curious theory wherein the name itself suggests an indifference to mischief created by polluters if such pollution is inconvenient to abate.[35] Rigid theories related to "riparian land owners" caused many jurists to adopt a "reasonable use doctrine," wherein upstream polluters are permitted to pollute water streams unobstructed if such pollution is not "unreasonable." [36] Such pollutions, however, invariably continue and increase, leaving the problem of abatement to a future generation.

Many courts experience considerable difficulty in resolving the equities in view of contributions made by industry to communities, such as providing employment and paying taxes.[37] For example, a steel galvanizing plant expelling noxious injurious fumes,[38] a coke plant belching harmful gases and odors,[39] a chemical plant releasing deadly chlorine gas,[40] and an aluminum smelting plant discharging corrosive fluorides,[41] all were found to have value to the community and to provide security to the nation and, accordingly, their continued operations and pollution aggravation were held to supersede any public policy arguments for environmental health. Nominal damages, if any, were awarded, and injunctions were uniformly denied.[42]

The result of these practices, therefore, has been to perpetuate and compound environmental pollution, to the detriment of future generations. Many polluters have blatantly adopted the callous attitude that it is cheaper to pay claims than to control pollution,[43] and other industries have simply refused to abate pollution practices in any way whatsoever.[44]

(b) Environmental Pollution; Nuisance; Damages

Liability for environmental pollution has been based upon a variety of forms of actions including negligence, nuisance, and trespass.[45] Contemporary law stresses wrongful conduct, with due consideration as to whether an invasion of interest exists which is intentional, negligent, or ultrahazardous.[46] The great majority of recent cases, however, characterize nuisance as an intentional invasion of the complainant's interests without regard to procedural technicalities associated with trespass and negligence.[47]

A nuisance concept encompassing both tortious conduct and invasion of property interests has developed in which a distinction has emerged between public and private nuisance. Both public and private nuisance, however, require a substantial interference and not merely an inconvenience or an offense to aesthetic senses.[48] Accordingly, a commercial activity may diminish the value of land, but damages are not recoverable unless such activity is a nuisance.[49]

Environmental pollution constituting a nuisance may be remedied by awarding damages; or, when damages at law are inadequate or irreparable harm is threatened, equitable relief or injunction are available.[50]

Air and water pollution which is not readily corrected or abated is termed a permanent nuisance.[51] Individuals specifically injured by uncontrollable pollution may recover damages, measured by diminution or depreciation in property value.[52] Thus, an oil refinery wrongfully polluting a stream created a permanent nuisance and was assessed damages measured by the difference in market value of adjoining land immediately before and immediately after the injury.[53] An incinerator operated by a furniture mill caused permanent damages to neighboring property justifying an award for depreciation in property value.[54]

Environmental pollution due to an unreasonable use of property, causing substantial interference with another's interest, is termed a temporary nuisance.[55] Temporary nuisances are abatable and, therefore, should be abated.[56] A steel galvanizing plant emitting obnoxious fumes and odors, for example, constituted a temporary nuisance and was compelled to make all reasonable efforts to abate the nuisance.[57] An aluminum reduction plant expelling corrosive fluorides into the air was compelled to install proper hoods and electronic precipitators despite the high cost of installing these controls.[58] In addition to abatement, damages may be assessed for the loss of rental value or use value of the property affected.[59] Thus, ammonia gas escaping unreasonably from an ice manufacturing facility was found to be a substantial interference with neighboring apartments and, accordingly, damages measured by loss of rental value were awarded.[60] Continued pollution is a renewable wrong and, therefore, successive damages are recovered until abated.[61]

Special damages proximately caused by environmental pollution are recoverable for personal discomfort, annoyance, or inconvenience, injury to health, or reasonable expenses incurred.[62] Thus, a chemical plant emitting carbon black into the atmosphere was found to be a nuisance, entitling the complainant to a $500 personal award of damages in addition to compensatory damages for depreciation of his property and for repainting of structures.[63]

Punitive damages may be awarded when wrongful pollution is intentionally and persistently maintained with a reckless disregard for others.[64] Intentional pollution of a stream by an oil refinery with full knowledge thereof was

held to be malicious conduct warranting liability for punitive damages.[65] Atmospheric pollution continued unabated
despite numerous complaints and, therefore, an asphalt
plant was held liable for punitive damages based on the
willful disregard of surrounding homeowners' property.[66]
An aluminum smelting plant which was fully cognizant
that corrosive fluorides were being expelled into the atmosphere further acknowledged a prevailing management view
that payment of claims was cheaper than installation of
proper pollution abatement equipment. Accordingly, treble
punitive damages were assessed.[67]

Damages are recoverable for wrongful pollution even
though injunctive relief has been granted.[68] Thus, environmental pollution may be enjoined and further proceeded
against for damages at law and, therefore, the remedies are
concurrent and not exclusive.[69]

(c) Equitable Relief—Injunctions

Equity will intervene and abate environmental pollution
by injunction when such pollution is continuous and permanent, when the injury is irreparable, or when damages
are an inadequate remedy.[70] Mere diminution in property
value without irreparable injury, however, is an insufficient basis for granting equitable relief.[71] But equity, like
relief at law, will not interfere with or enjoin an activity
which merely offends the sentimental, psychological, aesthetic, or artistic sensibilities.[72]

A court of equity will intervene and prevent harmful
gases and nauseating odors from being dispelled into the
atmosphere to the detriment of surrounding property owners.[73] Hence, an oil refinery may be enjoined from discharging nauseating gases into the air.[74] Granting an injunction against a chemical company discharging deadly
chlorine gas was held not to be an abuse of discretion when
the wrongdoer would have continued releasing chlorine
unless restrained.[75] Notwithstanding substantial installation costs, an aluminum reduction plant was required to
install available pollution abatement controls or, alternatively, be enjoined from continuing an operation which

emitted excessive quantities of corrosive fluorides into the atmosphere.[76]

When science and engineering provide methods for abating pollution, failure to employ such methods is a basis for enjoining a manufacturing operation.[77] An equitable decree is confined to issuing an injunction, and the burden is upon the tort-feasor to engineer a method for abating the pollution.[78] Although most states have enacted pollution control legislation, administrative proceedings related therewith are not a condition precedent to obtaining equitable injunctive relief.[79]

(d) Group Actions

A private citizen may enjoin environmental pollution constituting a nuisance if a special injury not common to the community[80] is suffered by the complainant. Two or more complainants may join in a class action to abate pollution when the property of each is similarly affected, even though the respective properties may be separate and distinct.[81] Hence, a class action brought by six property owners joined to abate the emission of noxious fumes and smoke was not invalidated by a failure of other members of such class to join the action.[82] Likewise, there was not a misjoinder of plaintiffs when fifty-five residents of a village sought to enjoin the operation of four stone quarries.[83]

(e) Public Nuisances—Powers and Responsibilities of Municipalities

Air and water pollution interfering with the health and well-being of an entire community is a public nuisance for which the wrongdoer may be subjected to criminal prosecution.[84] Generally, municipalities derive police power to abate environmental pollution from the state, either through a general statutory enactment, or by the charter granted to the municipality.[85] Accordingly, power to abate environmental pollution is a portion of the police power incidental to, and necessarily vested in, municipalities by the state.[86]

The law is well settled that municipalities are liable for environmental pollution created and maintained by them, even though such pollution may be pursuant to exercising a governmental function.[87] Thus, cities have been held liable for creating a nuisance by maintaining garbage dumps and sewer treatment plants.[88]

Municipalities, however, remain immune to liability for failure to abate environmental pollution created or maintained by third parties.[89] The few exceptions to governmental immunity are limited to interferences with public right-of-ways or to nuisances existing on property owned or maintained by the municipality.[90] It is conceivable that pollution of air or of a waterway may be so acute as to be an interference with a public right-of-way.[91]

A few jurisdictions have held that a municipality having power to abate a nuisance must exercise such power, and this accordingly reflects the view that a legislative mandate is imposed upon the municipality to discharge a municipal function.[92] If the duty to abate environmental pollution is imposed by statute, a municipality may be held liable for a negligent failure to abate, since liability is predicated on failure to exercise a ministerial duty imposed by statute.[93]

Municipal officers are ordinarily immune from liability for negligence in carrying out "discretionary" duties as long as such duties are carried out in good faith.[94] Duties imposed by law involving less personal judgment are classified as "ministerial," and municipal officers may be held liable for misfeasance and nonfeasance in carrying out such duties.[95] Due consideration should be extended, therefore, to determining whether duties imposed upon public officials to enforce antipollution laws are discretionary or ministerial.

Statutes and ordinances directed against environmental pollution at the time of their enactment encounter strict constitutional restraints wherein enacted laws must afford due process and provide equal protection to all citizens.[96] City ordinances, for example, have been held unconstitutional and void on the basis of vesting unlawful discretion to summarily abate a smoke nuisance without defining the terms and conditions under which abatement could be effected.[97] Valid statutes and ordinances directed at abating environmental pollution practices, therefore, must prescribe definite standards to guide administrative agencies in exercising the power delegated.[98]

Accordingly, due to constitutional restrictions, discretionary powers vested in public officials are limited, and duties imposed by pollution abatement laws are primarily ministerial.[99] The conclusion is apparent, therefore, that public officials charged with the duty of abating environmental pollution are susceptible to liability for neglect of their official duties.[100]

(f) Use of Science

An interested citizens' group in Montana recently brought suit to enjoin a paper pulp mill operation and compel the facility to "at least conform to the state of the art." [101] Failure to utilize advanced engineering techniques is a sufficient basis for granting an injunction, and the burden of pollution abatement costs is not a defense.[102] The United States Supreme Court upheld a Detroit air pollution ordinance and noted that expenditures for pollution controls were not unreasonable.[103] Public pollution abatement laws, however, are invalid to the extent that compliance therewith is impossible due to nonavailability of modern abatement controls.[104]

Accordingly, a deficiency in scientific know-how may be a good defense against enforcement of public pollution laws. However, a lack of suitable pollution controls is not a defense to a nuisance action initiated by a private citizen.

• • •

2.4 New Theories for Private Pollution Suits

In the face of chronic underenforcement of existing antipollution laws, the private citizen may wonder if he can do anything to stop the assault on his environment and health by industrial polluters. Surprisingly, large-scale results might be achieved through private litigation, the author argues, by plaintiffs who can marshal both the evidence of violations of established standards and the growing body of data on the effects of pollution. Mr. Esposito then offers a few suggestions for extensions of traditional doctrines of law which would facilitate such remedies.

AIR AND WATER POLLUTION: WHAT
TO DO WHILE WAITING FOR
WASHINGTON*

by John C. Esposito†

In 1308 a luckless resident of the city of London was
executed for violating a Royal Proclamation prohibiting
the burning of coal in furnaces.[105] Since that time, it is safe
to say, there has been something of a decrease in the severi-
ty of public sanctions applied against the polluters of our
environment. . . . But we are just now entering an era
which will witness an unprecedented—and long overdue—
consciousness of the threat to our environment. The courts
will be obliged to rethink much of the conventional legal
wisdom relating to judicial policy vis-à-vis ecological questions. Holmes said that ". . . if old implements could not be
adjusted to new uses, human progress would be slow.[106]
With regard to environmental questions, one might go
further and say that human life—not to mention human
progress—may end completely if new uses cannot be made
from old legal implements.

(a) The Legal Implications of the Failure to Utilize the Latest Pollution Control Technology

There are probably several hundred companies engaged
in producing air and water pollution control equipment.
Many of these companies were canvassed for our study
and the almost universal complaint was that industry was
not willing to invest in the latest, most adequate control
technology. The following response, from a manufacturer
of water pollution controls, is typical:

> . . . we have found it very hard to place our equip-
> ment out in the field, mostly because industries refuse
> to spend any money for this cause. The attitude toward
> cleaning up the waste water is very negative, and they

* Reprinted with permission from 5 *Harvard Civil Rights–Civil
Liberties Law Review* 32 (1970). Some sections have been omitted
and section headings changed. The footnotes have been renumbered.
† A.B. Long Island University; M.A. Rutgers University; J.D.
Harvard University; Member, District of Columbia Bar; Staff Con-
sultant, Center for the Study of Responsive Law, Washington, D.C.

feel that they are paying for something in which there is no profit available to them. Therefore, unless they are forced into doing something about it, my opinion is that they are going to continue to stall, either by pulling political strings or denying that there is any purification equipment available.[107]

From the economic point of view of the corporate polluter, this is, of course, eminently sensible. Pollution is what economists call an external diseconomy[108]—i.e., it is a cost of production (the use of air and water as a depository of industrial waste) which is borne not by the profit seeker but by society at large. Why then, absent compulsion, should the corporate executive "internalize" this cost, and thereby surrender what is in effect a public subsidy, by investing in profit-reducing pollution control equipment? Such investments are embarrassing expenditures on the company's annual income statements.

This public subsidy conferred upon the polluter not only results in an economic windfall to him; it leads also to misallocation of economic resources because the costs of his activity are not accurately reflected in the company's income statement. If on the other hand the polluter had to pay, through the imposition of money damages, for the mental, physical, and ecological damage caused by him, several results would appear. First, if the costs of the penalties assessed against polluters were greater than the costs of pollution control equipment, the polluter would rationally choose to increase net profits by purchasing such equipment. Second, if all polluters were assessed these costs, a highly innovative pollution control industry would be created in response to the great demand for cheaper and more efficient pollution control devices. Third, in the long run the forced internalization of pollution costs would increase the sales of nonpolluting industries since consumer demand, unless inelastic, would shift toward goods whose price did not include the costly surcharge of court-imposed pollution damages.

The social costs imposed by private profit seeking have not gone completely unnoticed by the common law. Historically, an individual whose person or property has been adversely affected by the use to which his neighbor has devoted his property has been able to sue for damages or injunctive relief on the theories of nuisance, negligence, or trespass.[109] In an earlier age, these were discreet, tightly compartmentalized legal concepts which must have provided eighteenth century legal lexicographers many joyful, hairsplitting hours. But under modern development they have all merged to a great extent; the lines between each have become twisted,[110] and no attempt will be made to unravel them here.

The important point for the purposes of the present discussion is to recognize that the concepts of nuisance, negligence, and trespass represent the common law's rudimentary attempts to redress identifiable injuries caused by external diseconomies. What this means in the context of air and water pollution is that when a plaintiff can show that the activities of his corporate neighbor are sufficiently noxious to satisfy certain technical requirements the courts will order the defendant to pay damages or will enjoin his activities. The defendant is thereby forced to internalize a cost of production—the polluting of clean air and water —by paying damages, by ceasing his noxious operations, or by buying off the plaintiff. If these "internalizing" suits become widespread enough, they may provide effective deterrents to the industrial pollution of our environment. That is the potential of this crude common law device.

One reason why the potential of this private nuisance action has not been realized is that damages alleged by the plaintiffs, who are typically one or a few homeowners situated near an industrial smokestack, have seldom reflected the entire social cost resulting from the defendant's pollution. Although the particular plaintiffs who step forward with a lawsuit may be grievously injured, an even stronger case could be made against the polluter if plaintiffs could, in a class action, represent the claims of all persons victimized by the pollution in any manner, including injuries to mental and physical health and ecological damage. Then the court would be presented with the true social costs of the defendant's pollution in balancing that cost against the cost to the polluter of purchasing control equipment.

From this point of view, then, the class action can be an effective device for demonstrating, through strength of numbers, the weight of the equities on the side of environmental safety. Otherwise, faced with only a few plaintiffs claiming relatively minimal damages, corporate polluters may say, as did one executive of Reynolds Metals Company, "It is cheaper to pay claims than it is to control fluorides.[111]

Unfortunately, Federal Rule 23 [112] may never be developed as a vehicle to aggregate the relatively small monetary claims of numerous pollution victims in light of the Supreme Court's recent decision in *Snyder v. Harris*.[113] State class action doctrines are presently even less viable than was the federal provision before *Snyder*, although there may remain considerable room for innovation in the state courts. In purely practical terms, relatively small individual nuisance actions do not offer the contingent fee potentials to induce lawyers to act as "private attorneys general" in the effort to abate pollution. Expanding the class action concept will be a challenge both to the ingenuity of lawyers and to the ability of our legal system to adapt its procedures to the new varieties of social injuries produced by modern technology.

Even if representative plaintiffs could maintain such suits, they would still be faced with the immense, possibly insurmountable, scientific problem of proving causation where there are multiple polluters. Conservation action groups, such as the Environmental Defense Fund and others, can provide technical information in this area, as can the massive data now being collected by federal and state pollution control agencies. In addition, many of the problems of causation might be avoided by adapting the tort doctrine of joint and several liability to multiple polluters as class defendants.

While resolution of class action and causation problems may not be achieved soon, the increasing availability of improved pollution control devices may have a more immediate impact on the effectiveness of the traditional private nuisance suit. In *Renken v. Harvey Aluminum*,[114] the defendant's failure to keep industrial processes abreast of the latest pollution control technology was the basis for an injunction ordering the adoption of certain controls. The court was unmoved by the contention that the cost of these new controls might exceed $2 million,[115] an amount equal to five percent of the original plant cost. In *McElwain v. Georgia-Pacific*,[116] an action which sounded in nuisance, the court held that punitive damages would lie if the jury "found that the defendant had not done everything reasonably possible to eliminate or minimize damage to adjoining property." [117] One of the most interesting aspects of the *Georgia-Pacific* opinion is that the court used none of the harsh words—like "willful," "wanton," and "reckless disregard"—which are commonly heard in connection with punitive damages. The court seemed to be saying that a manufacturer who pollutes the atmosphere is charged with a duty to keep abreast of and utilize the most adequate technology, and that failure to do so will not simply bear on the determination of whether a wrong has been committed—negligence, trespass—or whether an action for damages due to nuisance will lie; rather, given the special knowledge and expertise of the defendant, a failure to keep abreast will result in punitive damages above and beyond the ordinary form of relief.

The expansion of the reasoning of these two cases may, with adequate empirical investigation, breathe new life into the concepts of nuisance, negligence, and trespass as they relate to pollution problems. Expert testimony that the defendant has not adopted the latest available technology —and our study indicates that this is a widespread phenomenon—may provide a basis for the court to issue a specific timetable for the adoption of appropriate controls, as in *Renken*. But even when the court may be reluctant to prescribe exact methods and timetables or to calculate speculative pollution damages, the possibility of extensive punitive damages may persuade the industry that there is no comparative advantage to be achieved by not investing in pollution control equipment. Many industries have until

now been content to take their chances by pay
quent and barely burdensome damages.

(b) Product Liability Suits

The product liability suit has great potential with respect
to air pollution.[118] Probably the most powerful case for
negligent manufacture as it relates to air pollution can be
made against the automobile companies. Although esti-
mates vary, it is clear that emissions from automobiles
account for between forty and sixty percent of all air pollution, and that figure is much higher in some cities.[119] There
is abundant documentation of the adverse health effects of
carbon monoxide, hydrocarbons, oxides of nitrogen and
lead—pollutants for which the automobile is largely or
almost totally responsible.[120]

The law is clear, as a result of *MacPherson v. Buick
Motor Company*[121] and the innumerable cases which
embellished on that pioneering opinion of Mr. Justice
Cardozo, that the negligent manufacturer of a product is
liable for the injury resulting from the use of his defective
product.[122] And the Restatement of Torts makes clear that
this duty of care on the part of the manufacturer extends
"to those whom he should expect to be endangered by its
probable use." [123] In the case of an automobile negligently
manufactured so as to emit dangerous exhaust fumes, the
duty would extend to anyone who breathes, presumably
the entire population. However, causation may prove to be
a problem for most citizens since it is often difficult to
separate out the effects of the many different kinds of
pollutants in the ambient air of any metropolitan area. Yet,
certain groups which experience an inordinate exposure
to motor vehicle fumes may be in a strong position to
prosecute such actions successfully. The most obvious
examples would be tunnel policemen, toll takers, taxi
drivers, etc.[124] But of course the mere fact of exposure to
dangerous emissions and consequent injury is not enough
to prove liability. The plaintiff in a product liability suit
against the automakers would have to show that they had
failed to exercise due care to minimize these dangerous

emissions.[125] That difficult problem of proof may soon be overcome.

The automobile industry has been criticized for some time for its failure to improve pollution control devices.[126] A resolution by the Los Angeles County Board of Supervisors declared that if the automobile companies had sincerely devoted their energies to dealing with the air pollution problem during the years 1953 to 1956, "air pollution from motor vehicles would have ceased to be a problem by 1966. . . ." [127] These critics found some support for their position in January of 1969 when the Department of Justice filed a civil antitrust complaint against the four major motor vehicle manufacturers and their trade association, the Automobile Manufacturers Association (AMA). The complaint alleged that the manufacturers, under the auspices of the AMA, agreed to pursue research, development, manufacture, and installation of pollution control equipment on a noncompetitive basis, that they agreed to seek joint appraisal of patents submitted by third parties, and that they agreed on at least three occasions— 1961, 1962, and 1964—to attempt to delay installation of motor vehicle air pollution control equipment.[128]

If a judgment were won against the companies for consciously conspiring to delay the introduction of more efficient control devices, private plaintiffs who could show causation and damages would be able to establish negligent or intentional conduct on the part of the defendants. Indeed, even punitive damages might be recoverable for intentional, conscious disregard of the interests of others in conspiring to delay the introduction of such devices.[129] Unfortunately, the Justice Department has entered into a consent judgment in that case,[130] which does not operate as an adjudication of the defendants' conduct; but some local governments are proceeding with their own actions based on the same set of allegations.[131]

(c) Stockholder Suits

Until now, corporate polluters have been generally free from internal pressure to desist from their exploitation of the environment. There is, of course, good reason for this.

Stockholders do not generally include altruism among their motives for investing. The business of business is making money. Pollution control costs money and consequently reduces the fund available for dividends. Executives, therefore, do not view pollution control as a crowd pleaser at the annual stockholders' meeting. Rare verbal exuberances of corporate public-spiritedness have not been kindly received by the courts either. Henry Ford once announced that he was putting the majority of profits back into the business "in order to spread the benefits of this industrial system to the greatest possible number, to help them build their lives and their homes." [132] He was forcefully remonstrated by the Supreme Court of Michigan for this heretical notion that the corporation has a responsibility to the public at large which may be more important than stockholder dividends:

> There should be no confusion . . . of the duties which Mr. Ford conceives that he and the stockholders owe the general public and the duties which in law he and his directors owe to protesting, minority stockholders. A business corporation is organized and carried on primarily for profit.[133]

Yet, there are indications that the situation is changing and that considerable stockholder pressure may be brought to bear on corporate polluters. A recent issue of the *Wall Street Journal* reported that:

> Pollution issues also will be a prime concern of a new stockholders' pressure group, called Proxies for People, being organized by Saul D. Alinsky, the Chicago-based social activist. Mr. Alinsky plans to start soliciting proxies from stockholders throughout the country late next summer and use them to "play a bit of corporate jujitsu" at annual meetings of companies that cause pollution and contribute to other social ills.[134]

Notwithstanding serious economic and political objections to such unlikely corporate altruism, S.E.C. proxy rules do not require management to submit to the shareholders proposals "primarily for the purpose of promoting general economic, political, racial, religious, social, or similar causes.[135] However, if the stockholder can point to some specific economic detriment which might result from the corporation's continuing pollution, such as a possible damage judgment, then the above proxy rule exception would seem not to apply.

Since a majority of stockholders are not likely to approve such resolutions to cease pollution in any event, a stockholder derivative suit against the corporate directors for breach of fiduciary duties would seem a more promising approach. Ordinarily the stockholder would proceed upon the theory of waste of corporate assets through the directors' failure to purchase and install pollution control equipment, so long as the predictable damage judgment in favor of pollution victims would be greater than the cost of such control equipment. Regardless of any waste of corporate assets, pollution exceeding government-established emission levels might constitute a *per se* breach of fiduciary duty as being violative of law or public policy.[136] Whether where it was held that a director would be in breach of his fiduciary duty to the corporation if it could be shown that he used company property in order to defeat the public policy embodied in the National Labor Relations Act.

public-spirited stockholders exist in sufficient numbers to make this device a viable one is problematical. The stockholder suit may, however, bring about tangible results in isolated cases.

(d) Actions against Public Officials for Failure to Abate Pollution Nuisances

As already indicated,[137] the rolls are replete with antipollution laws at every level of government. Although most are by no means strong or pervasive enough, they might be the basis for beginning the enormous process of reversing alarming trends in environmental pollution. Unfortunately, however, many public agencies charged with pollution control and abatement provide notoriously classic examples of conscious nonenforcement of the law. At times the failure to enforce may be traced directly to possible conflicts of interest on the part of the putative enforcers and sometimes to outright disregard and contempt for the public.[138] Many agencies have detailed information concerning the contribution of local industries to the total pollution problem and have permitted these files to accumulate bureaucratic dust for as long as fifteen years.[139] To take one example of active nonenforcement—one which is all too typical—the Boston Metropolitan Air Pollution Control District receives from seven to eight hundred complaints per year. Yet there have been a scant four prosecutions under the state's criminal antipollution statute and only one of these has resulted in conviction.[140]

How can the private citizen respond to such official dereliction in order to force his protectors to be more responsive to public needs? The treatises tell us that remedies against nonfeasant public officials are almost nonexistent in the field of pollution control. The general rule, we are told, is that there can be no recovery for the negligent failure of officials to abate a public nuisance.[141] This no-liability rule is premised on the notion that nuisance abatement is "governmental," "legislative," "quasi-judicial." In short, it is a discretionary function left to the administrative agency, and the courts will adopt their traditional stance of deference to the decisions of the agency, including decisions not to enforce.

Generally, the same reasoning would apply to an application for a writ of mandamus to compel officials to enforce the pollution abatement statutes. Since the conventional formulation holds that mandamus lies to compel the performance of ministerial duties but not where the action involves discretion,[142] superficial analysis might lead the courts to deny the writ in cases of nonenforcement of environmental protection statutes.

One court, in another context, neatly characterized the sophistry inherent in this ministerial-discretionary distinction: "It would be difficult to perceive of any official act, no matter how directly ministerial, that did not admit of some discretion in the manner of its performance, even if it involved only the driving of a nail." [143] Other writers have found that the distinctive is artificial and abstruse,[144] and nowhere is this more true than in the area of pollution abatement. A hard-headed analysis of the real-life dynamics of many pollution control agencies would reveal

that a strong case can be made for mandamus and the
negligence action against officials as remedial devices as
well as deterrents to future inaction.

First of all, it is important to note that many state
statutes embody clear, albeit primitive, standards, such as
the Ringlemann Smoke Chart.[145] Frankly, it requires no
great exercise of expertise or discretion to determine
whether the density of smoke from stack emission exceeds
the maximums allowed under these standards. As one
court said, in reviewing enforcement under a New York
law incorporating the Ringlemann Smoke Chart, "it would
appear that any dense emission would be a violation." [146]
It is submitted that official judgments under such statutes
require only the slightest bit more discretion than the driving of a nail, and that a writ of mandamus or an action
for negligent nonfeasance should lie to compel enforcement. The example given may strike some as a somewhat
palliative approach to air pollution control, and it may
be since smoke is a minute part of the overall problem.
But it is important to note that even this rudimentary enforcement could contribute significantly to the abatement
of other pollutants since many are constituent elements
of what is generically referred to as "smoke."

Turning toward those areas where the pollution picture
may be more complicated and the pollutants involved
more exotic, a similarly strong case can be made for official
liability for negligence or the writ of mandamus. Our
study has convinced us that the plaintiff in many cases
can show that official inaction flies in the face of detailed
information which the agency may have in its files with
respect to violations, and that the agency has failed to use
its full powers under the applicable law to demand specific
cleanup measures by the polluters. In a broader sense,
our studies and those of other task forces[147] have consistently found chronic nonenforcement—not the lack of
desirable substantive regulations—to be the central characteristic of administrative agency failure to protect the
public interest.

If judicial control of administrative action is to be effective, the concept of abuse of discretion must be applied

to agency inaction as well as to agency action, to decisions whether to prosecute violators as well as to decisions defining substantive violations. A pattern of selective enforcement may deny equal protection of the laws[148] and can be raised as a defense by the person selectively prosecuted.[149] Likewise, persons who lose the protection of a statute enacted for their benefit ought to have a judicial remedy of selective nonenforcement as a denial of equal protection. It is no answer that the statute conferring the benefit might only grant a "privilege" instead of a "right" guaranteed by the Constitution; for even a privilege may not be conferred or withheld on the basis of whim.[150] Some rational basis, grounded in the governing statute, valid substantive regulations, or a properly delimited administrative "expertise," should be required for every constitutionally permissible agency decision not to enforce the law.

A traditional objection to judicial review of prosecutorial discretion has been that an agency with a limited budget cannot prosecute all violators. Thus the agency might legitimately rely upon its expertise to determine enforcement priorities according to some rational cost-benefit analysis consistent with its peculiar statutory mandate. But scarcity of enforcement resources should not entitle a prosecuting agency to base nonenforcement of the law upon whim, laziness, the political power of violators, or their greater access to agency personnel.

By refusing even to adopt clear prosecutorial priorities, an agency flouts due process just as if it defined substantive offenses in an arbitrary and capricious manner. Under this theory the role of administrative expertise would be the same whether judicial review related to agency action or inaction.[151] Far from being an undesirable influence, judicial review of prosecutorial discretion would have the salutary effect of breaking through a wall of immunity which has shielded the many pollution control officers for whom nonfeasance and consistent disregard for public health have become a way of life.

(e) The Constitutional Right to Clean Air and Water

• • •

So we are dealing with a problem which, if not dealt

with quickly, may result in the end of mankind. There is no circumspect way to put the problem; it is simply that serious. Against this setting, it is difficult for an American lawyer to accept the proposition that the widespread threat of total human extinction is not somehow addressed by the panoply of rights delineated in the central legal document of our nation, the Constitution of the United States of America. Of course, the Constitution says nothing explicitly about the right to be free from pollution, yet one feels certain that the general concern for the sanctity of the person which pervades that document would remind the Justices of the Supreme Court of the famous words of Mr. Justice Holmes in the case of *Missouri v. Holland*.[152]

> ... when we are dealing with words that are also a constituent act, like the Constitution of the United States, we must realize that they have called into life a being the development of which could not have been forseen completely by the most brilliant of its begetters. It was enough for them to realize or to hope that they had created an organism; it has taken a century and cost their successors much sweat and blood to prove that they created a nation. The case before us must be considered in the light of our whole experience, and not merely in that of what was said a hundred years ago.[153]

In *Griswold v. Connecticut*,[154] for instance, holding unconstitutional a statute prohibiting the use of a birth control device or drug, Justice Douglas confronted the issue that the Constitution does not explicitly provide a right of privacy in marriage. He pointed out that the explicit guarantees of the Bill of Rights have always been interpreted as carrying with them certain implicit correlative guarantees. The specific guarantees actually are nuclei of a constellation of closely related rights. "Various guarantees create zones of privacy." [155] By violating this implicit zone of privacy, the statute exceeded constitutional bounds.

Almost parenthetically, Justice Douglas mentioned the stepchild of the Bill of Rights, the Ninth Amendment.[156] He relied upon that Amendment as evidence that the rights correlative with those specifically delineated are not negated by the absence of explicit guarantees.

The rule of construction embodied in the Ninth Amendment could be the foundation for a declaration by the Supreme Court of a constitutional right to an uncontaminated environment. Perhaps no principle is as fundamental as the preciousness of every human life. The Fifth and Fourteenth Amendments offer no less protection to "life" than to "liberty." Surely liberty and the various rights specifically enumerated in the Constitution are meaningless abstractions if life itself is ended through pollution's often invisible but unrelenting and imminently cataclysmic environmental assault on the human body.

Delimiting the precise scope and nature of a constitutional right to an uncontaminated environment will be extremely problematical. Whether the source of the right is imminent threat to human life or invasion of privacy, the constitutional protection would extend only to some degree of pollution deemed "unreasonable." Moreover, a reasonableness standard is consistent with the explicit constitutional provisions to which the new right is related —e.g., the "due" process of the Fifth Amendment, the prohibition of "unreasonable" searches and seizures of the Fourth Amendment.

A second issue is whether the constitutional protection would run only against government pollution or against private polluters as well. Here again the explicit constitutional provisions from which the right might be said to arise grant protection only against state action. Although the government is indeed a major polluter itself,[157] a constitutional right not extending to protection from the most important—i.e., private—pollution would be illusory. Perhaps this new constitutional right would only empower, not command, the Congress to enact antipollution legislation. Nevertheless, an affirmative duty upon government not to facilitate private pollution could have far-reaching effects. And this constitutional right might impose new duties severely limiting the scope of administrative discretion not to abate pollution. A duty would likewise be imposed upon other government agencies not directly concerned with pollution control to avoid approving, promoting, or even indirectly facilitating private pollution.[158] For example, the Atomic Energy Commission could no longer approve site locations for nuclear-powered electric generating plants without considering the effects of thermal pollution.[159]

Moreover, *Monroe v. Pape*[160] eliminates any doubt that the "under color of law" provision of 42 U.S.C. §1983[161] was intended to reach state *non*enforcement which compromises federally guaranteed rights.

> The [congressional] aim was to provide a federal remedy where the state remedy, though adequate in theory, was not available in practice. . . . [I]t is abundantly clear that one reason the legislation was passed was to afford a federal right in federal courts because, by reason of . . . *neglect* . . . state laws might not be enforced and the claims of citizens to the enjoyment of rights, privileges, and immunities guaranteed by the Fourteenth Amendment might be denied by state agencies.[162]

This situation is on all fours with the type of negligent disregard of public duty which has been discussed earlier[163] and would afford a federal cause of action under §1983 against nonfeasant state pollution control officials without regard to diversity or jurisdictional amount.[164]

If government is not required to act directly, then it at least might be compelled to facilitate efforts of private citizens to combat pollution through the courts. For one thing, it is reasonable to conclude that court action against pollution is not feasible unless class plaintiffs can reflect the total damage resulting from the pollution and unless multiple polluters can be joined as class defendants.[165] State procedural rules might be voided which prevent maintenance of such class actions. In addition, courts might be constrained from applying unreasonably restrictive nuisance doctrines in private actions to abate pollution.

The "precedent" for this reshaping of state tort law and procedural rules is *Shelley v. Kraemer*.[166] There, the Supreme Court held that judicial enforcement of a racially discriminatory restrictive covenant constituted state action in violation of the equal protection clause. Extension of *Shelley* beyond the voiding of restrictive covenants has not been looked upon favorably by commentators.[167] With but little imagination, a literal application of the Court's statement that "[t]he power of the state to create and enforce property interests must be exercised within the boundaries defined by the Fourteenth Amendment[168] could radically reshape much state law traditionally considered beyond the reach of federal power.

The possibility of asserting a constitutional right to a clean environment directly against private polluters provides a potentially monumental opportunity to dramatize, only in the way that groundbreaking Supreme Court cases can, the responsiveness of our legal system to modern exigencies. A victory on this point would result in a decision which would stand alongside *Brown v. Board*[169] in the history of American constitutional law and might lead the way to truly effective legislative and executive recognition of the scope of the environmental problem.[170]

(f) Summary

> *The business of America is business.*
>
> —Calvin Coolidge

We live in a business culture. That culture has shaped the prevailing values of our society to meet the requirements of the corporate system and has fed the mystique of progress. Judges are part of our society and they have often afforded special solicitude to those enterprises which promised to increase the productive base of the nation or the locality.

The common law has articulated a doctrine, commonly used in nuisance cases, known as "balancing the equities" —weighing the social utility of the defendant's behavior against the injury to the plaintiff. When the social utility is determined to be substantial enough, i.e., when there is a prospect for "progress," the plaintiff's injury is more likely to be thought of as an inconvenience. But this is only one aspect of the problem.

Legal realism requires us to recognize that "balancing the equities" is a judicial evaluative process which extends far beyond the bounds of nuisance law, even though its determinative force in other areas of decision is unacknowledged. Whether the question before a court concerns the existence of a constitutional right to clean air and water, or perhaps whether substantial product liability suits will lie against the automobile companies, the courts will, either explicitly or *sub silentio,* consider the resolution of these questions in the light of their possible effects on "progress." But unless advancement in the economic sense is placed in juxtaposition with the probable costs in human lives resulting from pollution, "progress" is an empty and illusory idea.

This essay has assumed that, for the present at least, the courts have the greatest potential to innovate, to dramatize, and to provide redress insofar as our environmental crisis is concerned. Yet, it is sobering to remember that for almost two hundred years the courts have generally balanced the equities in favor of industrial exploitation of the environment. In a statement distinguished for its candor if not for its wisdom, one judge has said:

> . . . one's bread is more important than the landscape or clear skies. Without smoke, Pittsburgh would have remained a pretty village.[171]

It is time for the courts to abandon this brand of judicial mercantilism and set out to redress the imbalance of the last two hundred years.

2.5 Actions by Incorporated Citizens' Groups

This report illustrates the service which lawyers can render to local groups, such as the League of Women Voters. While some reference is made to Texas law, virtually identical provisions exist under the laws of every state.

WHAT CAN THE CITIZEN DO ABOUT
AIR POLLUTION*

*by Richard T. Marshall
and Larry H. Schwartz†*

Not only does a private citizen or incorporated Clean
Air Committee have a right to bring a lawsuit or a *class
action* against the polluter, but under certain theories of
law the private citizen or group can sue the state, the
county, or the city.

1. In many states the local Clean Air Committee can
appear as an intervenor in an enforcement lawsuit brought
by the State Air Control Board against an offending polluter. In some states the burden is upon the State Air
Control Board to go to court if the polluter ignores a Board
order. In other states the burden is upon the polluter to
go to court to attempt to set aside a Board order. In either
such type of lawsuit there is no reason why interested
individuals and organizations cannot enter the suit to
assert their rights in seeing that the polluter is shut down
until such time as he can operate without damaging and
despoiling the atmosphere.

2. Under the *trust doctrine*, the state, county or city,
or even the federal government, may be considered a
fiduciary for the people, with the affirmative duty to protect
and preserve their proprietary rights, including their right
to a clean environment. Citizens or groups may thus sue a
government unit under the *trust doctrine* to assert their
property rights in a clean environment. The U.S. Supreme
Court stated as early as 1892 that "the state holds the title
to the lands under the navigable waters . . . in trust for
the people of the state that they may enjoy the navigation
of the waters, carry on commerce over them, and have
liberty to fishing therein freed from the obstruction or
interference of private parties."[172] The Supreme Court of
the State of Florida has also established this trust right in

* Prepared by the authors for the El Paso League of Women
Voters. Several sections omitted.

† Practicing attorneys in El Paso, Texas. Mr. Marshall's role in
a suit against the American Smelting and Refining Company is
described in §5.5 below.

the people to force governmental units to protect their rights in the enjoyment of their environment.

3. The right of the people to enjoy the environment is also said to be a *civil right,* stemming from the Bill of Rights and the Fourteenth Amendment to the Constitution of the United States. In 1871 Congress enacted a Civil Rights Act which many attorneys believe may be invoked to protect citizens' civil rights against poisonous pollution of the environment. Constitutionally, it has been said that, in addition, the unenumerated rights of the people under the Ninth Amendment, the "forgotten amendment" in the Bill of Rights, include environmental rights. A suit against a local governmental unit under the Civil Rights Act of 1871 might also be brought under the Ninth Amendment and, furthermore, the Fourteenth Amendment upon an allegation that the state, county or city is by its own inaction failing to enforce the federally protected civil rights of its inhabitants to a clean environment, and thus aiding and abetting the taking of their property rights without due process of law. Further, it may be argued that a state which either affirmatively or permissively sanctions the pollution of the environment thus grants a property right to a polluter to do as he pleases, while failing to protect the rights of other citizens to a clean environment. Such action by a state, county or city in effect is a denial of the equal protection of the laws to its citizens as well as a taking of their property right without due process of law, all in violation of the Fourteenth Amendment.

There is no question that a private organization or citizens' group may be most effective if it is incorporated. Under the Texas Non-Profit Corporation Act, such an educational and public-spirited organization may be chartered as a nonprofit corporation by the State of Texas. Under the Internal Revenue Code, such a corporation may qualify as a tax-exempt organization, contributions to which may be tax-deductible. So long as such organization does not actively participate in damage suits for private plaintiffs, it may enjoy this tax-free status, even though it appears as a litigant in public lawsuits and in private injunction lawsuits.

[1] Serious statute of limitations problems may be involved in pollution cases, especially where chronic inhalation occurs. On these problems, see discussion in Rheingold, "Solving Statutes of Limitation Problems," 4 *Am. Jur. Trials* 441 (1966).

[2] *United Verde Copper Co. v. Jordan,* 14 F.2d 299 (9th Cir. 1926) (smelter); *Asphalts Products Co. v. Marable,* 65 Ga. App. 877, 16 S.E.2d 771 (1941); *Kelley v. National Lead Co.,* 240 Mo. App. 47, 210 S.W.2d 728 (1948) (chemical plant) (judgment was reversed for the defendant with leave given to the plaintiff to amend his complaint from negligence to nuisance). For collected cases, see 54 A.L.R.2d 764.

[3] Private nuisance is predicated on the theory of an interference with one's use and enjoyment of his own property. Incident to ownership of land is the right to enjoy it free from disturbances. See Prosser, *Torts* 611 (3rd ed., 1964). Also see *Morgan v. High Penn Oil Co.,* 238 N.C. 185, 77 S.E.2d 682 (1953) (oil refinery as a nuisance) (reversed and new trial granted because of unclear charge to jury as to essential elements of private nuisance); *Combs v. Crawford,* 258 Ky. 405, 80 S.W.2d 46 (1935) (dump as a nuisance). See generally 86 A.L.R.2d 1322 (oil refinery as a nuisance); 52 A.L.R.2d 1134 (public dump as a nuisance).

[4] *Reynolds Metals Co. v. Lampert,* 324 F.2d 465 (9th Cir. 1963).

[5] *Smith v. Weber,* 70 S.D. 232, 16 N.W.2d 537 (1944) (landlord's liability); *Thomaspolsky v. Gabriel Real Estate Corp.,* 247 App. Div. 776, 286 N.Y. Supp. 285 (1936) (landlord's liability); *Tomko v. Feldman,* 128 Pa. Super. 429, 194 Atl. 338 (1937) (innkeeper's liability).

[6] *Young v. Lee,* 310 Mich. 42, 16 N.W.2d 659 (1944) (liability of an installer); *Ferguson v. Boston Gaslight Co.,* 170 Mass. 182, 49 N.E. 115 (1898) (liability of a repairman); *Donoughe v. East Ohio Gas Co.,* 89 Ohio App. 411, 46 Ohio Op. 244, 102 N.E.2d 881 (1950) (liability of an inspector); *Moran v. Pittsburgh-Des Moines Steel Co.,* 166 F.2d 908 (3d Cir. 1948), cert. denied, 334 U.S. 846 (1948).

[7] *Koch v. Southern Cities Distrib. Co.,* 18 La. App. 664, 138 So. 178 (1931); *Westfield Gas Corp. v. Hill,* 131 Ind. App. 558, 169 N.E.2d 726 (1960); cf. 26 A.L.R.2d 136 (same for escape from service lines).

[8] *Tampa Drug Co. v. Wait,* 103 So.2d 603 (Fla. 1958); *Maize v. Atlantic Refining Co.,* 352 Pa. 51, 41 A.2d 850 (1945); *Ricciuti v. Voltarc Tubes, Inc.,* 277 F.2d 809 (2d Cir. 1960); *Chapman Chemical Co. v. Taylor,* 215 Ark. 630, 222 S.W.2d 820 (1949) (ultrahazardous basis for liability).

[9] *Barnard Bus Lines v. Weeks,* 156 Va. 465, 158 S.E. 870 (1931). *Gluckstein's Admrx. v. Martin,* 244 App. Div. 39, 278 N.Y. Supp. 129 (1935); cf. 56 A.L.R.2d 1099 (private motor vehicles).

[10] *Coastal Coaches v. Ball,* 234 S.W.2d 474 (Tex. 1950).

[11] See 58 *Am. Jur. Workmen's Compensation* §252 (1948). Where there is a single, sudden exposure which causes the damage, the action is generally brought under the regular workmen's compensation provisions.

[12] There is another assumption in this situation: that expert evidence will be able to show that these pollutants were a substantial cause of the emphysema. It would be possible to be the main source of the pollutants per se but not of the pollutant-induced injuries, where different pollutants had a different potential for lung injury.

[13] *Hagy v. Allied Chemical & Dye Co.* 122 Cal. App.2d 361, 265 P.2d 86 (1954).

[14] See supra note 3.

[15] *Reynolds Metals Co. v. Lampert,* supra note 4.

[16] *Luthringer v. Moore,* 31 Cal.2d 489, 190 P.2d 1 (1948). Assumption of the risk here would seem to be a strong defense because, unlike a cigarette smoker, the air inhaler is not aware of the attendant risks.

[17] The discussion in 38 *Am. Jur. Municipal Corporations* §603 (1941) makes it clear that it is only the minority of states which would create liability on the part of municipalities for failure to pass or enforce ordinances or the like.

[18] Most of the actions brought against the United States under the Federal Torts Claims Act for failure to predict the weather accurately or for giving negligent forecasts have failed, apparently on the basis that a discretionary activity was engaged in. See *National Mfg. Co. v. United States,* 210 F.2d (8th Cir. 1954), cert. denied, 347 U.S. 967 (1954); Jayson, *Handling Federal Tort Claims,* at 12–42 (1964).

[19] Hueter, 12 Arch. Env. H. 553 (1966).

[20] See generally note 8 above.

[21] A case in point is *J. C. Lewis Motor Co. v. Williams,* 85 Ga. App. 538, 69 S.E.2d 816 (1952), where liability for the death from asphyxiation of a farm hand on a tractor was predicated on so designing the exhaust of the tractor as to put the opening near a place where a worker would presumably stand.

[22] Nader, *Unsafe at Any Speed* (1965); *The New York Times,* May 1, 1966, p. 1; *Medical World News,* Jan. 5, 1962, p. 15.

[23] *The New York Times,* supra note 22. If it could be shown that the gasoline presently in use is formulated to produce unnecessary pollutants upon combustion, the gasoline producers might be similarly liable.

[24] *Tidal Oil Co. v. Pease,* 153 Okla. 137, 5 P.2d 389 (1931); *Harper-Turner Oil Co. v. Bridge,* 311 P.2d 947 (Okla. 1957).

[25] Prosser, *Torts* §42 (3d ed., 1964). Other cases have held that the burden is on the plaintiff to prove what part of the damage was

attributable to each defendant sued, on the theory that the liability is several, and the damage each polluter did was separate. See, e.g., involving pollution, *Vaughn v. Burnette*, 211 Ga. 206, 84 S.E.2d 568 (1954); *Maas v. Perkins*, 42 Wash.2d 38, 253 P.2d 427 (1953); *O'Neal v. Southern Carbon Co.*, 216 La. 96, 43 So.2d 230 (1949).

[26] Restatement (Second), Torts §431 (1965).

[27] Prosser, *op. cit.* supra note 26, §41 at 247.

[28] *Summers v. Tice*, 33 Cal. 2d 80, 199 P.2d 1 (1948); *Landers v. East Texas Salt Water Disposal Co.*, 151 Tex. 251, 248 S.W.2d 731 (1952) (water pollution case).

[29] New Section 433A of the Restatement of Torts (Second) presents a number of suggested rules which are of great help in this area. Where the negligence or wrongs of several persons combine to cause one indivisible harm such as a personal injury, and each person sued contributed substantially to the whole damage, the Restatement would allow recovery against any one tort-feasor for the whole damage. If any rational division could be made between the relative contributions of the various persons, however, the Restatement would authorize such a split. For example, if forty percent of the pollution was due to the acts of A and sixty percent due to the acts of B, A would be liable for forty percent of the whole harm done to the plaintiff. See also the numerous cases cited in support of these propositions in the Restatement (Second), Torts, Appendix §433A (1965).

[30] Haar, *Land-Use Planning* (1st ed., 1959), p. 131.

[31] *Arizona Copper Co. v. Gillespie*, 230 U.S. 46, 33 S.Ct. 1004, 57 L.Ed. 1384 (1913).

[32] *City of Harrisonville v. W. S. Dickey Clay Mfg. Co.*, 289 U.S. 334, 53 S.Ct. 602, 77 L.Ed. 1208 (1933).

[33] *Hofstettler v. Myers*, 170 Kan. 564, 228 P.2d 522 (1951).

[34] *De Lahunta v. City of Waterbury*, 134 Conn. 630, 59 A.2d 800 (1948).

[35] *Milling v. Berg*, 104 S.2d 658 (Fla.App. 1958); *Costas v. City of Fond Du Lac*, 24 Wis.2d 409, 129 N.W.2d 217 (1964).

[36] *Kennedy v. Moog, Inc.*, 48 Misc.2nd 107, 264 N.Y.S.2d 606 (1965); *Parsons v. City of Sioux Falls*, 65 S.D. 145, 272 N.W. 288 (1937); *Vestal v. Gulf Oil Corp.*, 149 Tex. 487, 235 S.W.2d 440 (1951).

[37] *De Blois v. Bowers*, 44 F.2d 621 (D.Mass. 1930).

[38] *Ibid.* Although declared a nuisance, an injunction was denied and plaintiffs were awarded damages.

[39] *Bove v. Donner-Hanna Coke Corporation*, 236 App. Div. 37, 258 N.Y.S. (Sup. Ct. 1932).

[40] *Fritz v. E. I. DuPont de Nemours & Co.*, 45 Del. 427, 75 A.2d 256 (1950).

[41] *Arvidson v. Reynolds Metals Co.*, 236 F.2d 224 (9th Cir. 1956), affirming 125 F.Supp. 481 (W.D. Wash. 1954).

[42] *De Blois v. Bowers*, 44 F.2d 621 (D.Mass. 1930), noted in 38 above.

[43] *Reynolds Metals Company v. Lampert*, 324 F.2d 465 (9th Cir. 1963).

[44] "Pollution," Chemical and Engineering News (Feb. 10, 1969), p. 17.

[45] *Schindler v. Standard Oil Co. of Indiana*, 207 Mo.App. 190, 232 S.W. 735 (Mo.App. 1921); *Eastern Air Lines, Inc. v. American Cyanimide Co.*, 321 F.2d 683 (9th Cir. 1963); *Reynolds Metals Company v. Martin*, 337 F.2d 780 (9th Cir. 1964); fluoride fumes and particles emitted held to be both a trespass and a nuisance, under Oregon law.

[46] Haar, *op. cit. supra* note 30, at p. 95.

[47] Prosser, Law of Torts 598 (3rd ed. 1964).

[48] *Amphitheaters, Inc. v. Portland Meadows*, 184 Ore. 336. 198 P.2d 847 (1948): substantial interference required; *Frederick v. Brown Funeral Home*, 222 La. 57, 62 S.2d 100 (1952): mere inconvenience does not constitute a nuisance; *Livingston v. Davis*, 243 Iowa 21, 50 N.W.2d 592 (1951): unsightly, or offending aesthetic sense, is not a nuisance, but see, *State v. Buckley*, 16 Ohio St.2d 128 (1968): requiring fencing of junkyard is valid.

[49] *McOuail v. Shell Oil Company*, 40 D.Ch. 410, 183 A.2d 581 (1962); *Bostick v. Smoot Sand and Gravel Corp.*, 154 F.Supp. 744 (D.Md. 1957).

[50] *Purcell v. Davis*, 100 Mont. 480, 50 P.2d 255 (1935); *Costas v. City of Fond du Lac*, *supra* note 35.

[51] *Roddenberry Co., Inc. v. Carter*, 192 F.2d 448 (5th Cir. 1951).

[52] *City of Shawnee v. Bryant*, 310 P.2d 754 (Okla. 1957); *City of Harrisonville v. Dickey Clay Mfg.*, *supra* note 32. See, Oleck, Cases on Damages, c. 24 (1962).

[53] *Sinclair Prairie Oil Co. v. Seebeck*, 182 Okla. 436, 78 P.2d 282 (1938); *Hancock v. Moriarity*, 215 Ga. 274, 110 S.E.2d 403 (1959): prospective damages considered when permanent nuisance devalues land.

[54] *Economy Furniture, Inc. v. Jirasek*, 345 S.W.2d 951 (Tex. 1961).

[55] *Ritter v. Keokuk Electro-Metal Company*, 248 Ia. 710, 82 N.W.2d 151 (1957); *Jones v. Trawick*, 75 S.2d 785 (Fla. 1954).

[56] *Commonwealth v. Hanzlik*, 400 Pa. 134, 161 A.2d 340 (1960): the proper remedy is to abate the pollution and not merely regulate it.

[57] *De Blois v. Bowers*, *supra* note 42.

⁵⁸ *Renken v. Harvey Aluminum, Inc.*, 226 F.Supp. 169 (D.Ore. 1963): evidence established that proper pollution controls would greatly reduce, if not eliminate, escape of fluorine.

⁵⁹ *Greer v. City of Lennox*, 107 N.W.2d 337 (S.D. 1961). See, Oleck, Cases on Damages, c. 24 (1962).

⁶⁰ *Garber v. Rubel Corp.*, 160 Misc. 716, 290 N.Y.S. 632 (1936).

⁶¹ *Reynolds Metals Company v. Wand*, 308 F.2d 504 (9th Cir. 1962): the emission of noxious fumes and gases was abatable and, therefore, successive actions permissible.

⁶² *Parsons v. Sioux Falls, supra* note 36: a $5,000 award was held to not be excessive damages to a riparian landowner for discomfort and annoyance.

⁶³ *Cooper Tire & Rubber Co. v. Johnston*, 234 Miss. 432, 106 S.2d 889 (1958).

⁶⁴ *Newman v. Nelson*, 350 F.2d 602 (10th Cir. 1965): persistent maintenance of water pollution is a nuisance.

⁶⁵ *Donley v. Amerada Petroleum Corporation*, 152 Kan. 518, 106 P.2d 652 (1940); *Southland Co. v. Aaron*, 224 Miss. 780, 80 S.2d 823 (1955).

⁶⁶ *Claude v. Weaver Construction Co.*, 158 N.W.2d 139 (Iowa 1968).

⁶⁷ *Reynolds Metals Company v. Lampert, supra* note 43: on crossexamination, the plant manager commented: "It is cheaper to pay claims than it is to control fluoride gases."

⁶⁸ *Guttinger v. Calaveras Cement Company*, 160 Cal.App.2d 460, 325 P.2d 145 (1958).

⁶⁹ *City of Northlake v. City of Elmhurst*, 41 Ill.App.2d 190, 190 N.E.2d 375 (Ill.App. 1963).

⁷⁰ *Wilmont Homes, Inc. v. Weiler*, 202 A.2d 576 (Del. 1964); *Crushed Stone Co., Inc. v. Moore*, 369 P.2d 811 (Okla. 1962); *Christopher v. Jones Chemicals, Inc.*, 41 Cal. Rptr. 828 (Cal.App. 1964).

⁷¹ *Dill v. Excel Packing Company, Inc.*, 183 Kan. 513, 331 P.2d 539 (1958).

⁷² *Kennedy v. Moog, Inc., supra* note 36. But see, *State v. Buckley, supra* note 48.

⁷³ *Sarraillon v. Stevenson*, 153 Neb. 182, 43 N.W.2d 509 (1950).

⁷⁴ *Morgan v. High Penn Oil Co.*, 238 N.C. 185, 77 S.E.2d 682 (1953); *Causby v. High Penn Oil Co.*, 244 N.C. 235, 93 E.E.2d 79 (1956).

⁷⁵ *Christopher v. Jones Chemicals, Inc., supra* note 70.

⁷⁶ *Renken v. Harvey Aluminum, Inc., supra* note 58.

⁷⁷ *Herring Motor Company v. Walker Company, Inc.*, 409 Pa. 126, 185 A.2d 565 (1962).

[78] *Rode v. Sealtite Insulation Mfg. Corp.*, 3 Wis.2d 286, 88 N.W.2d 345 (1958).

[79] *Pottock v. Continental Can Co., Inc.*, 210 A.2d 295 (Del. 1965); *Diercks v. Hodgdon*, 237 Ore. 186, 390 P.2d 935 (1964). But, see: *Schofield v. Material Transit, Inc.*, 206 A.2d 100 (Del. 1960). See also: "A Complete Guide to Pollution Control," Chemical Engineering (October 14, 1968), p. 13, particularly pp. 25–49.

[80] *Hill v. Stokely-Van Camp, Inc.*, 260 Minn. 315, 109 N.W.2d 749 (1961).

[81] *Griffin v. Hurt*, 200 Tenn. 133, 291 S.W.2d 271 (1956).

[82] *Ritter v. Keokuk Electro-Metals Company, supra* note 55.

[83] *Brainin v. Great Lakes Supply Corporation*, 9 Ill.App.2d 560, 133 N.E.2d 730 (1956): there was no misjoinder with respect to injunctive relief; however, there was a misjoinder of defendants in regard to seeking damages since the four quarry owners had no connection.

[84] *Donley v. Amerada Petroleum Corporation, supra* note 65: persistently calling the defendant oil company "criminals," however, was unnecessary.

[85] *Penn-Dixie Cement Corporation v. City of Kingsport*, 189 Tenn. 450, 225 S.W.2d 270 (1949); *Ballen v. Nester*, 164 S.W.2d 378 (Mo. 1942).

[86] *Nourse v. City of Russelville*, 257 Ky. 525, 78 S.W.2d 761 (1935). See also Federal Clean Air Act, wherein the Dept. of Health, Education and Welfare is empowered to request the Dept. of Justice to initiate legal action when air pollution results from operations in another state. See Civil Case No. 19274 in the U.S. District Court for the District of Maryland.

[87] 56 A.L.R.2d 1415, at 1415 (Sec. 3).

[88] *City of Decatur v. Parham*, 268 Ala. 585, 109 So.2d 692 (1959); *City of Harrisonville v. W. S. Dickey Clay Mfg. Co., supra* note 32.

[89] 56 A.L.R.2d 1415, at 1422 (Sec. 4); *Galleher v. City of Wichita*, 179 Kan. 513, 296 P.2d 1062 (1956).

[90] 63 C.J.S., Municipal Corporations, Sec. 770 (1950); *Fowler v. Board of County Commissioners of Prince George's County*, 230 Md. 504, 187 A.2d 856 (1963).

[91] *Ibid.* §886. A municipality may be liable when sewage is emptied into a culvert by a third person with permission or by authority of the municipality. The municipality will become liable if it fails to abate the nuisance after having knowledge thereof.

[92] 38 Am. Jur., Municipal Corporations, Sec. 651 (1954). Compare footnotes 39-41. A municipal function is distinguished from a governmental function.

[93] *Ibid.*

[94] *Nelson v. Knox*, 256 F.2d 312 (6th Cir. 1958).

[95] *Whitt v. Reed*, 239 S.W.2d 489 (Ky. App. 1951): imperative or ministerial duties; *Farmer v. State*, 224 Miss. 96, 79 So.2d 528 (1955).

[96] *Ballentine v. Nester*, 350 Mo. 58, 164 S.W.2d 378 (1942); *People v. International Steel Corp.*, 102 Cal.App.2d 935, 226 P.2d 587 (1951).

[97] *City of Kankakee v. New York Central R. Co.*, 387 Ill. 109, 55 N.E.2d 87 (1944).

[98] *Ibid.*, *Board of Health of Weehawken Tp. v. New York Central R. Co.*, 4 N. J. 293, 72 A.2d 511 (1950).

[99] *Huron Portland Cement Co. v. Detroit*, 362 U.S. 440, 80 S.Ct. 813, 4 L.Ed.2d 852 (1960).

[100] There is no doubt that there would be no immunity when neglect of duty was willful and malicious. See Prosser, *op. cit. supra* note 47, at 1013–1019.

[101] "Right to Clean Air," Chemical and Engineering News (Feb. 10, 1969), p. 18. Basis of suit was that the "right to clean air" is one of the unnamed rights guaranteed by the 9th Amendment to the United States Constitution.

[102] *Herring v. Walker*, *supra* note 77; *Huron Portland Cement v. Detroit*, *supra* note 99; The Ohio Engineer (March, 1969), pp. 21–24, notes that two of the "Seven Engineering Wonders of Ohio for 1968" were pollution control facilities.

[103] *Huron Portland Cement Co. v. Detroit*, *supra* note 99.

[104] *Ibid. People v. Cunard White Star*, 280 N.Y. 413, 21 N.E.2d 489 (1939): smoke regulation law valid only to the extent that compliance therewith is possible with modern appliances and practicable methods.

[105] C. Haar, Land Use Planning 131 (1959).

[106] O. Holmes, THE COMMON LAW 33 (Little Brown ed. 1963).

[107] Confidential correspondence from the manufacturer.

[108] *E.g.*, A. Pigou, THE ECONOMICS OF WELFARE 160-161 (1932).

[109] Juergensmeyer, *Control of Air Pollution Through Assertion of Private Rights*, 1967 DUKE L.J. 1126.

[110] *See generally* W. Prosser, THE LAW OF TORTS 592-633 (1964) [hereinafter cited as Prosser].

[111] *Quoted in Reynolds Metals Co. v. Lampert*, 324 F. 2d 465, 466 (9th cir. 1963).

[112] Fed. R. Civ. P. 23(b).

[113] 394 U.S. 332 (1969), holding that class members may aggregate individual claims to reach the $10,000 federal question juris-

dictional amount of 28 U.S.C. §1331(a) (1964) only when those
individuals share a "common and undivided" interest; *noted in* 83
HARV. L. Rev. 202 (1969).

[114] 226 F. Supp. 169 (D. Ore. 1963).

[115] *Id*. at 175.

[116] 245 Ore. 247, 421 P.2d 957 (1967).

[117] *Id*. at 251-52, 421 P.2d at 959.

[118] Rheingold, *Civil Cause of Action for Lung Damage Due to
Pollution of the Urban Atmosphere,* 33 BROOKLYN L. REV. 17,
19 (1967).

[119] *See, e.g.,* STAFF REPORT OF THE SENATE COMMERCE
COMMITTEE ON THE SEARCH FOR A LOW-EMISSION
VEHICLE, 91st Cong., 1st Sess. 2 (1969).

[120] *See, e.g.,* REPORT OF THE SURGEON GENERAL TO
THE U.S. CONGRESS—MOTOR VEHICLES, AIR POLLUTION
AND HEALTH, DOC. NO. 489, 87th Cong., 2d Sess. (1962).

[121] 217 N.Y. 382, 111 N.E., 1050 (1916).

[122] Prosser, *supra* note 110, at 660-61.

[123] RESTATEMENT (SECOND) OF TORTS §395 (1965).

[124] *See, e.g., Triborough Agrees to Plan for Study of Tunnel
Fumes,* New York Times, Aug. 19, 1969, at 85, col. 1.

[125] On the other hand, developments in the rapidly changing law
of strict product liability might enable a victim of automobile pollution to recover damages without having to prove negligence.
Traditionally, only actual consumers or users of the hazardous
product, and not innocent bystanders, have been able to recover
under this theory. Prosser, *supra* note 110, at 682-83. However,
there seems no good reason to distinguish between buyers and other
persons injured by automobile exhaust, especially where such pollution is known to be hazardous and damage to health is readily
predictable.
"There may be no essential reason why such plaintiffs [non-users
and non-consumers] should not be brought within the scope of the
protection afforded, other than that they do not have the same
reasons for expecting such protection as the consumer who buys
the marketed product; but the social pressure which has been
largely responsible for the development of the rule stated has been
a consumer's pressure, and there is not the same demand for the
protection of casual strangers." RESTATEMENT (SECOND) OF
TORTS §402A, comment *o* at 356-57 (1965).

[126] R. Nader, UNSAFE AT ANY SPEED (1965).

[127] Los Angeles County Bd. of Supervisors, Res. No. 180 (Jan.
26, 1965).

[128] *United States v. American Auto. Mfrs. Ass'n,* Civil No. 69-75-
JWC, Trade Reg. Rep. ¶ 45,069 (C.D. Cal., filed Jan. 10, 1969).

[129] Prosser, *supra* note 129, at 10.

[130] *United States v. American Auto. Mfrs. Ass'n,* Civil No. 69-75-JWC, Trade Reg. Rep. ¶ 72,907 (C.D. Cal., entered Oct. 29, 1969).

[131] 115 CONG. REC. E7662 (daily ed. Sept. 19, 1969).

[132] *Quoted in Dodge v. Ford Motor Co.,* 204 Mich. 459, 170 N.W. 668 (1919).

[133] *Id.* at 507, 170 N.W. at 684.

[134] Wall Street Journal, Nov. 21, 1969, at 39, col. 4.

[135] 17 C.F.R. §240.14a-8(c)(2)(1968).

[136] *Cf. Abrams v. Allen,* 297 N.Y. 52, 74 N.E.2d 305 (1947),

[137] See §(a) above.

[138] Consider the statement made by Atomic Energy Commission member James T. Ramey before the Joint Committee on Atomic Energy. In response to a question put to him about citizen concern over nuclear-powered electric generating stations, Mr. Ramey said that this concern was due to "professional stirrer-uppers" and radical scientists. Hearing, October 30, 1969. No transcript of that hearing is yet available.

[139] Confidential interview with a state assistant attorney general.

[140] Kovel, *A Case for Civil Penalties: Air Pollution Control* 46 J. URBAN L. 153, 154 (1969); Jost, *Cold Facts on Hot Water: Legal Aspects of Thermal Pollution,* 1969 WIS. L. REV. 253.

[141] 38 Am. Jur. §651 (1941). But this same section does point out that there is a minority of jurisdictions which do permit official liability for failure to abate a nuisance. Also, it should be noted that some jurisdictions charge public officials with a duty to abate nuisances in public places, and that nonfeasance in this situation would result in liability to injured parties. 56 A.L.R.2d 1415 (1957).

[142] L. Jaffe, JUDICIAL CONTROL OF ADMINISTRATIVE ACTION 181 (1965).

[143] *Ham v. Los Angeles County,* 46 Cal. App. 148, 162, 189 P. 462, 468 (Dist. Ct. App., 2d Dist. 1920).

[144] Prosser, *supra* note 110, at 1013-19.

[145] The Ringlemann chart is actually a series of five charts; each chart has a rectangular grid of black lines on a white background. The spacing between the lines decreases systematically from chart 1 through chart 5. The charts are used to measure the blackness of smoke emissions.

[146] *People ex rel. Aubertel v. Consolidated Edison Co. of New York,* 116 N.Y.S.2d 555, 558 (N.Y.C. Mun. Ct. 1952).

[147] *E.g.,* E. Cox R. Fellmeth, J. Schultz, THE 'NADER REPORT' ON THE FEDERAL TRADE COMMISSION (1969).

[148] *Yick Wo v. Hopkins,* 118 U.S. 356 (1886); *cf. Hadnot v. Ames,* 89 S. Ct. 1101, 1104-05 (1969).

[149] *Yick Wo v. Hopkins,* 118 U.S. 356 (1886); cf. *Lenske v. United States,* 383 F.2d 20, 27 (9th Cir., 1967).

[150] *E.g., United States v. Robel,* 389 U.S. 258 (1967); *Schware v. Board of Bar Examiners,* 353 U.S. 232, 238-39 (1957). See generally Van Alstyne, *Demise of the Right-Privilege Distinction in Constitutional Law,* 81 HARV. L. REV. 1437 (1968); Cahn & Cahn, *The New Sovereign Immunity,* 81 HARV. L. REV. 929 (1968); Reich, *The New Property,* 73 YALE L.J. 733 (1964).

[151] *Cf.* Jennings, *Tort Liability of Administrative Officers,* 21 MINN. L. REV. 263 (1937).

[152] 252 U.S. 416 (1920).

[153] *Id.* at 433.

[154] 381 U. S. 479 (1965).

[155] *Id.* at 484.

[156] *Id.* The Ninth Amendment reads: "The enumeration in the Constitution, of certain rights, shall not be construed to deny or disparage others retained by the people."

[157] *See, e.g.,* HOUSE COMM. ON GOVERNMENTAL OPERATIONS, 1966-68 SURVEY OF WATER POLLUTION CONTROL AND ABATEMENT AT FEDERAL INSTALLATIONS, H.R. REP. No. 91-75, 91st Cong., 1st Sess. (1969).

[158] *Cf. Reitman v. Mulkey,* 387 U.S. 369 (1967); *Evans v. Newton,* 382 U.S. 296 (1966); *Burton v. Wilmington Parking Authority,* 365 U.S. 715 (1961); *Shelley v. Kraemer,* 334 U.S. 1 (1948). Local zoning regulations, by which industrial polluters often become concentrated in certain areas, have served to exacerbate pollution problems rather than to isolate residential areas from environmental fallout. Not only are those who reside within the industrial area often deemed to have forgone any nuisance claims, but those who live outside the area are subjected to increasing amounts of pollution in the aggregate, but from increasingly numerous, remote, and unidentifiable sources. To the extent that these state-enforced zoning schemes result (however unintentionally) in frustrating the pollution victim's effort to identify proper defendants, joint and several liability of class defendant polluters might be constitutionally required as a remedy. *Cf. Ybarra v. Spangard,* 25 Cal. 2d 486, 154 P.2d 687, 162 A.L.R. 1258 (1944).

[159] *See, e.g., New Hampshire v. A.E.C.,* 406 F.2d 170 (1st Cir. 1969).

[160] 365 U.S. 167 (1961).

[161] (1964). "Every person who, under color of any statute, ordinance, regulation, custom, or usage of any state . . . subjects, or causes to be subjected, any citizen of the United States or other person within the jurisdiction thereof to the deprivation of any rights, privileges, or immunities secured by the Constitution and laws, shall be liable to the party injured in an action at law, suit in equity, or other proper proceeding for redress." *Id.*

[162] 365 U.S. at 174 (emphasis supplied).

[163] *See* text, *supra* at 136; *cf. Reitman v. Mulkey,* 387 U.S. 369 (1967); *Symkowski v. Miller,* 294 F. Supp. 1214 (E.D. Wis. 1969); *Cottonreader v. Johnson,* 252 F. Supp. 492 (M.D. Ala. 1966).

[164] 28 U.S.C. §1343(4) (1964).

[165] *See* text, *supra* at note 110.

[166] 334 U.S. 1 (1948).

[167] *See, e.g.,* Wechsler, *Toward Neutral Principles of Constitutional Law,* 73 HARV. L. REV. 1, 29-31 (1959).

[168] 334 U.S. at 22.

[169] 347 U.S. 483 (1954).

[170] One of the country's leading environmental trial lawyers, Victor J. Yannacone, recently said, "Every piece of enlightened social legislation that has come down in the past 50 or 60 years has been preceded by a history of litigation in which lawyers around the country have focused forcibly the attention of the legislature on the inadequacies of existing legislation." Christian Science Monitor, Oct. 2, 1969, at 3, col. 1.

[171] *Waschak v. Moffat,* 379 Pa. 441, 453, 109 A.2d 310, 316 (1954).

[172] *Illinois Central Railroad Company v. Illinois,* 146 U.S. 1018, 1042 (1892).

CHAPTER 3

WHAT LAWS ARE ON THE BOOKS
RELATING TO POLLUTION

CHAPTER 3

WHAT LAWS ARE ON
THE BOOKS RELATING
TO POLLUTION

There are numerous statutes on the books—at every level
of government—dealing with virtually every phase of pollution. There are so many, in fact, that within one state
there are often conflicts and overlaps, just as conflicts and
overlaps exist between the federal and state laws on any
subject. These laws are relevant, as we have already
pointed out (§1.6) for three reasons: they form the basis
of the power of the government to deal with pollution;
they establish a public policy toward the eradication of
pollution; and in some instances they form the basis for
the type of private suit which is at the heart of this book.

We can do no more here than give summaries of the
pertinent federal laws (§3.1), and suggest the type of state
and local laws and regulations which may exist in your
area (§§3.3 and 3.4). And, since there is so much ferment, we will cover some of the major law changes being
suggested (§3.2).

3.1 The Federal Legal Framework

(a) National Environmental Policy Act of 1969,
83 Stat. 852

This act, which became effective in 1970, represents
a major statement of purposes of Congress in this area,
and has been said to amount to a Bill of Rights in the environmental area. §101(c) states:

The Congress recognizes that each person should enjoy a healthful environment and that each person has a responsibility to contribute to the preservation and enhancement of the environment.

The act then instructs all federal agencies to conduct their business in accordance with the general aims of the act and to consider the impact on the environment of each of its activities. The act also creates the Council on Environmental Quality within the Executive Office of the President. The role of the council is to review governmental programs in the light of the policy of the act, and to give advice to the President and others on environmental protection.

(b) Water Quality Improvement Act of 1970, Public Law 91-224

This act greatly amended the Water Pollution Control Act described below. It deals with pollution due to oil spillage, to sewage from vessels, and to mine wastes. It has specific provisions for the Great Lakes and for co-operation among agencies. It replaces the Oil Pollution Act of 1924, and not only increases penalties for oil spills but makes polluters absolutely liable for the cost of cleaning up spills. A second section of the law is known as the Environmental Quality Improvement Act of 1970 and deals with all types of pollution. It establishes an Office of Environmental Quality.

(c) Clean Air Act of 1967, 42 U.S.C. §1857

This act provides for many federal steps to clean ambient air. It creates a National Air Pollution Control Administration, part of the Department of Health, Education, and Welfare. This act also covers Motor Vehicles Emission Standards. Many proposed amendments to this act are before Congress. The purposes of the act are described as follows (§1857):

(1) to protect and enhance the quality of the nation's air resources so as to promote the public health and welfare and the productive capacity of its population;

(2) to initiate and accelerate a national research and development program to achieve the prevention and control of air pollution;

(3) to provide technical and financial assistance to state and local governments in connection with the development and execution of their air pollution prevention and control programs; and

(4) to encourage and assist the development and operation of regional air pollution control programs.

(d) Solid Waste Disposal Act of 1965, 42 U.S.C. §3251

This act sets up grants to states and interstate agencies for planning, and encourages research and training in waste disposal. Its stated purpose is [§3251 (*b*)]:

(1) to initiate and accelerate a national research and development program for new and improved methods of proper and economic solid-waste disposal, including studies directed toward the conservation of natural resources by reducing the amount of waste and un-salvageable materials, and by recovery and utilization of potential resources in solid wastes; and

(2) to provide technical and financial assistance to state and local governments and interstate agencies in the planning, development, and conduct of solid-waste disposal programs.

This law was substantially added to by the Resource Recovery Act of 1970 (84 Stat. 1227).

(e) Water Pollution Control Act of 1948, as amended, 33 U.S.C. §466

This act covers administrative oversight, interstate cooperation, research, grants for pollution control programs, and the establishment of a Water Pollution Control Administration and Advisory Board. The Congressional declaration for this act provides in part (§466):

(*a*) The purpose of §§466–466*g* and 466*h*–466*k* of this title is to enhance the quality and value of our water resources and to establish a national policy for the prevention, control, and abatement of water pollution.

(*b*) In connection with the exercise of jurisdiction over the waterways of the nation, and in consequence of

the benefits resulting to the public health and welfare
by the prevention and control of water pollution, it is
declared to be the policy of Congress to recognize,
preserve, and protect the primary responsibilities and
rights of the states in preventing and controlling water
pollution, to support and aid technical research relating
to the prevention and control of water pollution, and to
provide federal technical services and financial aid to
state and interstate agencies and to municipalities in
connection with the prevention and control of water
pollution . . .

(f) Clean Water Restoration Act of 1966, Pub. L. 89-753,
amending various sections, 33 U.S.C.

This act amended various sections of the Water Pollution Control Act [(e) above] and other provisions of water
pollution laws. Among other things, it provides for financial aid to cities to build modern sewage plants.

(g) Water Resources Research Act of 1964,
42 U.S.C. §1961

This law sets up water resources research institutes
in the states and related research on water resources. §1961
(c) provides for the making available of information. The
Congressional declaration is as follows (§1961):

In order to assist in assuring the nation at all times of
a supply of water sufficient in quantity and quality to
meet the requirements of its expanding population, it
is the purpose of the Congress, by this chapter, to stimulate, sponsor, provide for, and supplement present programs for the conduct of research, investigations,
experiments, and the training of scientists in the fields
of water and of resources which affect water.

(h) Water Resources Planning Act of 1965,
42 U.S.C. §1962

This law sets up a Water Resources Council and river
basins commissions. It gives grants to the state for comprehensive planning. The Congressional declaration was
as follows (§1962):

In order to meet the rapidly expanding demands
for water throughout the nation, it is hereby declared

to be the policy of the Congress to encourage the conservation, development, and utilization of water and related land resources of the United States on a comprehensive and coordinated basis by the federal government, states, localities, and private enterprise with the cooperation of all affected federal agencies, states, local governments, individuals, corporations, business enterprises, and others concerned.

(i) Saline Water Conservation Act of 1952, as amended in 1961, 42 U.S.C. §1951

This act authorized the Department of the Interior to act in this area. Its purposes are stated in §1951 as follows:

> In view of the increasing shortage of usable surface and ground water in many parts of the nation, and the importance of finding new sources of supply to meet its present and future water needs, it is the policy of the Congress to provide for the development of practicable low-cost means for the large-scale production of water of a quality suitable for municipal, industrial, agricultural, and other beneficial consumptive uses from saline water, and for studies and research related thereto.

(j) Marine Resources and Engineering Development Act of 1966, 33 U.S.C. §1101

This law sets up the National Council on Marine Researches and Engineering Development and a Commission on Marine Sciences, Engineering, and Resources. Subchapter II, §1121 *et seq.* deals with the establishment of sea grant colleges. §1101(*a*) is the Congressional declaration:

> It is hereby declared to be the policy of the United States to develop, encourage and maintain a coordinated, comprehensive, and long-range national program in marine science for the benefit of mankind to assist in protection of health and property, enhancement of commerce, transportation and national security, rehabilitation of our commercial fisheries, and increased utilization of these and other resources.

(k) Oil Pollution Act of 1961, 33 U.S.C. §1001

This act implements the provisions of the International

Convention for the Prevention of the Pollution of the Sea by Oil (1954).

(l) Rivers and Harbors Act of 1899, 33 U.S.C. §407

This is the section which requires a permit from the Army Corps of Engineers before any person can dump refuse into navigable waters. "Refuse" has been defined to include pollutants of all types. It has been widely used in the last year. §411 provides criminal sanctions and fines.

(m) Wilderness Act of 1964, 16 U.S.C. §1131

This act follows a congressional policy of protecting the wilderness in the United States. It creates a Wilderness Preservation System composed of federally-owned areas. The limited uses to which such lands may be put are itemized.

(n) Multiple Use-Sustained Yield Act of 1960, 16 U.S.C. §528

The stated purpose of this legislation is to put in effect the congressional policy that the national forests are to be used for recreation, range, timber, watershed, wildlife and fish purposes. To that end it advances the concepts of "multiple use" and "sustained yield." The former means that the various uses to which forest land may be put are to be coordinated and carried on concurrently; the latter concept means the striving for a high-level use without fundamentally impairing the land. Conservationists have been critical of both these aspects as likely to favor the interests of business over wildlife interests in the long run.

(o) Federal Insecticide, Fungicide and Rodenticide Act, 7 U.S.C. §135

The regulation of pesticides and similar "economic poisons" is carried out under this act. Among other things, it prohibits the sale of pesticides which have not been registered with the Secretary of Agriculture.

(p) Conservation Laws

There are many provisions on conservation in federal law, too numerous to discuss separately. Among the laws are:

Open Space Land, Urban Beautification and Historic
    Preservation Act, 42 U.S.C. §1500
Wetlands Act of 1961, 16 U.S.C. §715*k*
Laws to protect estuaries, 16 U.S.C. §1221
Migratory Bird Conservation Act, 16 U.S.C. §715
Wild Life Restoration Act, 16 U.S.C. §669
Fish and Wildlife Act of 1956, 16 U.S.C. §742*c*
Fish and Wildlife Coordination Act of 1965, 16 U.S.C.
    §662

(q) Environmental Education Act of 1970, 84 Stat.
    §1312

The act authorizes the Commissioner of Education to
establish educational programs to encourage environmental quality.

3.2 Proposed Future Federal Legislation and Governmental Action

President Nixon set forth the ground plan for future
governmental laws and actions in his annual State of the
Nation's Environment report Feb. 8, 1971. To combat
pollution, he proposed a $12 billion water pollution pre-
vention program, a tax on leaded gasoline, regulation of
noise pollution, regulation of toxic substances, controls on
ocean dumping, a federal recycling of paper program, and
improved pesticide control authority. The President also
proposed many advances in land use decisions, including
a new, national land-use policy, expanded open spaces in
urban areas, expansion of wilderness preservation systems,
and control of surface and underground mining. Looking
still more widely, the President suggested establishing an
Environmental Institute to conduct studies, expand international cooperation, and a World Heritage Trust to preserve areas of unique cultural value throughout the world.

Much work awaits all of the federal organizations
charged with responsibility in the ecology area. It is imperative that high national standards be formulated in many
areas, so that deviation from the standards may be used
both as measures of criminal conduct and civil violations.
There are, for example, obvious deficiencies in the area of

automobile exhaust and radiation emissions. Part of the solution will have to be increased staffs and budgets for these agencies.

3.3 State Laws

Every state has its own legislative treatment of the environmental areas, and it would be of no value, we feel, to explain the laws of any one or a number of states. Further, so rapid are the modifications of environmental law going on in this country that to attempt to explain any one system in detail might be an exercise in history by the time you read this.

An example of the rethinking and revision in the state legal frameworks is the new New York State antipollution law passed April 1970. That act abolishes a proliferation of state agencies which had been dealing piecemeal with pollution problems. In their stead, it sets up a Department of Environmental Conservation, with overall control, except for the tasks assigned to a newly created Office of Parks and Recreation.

The New York law delegates to the new department the power to set environmental standards for air, water, and other matters. It is given many other broad powers, including the authority to shut down at once any pollution source which is an imminent danger to health or welfare.

A complete picture of the New York law (or of any other state) would include noting participation by the state, by statute, in interstate compacts, such as the Interstate Sanitation Commission in New York (Public Health Law §1299). Also, in examining state law, attention should be paid to the constitution of the state. One of the most comprehensive constitutional provisions in this nation dealing with conservation appears in New York, Art. XIV, §4 of the constitution, which reads as follows:

> The policy of the state shall be to conserve and protect its natural resources and scenic beauty and encourage the development and improvement of its agricultural lands for the production of food and other agricultural products. The legislature, in implementing this policy,

shall include adequate provision for the abatement of air and water pollution and of excessive and unnecessary noise, the protection of agricultural lands, wetlands and shorelines, and the development and regulation of water resources. The legislature shall further provide for the acquisition of lands and waters, including improvements thereon and any interest therein, outside the forest preserve counties, and the dedication of properties so acquired or now owned, which, because of their natural beauty, wilderness character, or geological, ecological, or historical significance, shall be preserved and administered for the use and enjoyment of the people. Properties so dedicated shall constitute the state nature and historical preserve, and they shall not be taken or otherwise disposed of except by law enacted by two successive regular sessions of the legislature.

The interrelation of federal and state statutes should be noted. In some limited instances, the states merely mirror the federal law. When a new statute is added to the federal laws, a state will pass the same law. For example, the United States statutes relating to drugs, cosmetics, foods and pesticides have often been reenacted on the state level. On the other hand, in some areas the states have been more progressive than the Congress, and have either entered areas where the federal government has not gone, or have gone further in the protection of the environment than the federal government has in the same area. This is sometimes due to the fact that one national law would not be appropriate, and the better approach is a state-by-state system of laws. State progress has been notable in recent years in the area of strip mining, billboard laws and noise pollution.

3.4 City Level Legislation

It is on the local, grass-roots level that the concerned citizen can make perhaps his greatest contribution to the legal process. A great variety of laws await enactment at the city and state level. As a pressure group of one, or as a leader in a local citizens' committee, the citizen can press for the revision of the laws in order to support governmental action against pollution. And, of course, grass-roots efforts are not limited to legislation. Local action can consist of lawsuits, conducting educational programs, and meeting with local politicians and law enforcement officials.

An example of the type of law which a citizen can seek to have enacted and which will make a direct impact on his immediate environment, is the model law we set out below. It is one proposed by the State of New Jersey for adoption by its various localities.

The New Jersey Model

AN ORDINANCE ESTABLISHING AN AIR POLLUTION
    CONTROL FOR THE CITY OF _____

• • •

1:2 *FINDINGS AND DECLARATION OF POL-ICY:* It is hereby declared that pollution of the atmosphere by smoke, cinders, soot, fly ash, gases, fumes, vapors, odors, dust, and other contaminants is a menace to the health, welfare, and comfort of the residents of _____ and a cause of substantial damage to property. For the purpose of controlling and reducing atmospheric pollution, it is hereby declared to be the policy of the _____ to minimize air pollution as herein defined and prohibit excessive emission of the same, to establish standards governing the installation, maintenance, and operation of equipment and appurtenances relating to combustion which are a source or potential source of air pollution, and in furtherance of this purpose to cooperate and coordinate these efforts with the State Department of

_____.

2: *DEFINITIONS*

• • •

AIR POLLUTION: The presence in the outdoor atmosphere of one or more air contaminants in such quantities and duration as are, or tend to be, injurious to human health or welfare, to animal or plant life, or to property, or would unreasonably interfere with the enjoyment of life or property throughout the _____ as shall be affected thereby, and excludes all aspects of employer-employee relationship as to health and safety hazards.

ECONOMIC POISONS: Those chemicals used as insecticides, rodenticides, fungicides, herbicides, nematocides, or defoliants.

FUEL-BURNING EQUIPMENT: Any furnace, boiler, water heater, device, mechanism, stoker, burner, stack, oven, stove, kiln, still, or other apparatus, or a group or collections of such units in the process of fuel-burning for the generation of heat or power. Refuse-burning equipment shall be considered incinerators as herein defined and not as fuel-burning equipment under this definition. Ovens, stoves, or ranges used exclusively for domestic cooking purposes are not included herein.

INCINERATOR: Any device, apparatus, equipment, or structure used for destroying, reducing, or salvaging by fire any material or substance, including but not limited to refuse, rubbish, garbage, debris, or scrap or facilities for cremating human or animal remains.

ODOR: A property of a substance which affects the sense of smell.

OPEN BURNING: Any fire wherein the products of combustion are emitted into the open air and are not directed thereto through a stack or chimney.

• • •

REFUSE: All putrescible and non-putrescible wastes (except body wastes), and shall include but not be limited to garbage, rubbish, yard trimmings, leaves, ashes, street cleanings, dead animals, abandoned automobiles, and solid market and industrial wastes.

RINGELMANN SMOKE CHART: Ringelmann's Scale for Grading the Density of Smoke, published by the United States Bureau of Mines, or any chart, recorder, indicator, or device for the measurement of smoke density which is approved by the State Department of Health of the State of New Jersey, as the equivalent of said Ringelmann's Scale.

RUBBISH: Solids not considered to be highly flammable or explosive, and shall include but not be limited to rags, old clothes, leather, rubber, carpets, wood, excelsior, paper, ashes, tree branches, yard trimmings, furniture, tin cans, glass, crockery, masonry, and other similar materials.

•　•　•

SMOKE: Small gas-borne and air-borne particles arising from a process of combustion in sufficient number to be observable.

•　•　•

3:　*PROHIBITION OF OPEN AIR BURNING*

3:1　No person shall cause, suffer, allow, or permit, open burning of refuse or plant life, nor conduct a salvage operation by open burning, except as provided in Section 3:2.

3:2　The open burning of trade waste is not prohibited where no other known method of disposal can be used without hazard to health or property and the required affidavit has been filed with and approved by the Commissioner of the New Jersey State Department of Health in accordance with Chapter II, Section 1.4, of the New Jersey Air Pollution Control Code.

4.　*SMOKE EMISSIONS FROM FUEL-BURNING EQUIPMENT*

4:1　No person shall cause, suffer, allow, or permit, smoke from any fuel-burning equipment, the shade or appearance of which is darker than No. 1 of the Ringelmann Smoke Chart, to be emitted into the open air.

4:2　The provisions of this section shall not apply to:
　　(a) Smoke emitted during the cleaning of a fire box or the building of a new fire, the shade or appearance of which is not darker than

No. 2 of the Ringelmann Smoke Chart, for a period or periods aggregating no more than three minutes in any fifteen consecutive minutes.

5: *INCINERATOR REGULATION*

5:1 *SMOKE EMISSIONS:* No person shall cause, suffer, allow, or permit, smoke from any incinerator, the shade or appearance of which is darker than No. 1 of the Ringelmann Smoke Chart, to be emitted into the open air; or emissions of such opacity within a stack or chimney, or exclusive of water vapor, of such opacity leaving a stack or chimney to a degree greater than the emission designated as No. 1 of the Ringelmann Smoke Chart.

5:2 *NEW FIRES:* The provisions of Section 5.1 shall not apply to smoke emitted during the building of a new fire, the shade or appearance of which is not darker than No. 2 of the Ringelmann Smoke Chart, for a period of no longer than three consecutive minutes; or to emissions of such opacity within a stack or chimney or exclusive of water vapor, of such opacity leaving a stack or chimney to a degree which is not greater than the emissions designated as No. 2 of the Ringelmann Smoke Chart, for a period no longer than three consecutive minutes.

5:3 *VISIBLE PARTICLES:* No person shall cause, suffer, allow, or permit, the emission of particles of unburned waste or ash from any incinerator which are individually large enough to be visible while suspended in the atmosphere.

5:4 *ODORS:* No person shall construct, install, use, or cause to be used any incinerator which will result in odors being detectible by sense of smell in any area of human use or occupancy.

•   •   •

6: PROHIBITION OF AIR POLLUTION

6:1 No person or owner of property, and no person having possession or control of property, shall cause, suffer, allow, or permit, to be emitted into the open air substances in such quantities as shall result in air pollution. The provisions of this section shall not apply to the use of economic poisons.

• • •

8:1 Any person who shall violate any of the provisions of this Code, or who shall fail to comply therewith or with any of the requirements thereof, shall be punishable _____.

CHAPTER 4

WHAT THE COURTS HAVE DONE SO FAR FOR THE ENVIRONMENT

CHAPTER 4

WHAT THE COURTS HAVE DONE SO FAR FOR THE ENVIRONMENT

In this chapter we analyze the leading cases in the area of environmental law. There are literally thousands of "pollution" cases of all sorts on the books from every state in the Union. We present here digests of the ones which we feel are the key decisions in the developing law of environmental protection. In not all of these did the person suing for pollution eradication win, or receive exactly the relief which he sought. In not all of these was a private person suing, for that matter; in some the government had brought the suit.

We have already pointed out in Chapter 1 that a "case" means any number of things to a lawyer. The type of case we have digested here is a precedent—a decision from a court which has given due consideration to the issues in the case. The type of case which has been filed and is pending—the work in the trial courts right now—is the subject of Chapters 5 and 6. While most of the cases are digested quite briefly, we have judged four to be of such significance as to demand quotation at length from the opinions of the court. These are set forth in a final section of the chapter.

4.1 Cases Illustrating the Power of Injunction in Nuisance Abatement

(a) Million-Dollar Pulp Mill Could Be Shut Down When It Polluted Farmer's Stream and Did $100 Damage

The plaintiff in *Whalen v. Union Bag and Paper Company*, 208 N.Y. 1, 101 N.E. 805 (1913), owned a 250-

acre farm through which there ran a stream. Plaintiff claimed that defendant company, operator of a pulp mill upstream, caused the discharge of sulfuric acid, lime, and sulfur into the stream, thus rendering it impure and damaging the land. An injunction was sought.

The New York court grappled with the problem of comparative injuries. The mill represented an investment in excess of $1 million, and it provided employment for more than four hundred persons. The court found that the harm done to the plaintiff was about $100, but was not insubstantial if one considered the harm done to animal and vegetable life. The defendant did not show that the nuisance would become less injurious in the future. Thus, despite the relatively great expense of abating the injury, the court found that the mill clearly comprised a nuisance which invaded the plaintiff's property rights. Judgment was rendered for the plaintiff and an injunction issued.

(b) Injunction Granted for Trespass of Fluorides to Orchards—Damages Inadequate Remedy

In *Renken v. Harvey Aluminum, Inc.*, 226 F. Supp. 169 (D. Ore. 1963), the plaintiffs, owners of orchard land, sought to enjoin an aluminum reduction plant from operating as a nuisance. The constant settling of fluorides on plaintiffs' property resulted in a continuous trespass, an actionable wrong which the court considered interchangeable with "nuisance." Evidence clearly indicated that fluorine escaping from the plant damaged the plaintiffs' orchards. It was also proven that the installation of cell hoods, such as used elsewhere in the industry, would have greatly reduced the escape of harmful material from the plant.

The principal issue was whether damages for past and prospective trespasses would be an adequate relief, or whether an injunction should be issued. The federal court in Oregon determined that the plaintiffs would be pursuing a "judicial merry-go-round" if they were relegated to continuously suing for monetary relief. On the other hand, the defendant was unable to prove that the use of its property which caused the injury was unavoidable or that the injury-causing condition could be alleviated only by vast expenditures, such as would constitute a deprivation of use of property. The court ordered the defendant to install proper cell hoods within one year or the injunction against operation of the plant would issue.

4.2 Case Illustrating Awarding of Damages for Nuisances

(a) Nuisance Action for Air Pollution—Damages for Sulfuric Acid Fumes

In *Kelly v. National Lead Company,* 210 S.W.2d 728 (Mo. 1948), plaintiffs, husband and wife, sued to recover compensation for personal injuries and property damage allegedly caused by defendant's negligent operation of its plant. The plaintiffs claimed that defendant company negligently and carelessly caused large quantities of noxious gases, fumes, and particles of sulfuric acid to be discharged from its plant, which were then deposited by the wind on plaintiffs' property.

The Missouri appellate court held that negligence was the wrong theory for the plaintiffs to proceed under. To prove negligence the plaintiffs attempted to show that defendant failed to observe a statutory duty to use an antipollution device in its plant. However, the plaintiffs failed to establish the existence of such a duty because the antipollution device in question was not yet out of the experimental stages and available on the market.

The plaintiffs should have proceeded on the theory of nuisance. The court recognized as well established the principle that one who permits fumes and gases to escape from his premises, and be deposited on the premises of another so as to cause injury, commits an actionable nuisance. That theory best fit the facts established by the plaintiffs. Therefore, the court ordered a new trial on the nuisance theory.

4.3 Cases Illustrating Use of Punitive Damages Awards in Halting Pollution

(a) Punitive Damages Against Air Pollution—"It Is Cheaper to Pay Claims Than Control Fluorides"

In *Reynolds Metals Company v. Lampert,* 324 F.2d 465 (9th Cir. 1963), the plaintiff was denied punitive damages and appealed. His injury was caused by fallout of fluorides onto his fields. The trial transcript revealed that the defendant had knowledge that its plant had caused such injury in the past. The transcript also revealed that the jury was not permitted to hear testimony of a chemical engineer who claimed that it was possible to remove ninety-eight to ninety-nine percent of the fallout. The jury had been told to disregard a statement by the defendant's manager that "it is cheaper to pay claims than to control fluorides."

The federal appellate court found that there was enough evidence to submit the issue of punitive damages to the jury to determine if the defendant had acted in wanton disregard of property rights of others, or recklessly so as to imply a disregard of social obligations.

(b) Punitive Damages Can Be Awarded to Punish Paper Mill Which Knowingly Permitted Pollution

In *McElwain v. Georgia-Pacific Corporation,* 245 Ore. 247, 421 P.2d 957 (1966), the plaintiff sought $35,000 compensatory damages and $20,000 punitive damages from the defendant on the claim that effluents and noxious gases from the defendant's paper mill were continuously being deposited on plaintiff's dwelling and garden. The jury was not permitted by the trial judge to determine the issue of punitive damages. The appellate court found, however, that there was adequate evidence for a jury to award punitive damages. A retrial was ordered.

In the Oregon court's view, punitive damages were appropriate whenever there was a wrongful act, done intentionally, with knowledge that it would cause harm to a particular person. The court was satisfied that the defendant knew when it built its paper mill that there might be damage to adjoining property. This was evidenced by the substantial use of air pollution devices by the defendant. The defendant itself introduced evidence that after seven years of operation it raised its smokestack to 290 feet to effectuate a high-level discharge of gases. To the court this indicated a strong possibility that the defendant did not do everything within its power to control pollution from the time it opened the plant.

Three of the seven-man court dissented on the ground that the evidence presented did not indicate that the plant was unreasonably operated. To the dissenters it was immaterial that the defendant did not do everything possible to prevent damages, or even that the defendant acted intentionally. To impose punitive damages the dissenters required malice on the part of the defendant. They felt that punitive damages were inappropriate in this case where the defendant apparently acted only negligently.

4.4 Cases Illustrating Actions Against Cities for Pollution

(a) City Stopped by Motel Owner from Emitting Gas— Irreparable Injury Even Though Business Was Prospering

In *Costas v. City of Fond Du Lac,* 24 Wis.2d 409, 129 N.W.2d 217 (1964), a city was enjoined from permitting impure gases with offensive odors from emanating from its sewage disposal plant. The escape of impure gases constituted a nuisance to the plaintiff's property—a motel with an outdoor restaurant and swimming pool. The defendant claimed that plaintiff suffered no irreparable injury because his business was prospering.

The Wisconsin court ruled that the fact that plaintiff had not been forced to go out of business was not conclusive of an absence of irreparable injury. While it is true that if plaintiff had gone out of business precise pecuniary damages could have been ascertained and an injunction would have been unnecessary, it was precisely because the money damages were not ascertainable that an injunction should issue to abate the nuisance.

It was also within the court's equity powers to go beyond a mere abatement order and provide in detail how the nuisance should be abated. The court ordered the municipality to provide funds to modernize the sewage plant unless the defendant could devise another suitable means of abatement.

(b) Person Living Near City Dump Could Have It Shut Down as a Nuisance

The plaintiffs in *Steiffer v. Kansas City*, 175 Kan. 794, 267 P.2d 474 (1954), sought to enjoin the city from maintaining a public dump which was alleged to be a nuisance. The plaintiffs claimed that noxious odors from the dump made their dwelling place, which was located about 700 feet from the dump, unfit for occupation, and that it impaired their personal health as well as the value of their land. Fires had occurred frequently in the dumping grounds and smoke and burning trash had been blown about the grounds of the plaintiffs. Furthermore, the dump became increasingly infested with rodents and insects.

The Kansas court first decided that the immunity of municipalities did not extend to acts done which create or maintain a nuisance, so that the city could be sued. The court then defined nuisance as any use of property which gives offense to or endangers life or health, violates the laws of decency, unreasonably pollutes the air with foul, noxious, offensive odors or smoke, or obstructs the reasonable and comfortable use and enjoyment of the property of another. The allegation that the city dump constituted a nuisance was sustained.

(c) Supreme Court Refuses to Enjoin Water Pollution by City—Damages Awarded for Nuisance

In *Harrisonville v. Dickey Clay Company*, 289 U.S. 334 (1932), the United States Supreme Court refused to enjoin the use of a stream on pasture land for the discharge of sewage by a municipality. The injunction would work a disproportionate hardship upon the defendant by causing it to construct a new or auxiliary plant at great expense. The public interest would be prejudiced by that result. Substantial redress by payment of money damages equal to depreciation in value of the pasture land because of the nuisance was available to the plaintiff landowner. Denial of the injunction and payment of money damages were consistent with the municipality's right of condemnation.

The court further held that the pollution of the stream

was not a "permanent nuisance," i.e., one that is relatively enduring and not likely to be abated voluntarily or by time. This concept affords a plaintiff immediate recovery of the total diminution of value of land afflicted permanently. Though a permanent nuisance did not exist because the municipality could always terminate it, the plaintiff was awarded depreciation damages out of considerations of fairness.

4.5 Cases Illustrating Power of Government To Abate Pollution

(a) Power of Federal Government to Enjoin Interstate Pollution Upheld—Socially Desirable Goals of Clean Air Act

In *United States v. Bishop Processing Company*, 287 F.Supp. 624 (D.Md. 1968), the government sought an injunction under the federal Clean Air Act, 42 U.S.C. §1857, against the operator of a rendering plant in Maryland which allegedly discharged malodorous pollutants which moved across the state line to affect air around Selbyville, Delaware. The defendant moved to dismiss the action claiming that the Clean Air Act was unconstitutional for it regulated purely intrastate as opposed to interstate activities.

The federal court found that the movement of pollutants across state lines constituted interstate commerce which was subject to the regulation of Congress according to the Constitution. Furthermore, the originator of the pollution need not have intended the pollution to cross state lines, nor was it necessary to show that the pollutants interfered with interstate commerce.

When considering the basis for the regulation, the court said that "the commerce power may be exercised to achieve socially desirable objectives even in the absence of economic considerations." However, economic considerations were present. In addition to the fact that the pollution crossed state lines, it affected business conditions, property values, and impeded industrial development. This provided a sufficiently rational basis for Congressional regulation. The defendant's motion to dismiss was denied. Decision affirmed by U.S. Supreme Court, May 18, 1970.

(b) Power of City to Ban Cesspools, Without Proof That Any Cesspool Was a Nuisance

In 1935, the city of Russelville, Kentucky, passed blanket ordinances which established a modern sewer system and outlawed cesspools and privy vaults as nuisances because they contaminated the soil. In *Nourse v. City of Russelville,* 275 Ky. 525, 78 S.W.2d 761 (1936), the plaintiff sought to enjoin the implementation of the ordinances with respect to his land. He established that the sewage disposal and cesspool equipment on his land were sanitary. The city, however, was able to demonstrate the unsanitary conditions and practices in the city generally.

The Kentucky court held that municipalities may abate nuisances pursuant to the reasonable exercise of its police powers. The city may enact laws to preserve and promote the health, morals, security, and general welfare of its citizens as a unit. Since the benefits of a sanitary sewage system would be lost unless the inhabitants could be compelled to abandon the threatening archaic structures, it was reasonable to compel all owners of the unsanitary equipment to discontinue their use. It was not necessary for the city to demonstrate that each old unit was in fact an existing nuisance. Hence, plaintiff's action for an injunction failed.

(c) Power of City to Abate Pollution from Steamboats Operating with Federal License

In *Huron Cement Company v. Detroit,* 362 U.S. 440 (1960), the United States Supreme Court considered the constitutionality of Detroit's Smoke Abatement Code. The code set a maximum standard for smoke emissions within the city. The issue was whether the standards were applicable to the appellant. The appellant operated steamships on the Great Lakes in accordance with federal standards for boiler apparatus. The appellant claimed that the Detroit statute squarely conflicted with a comprehensive scheme of federal legislation, and that it materially affected interstate commerce where uniformity is necessary.

The Supreme Court, however, viewed the federal legislation as aiming at maritime navigation and therefore there
was no overlap by the Detroit ordinance which was aimed
exclusively at air pollution. Also, the mere fact that the
appellant's ships were federally licensed did not immunize
the vessel from the operation of local police powers. Such
powers did not constitute a direct regulation of commerce.
The ordinances intended to promote the health and welfare
of the city's inhabitants.

In the exercise of these police powers, the Court said
the "states and their instrumentalities may act, in many
areas of interstate commerce and maritime activities, concurrently with the federal government." When the Constitution conferred upon Congress the power to regulate
commerce, it was not intended to cut the states off from
legislating on matters relating to safety of their citizens,
though the legislation might indirectly affect the commerce
of the country.

4.6 Cases Illustrating Standing of Conservationist Groups and Others To Sue for Pollution

(a) Conservation Group Has Standing to Intervene in Administrative Award of License to Power Company— Famous Scenic Hudson–Storm King Case

In *Scenic Hudson Preservation Conference v. Federal
Power Commission,* 354 F. 2d 608 (2d Cir. 1965), *cert.
den.* 384 U.S. 941 (1966), a case resulting from the cele-
brated dispute between Consolidated Edison Company of
New York (Con Ed) and conservationists, the federal
court ordered the Federal Power Commission (FPC) to
withdraw a license to construct a pumped storage hydroelectric project on the Hudson River at Storm King that
had been granted to Con Ed.

The federal court determined that the conservation
group had the right to intervene in the FPC hearings as
an "aggrieved party," although it had no appreciable
economic interest in the area. "Special interests" such as
the preservation of the scenic beauty, fish, and wildlife
were sufficient. The plaintiff was able to have the court

compel the FPC to adduce additional evidence on the absence of alternative available areas for Con Ed, on the effect of the plan on the fish resources of the Hudson River, and on the effect on the natural beauty and national historic shrines in the Hudson Valley.

Thus, the license granted by the FPC to Con Ed was withdrawn and the matter returned to the FPC to re-evaluate the application for the license. At the time of this writing, the matter is still before the FPC.

(b) Damage to Cattle Ranch from Fluoride Fumes— Courts Have Power to Consider Action Even Though State Administrative Agency Had Not Acted

In *Reynolds Metals Company v. Martin,* 337 F. 2d 780 (9th Cir. 1964), the action was brought by Martin for alleged contamination of his 1500-acre cattle ranch by fluoride fumes and particulates from the nearby Reynolds aluminum reduction plant. This particular proceeding was brought by Reynolds Company to have the case dismissed for lack of jurisdiction. Its claim was that the state Sanitary Authority, an administrative body, was required by law to pass initially on questions of air pollution, not the courts. The court found a state law exception to this administrative jurisdiction in case of public and private nuisance. Martin's action, however, was brought on trespass grounds to take advantage of the longer statute of limitations.

The federal court resolved the issue by noting the overlap between nuisance and trespass. Nuisance is "an actionable invasion of a possessor's interest in the use and enjoyment of his land"; trespass is "an actionable invasion of a possessor's interest in the exclusive possession of land." Thus a trespass interfering with interest in the exclusive possession of land, if it is of a continuing nature, will also interfere with the use and enjoyment of land, and thereby constitute a nuisance. Therefore, Martin's action, for purposes of administrative jurisdiction, was brought in nuisance though it was considered an action in trespass for the statute of limitations. Motion to dismiss by Reynolds was denied.

4.7 Cases Illustrating New Legal Theories of Liability of Polluters

(a) Strict Liability for Use of Hydrocyanic Acid Gas— Ultrahazardous Activities

In *Luthringer v. Moore,* 31 Cal. 2d 489, 190 P.2d 1 (1948), the plaintiff, a drugstore employee, was injured by lethal hydrocyanic acid gas which was being used as an exterminant in the basement of an adjacent restaurant. The plaintiff was awarded $10,000 in damages. At issue was whether the plaintiff's lawsuit could be based upon the legal concept of absolute liability, i.e., liability for engaging in an ultrahazardous activity even where no negligence was present.

The California Supreme Court upheld judgment for the plaintiff. The important factor was that certain activities may be so hazardous to the public—and of relative infrequent occurrence so that the public is not aware of the hazard so as to protect itself—to warrant application of absolute liability as a public policy. An activity is ultrahazardous if it necessarily involves a risk of serious harm to the person or property of others which cannot be eliminated by the exercise of the utmost care. Under this standard, the court found that the use of highly penetrative hydrocyanic acid gas for extermination was an ultrahazardous activity, for the public was not familiar with the use of the gas, and no amount of care by the exterminator such as sealing off the room would be sufficient to prevent injury from escaping gas. The exterminator was deemed to know, or should have known, that injury was likely to result.

(b) Antitrust Action by Government Against "Big Four" Automobile Manufacturers for Delaying Use of Pollution Devices—Subsequent Actions

In an action entitled *United States v. Automobile Manufacturers Association, Inc.,* 1969 Trade Cases 72,907 (C.D. Cal.), the Department of Justice filed an antitrust suit in Los Angeles alleging that the four major automobile producers (General Motors, Ford Motor, Chrysler, and American Motors) unlawfully conspired to delay the development and installation of antipollution devices for motor vehicles. This was alleged as to the Automobile Manufacturers Association, too. It was alleged that the defendants could have installed "positive crankcase ventilation" in 1962 models but agreed amongst themselves to install them uniformly in 1963. It was alleged that the defendants agreed, through a cross-licensing agreement, to restrict the price they would pay for patents developed by outsiders.

The federal district court in October 1969 enjoined the defendants from combining or conspiring to hinder or limit the development, manufacture, installation, and distribution of antipollution devices. The cross-licensing agreement was also invalidated. The defendants submitted to the judgment, as it could under the Sherman Antitrust Act, without a trial or a finding of any fact, and without the judgment constituting an admission by any of them. This is known as a consent decree.

This consent decree did not, however, please all of the persons involved with the suit. New York City appealed the decision of the district court on the basis that it wanted a clause in the decree that would make it more useful to private suits for treble damages which many cities and persons were considering. This clause would make the court decree admissible evidence that the charges brought by the federal government were true, whereas the consent decree as entered would not have that effect. In March 1970 the Supreme Court of the United States affirmed the district court's ruling, denying the request of New York City. Thus, while private suits can still be brought, the burden of proof is much greater than it would have been under the decree New York City sought.

In its appeal, New York City was joined by Los Angeles County, Baltimore, and five Philadelphia cities as *amici curiae*—friends of the court. The American Civil Liberties Union, two Chicago aldermen, and a number of individuals also joined in the appeal, or brought one of their own. In an appeal by two individuals, Grossman and Tamkin, the suit was brought on behalf of a class of persons—the nation. The Supreme Court's ruling disposed of all of these cases.

Quite a number of private civil suits for treble damages have been filed. In September, 1970, a federal court in Los Angeles held that the plaintiffs in these actions, a group that included a number of cities, could claim a violation of antitrust laws even though they were not buyers of the automobiles.

4.8 Cases Illustrating Problems in Proving a Pollution Case

(a) Aggravation of Cancer Due to Release of SO₂ During Weather Inversion—Proof of Use of Gas Masks

In *Hagy v. Allied Chemical and Dye Corporation*, 122 Cal.App. 2d 361, 265 P.2d 86 (1954), the California court applied the legal concept that a negligent person is responsible for the full extent of an injury caused by him even though the injury is greatly magnified by the peculiar physical condition of the injured party. Defendant's factory had permitted a dense smog of sulfur dioxide and trioxide to accumulate in an area around the plant for several hours during a known atmospheric inversion which prevented the clouds from rising.

The plaintiffs, husband and wife, breathed in the fumes while driving by the factory, became ill, and were hospitalized. Subsequently, the wife lost her voice. Her illness progressed and was diagnosed as cancer of the larynx, a condition which, in a dormant state, had existed prior to the incident complained of. A laryngectomy was performed four months after the incident resulting in a permanent loss of voice. The jury allowed recovery for aggravation of the preexisting cancer on the theory that the injury caused by defendant to plaintiff's throat also caused the cancerous tendency to "light up." The wife recovered $25,000; the husband $5000 for aggravation of a preexisting heart condition and loss of his wife's "society."

Some of the facts of this case are most interesting. The proof by the plaintiffs that the personnel in the factory were aware of the continuing risk of putting new pollutants into the air during the thermal inversion consisted in part of evidence that employees had been seen leaving the factory wearing gas masks! This was at 7:45 P.M. The acid was being manufactured with fumes released, from 6:25 to 8:25 P.M. Plaintiffs drove through the clouds of gas shortly after 8:25 P.M.

(b) Beryllium Emissions—Proof of Injury to One Who Resided Near Factory

Heck v. Beryllium Corporation, 424 Pa. 140, 226 A.2d 87 (1966), involved an action for personal injury caused by the emission of beryllium into the atmosphere. Plaintiff resided several miles from the defendant's plant and had inhaled beryllium from 1939 to trial (1955). In 1950, the Atomic Energy Commission established a toxicity level for beryllium that should not be exceeded in out-plant areas. From 1951 to 1955 defendant's emissions exceeded the minimum of the permissible range for the area where the plaintiff resided. Defendant was adjudged negligent, but received a judgment notwithstanding the verdict on the basis of expert testimony that plaintiff's illness could only have been caused by the level of toxic emissions between 1951 and 1955 if she had been exposed prior to 1951.

On appeal, the judgment for the defendant was set aside by the Pennsylvania court. A defendant may be liable for all the harm caused by its negligent act though the injury is enhanced by an unknown physical condition. In determining whether the emissions from 1951 to 1955 were negligent the trial court should have considered the susceptibility of the plaintiff to beryllium poisoning caused by emissions prior to 1951 even though such emissions may not have been negligent. Because of the unknown degree of exposure for eleven years prior to the AEC ruling and the highly dangerous nature of the substance, emissions from 1951 to 1955 exceeding the minimum of the permissible range could constitute negligence. A new trial was awarded to the plaintiff.

(c) Nuisance Action by Airline Against Factory for Plane Crash—Failure of Proof

In *Eastern Airlines, Inc. v. American Cyanamid Company,* 321 F.2d 683 (5th Cir. 1963), the airline brought the action for damage to an airplane which crashed, allegedly because the airport runway was obscured by smoke from the defendant's plant. The action was based on both nuisance (which approaches strict liability without negligence) and negligence. The jury did not find that the operation of defendant's plant unreasonably interfered with Eastern's use of the airport. That is, although the defendant's plant did constitute a nuisance as to neighbors in the vicinity of the plant, it was not established that the pollution caused Eastern's plane to crash. This would have to be shown to establish liability on a nuisance theory. Furthermore, both parties were deemed negligent with regard to the particular crash. Judgment was rendered for defendant by the federal court.

(d) Proof of Fluoride Poisoning—Factory Presumed to Be Careless—Not a Defense That Modern Pollution Devices Were in Use

In *Reynolds Metals Company v. Yturbidé,* 258 F.2d 321 (9th Cir.), *cert. den.* 358 U.S. 840 (1958), Yturbide sought damages for personal injuries caused by fluoride poisoning. The fluoride, it was alleged, emanated from Reynolds' plant and was carried by winds over to plaintiff's farm where it was inhaled and ingested with food grown for domestic use. At issue was whether the fluoride came from defendant's plant, and whether the defendant was negligent in allowing the fluoride to escape in quantity so as to injure the plaintiff.

The federal court permitted a presumption of negligence to be raised against the defendant because (1) the injuries complained of were conclusively proven to have been caused by fluorides; (2) it was, therefore, inferable that excessive amounts of fluoride reached the plaintiff's farm from somewhere; (3) the instrumentality that produced fluorides was solely within the defendant's control; and (4) such accidents did not commonly occur where ordinary care was exercised. This presumption of negligence (*res ipsa loquitur*) required the defendant to prove to the jury that it exercised reasonable care.

Proof that the plant was equipped with modern means of controlling fluoride emissions did not, as a matter of law, rebut the presumption of negligence. The question of whether due care was exercised remained a question of fact for jury determination. Judgment for plaintiffs was affirmed.

4.9 Case Illustrating Power of Government to Refuse Permission to Fill Wetlands

The United States Army Corps of Engineers has had its own way for too long. We present here a landmark decision by Chief Judge Brown of the United States Court of Appeals for the Fifth Circuit, New Orleans, La. The decision deals with Boca Ciega Bay, an area that is navigable, the home of a great many unique fish and birds, an endless variety of trees and plants, and of remarkable natural beauty, as is set forth in the judge's decision rendered July 16, 1970 that follows:

(a) Decision of Court

UNITED STATES COURT OF APPEALS
FOR THE FIFTH CIRCUIT
ALFRED G. ZABEL and DAVID H. RUSSELL,
Plaintiffs-Appellees,

versus

R. P. TABB, COLONEL, CORPS OF ENGINEERS,
DISTRICT ENGINEER, DEPARTMENT OF THE ARMY,
JACKSONVILLE, FLORIDA, DISTRICT;
STANLEY R. RESOR, SECRETARY OF THE ARMY;
AND UNITED STATES OF AMERICA,
Defendants-Appellants.

July 16, 1970

276 F.2d 764 (5th Cir.) Certeriori denied, Feb. 22, 1971
U.S. Supreme Court.

BROWN, Chief Judge: *It is the destiny of the Fifth Circuit to be in the middle of great, oftentimes explosive issues of spectacular public importance. So it is here as we enter in depth the contemporary interest in the preservation of our environment.** By an injunction requiring the issu-

ance of a permit to fill in eleven acres of tidelands in the beautiful Boca Ciega Bay in the St. Petersburg-Tampa, Florida area for use as a commercial mobile trailer park, the District Judge held that the Secretary of the Army and his functionary, the Chief of Engineers, had no power to consider anything except interference with navigation. There being no such obstruction to navigation, they were ordered to issue a permit even though the permittees acknowledge that "there was evidence before the Corps of Engineers sufficient to justify an administrative agency finding that [the] fill would do damage to the ecology or marine life on the bottom." We hold that nothing in the statutory structure compels the Secretary to close his eyes to all that others see or think they see. The establishment was entitled, if not required, to consider *ecological factors* and, being persuaded by them, to deny that which might have been granted routinely five, ten, or fifteen years ago before man's explosive increase made all, including Congress, aware of civilization's potential destruction from breathing its own polluted air and drinking its own infected water and the immeasurable loss from a silent-spring-like disturbance of nature's economy. We reverse.

I. Genesis: The Beginning

In setting the stage we draw freely on the Government's brief. This suit was instituted by Landholders, Zabel and Russell, on May 10, 1967, to compel the Secretary of the Army to issue a permit to dredge and fill in the navigable waters of Boca Ciega Bay, in Pinellas County near St. Petersburg, Florida. On August 15, 1967, the United States and its officers, Defendants-Appellants, filed a motion to dismiss the suit for lack of jurisdiction which was denied. The United States and other defendants then answered the

* Emphasis added.

complaint alleging lack of jurisdiction and that the Court
lacks power to compel a discretionary act by the Secretary
of the Army. The United States and other defendants
moved for summary judgment. Landholders, Zabel and
Russell, also moved for summary judgment. After a hearing, the District Court, on February 17, 1969, granted
summary judgment for Landholders and directed the Secretary of the Army to issue the permit. It granted a stay of
execution of the judgment until this appeal could be heard
and decided. We invert the summary judgments, reversing
Appellees and rendering judgment for the United States.

Landholders own land riparian to Boca Ciega Bay and
adjacent land underlying the Bay. It is navigable water of
the United States, being an arm of Tampa Bay which opens
into the Gulf of Mexico. The Zabel and Russell property
is located about one mile from the Intracostal Waterway.

Landholders desire to dredge and fill on their property in
the Bay for a trailer park, with a bridge or culvert to their
adjoining upland. To this purpose they first applied to the
state and local authorities for permission to perform the
work and obtained the consent or approval of all such
agencies having jurisdiction to prohibit the work, namely
Pinellas County Water and Navigation Control Authority
(which originally rejected permission, but ultimately issued
a permit pursuant to state Court order), Trustees of the
Internal Improvement Fund of the State of Florida, Central
and South Florida Flood Control District, and Board of
Pilot Commissioners for the Port of St. Petersburg.

Landholders then applied to the Corps of Engineers for
a federal permit to perform the dredging and filling. The
Pinellas County Water and Navigation Control Authority
(which originally rejected permission, but ultimately issued
a permit pursuant to state Court order) continued to op-
pose the work as did the Board of County Commissioners
of Pinellas County, who also comprise the Pinellas County
Water and Navigation Control Authority, the County
Health Board of Pinellas County, the Florida Board of
Conservation, and about 700 individuals who filed protests.
The United States Fish and Wildlife Service, Department

of the Interior, also opposed the dredging and filling because it "would have a distinctly harmful effect on the fish and wildlife resources of Boca Ciega Bay."

A public hearing was held in St. Petersburg in November, 1966, and on December 30, 1966, the District Engineer at Jacksonville, Florida, Colonel Tabb, recommended to his superiors that the application be denied. He said that "The proposed work would have no material adverse effect on navigation" but that:

> "Careful consideration has been given to the general public interest in this case. The virtually unanimous opposition to the proposed work as expressed in the protests which were received and as exhaustively presented at the public hearing have convinced me that *approval of the application would not be in the public interest*. The continued opposition to the U.S. Fish & Wildlife Service despite efforts on the part of the applicants to reduce the extent of damage leads me to the conclusion that approval of the work would not be consistent with the intent of Congress as expressed in the Fish & Wildlife Coordination Act, as amended, 12 August 1958. Further, the opposition of the State of Florida and of county authorities as described in paragraph 5 above gives additional support to my conclusion that the work should not be authorized."

The Division Engineer, South Atlantic Division, Atlanta, Georgia, concurred in that recommendation stating: "In view of the wide spread opposition to the proposed work, it is apparent that approval of the application would not be in the public interest." The Chief of Engineers concurred for the same reasons. Finally, the Secretary of the Army denied the application on February 28, 1967, because issuance of the requested permit:

1. Would result in a distinctly harmful effect on the fish and wildlife resources in Boca Ciega Bay,
2. Would be inconsistent with the purposes of the Fish and Wildlife Coordination Act of 1958, as amended (16 U.S.C. 662),
3. Is opposed by the Florida Board of Conservation on behalf of the State of Florida, and by the County

Health Board of Pinellas County and the Board of County Commissioners of Pinellas County, and
  4. Would be contrary to the public interest.

Landholders then instituted this suit to review the Secretary's determination and for an order compelling him to issue a permit. They urged that the proposed work would not hinder navigation and that the Secretary had no authority to refuse the permit on other grounds. They acknowledged that "there was evidence before the Corps of Engineers sufficient to justify an administrative agency finding that our fill would do damage to the ecology or marine life on the bottom." The Government urged lack of jurisdiction and supported the denial of the permit on authority of §10 of the Rivers and Harbors Act of March 3, 1899, 30 Stat. 1121, 1151, 33 U.S.C.A. §403, giving the Secretary discretion to issue permits and on the Fish and Wildlife Coordination Act of March 10, 1934, Stat. 401, as amended, 16 U.S.C.A. §§661 and 662 (a), requiring the Secretary to consult with the Fish and Wildlife Service and state conservation agencies before issuing a permit to dredge and fill.

The District Court held that it had jurisdiction, that the Fish and Wildlife Coordination Act was not authority for denying the permit, and that:

> "The taking, control or limitation in the use of private property interests by an exercise of *the police power of the government* or the public interest or general welfare should be authorized by legislation which clearly outlines procedure which comports to all constitutional standards. This is not the case here.
>
> As this opinion is being prepared the Congress is in session. Advocates of conservation are both able and effective. The way is open to obtain a remedy for future situations like this one if one is needed and can be legally granted by the Congress."

The Court granted summary judgment for Landholders and directed the Secretary of the Army to issue the permit. This appeal followed.

The question presented to us is whether the Secretary of the Army can refuse to authorize a dredge and fill project in navigable waters for factually substantial ecological reasons even though the project would not interfere with navigation, flood control, or the production of power. To answer this question in the affirmative, we must answer two intermediate questions affirmatively. (1) *Does Congress for ecological reasons have the power to prohibit a project on private riparian submerged land in navigable waters?* (2) *If it does, has Congress committed the power to prohibit to the Secretary of the Army?*

II. Constitutional Power

The starting point here is the Commerce Clause and its expansive reach. The test for determining whether Congress has the power to protect wildlife in navigable waters and thereby to regulate the use of private property for this reason is whether there is a basis for the Congressional judgment that the activity regulated has a substantial effect on interstate commerce. *Wickard v. Filburn,* 1942, 317 U.S. 111. That this activity meets this test is hardly questioned. *In this time of awakening to the reality that we cannot continue to despoil our environment and yet exist,* the nation knows, if Courts do not, that the destruction of fish and wildlife in our estuarine waters does have a substantial, and in some areas a devastating, effect on interstate commerce. Landholders do not contend otherwise. Nor is it challenged that dredge and fill projects are activities which may tend to destroy the ecological balance and thereby affect commerce substantially. Because of these potential effects Congress has the power to regulate such projects.

III. Relinquishment of the Power

Landholders do not challenge the existence of power. They argue that Congress in the historic compromise over the oil rich tidelands controversy abandoned its power over other natural resources by the relinquishment to the states in the Submerged Lands Act. By it they urge the Government stripped itself of the power to regulate tidelands property except for purposes relating to (i) navigation, (ii) flood control, and (iii) hydroelectric power. This rests on the expressed Congressional reservation of control for these three purposes over the submerged lands, title to and power over which Congress relinquished to the states.

The argument assumes that when Congress relinquished title to the land and the right and power to manage and use the land, it relinquished its power under the commerce clause except in particulars (i), (ii), and (iii). It also assumes that reservation of these three enumerated aspects of the commerce power implied that Congress gave up its plenary power over the myriad other aspects of commerce. See, e.g., *Heart of Atlanta Motel, Inc. v. United States,* 1964, 379 U.S. Congress clearly has the power under the Commerce Clause to regulate the use of Landholders' submerged riparian property for conservation purposes and has not given up this power in the Submerged Lands Act.

IV. Prohibiting Obstructions to Navigation

The action of the Chief of Engineers and the Secretary of the Army under attack rests immediately on the Rivers and Harbors Act, 33 U.S.C.A. §403, which declares that "the creation of any obstruction *** to the navigable capacity of any of the waters of the United States is prohibited." The Act covers both building of structures and the excavating and filling in navigable waters.

Another case holds that the Corps has a duty to consider factors other than navigational. *Citizens Committee for the Hudson Valley v. Volpe,* S.D.N.Y., 1969, 302 F.Supp. 1083. There the District Court held that the Corps must consider a fill project in the context of the entire expressway project of which it was a part rather than just considering the fill and its effect on navigation. The reasoning was that the approval of the Secretary of Transportation was necessary before a proposed causeway could be constructed. The causeway, along with the fill, was an integral part of the expressway project. However, if the Corps and Secretary of the Army approved the fill and the State completed it, the Secretary of Transportation, considering the enormous expense of the fill, would have no choice, other than approving the causeway. The Army thus had exceeded its authority in approving the fill on only navigational considerations since approval of the fill was effectually approval of the causeway.*

But such circuity is not necessary. Governmental agencies in executing a particular statutory responsibility ordinarily are required to take heed of, sometimes effectuate and other times not thwart other valid statutory governmental policies. And here the government-wide policy of environmental conservation is spectacularly revealed in at least two statutes, The Fish and Wildlife Coordination Act and the National Environmental Policy Act of 1969.

The Fish and Wildlife Coordination Act clearly requires the dredging and filling agency (under a governmental permit), whether public or private, to consult with the Fish and Wildlife Service, with a view of conservation of wildlife resources. If there be any question as to whether the statute directs the licensing agency (the Corps) to so consult it can quickly be dispelled. Common sense and reason dictate that it would be incongruous for Congress, in light of the fact that it intends conservation to be considered in private dredge and fill operations (as evidenced by the clear wording of the statute), not to direct the only federal agency concerned with licensing such projects both to consult and to take such factors into account.

The second proof that the Secretary is directed and authorized by the Fish and Wildlife Coordination Act to consider conservation is found in the legislative history. The Senate Report on the Fish and Wildlife Coordination Act states:

* The Court essentially held that the Corps, where approval of Transportation is also required, cannot be oblivious to the effect of fill projects on the beauty and conservation of natural resources. This inference arises from the fact that the Secretary of Transportation is statutorily required to consider conservation before granting a permit. But if the fill on which the causeway was to be built were completed at the time the permit for the causeway was requested, there would be no conservation factors for Transportation to consider. The Court held that the Corps could not blind itself to this fact and thereby cut off considerations of conservation by granting a fill permit without Transportation's approval of the causeway.

"Finally, the nursery and feeding grounds of valuable crustaceans, such as shrimp, as well as the young of valuable marine fishes, may be affected by dredging, filling, and diking operations often carried out to improve navigation and provide new industrial or residential land.

* * * *

Existing law has questionable application to projects of the Corps of Engineers for the dredging of bays and estuaries for navigation and filling purposes. More seriously, existing law has no application whatsoever to the dredging and filling of bays and estuaries by private interests or other non-Federal entities in navigable waters under permit from the Corps of Engineers. This is a particularly serious deficiency from the standpoint of commercial fishing interests. The dredging of these bays and estuaries along the coastlines to aid navigation and also to provide land fills for real estate and similar developments, both by Federal agencies or other agencies under permit from the Corps of Engineers, has increased tremendously in the last 5 years. Obviously, dredging activity of this sort has a profound *disturbing effect on aquatic life,* including *shrimp and other species of tremendous significance* to the commercial fishing industry. The bays, estuaries, and related marsh areas *are highly important as spawning and nursery grounds for many commercial species of fish and shellfish.*"

Congress intended the Chief of Engineers and Secretary of the Army to consult with the Fish and Wildlife Service before issuing a permit for a private dredge and fill operation.

This interpretation was judicially accepted in *Udall v. FPC:*

"Section 2(a), 16 USC §622(a), provides that an agency evaluating a license under which 'the waters of any stream or other body of water are proposed . . . to be impounded first shall consult with the United States Fish and Wildlife Service, Department of the Interior . . . with a view to the conservation of wildlife resources by preventing loss of and damage to such resources.' . . . Certainly the wildlife conservation aspect of the project must be explored and evaluated."

1967, 387 U.S. 428.

The meaning and application of the Act are also reflected by the actions of the Executive that show the statute authorizes and directs the Secretary to consult with the Fish and Wildlife Service in deciding whether to grant a dredge and fill permit.

In a Memorandum of Understanding between the Secretary of the Army and the Secretary of the Interior, it is provided that, upon receipt of an application for a permit to dredge or fill in navigable waters, the District Engineer of the Corps of Engineers concerned is required to send notices to all interested parties, including the appropriate Regional Directors of the Federal Water Pollution Control Administration, the Fish and Wildlife Service, the National Park Service and the appropriate state conservation, resources, and water pollution agencies. The District Engineer is given the initial responsibility of evaluating all relevant factors in reaching a decision as to whether the particular permit involved should be granted or denied. The Memorandum also provides that in case of conflicting views the ultimate decision shall be made by the Secretary of the Army after consultation with the Secretary of the Interior.

This Executive action has almost a virtual legislative imprimatur from the November 1967 Report of the House Committee on Merchant Marine and Fisheries, in reporting favorably on a bill to protect estuarine areas which was later enacted into law. As a result of the effective operation of the Interdepartmental Memorandum of Understanding, the Interior Department and the Committee concluded that it was not necessary to provide for dual permits from Interior and Army.

The intent of the three branches has been unequivocally expressed: The Secretary must weigh the effect a dredge and fill project will have on conservation before he issues a permit lifting the Congressional ban.

The parallel of momentum as the three branches shape a national policy gets added impetus from the National Environmental Policy Act of 1969, Public Law 91-190. This Act essentially states that *every federal agency shall consider ecological factors when dealing with activities which may have an impact on man's environment.*

To judge the ebb and flow of the national tide, he can look to the Report of the House Committee on Government Operations. Although this perhaps lacks traditional standing of legislative history, it certainly has relevance somewhat comparable to an Executive Commission Report. On March 17, 1970, it approved and adopted a Report, based on a study made by its Conservation and Natural Resources Subcommittee, entitled *Our Waters and Wetlands: How the Corps of Engineers Can Help Prevent Their Destruction and Pollution.*

The heading of the Report reads:

> "The Corps of Engineers, which is charged by Congress with the duty to protect the nation's navigable waters, should, when considering whether to approve applications for landfills, dredging and other work in navigable waters, *increase its consideration* of the effects which the proposed work will have, not only on navigation, but also on *conservation of natural resources, fish and wildlife, air and water quality, esthetics, scenic view, historic sites, ecology, and other public interest aspects of the waterway.*"

> "In 1968, the Corps revised its regulations to state that the Corps, in considering an application for a permit to fill, dredge, discharge or deposit materials, or conduct other activities affecting navigable waters, will evaluate "all relevant factors, including the effect of the proposed work on navigation, fish and wildlife, conservation, pollution, esthetics, ecology, and the general public interest." 33 CFR 209.120(d)(1).

The first section stifles any doubt as to how this part of Congress construes the Corps' duty under the Rivers and Harbors Act. The section traces the historical interpretation of the Corps' power under the Rivers and Harbors Act. It commends the Corps for recognizing ecological considerations under the Act to protect against unnecessary fills and cites the instant case. But following the temper of the times, the report by bold face black type cautions against any easy overconfidence and charges the Corps with ever-increasing vigilance.

When the House Report and the National Environmental Policy Act of 1969 are considered together with the Fish and Wildlife Coordination Act and its interpretations, there is no doubt that the Secretary can refuse on conservation grounds to grant a permit under the Rivers and Harbors Act.

V. Due Process

Landholders next contend that the denial of a permit without a hearing before the Fish and Wildlife Service is a deprivation of property without due process of law. Administrative law requires that before an agency can regulate a party, it must allow that party to be heard. Here, Landholders were given such a hearing before the Corps of Engineers, the body empowered to grant or deny a permit. They were not entitled to a hearing before the Fish and Wildlife Service because it is not "the one who decides." *Morgan v. United States,* 1935, 289 U.S. 468, 481, 56 S.Ct. 906, 912, 80 L.Ed. 1288, 1295. They were allowed to rebut the findings and conclusions of the Fish and Wildlife Service before the deciding body and thus were not denied due process for lack of a hearing.

VI. Taking Without Compensation

Landholders' last contention is that their private submerged property was taken for public use without just compensation. They proceed this way: (i) the denial of a permit constitutes a taking since this is the only use to which the property could be put; (ii) the public use is as a breeding ground for wildlife; and (iii) for that use just compensation is due.

Our discussion of this contention begins and ends with the idea that there is no taking. The waters and underlying land are subject to the paramount servitude in the Federal government which the Submerged Lands Act expressly reserved as an incident of power incident to the Commerce Clause.

VII. Conclusion

Landholders' contentions fail on all grounds. The case is reversed and since there are no questions remaining to

be resolved by the District Court, judgment is rendered for
the Government and the associated agent-defendants.

REVERSED and RENDERED.

(b) Postscript: U.S. Supreme Court affirmed Feb. 22,
1971.

4.10 Cases Illustrating Citizens' Action Group on DDT—Breaking Through Administrative Delay—EDF Cases

On May 28, 1970 two landmark decisions were handed
down by the United States Court of Appeals for the District
of Columbia Circuit. In the first decision, Chief Judge
Bazelon stated: "At some point administrative delay
amounts to a refusal to act, with sufficient finality and ripeness to permit judicial review." The Environmental Defense Fund, in an attempt to stamp out the remaining
dangers of DDT, requested that the Department of Health,
Education and Welfare set a zero tolerance for this pesticide, and it cited the Food, Drug, and Cosmetic Act and
referred to the Delaney amendment to back its position.
The Secretary refused to act, and he was reversed in this
decision and directed to publish the petitioner's proposal in
the Federal Register. At the same time, the Environmental
Defense fund requested that the Secretary of Agriculture
cancel DDT's permit, suspend its registration, and suspend
all production of DDT pending the conclusion of the cancellation proceedings. It cited the Federal Insecticide, Fungicide and Rodenticide Act which holds that misbranding
of an economic poison can result in cancellation of its registration. The decision out of the same court on the same day
by Circuit Judge Wright held that the Secretary of the
Department of Health, Education and Welfare should cancel the permit or specifically show why it should not be can-
celed. The problem of standing is clearly enunciated, analyzed and concluded in favor of petitioner in both cases.

The administrative buck-passing between the Department of Health, Education and Welfare and the Department of Agriculture would make an amusing Laurel and
Hardy skit of they were not dealing with such a dangerous

problem. DDT is a danger; it has caused death to birds, and threatened certain species with extinction. It has long-range effects on man because of biological multiplication, that is, the buildup of DDT parts per million. For instance, although the lower forms of aquatic life retain 10 DDT parts per million, 15 parts per million have been found in trout and salmon in the Great Lakes area. These fish may, in turn, be eaten by otters or muskrats who will retain 20 to 30 parts per million in their bodies—and so on up the animal ladder, with increasing concentrations maintained, and all of the adverse effects not yet known.

Because the administrative agencies have such a crucial part to play in putting action behind the drive for environmental quality, we set forth here substantial portions of the May 28, 1970 decisions which are of monumental importance.

USDA (United States Department of Agriculture) was directed to suspend such registrations within 30 days, or give the court their reasons for failing to do so. USDA chose the latter. Supported by their response of June 29, 1970, which EDF considered incompetent and largely irrelevant, USDA stood firm on all registrations. However, the Court in January 1971 ordered the Environmental Protection Agency (which had assumed governmental pesticide responsibility) to issue cancellation notices on the uses of DDT in question and to consider suspension of all other uses. In March 1971, the EPA took these steps, but refused to ban DDT and 2,4,5-T completely, as not an imminent hazard to humans.

The DDT litigation has become a major environmental test case. In addition to the original copetitioners (Sierra Club, National Audubon Society, and West Michigan Environmental Action Council), EDF has been joined by the Izaak Walton League of America and the State of New York as intervenors. USDA was joined by the Montrose Chemical Company (the major manufacturer of DDT) and the National Agricultural Chemicals Association. EDF attorneys in the case have been James W. Moorman, Edward Berlin, Edward Lee Rogers, and Charles R. Halpern, with scientific support primarily from Dr. Charles F. Wurstur of the State University of New York at Stony Brook.

(a) Decision in Department of Agriculture Case

UNITED STATES COURT OF APPEALS
FOR THE DISTRICT OF COLUMBIA CIRCUIT

ENVIRONMENTAL DEFENSE FUND,
INCORPORATED, *et al.*,
PETITIONERS

V.

CLIFFORD H. HARDIN, SECRETARY
OF AGRICULTURE,
UNITED STATES DEPARTMENT
OF AGRICULTURE, RESPONDENTS
ISAAK WALTON LEAGUE
OF AMERICA, INTERVENOR

Decided May 28, 1970
428 F.2d 1093
(footnotes omitted).

Messrs. James W. Moorman and *Charles R. Halpern* were on the motion for petitioners.

BAZELON, *Chief Judge*: This case requires the court to consider under what circumstances there may be a judicial remedy for the failure of an administrative agency to act promptly, and what form that remedy may take.

The shipment of pesticides in interstate commerce is regulated by the Federal Insecticide, Fungicide, and Rodenticide Act (FIFRA), which is administered by the Secretary of the Department of Agriculture. The Act requires pesticides and other "economic poisons" to carry labels bearing certain information, including any warnings necessary to prevent injury to people. A pesticide which fails to comply with the labelling requirement, or which cannot be rendered safe by any labelling, is "misbranded," and the Secretary must refuse or cancel its registration as an economic poison approved for shipment in interstate commerce.

The statute establishes an elaborate procedure by which a registration may be cancelled, that begins when the Secretary issues a notice of cancellation to a registrant. Since the statutory procedures can easily occupy more than a year, the statute also gives the Secretary the power to suspend a registration immediately if he finds such action "necessary to prevent an imminent hazard to the public." Such an interim suspension triggers an expedited version of the procedure that can lead to cancellation.

Petitioners here are five organizations engaged in activities relating to environmental protection. On the basis of extensive evidence of the harmful effects of the pesticide DDT on human, plant, and animal life, they filed a petition with the Secretary of the Department of Agriculture requesting (1) the issuance of notices of cancellation for all economic poisons containing DDT, and (2) the suspension of registration for all such products pending the conclusion of cancellation proceedings. The Secretary issued notices of cancellation with respect to four uses of DDT, solicited comments concerning the remaining uses, and took no action on the request for interim suspension. Petitioners filed this appeal, seeking to compel the Secretary to comply with their request.

The Secretary moved to dismiss for lack of jurisdiction, asserting that petitioners lack standing to complain of his failure to act, that *there is no final order ripe for review,* that any final order would nevertheless be unreviewable because it involves questions committed by law to agency discretion, and that any available relief can be afforded only by the district court on a writ of mandamus, and not by the court of appeals. Since we can accept none of those conclusions, the motion to dismiss must be denied, and the case remanded to the Secretary to provide this court with the record necessary for meaningful appellate review.

I. STANDING

The legislative history of the FIFRA refutes respondents' contention that only registrants and applicants for registration have standing to challenge the Secretary's determinations under the Act. The statute affords a right of review to "any person who will be adversely affected" by an order. An amendment that would have limited review to registrants and applicants was considered and rejected. The "zone of interests" sought to be protected by the statute includes not only the economic interest of the registrant but also the interest of the public in safety. Thus petitioners have standing if they allege sufficient injury in fact to create a constitutionally justiciable case or controversy. .

The injury alleged by petitioners is the *biological harm to man and to other living things resulting from the Secretary's failure to take action which would restrict the use of DDT in the environment.* Numerous scientific studies and several reports to government agencies have concluded that *DDT has a wide spectrum of harmful effects on nontarget plant and animal species; it increases the incidence in animals of cancer and reproductive defects*; and its residues persist in the environment and in the human body long enough to be found far in time and space from the original application.

Consumers of regulated products and services have standing to protect the public interest in the proper administration of a regulatory system enacted for their benefit. The interest asserted in such a challenge to administrative action need not be economic. Like other consumers, those who "consume"—however unwillingly—the pesticide residues permitted by the Secretary to accumulate in the environment are persons "aggrieved by agency action within the meaning of a relevant statute." Furthermore, the consumers' interest in environmental protection may properly be represented by a membership association with an organizational interest in the problem.

On the basis of petitioners' uncontroverted allegations, it appears that they are *organizations with a demonstrated interest in protecting the environment from pesticide pollution. Therefore they have the necessary stake in the outcome of a challenge to the Secretary's inaction to contest the issues with the adverseness required by Article III of the Constitution.*

II. REVIEWABILITY

Related to the question of standing is respondents' argument that the decision to suspend the registration of a pesticide as an "imminent hazard" is committed by statute to unreviewable administrative discretion. Even if petitioners have standing to seek review of some administrative decisions under the FIFRA, respondents contend that they cannot seek review of a decision on emergency suspension. Preclusion of judicial review is not lightly to be inferred, however; it requires a showing of clear evidence of legislative intent. That evidence cannot be found in the mere fact that a statute is drafted in permissive rather than mandatory terms. Although the FIFRA provides that the Secretary "may" suspend the registration of an economic poison that creates an *imminent hazard to the public,* we conclude that his decision is not thereby placed beyond judicial scrutiny.

III. RIPENESS

The main thrust of respondents' argument is that the Secretary has issued no final order reviewable in this court. Petitioners asked the Secretary to take certain actions; he complied in part, and indicated that he was considering further compliance. Since he has neither granted nor denied much of the relief requested, respondents contend that his response to petitioners' request has not yet ripened into a reviewable order.

An order expressly denying the request for suspension or for cancellation would clearly be ripe for review. The doctrines of ripeness and finality are designed to prevent premature judicial intervention in the administrative process, before the administrative action has been fully considered, and before the legal dispute has been brought into focus. No subsequent action can sharpen the controversy arising from a decision by the Secretary that the evidence submitted by petitioners does not compel suspension or cancellation of the registration of DDT. In light of the urgent character of petitioners' claim, and the allegation that delay itself inflicts irreparable injury, the controversy is as ripe for judicial consideration as it can ever be.

Respondents suggest that the district court is the proper forum for any review that may be available, characterizing the petition as one for relief in the nature of mandamus. We find it unnecessary to decide whether petitioners could have obtained relief from the district court, since the availability of that extraordinary remedy for the failure of an officer to perform his statutory duty need not bar statutory appellate review of the failure to act, when exigent circumstances render it equivalent to a final denial of petitioners' request. There is some authority to the effect that only a trial court is capable of reviewing orders issued without benefit of formal factfinding based on a record. That view has been criticized, however, for dividing between two courts the review of the various orders involved in a single administrative proceeding. Whatever its continuing vitality, that line of authority is especially inappropriate here, where the facts in issue lie peculiarly within the special competence of the Secretary. The district court could do no more than remand to the Secretary, as we do here; there seems to be no reason to inject another tribunal into the process.

It remains for us to determine whether, in the circumstances of this case, administrative inaction is the equivalent of an order denying relief. Clearly relief delayed is not always equivalent to relief denied. There are many factors that result in delay, and a court is in general ill-suited to review the order in which an agency conducts its business. But *when administrative inaction has precisely the same impact on the rights of the parties as denial of relief,** an agency cannot preclude judicial review by casting its decision in the form of inaction rather than in the form of an order denying relief.

A. With regard to the request for interim suspension of the registration of DDT, we agree that inaction is tantamount to an order denying suspension. The suspension power is designed to protect the public from an "imminent hazard"; if petitioners are right in their claim that DDT presents a hazard sufficient to warrant suspension, then even a temporary refusal to suspend results in irreparable injury on a massive scale. The controversy over interim relief is ripe for judicial resolution, because the Secretary's inaction

* Emphasis added.

results in a final disposition of such rights as the petitioners and the public may have to interim relief.

Nevertheless, meaningful appellate review of the refusal to suspend DDT's registration is impossible in the absence of any record of administrative action. The suspension decision is committed by statute to the Secretary; the role of the court is merely to ensure that he exercises his discretion within a reasonable time, and to ensure that his decision is supported by the record. Therefore, we must remand the case to the Secretary, either for a fresh determination on the question of suspension, or for a statement of reasons for his silent but effective refusal to suspend the registration of DDT. If he persists in denying suspension in the face of the impressive evidence presented by petitioners, then the basis for that decision should appear clearly on the record, not in conclusory terms but in sufficient detail to permit prompt and effective review. In view of the emergency nature of the claim, we retain jurisdiction to permit respondents to provide us, within thirty days, with the record necessary for review.

B. With respect to the request for notices of cancellation, we are more reluctant to equate a tentative and equivocal delay with an outright denial of the request. The Secretary has made a few feeble gestures in the direction of compliance with the request, and further action is apparently under consideration. But the statutory scheme of the FIFRA itself contemplates a lengthy inquiry into the conditions for the safe use of an economic poison before its registration may finally be cancelled. Since the issuance of cancellation notices merely triggers that administrative mechanism, it is questionable whether the Secretary may properly defer the decision to issue notices in order to engage in a preliminary inquiry not contemplated by the statute.

At some point *administrative delay amounts to a refusal to act, with sufficient finality and ripeness to permit judicial review*. The present record does not permit us to determine whether that point has been reached here. On remand, the Secretary should either decide on the record whether to issue the remaining requested cancellation notices, or explain the reasons for deferring the decision still further. In the light of that record, and in view of his disposition of the request for interim relief, the court will be in a better position to evaluate the impact of any further delay and decide whether judicial relief is appropriate.

Remanded for further proceedings in accordance with this opinion.

(b) Decision in HEW Case

UNITED STATES COURT OF APPEALS FOR THE DISTRICT OF COLUMBIA CIRCUIT

ENVIRONMENTAL DEFENSE FUND, INC., *et al.*, PETITIONERS

V.

UNITED STATES DEPARTMENT OF HEALTH, EDUCATION AND WELFARE, ROBERT H. FINCH, SECRETARY, RESPONDENTS

Decided May 28, 1970
428 F.2d 1083
(footnotes omitted).

Mr. Edward Berlin, Mr. James W. Moorman on the brief, for petitioners.

WRIGHT, *Circuit Judge*: The pesticide DDT has been one of the most widely used chemicals to control various insect populations and to protect agricultural crops from destruction by insects. Recent scientific studies have, however, raised serious questions about the effect on the environment and on human health of the continued use of DDT. Some experiments have demonstrated that DDT increased the incidence of cancer in mice, and a recent Government commission on pesticides concluded that "[t]he evidence for the carcinogenicity of DDT in experimental animals is impressive."

Petitioners are six individuals and a corporation. The individual petitioners include five young mothers who presently or intend in the future to breastfeed their babies; these mothers seek elimination of DDT because mothers' milk presently contains excessive DDT residues up to twice the maximum average daily intake recommended as safe by the United Nations World Health Organization. Mrak Commission Report at 374. The sixth individual petitioner is an agricultural worker required to come into frequent—and allegedly dangerous—contact with DDT as a consequence of his occupation. Environmental Defense Fund, Inc., a nonprofit New York corporation, is made up of scientists and other citizens dedicated to the protection of man's environment and "seeks to assure the preservation or restoration of environmental quality on behalf of the general public."

On the basis of these recent studies, petitioners here filed a petition with the Secretary of Health, Education and Welfare, under applicable statutory provisions, proposing that the Secretary establish a "zero tolerance" for DDT residues in or on raw agricultural commodities. The Secretary rejected the petition as legally insufficient since petitioners had not shown any "practicable method" of removing the residues of the persistent pesticide DDT from raw agricultural commodities. Consequently, he refused to publish petitioners' proposal in the Federal Register, an action which would have triggered a series of informal and formal administrative procedures, including study of the proposal by a specially appointed committee of scientists and formal administrative hearings open to all interested parties.

In this court, petitioners urge that the Secretary's order refusing to publish their proposal should be reversed on two grounds. First, they argue that their petition, properly interpreted, met all the statutory requirements, including that of "practicability." Second, they urge that the 1958 amendment to the Food, Drug and Cosmetic Act, which requires the Secretary to ban any food additive which is found to induce cancer in experimental animals (the Delancy amendment), must be read to require the Secretary not merely to publish their proposal but to establish the "zero tolerance" forthwith.

I

At the outset, we reject respondents' position that any action by HEW on petitioners' proposal must await action, in the first instance, by the Department of Agriculture. The federal government regulates the use of pesticides through two statutes, the Food, Drug and Cosmetic Act (FDCA), administered by the Secretary of HEW, and the Federal Insecticide, Fungicide and Rodenticide Act (FIFRA), administered by the Secretary of Agriculture.

FIFRA regulates the shipment of pesticides, called *"economic poisons," in interstate commerce*. Under the provisions of that Act, every economic poison marketed in interstate commerce must be registered. To be registered, an economic poison must meet certain requirements relating to labeling, agricultural usefulness, and safety. These requirements apply to all pesticides, whether or not used on food crops. FDCA regulates pesticides only to the extent of controlling the residue of a pesticide which can safely remain in or on raw agricultural commodities. The Act first prohibits shipment in interstate commerce of "adulterated" crops. 21 U.S.C. §331. Raw agricultural commodities are considered "adulterated" if there are residues of pesticide chemicals in or on them. 21 U.S.C. §342(a)(1). However, the Secretary of HEW is authorized to establish maximum permissible amounts, called tolerances, for pesticide residues; if the pesticide residue is below the tolerance, the commodity is not considered "adulterated." 21 U.S.C. §346a.

The heart of the regulatory scheme lies in the establishment of these tolerances. Without detailing the elaborate procedures involved, we note that the Act provides two general commands to the Secretary of HEW in establishing tolerances. First, the Act directs the Secretary of HEW to establish tolerances *"to the extent necessary to protect the public health."* 21 U.S.C. §346a(b). In making this judgment, the Secretary is required by the Act to consider the necessity for an adequate food supply, other ways in which the consumer might be affected by the same pesticide, and the opinion of the Secretary of Agriculture as to the agricultural usefulness of the pesticide involved. *Ibid.* Second, the general instruction to establish tolerances is modified by the authorization to establish a zero tolerance—a ban on any residue at all—"if the scientific data before the Secretary does not justify the establishment of a greater tolerance." *Ibid.* In the words of both Senate and House Reports on this legislation:

> "Before any pesticide-chemical residue may remain in or on a raw agricultural commodity, scientific data must be presented to show that the pesticide-chemical residue is safe from the standpoint of the food consumer. *The burden is on the person proposing the tolerance or exemption to establish the safety of such pesticide-chemical residue.*"

While it is obvious that the responsibilities of the two Secretaries are interrelated and ought to be coordinated, we think their individual responsibilties are quite clear and quite separate. The Secretary of HEW is given the primary responsibility for determining the amount of residue of a pesticide which can safely—from the viewpoint of the food consumer—be left on raw agricultural commodities. It is true that in establishing a tolerance the Secretary of HEW must take into account the Agriculture Secretary's opinion regarding the agricultural usefulness of the pesticide, but that is only one of many factors which HEW must consider. In our judgment, the Act's language requires that HEW make its own independent judgment, based on public health considerations, as to the tolerance which should be set for pesticide residues on raw agricultural commodities and not abdicate its responsibility to the Department of Agriculture.

The legislative history supports this conclusion and makes clear beyond peradventure that Congress intended to lodge primary responsibility for public health considerations with the Secretary of HEW. The present pesticide provisions of the FDCA were added by amendment in 1954. The reports of both Houses of Congress on the 1954 amendments stressed that one of the main goals of that legislation was to define clearly departmental responsibilities:

"The principal respects in which this bill would change and improve existing law are—

*   *   *   *

"2. The determination of questions of agricultural usefulness and probable residue levels involved in the establishment of tolerances, is made a function of the Department of Agriculture; while the determination of questions of a public health nature remains a function of the Department of Health, Education, and Welfare. * * *"

If Congress intended that either department defer to the other, the House and Senate reports suggest that ordinarily Agriculture's decisions as to whether to register a pesticide under FIFRA for use on food crops should depend upon HEW's decision to grant a tolerance.

Respondents suggest, however, that the problem posed by DDT's "persistence" somehow alters these basic responsibilities. They argue that, as a result of DDT's persistence, DDT remains in the air, water and soil for a sufficient length of time to be carried over from season to season and from one crop to another. As a result, according to this argument, DDT must first be deregistered by Agriculture, and the chemical allowed to gradually disappear, before HEW can reasonably enact zero tolerances. We note in passing that this argument would apparently mean that HEW would *never* have to act since, according to the argument's premise, DDT would have disappeared.

But, in any event, we do not see how the fact that there is a new, and quite difficult, dimension present in any decision to revise present DDT tolerances operates to relieve HEW of its statutory responsibility. DDT's persistence will obviously affect any action taken by HEW; in all probability it will require that agency to bring creativity and imagination to bear in the search for a workable solution to the problem. But HEW's present posture would require the Department of Agriculture to weigh all the public health concerns which Congress intended that HEW assess.

One of the strengths of administrative agencies has always been thought to be the expertise which reposes in specialized administrators. Presumably that was one of the reasons Congress thought it wise to divide responsibilities for different aspects of pesticide regulation between the Departments of Agriculture and HEW: each has a particular specialty and focus. For either department to relinquish its responsibility would destroy the regulatory scheme enacted by Congress. Consequently, we believe that HEW had and continues to have a responsibility to appraise the continuing safety of pesticide tolerance levels; it should, of course, continue to coordinate its operations with the Department of Agriculture, as it presently does. But it may not relinquish or evade its own responsibilities.

II

The Commissioner of Food and Drugs, acting as the delegate of the Secretary of HEW, rejected petitioners' petition on the ground that it did not satisfy Section 408 (d)(1)(E) of the FDCA, which requires data showing "practicable methods for removing residue which exceeds any proposed tolerance." This alleged deficiency also derives from the fact that DDT is a "persistent" pesticide, *i.e.*, it does not decay quickly, but remains in its toxic form in the environment (and increasingly in human bodies) for a period of years. Thus even if all applications of DDT were to cease tomorrow, substantial and detectable residues of DDT would apparently continue to exist in many raw agricultral commodities. Under these circumstances, establishing a zero tolerance for DDT on all commodities, effective immediately, would mean that a substantial proportion of food in the United States would still be "adulterated" within the meaning of the FDCA.

In their supplement to their petition, however, petitioners made clear that they were not seeking this infeasible, major disruption of the country's food supply. Specifically, they suggested:

> "* * * At a minimum, the Secretary should establish a zero tolerance for DDT and its residues on all raw agricultural commodities with the possible exemption from seizure of any commodities in which it can be established that any residues are the consequences of applications of DDT that were made prior to the announcement by the Secretary of the zero tolerance."

This is certainly one possible solution leading to the gradual elimination of a persistent pesticide from the environment.

In any event, we think HEW's emphasis on the "practicability" requirement is seriously misplaced, as disclosed by the most cursory examination of the legislative history of the provision. Both House and Senate reports emphasize that the formal requirements for a petition are to be flexibly administered in the interest of safeguarding the public health:

> "It is intended that a rule of reason should dictate the nature and extent of the information which should be submitted with a petition. What is contemplated is data adequate to permit an accurate appraisal of safety to protect the public health. In this respect the data as to a particular chemical will depend upon many variable factors, including its physical and chemical properties, recommended purpose, toxicity, and rate of disappearance. The emphasis to be placed on any such factor will similarly depend on the particular pesticide chemical under consideration and its proposed usage."

In our judgment, the Commissioner of Food and Drugs failed to apply a "rule of reason" in assessing the present petition. Instead of publishing petitioners' proposal, which would begin an administrative process designed to bring forth constructive alternatives for dealing with an admittedly difficult but vitally important problem, the Commissioner chose to stop petitioners at the door. Moreover, he chose to rely on a requirement which cannot be applied literally to the present case. Everyone agrees that there is no way to remove DDT from the environment *immediately*. *The questions to be answered are how great is the present danger and what steps ought to be taken immediately in response to that danger.*

These are basically matters for exploration and judgment which in the last analysis will rest with HEW. But there was no further information or data regarding these matters which HEW could reasonably seek to have petitioners produce. They have already submitted "data adequate to permit an accurate appraisal of safety to protect the public health." What remains to be developed are reasonable approaches to the problem. Petitioners in fact endeavored to suggest one—a zero tolerance with exemptions for residues attributable to DDT applications made before the establishment of the tolerance. Another approach, suggested by the Secretary's Commission on Pesticides and Their Relationship to Environmental Health and quoted in respondents' brief, is to announce immediately a gradual stepwise reduction of permissible residue levels to be effective on a prospective basis. Yet another approach might be to announce a zero tolerance level to be effective at some time in the future.

Moreover, it is clear from the present regulations that the effect of the present level of environmental contamination does not affect all foods similarly, since there are, at present, different levels of DDT tolerances for different commodities. Therefore, it may also be possible to deal differently with different categories of foodstuffs.

None of these alternatives has been considered in specific detail, with opportunity for comment and study by all interested parties. The administrative process, the process which Congress intended to focus on and illuminate these problems, has not been permitted to begin. In our view, the petition does comply with all statutory prerequisites, and this case must, therefore, be remanded to the Secretary of HEW with directions to file petitioners' proposal and to publish it in the Federal Register, as provided in 21 U.S.C. §346a(d)(1).

III

Petitioners here argue that any remand order should not permit the Secretary to consider "whether it is appropriate to continue, for any period of time, using DDT; rather, the Secretary should consider only the solution that should be implemented to afford the consuming public the greatest possible protection from continued exposure to that cancer-producing poison." Petitioners contend that this result is compelled by 21 U.S.C. §348(c)(3)(A), the so-called Delaney amendment, which requires the Secretary to ban any *food additive* which has been found to cause cancer in

experimental animals. Since we have decided that a remand is necessary, we think it appropriate to indicate our
views on this question.

DDT tolerances range from 50 parts per million in or
on peppermint hay and spearmint hay which are not to be
used for feeding livestock down to one part per million on
artichokes, asparagus and other foods, and down to 0.05
part per million in milk.

Several related events which occurred in the late 1950's
form the basis for petitioners' argument that the Delaney
amendment, or at least the principle it embodies, applies to
pesticide chemicals. Just prior to Thanksgiving 1959, HEW
seized substantial proportions of that year's cranberry crop
because the cranberries contained residues of the weed
killer pesticide aminotriazole. In announcing the legal basis
for the Department's action, then Secretary of HEW
Arthur Flemming took the following position:

> "* * * Research has established the fact that the
> weed killer, aminotriazole, causes cancer in the thyroid
> of rats when it is contained in their diet.
>
> "It is the Department's position that because such a
> chemical is unsafe, we cannot issue a regulation setting
> a tolerance for it when it causes cancer in man or
> animal. * * *
>
> "This policy is basic in our food and drug law, and
> it was spelled out in the law itself when Congress re-
> cently passed the Food Additives Amendment. This
> included the following provision:
>
> "[Delaney Amendment set out]
>
> *"In endorsing this language, we told Congress this
> policy was already in force under the pesticide chemi-
> cals law without the above-quoted language."*

Shortly after the cranberry seizure, Secretary Flemming
appeared before a congressional committee to testify in
support of an extension of the Delaney amendment to the
color additives portion of the FDCA. (The original Delaney amendment applied to food additives.) In his testimony, Secretary Flemming emphasized that scientifically
there was no way to determine a "safe" level for a substance known to produce cancer in animals. Relying on

this scientific finding, Flemming again told Congress that HEW would be required to apply the no-carcinogen policy even absent the explicit statutory command:

> "According to the advice of our scientists, the principle of the * * * anticancer (Delaney) proviso of the Food Additives Amendment reflects, basically, the current state of scientific knowledge and we would therefore, except as noted below, feel constrained to apply the same principle even in the absence of this proviso, *and we do in fact apply it in the administration of the Pesticide Chemicals Amendment which does not contain the proviso.*"

While we agree that these events are not without legal significance, we do not think the Delaney anticancer amendment can be held to apply full force to pesticide chemicals. The Delaney clause was added, as we have noted, to the FDCA as part of the Food Additives Amendment of 1958 and reads, in pertinent part, as follows:

> "* * * [N]o additive shall be deemed to be safe if it is found to induce cancer when ingested by man or animal, or if it is found, after tests which are appropriate for the evaluation of the safety of *food additives,* to induce cancer in man or animal * * *."

Two years later, in 1960, Congress added a similar prohibition on color additives which were found to induce cancer in test animals. But in both instances the statute explicitly excludes pesticide chemicals from the definition of the terms "food additive" and "color additive." This does not, however, end the matter. Rather, it means that the statutory standards to be applied are not the specific commands of the anticancer amendments, but the general command contained in Section 408 of the FDCA, 21 U.S.C. §346a.

Section 408 of the FDCA authorizes the Secretary of HEW to establish tolerances for pesticide residues on or in raw agricultural commodities "to the extent necessary to protect the public health." The section also authorizes the setting of a zero tolerance (no residue) level "if the scientific data before the Secretary does not justify the establishment of a greater tolerance." We need not pause to plumb the obvious ambiguities in this language since both Senate and House Committee Reports make the intended meaning of this section indisputably clear:

> "Before any pesticide-chemical residue may remain in or on a raw agricultural commodity, scientific data must be presented to show that the pesticide-chemical residue is safe from the standpoint of the food consumer. The burden is on the person proposing the tolerance or exemption to establish the safety of such pesticide-chemical residue."

In this context, we think the events of the late 1950's indicate administrative action entirely consistent with, if not required by, Congress' expressed intent. At that time, Secretary Flemming indicated that there was no scientific basis for determining a "safe" residue level for a chemical known to produce cancer in experimental animals. Under such conditions, it would obviously be impossible to meet the congressionally imposed burden of establishing the safety of a residue of such a pesticide. On remand, therefore, the Secretary must consider the scientific evidence presented and determine whether continued tolerances for DDT are consistent with the intent of Congress. If the evidence demonstrates that DDT is a carcinogen and the Secretary proposes to continue in effect any DDT tolerances on raw agricultural commodities, he would, of course, be required to explain the basis on which he determined such tolerances to be "safe."

The petition for review is granted, the order of the Secretary of HEW is reversed, and the case is remanded with instructions to publish petitioners' proposal in the Federal Register and commence the administrative process contemplated by the provisions of the Food, Drug and Cosmetic Act.

SO ORDERED.

4.11 Case Illustrating the Eradication of Municipal Water Pollution—ISC Cases

Connecticut, New York, and New Jersey had joined together and formed a compact creating an Interstate Sanitation Commission with powers to regulate the water within an approximate fifty-mile radius of the city of New York, as shown in the exhibit attached to the complaint against the village of Port Chester. Despite the fact that the judge found no concession by the town of Brookhaven at all as to their pollution, he did grant the relief requested by the plaintiff, that of injunctive relief unless and until defendants complied with the standards of treatment.

In the case of the Interstate Sanitation Commission against the Port Jefferson Sewer District, the issues were reduced by stipulation of the parties to four:

1. Pollution
2. Acknowledgment of the pollution by defendant
3. Whether appeals had been taken from the administrative orders of the Interstate Commission
4. Whether the defendants failed to abate pollution

That case was tried under Article 12-B of the Public Health Law of the State of New York (now §1299, Public Health Law). After a full trial, the judge rendered an opinion finding the defendants permitted inadequately treated sewerage and other polluting matters to flow into the waters embraced within the Interstate Sanitation Commission district. In this particular case, the Long Island Sound was being adversely affected.

A copy of the judgment entered under calendar number 4839 of the county of Suffolk bearing index number 77612 for the year 1962 follows.

(a) Interstate Sanitation Commission v. Town of Brookhaven and Port Jefferson Sewer District

This was the trial of an action brought by plaintiff, the Interstate Sanitation Commission, for an injunction restraining the defendants from continuing the pollution of waters known as Port Jefferson Harbor and embraced within the waters of the Interstate Sanitation District, by permitting the discharge of sewage and other polluting matters emanating from the Port Jefferson Sewer District into those waters in violation of the Tri-State Compact of the states of New York, New Jersey, and Connecticut, directing abatement of the pollution, and directing compliance by the defendants with an order issued by plaintiff on May 12, 1954, pursuant to the authoritative provisions of Article 12-B of the Public Health Law of the state of New York.

By stipulation read into the record by the attorneys for the respective parties at the inception of the trial, the issues raised by the complaint and answer were confined to (1) whether the defendants permitted untreated sewage and other polluting matters to flow into waters embraced within the Interstate Sanitation District in violation of the Tri-State Compact and the pertinent provisions of the Public Health Law of the State of New York; (2) whether the defendants, at the hearing conducted before the Interstate Sanitation Commission on March 5, 1954, acknowledged that untreated sewage and other polluting matters emanating from the Port Jefferson Sewer District were permitted to flow into waters of the Interstate Sanitation District in violation of the Tri-State Compact and the Public Health Law of the State of New York; (3) whether an appeal was taken by defendants from the order of the Interstate Sanitation Commission issued May 12, 1954; and (4) whether the defendants failed to abate the pollution and to make provision for the proper treatment of sewage by the construction of adequate facilities therefor as directed by the order of May 12, 1954.

Upon a preponderance of the credible evidence received at the trial the court resolved the issues by finding (1) that the defendants permitted inadequately treated sewage and other polluting matters emanating from the Port Jefferson Sewer District to flow into waters embraced within the Interstate Sanitation District in violation of the Tri-State Compact and the Public Health Law of the State of New York; (2) that there was no acknowledgment by defendants at the hearing conducted before the Interstate Sanitation Commission on March 5, 1954, that inadequately treated sewage and other polluting matters emanating from the Port Jefferson Sewer District were permitted to flow into waters embraced in the Interstate Sanitation District; (3) that no appeal was taken by defendants from the order of the Interstate Sanitation Commission issued May 12, 1954; and (4) that the defendants have failed to abate the pollution of waters embraced within the Interstate Sanitation District and to make provision for the proper treatment of sewage and other polluting matters emanating from the Port Jefferson Sewer District by the construction of adequate facilities therefor, as directed by the order of the Interstate Sanitation Commission issued May 12, 1954.

Upon these findings the court granted judgment in favor of the plaintiffs and against the defendants for the relief demanded in the complaint, and directs that the defendants abate the pollution and obey the directions of the order of the Interstate Sanitation Commission issued May 12, 1954, within sixty days after the date of this decision.

Submit judgment.

(b) Interstate Sanitation Commission v. Village of Port Chester

Greenwich, Connecticut, built a multimillion dollar water pollution control facility, and when the tide was right it worked well. The village of Port Chester used the Long Island Sound for its outfall from the Byram River. Untreated or inadequately treated sewage moved by the tidal flow swept into the Greenwich, Connecticut, area. Townships sharing a common body of water are more or less at the mercy of that municipality which lags behind in water pollution control because of the tidal movement. Complaints to the Interstate Sanitation Commission by the residents of Greenwich, Connecticut, resulted in administrative hearings. On May 3, 1961 an order was issued by the Commission setting forth the time schedule on which the village of Port Chester was to comply with pollution abatement requirements. A complaint was served by the Interstate Sanitation Commission, party plaintiff, against the village of Port Chester, and a full trial was heard before the Hon. Justice Joseph Gagliardi in which some 134 pages of testimony were taken. The author (N.L.) was trial counsel to the Commission.

Judge Joseph Gagliardi was familiar with the waters in this area and took several trips to the areas complained of, was familiar with the swimming, fishing, and sanitary conditions in the area, and, after hearing witnesses for both sides as well as the State and County Health Departments, handed down the following excellent and farseeing decision. Excerpts from the testimony of that trial are included in §7.2.

SUPREME COURT OF THE STATE OF NEW YORK
COUNTY OF WESTCHESTER

INTERSTATE SANITATION
COMMISSION,

Index No.
3598-1962

Plaintiff

v.

THE VILLAGE OF
PORT CHESTER,

Defendant

JUDGE JOSEPH GAGLIARDI:

This is an action brought pursuant to §1299-c of the Public Health Law by the Interstate Sanitation Commission. It is brought to compel defendant village of Port Chester to abate pollution of the waters of the Interstate Sanitation District, and to compel the village to construct such sewage treatment works as are necessary. It concerns pollution of the Byram River which flows through the defendant village into Long Island Sound.

By authority of the Compact between the states of New York, New Jersey, and Connecticut (see, Public Health Law, Art. 12-B), that portion of Long Island Sound has been denominated class A waters. As such they are to be primarily suitable for recreational purposes, shellfish culture, or the development of fish life, *ibid.*, Art. VI [1] [2]. This general purpose has been translated into specific prohibitions against discharge of sewage into such waters which have not been treated according to certain standards. Some of the standards are (*a*) removal of at least sixty percent of suspended solids; (*b*) reduction of intestinal bacilli to less than one per cubic centimeter in not more than fifty percent of samples; and (*c*) reduction of oxygen demand of sewage effluent to below fifty percent of saturation, *ibid.*, Art. VII.

On May 13, 1961, after a hearing, the Interstate Sanitation Commission ordered the village of Port Chester to construct necessary pollution control works. The primary issue in this action is whether the sewage treatment plant now in operation by the village complies with the requirement of removal of sixty percent of suspended solids. An additional issue is whether defendant village is failing to prevent discharge of prohibited industrial waste into the Byram River.

With respect to the latter issue, there is ample proof of discharge from a number of industrial plants of oil, grease, pickling liquors, carbon, and laundry waste in violation of the order of the Commission, as well as in violation of the village ordinance (ordinance regulating the use of Public Sewer Connections, etc., §IV).

With respect to the former issue, there is a factual dispute as to the amount of removal of suspended solids. Many samplings have been taken of the influent and effluent of the sewage treatment plant. There are some indications that at certain times the plant removes as high as sixty-nine percent of suspended solids. The defendant village adduced testimony indicating removal of fifty percent. That in itself falls short of the sixty percent requirement. Moreover, series of tests have established a removal rate of fifty-two percent, or perhaps only of 40.6 percent. The court finds that the present sewage treatment facilities do not comply with the requirements of the statute.

Therefore, judgment is awarded to the plaintiff. The complaint in this action was served in 1962. The testimony establishes that *these waters are so polluted as to pose a serious danger to the health of any person or animal life being in them.* Hence, the court directs that defendant (*a*)

LEGEND

FINE SCREENS OR EQUIVALENT
PRIMARY TREATMENT
INTERMEDIATE TREATMENT
COMPLETE TREATMENT
SHADED SEGMENT DENOTES TYPE
OF PLANT UNDER CONSTRUCTION
CLASS "A" WATERS
CLASS "B" WATERS

CONNECTICUT

NEW HAVEN

FAIRFIELD

LONG ISLAND SOUND

SUFFOLK

CONNECTICUT
NEW YORK

PUTNAM

ROCKLAND

NEW YORK/NEW JERSEY (BORDER)

SEWAGE TREATMENT PLANTS
IN THE
INTERSTATE SANITATION DISTRICT
NEW YORK NEW JERSEY CONNECTICUT

eliminate the discharge of industrial wastes within four months of service of the judgment herein; and (b) complete and staff all necessary plants and equipment in order to comply with all of the waste removal requirements of the Interstate Sanitation Commission within twenty-four months of service of the judgment herein.

4.12 Case Illustrating Balancing the Equities in Cement Plant Pollution—Boomer Case

Oscar Boomer enjoyed living in the town of Coeymans, New York, with his wife, Jane, and family, and they lived there eighteen years in peace and comfort. Then the At- lantic Cement Company moved in next door and every- thing hit the fan. Blasting at the rock quarry started with vibrations and noise. The cement company sent great volumes of dust and lime dust, coal dust, and other chemi- cal products into the air which coated the house and land, his equipment, and his wife, Jane. This dust adhered to the things it landed on and was difficult to wash off. Oscar Boomer decided to sue and found a good lawyer in David Duncan of Albany, New York. The trial lasted almost a month. All the issues were hotly contested and the decision on appeal was split. $185,000 was awarded for permanent damage for depreciation of property values and other damages, but no permanent injunction was granted. The majority opinion allowed the defendant to continue pol- luting the air and impair the peaceful quiet enjoyment of the property of plaintiffs upon payment of a fee, a unique if somewhat questionable holding. Nor did the majority of the court grant injunctive relief postponing the effective date eighteen months, thus allowing the de- fendant to effectively stop the harmful effects of their smokestack emissions. The court felt that "there would be no assurance that any significant taking or improve- ment would occur in the next eighteen months." The pres- sure on defendant, the possibility of their cement plant closing down would be the best incentive for them to find a method of curing the problem. Allowing the atmosphere to continue the impossible burden of absorb- ing tons of additional polluting matter daily upon payment of damages by the defendant seems to this writer to be a decision out of 1812. The court in Albany is not a great distance from this plant, and it takes no great imagination for the mind's eye to conceive of a cartoon showing a judge coughing, teary-eyed, handing down this decision to his sneezing, wheezing clerk. The court's uncertainty with their own decision is evident when the majority state that their decision "does not foreclose public health or other public agencies from seeking proper relief in a proper court."

(a) Oscar H. Boomer v. Atlantic Cement Company— Complaint

SUPREME COURT OF THE STATE OF NEW YORK COUNTY OF ALBANY

OSCAR H. BOOMER and
JANE C. BOOMER,

Plaintiffs

v.

THE ATLANTIC CEMENT
COMPANY, INC.,

Defendant

COMPLAINT
Index #4990/66

Plaintiffs, complaining of the defendant and for a first cause of action herein, allege:

FIRST: That the plaintiffs at all times hereinafter mentioned were and still are owners and occupants of certain lands in the town of Coeymans, etc.

SECOND: That said premises consisted of two parcels of real property with 480-foot frontage on New York State Route 9W . . . with certain buildings.

THIRD: That the said premises are located a very short distance northwesterly of the manufacturing plant of the defendant cement company.

FOURTH: That the plaintiffs have occupied the premises for upwards of eighteen years, etc.

FIFTH: That the above-named defendant is a corporation . . .

SIXTH: That for approximately two and a half years past, the above-named defendant . . . has been blasting the rock from its quarry, which quarry is located on a ridge approximately half mile west of the property of the plaintiffs herein.

SEVENTH: That the purpose of the quarry and its operation is to produce limestone for use by the above-named defendant in manufacturing cement.

EIGHTH: That the above-named defendant . . . has performed this operation in a negligent and careless, reckless, and unlawful manner as to damage the buildings of the plaintiffs to an extent to make necessary expensive repairs thereto.

NINTH: That the blast set off by the defendant had been of such terrific noise and force as to cause heavy vibrations, through the air and through the ground, to strike plaintiffs' buildings and thereby cause severe movement and shaking of said buildings and cause objects within the buildings to move about, and caused plaintiffs and their business invitees to be severely shaken, badly frightened, and nervously shocked thereby.

• • •

FIFTEENTH: That the defendant produces in great volume certain dust containing lime dust, coal dust, and other chemical products.

SIXTEENTH: That the above-mentioned dust is emitted by the said defendant corporation's quarry and permitted to be carried by the winds and is brought thereby onto the plaintiffs and carried upon the plaintiffs' grounds and buildings, roadways, doorways, windows, and into their buildings.

EIGHTEENTH: That the said dust upon adhering to the buildings, doors, windows, and other parts of said premises is for all practical purposes impossible of removal.

• • •

TWENTY-SECOND: That because of the herein-above-mentioned facts, defendant is maintaining a public nuisance . . .

TWENTY-THIRD: That the property of the plaintiffs

has become badly deteriorated and the plaintiffs have no adequate remedy at law.

WHEREFORE, plaintiffs pray for a judgment of this court.

(b) Dissenting Opinion of Judge Jasen
26 N.Y. 2d 219, 309 N.Y. Supp. 2d 312 (1970)

I agree with the majority that a reversal is required here, but I do not subscribe to the newly enunciated doctrine of assessment of permanent damages, in lieu of an injunction, where substantial property rights have been impaired by the creation of a nuisance.

It has long been the rule in this state, as the majority acknowledges, that a nuisance which results in substantial continuing damage to neighbors must be enjoined (*Whalen v. Union Bag and Paper Company*, 208 N.Y. 1; *Campbell v. Seaman*, 63 N.Y. 568; see also *Kennedy v. Moog*, 21 N.Y.2d 966). To now change the rule to permit the cement company to continuing polluting the air indefinitely upon the payment of permanent damages is, in my opinion, compounding the magnitude of a very serious problem in our state and nation today.

In recognition of this program, the legislature of this state has enacted the Air Pollution Control Act (Public Health Law, §§1264–1299-m) declaring that it is the state policy to require the use of all available and reasonable methods to prevent and control air pollution (Public Health Law, §1265[1]).

The harmful nature and widespread occurrence of air pollution have been extensively documented. Congressional hearings have revealed that air pollution causes substantial property damage, as well as being a contributing factor to a rising incidence of lung cancer, emphysema, bronchitis, and asthma.[2]

The specific problem faced here is known as particulate contamination because of the fine dust particles emanating from defendant's cement plant. The particular type of nuisance is not new, having appeared in many cases for at least the past sixty years [see *Hulbert v. Calif. Portland Cement Company*, 161 Cal. 239 (1911)]. It is interesting to note that cement production has recently been identified as a significant source of particulate contamination in the Hudson Valley.[3] This type of pollution, wherein very small particles escape and stay in the atmosphere, has been denominated as the type of air pollution which produces the greatest hazard to human health.[4] We have thus a nuisance which not only is damaging to the plaintiffs[5] but also is decidedly harmful to the general public.

I see grave dangers in overruling our long-established rule of granting an injunction where a nuisance results in substantial continuing damage. In permitting the injunction to become inoperative upon the payment of permanent damages, the majority is, in effect, licensing a continuing wrong. It is the same as saying to the cement company, you may continue to do harm to your neighbors so long as you pay a fee for it. Furthermore, once such permanent damages are assessed and paid, the incentive to alleviate the wrong would be eliminated, thereby continuing air pollution of an area without abatement.

It is true that some courts have sanctioned the remedy here proposed by the majority in a number of cases,[6] but none of the authorities relied upon by the majority are analogous to the situation before us. In those cases, the courts, in denying an injunction and awarding money damages, grounded their decision on a showing that the use to which the property was intended to be put was primarily for the public benefit. Here, on the other hand, it is clearly established that the cement company is creating a continuing air pollution nuisance primarily for its own private interest with no public benefit.

This kind of inverse condemnation (*Ferguson v. Village of Hamburg,* 272 N.Y. 234) may not be invoked by a private person or corporation for private gain or advantage. Inverse condemnation should only be permitted when the public is primarily served in the taking or impairment of property (*Matter of New York City Housing Authority v. Muller,* 270 N.Y. 333, 343; *The Pocantico Water Works Company v. Bird,* 130 N.Y. 249, 258). The promotion of the interests of the polluting cement company has, in my opinion, no public use or benefit.

Nor is it constitutionally permissible to impose servitude

on land, without consent of the owner, by payment of permanent damages where the continuing impairment of the land is for a private use (see *Fifth Ave. Coach Lines v. City of New York,* 11 N.Y.2d 342, 347; *Walker v. Hutchison City,* 352 U.S. 112). This is made clear by the State Constitution, Article I §7(*a*), which provides that "[p]rivate property shall not be taken for *public use* without just compensation" (emphasis added). It is, of course, significant that the section makes no mention of taking for a *private* use.

In sum, then, by constitutional mandate as well as by judicial pronouncement, the permanent impairment of private property for private purposes is not authorized in the absence of clearly demonstrated public benefit and use.

I would enjoin the defendant cement company from continuing the discharge of dust particles upon its neighbors' properties unless, within eighteen months, the cement company abated this nuisance.[7]

It is not my intention to cause the removal of the cement plant from the Albany area, but to recognize the urgency of the problem stemming from this stationary source of air pollution, and to allow the company a specified period of time to develop a means to alleviate this nuisance.

I am aware that the trial court found that the most modern dust control devices available have been installed in defendant's plant, but, I submit, this does not mean that *better* and more effective dust control devices could not be developed within the time allowed to abate the pollution.

Moreover, I believe it is incumbent upon the defendant to develop such devices, since the cement company, at the time the plant commenced production (1962), was well aware of the plaintiffs' presence in the area as well as of the probable consequences of its contemplated operation. Yet, they still chose to build and operate the plant at this site.

In a day when there is a growing concern for clean air, highly developed industry should not expect acquiescence by the courts, but should, instead, plan its operations to eliminate contamination of our air and damage to its neighbors.

Accordingly, the orders of the Appellate Division, insofar as they denied the injunction, should be reversed, and the actions remitted to Special Term to grant an injunction to take effect eighteen months hence, unless the nuisance is abated by improved techniques prior to said date.

● ● ●

The majority opinion balanced the "economic equities," rather than the "environmental equities." This decision should be challenged and reversed.

[1] See also Air Quality Act of 1967, 81 Stat. 485 (1967).

[2] See U.S. Cong., Senate Comm. on Public Works, Special Subcomm. on Air and Water Pollution, *Air Pollution 1966*, 89th Cong. 2d Sess., 1966, at 22–24; U.S. Congr., Senate Comm. on Public Works, Special Subcomm. on Air and Water Pollution, *Air Pollution 1968*, 90th Congr., 2d Sess., 1968, at 850, 1084.

[3] New York State Bureau of Air Pollution Control Services, *Air Pollution Capital District*. 1968, at 8.

[4] T. Ludwig, "Air Pollution Control Technology: Research and Development on New and Improved Systems," 33 *Law and Contemporary Problems*, 217, 219 (1968).

[5] There are seven plaintiffs here who have been substantially damaged by the maintenance of this nuisance. The trial court found their total permanent damages to equal $185,000.

[6] See *United States v. Causby* (328 U.S. 256); *Kentucky-Ohio Gas Company, v. Bowling* (95 S.W.2d 1, 5); *Northern Indiana Public Service Company v. Vesey* (200 N.E. 620); *City of Amarillo v. Ware* (120 Tex. 456, 40 S.W.2d 57, 61); *Pappenheim v. Metropolitan Elevated Railroad Company* (128 N.Y. 436); *Ferguson v. Village of Hamburg* (272 N.Y. 234).

[7] The issuance of an injunction to become effective in the future is not an entirely new concept. For instance, in *Schwarzenbach v. Oneonta Light and Power Company* (207 N.Y. 671), an injunction against the maintenance of a dam spilling water on plaintiff's property was issued to become effective one year hence.

CHAPTER 5

SUITS AGAINST INDUSTRY: AIR AND WATER POLLUTION

SUITS AGAINST INDUSTRY: AIR AND WATER POLLUTION

Water doesn't taste as good as it used to. Air doesn't "breathe" as good as it used to. Americans have been spoiled with what we thought was an unlimited resource of air and water, and we have continued to throw things away, into rivers, into the air, into the oceans, and a midwest professor recently said "There is no more *away*." We have failed to balance the environmental equities, and we are in trouble. Congressmen are drafting "Environmental and Conservation Bills of Rights." One recently stated that "the right of the people to clean air, pure water, freedom from excessive and unnecessary noise, and the natural scenic, historic and esthetic qualities of their environment shall not be abridged." What a jolt it is that laws are required to protect the air we breathe and the water we drink and, yet, some scientists say all our efforts may be too late.

Chapter 5 describes various court fights to halt the polluters. The plaintiffs in these actions range from the United States Government with all of its power and prestige to Mrs. Ruth Heck of Berks County, Pennsylvania. The United States Government sued the Florida Power & Light Co., and so far has lost. Mrs. Ruth Heck sued the big Beryllium Corp., and with Edward Wolf as attorney, she won. The Florida Power & Light Co. has so heated the waters around Turkey Point that only horseshoe crabs are seen on the bottom. The thermal death point for fish is 93°, and the water near the power plant has been measured at 100°.

The actions of a law school professor with his science department backing him up, and the enthusiastic applause of his law students, ended with a landmark decision from the Director of Puget Sound Air Pollution Control Agency in an administrative hearing which had the earmarks of David and Goliath, and with the same salutary result. The Department of Health of the State of New Jersey has brought an action which resulted in airlines updating their smoke control equipment and converting their jets to the most efficient smoke canisters, and that expert, swift and efficient action is described in §5.6.

The Environmental Defense Fund has attacked the leading cause of air pollution in a brief directed against lead pollution from automobile exhaust. We have therefore covered in this chapter the major sources of air and water pollution as well as methods of attack. The legal remedies used by the United States Government, the State of New Jersey, the City of El Paso, the United Automobile Workers and individual citizens, a law professor, a citizens' association, a group of attorneys, and an individual lawyer with the intention that these various methods of approach and attack will furnish some vehicle for the particular problem faced by the reader.

Substantive rights of all individuals seeking protection of the environment do not have to be created to be protected by American courts. Such rights to life, property and pursuit of happiness already exist. They are inherent and inalienable. They are protected from infringement and impairment by the federal government, state government and their political subdivisions, whether through executive, legislative or judicial action, the due process clause of the Fifth Amendment, the Ninth Amendment, or the due process, privileges and immunities, and equal protection clauses of the Fourteenth Amendment.

5.1 Government Puts Heat on Thermal Polluters

In March 1970 the United States of America (as party plaintiff) brought an action against the Florida Power and Light Company in Federal Court, Southern District of

Florida. Interior Department officials, who brought the suit through the Justice Department to block thermal pollution of Biscayne Bay by the Florida Light and Power Company, said it was the first time that a federal court had taken jurisdiction in such a case. Deputy Assistant Attorney General Walter Kichel, jr., asked the court to direct the defendant to submit plans within forty-five days demonstrating how pollution would be eliminated in its plant.

Judge C. Clyde Atkins based his precedent-setting decision to take jurisdiction in this thermal pollution case on recent Supreme Court interpretation of the Rivers and Harbors Act of 1899 [see §3.1(*l*)]. Government witnesses testified that nearly all living organisms in Biscayne Bay would be killed by the nuclear plant because the rate of flow through the installation would consume the entire volume of the bay every two or three weeks. In addition, the government claims that Florida Power and Light has reasonable alternative means of cooling the power plant. The complaint itself which follows, briefly sets forth the purpose of the Biscayne National Monument, and explains how the drawing of 550,000 gallons per minute through the power company's generating equipment in an attempt to cool the machinery would have a killing effect on plant and animal growth. It further states that 600 acres of Biscayne Bay area have already been heated up to the point where they are now barren of natural bay life.

The defendant's plan to build a canal involving the Card Sound, thus sending the heated effluent out into the ocean, would cause additional problems detrimental to the Biscayne National Monument, and would result in movement toward the monument of municipally and industrially polluted waters from northern Biscayne Bay. Affidavits from experts of national standing were used in this case, and thereafter their testimony was taken in court. Their areas of expertise are interesting: (1) Lee Purkerson, schooled in "atmospheric sciences" (a marine biologist); (2) John R. Thoman, with a degree in sanitary engineering, diplomate, American Academy of Environmental Engineers; (3) Clarence M. Tarzwell, an aquatic biologist,

Director of the National Marine Water Quality Laboratory, West Kingston, Rhode Island. This critically important case has been making headlines in the *Miami Herald* over the past several months and will continue to do so. Because of the landmark nature of the matter, extensive segments of the affidavits in support of, and the motion for preliminary injunction, as well as the memorandum, follow.

(a) Complaint in United States of America v. Florida Power and Light Company

IN THE UNITED STATES DISTRICT COURT FOR THE SOUTHERN DISTRICT OF FLORIDA

UNITED STATES OF
AMERICA,

Plaintiff

Civil Action

v.

FLORIDA POWER AND LIGHT
COMPANY,

Defendant

The United States of America, by its undersigned attorneys, by authority of the attorney general, and at the request of the secretary of the interior, alleges that:

I

This is a civil action to conserve the scenery, the natural and historic objects, and the wildlife, including marine life, within the area designated by Congress for the Biscayne National Monument, and to provide for the enjoyment of the same in such manner and by such means as will leave them unimpaired for the enjoyment of future generations. Jurisdiction over this action exists under 28 U.S.C. 1345.

II

On October 18, 1968, Congress enacted Public Law 90-606, 16 U.S.C. 450qq, authorizing the secretary of the interior to establish in the state of Florida, in Biscayne Bay, a navigable water of the United States, the Biscayne National Monument, "in order to preserve and protect for the education, inspiration, recreation, and enjoyment of present and future generations a rare combination of terrestrial, marine, and amphibious life in a tropical setting of great natural beauty . . ." A map required to be prepared by Section 1 of the Act of October 18, 1968, showing the boundaries of the Biscayne National Monument, is attached herewith, and marked as Exhibit 1.

●　　●　　●

VI

Florida Power and Light Company presently operates two fossil-fueled power plants located at Turkey Point, Dade County, Florida, adjacent to the Biscayne National Monument in Biscayne Bay. To operate these plants, the company draws saline water from Biscayne Bay at a rate in the neighborhood of 550,000 gallons per minute (i.e. 2.400 acre feet per day) for condensing and cooling purposes. As a result of passing through the heat exchangers, portions of the water drawn from the bay are exposed to the intense steam temperature of the heat exchangers and the total water drawn leaves the plant at 10 to 20° above ambient, killing micro and other small organisms in the water. The heated water, laden with dead organisms, is discharged through a complex of canals back into the Bay. At the point of discharge, this effluent has raised the surrounding Bay waters, including the waters within the Biscayne National Monument, to temperatures substantially higher than their natural condition.

VII

Defendant's fossil-fuel plants were put into full operation during the summer of 1967. The discharges since then of heated water laden with dead organisms discolor the waters of, and have had a visible destructive effect on marine ecology within, the Biscayne National Monument. A barren area of considerable magnitude surrounding the discharge point has resulted. In 1968 the area of damage was 300 acres, and during 1969, increased to more than 600 acres.

VIII

Defendant Florida Power and Light Company does not have any authorization from the Corps of Engineers, pursuant to the Rivers and Harbors Act of 1899, 33 U.S.C. 407, to discharge the heated waters, laden with dead organisms, into Biscayne Bay or any portion thereof, or into any other of the navigable waters of the United States.

IX

Further, to increase its production of electricity, defendant Florida Power and Light Company is in the process of constructing two nuclear reactors at Turkey Point, Dade County, Florida. The amount of water to be drawn from Biscayne Bay to cool these units, after they are completed and in operation, will increase to a total withdrawal of as much as 4,500,000 gallons per minute (i.e., approximately 20,000 acre feet per day). At this rate, water equivalent in volume to all of Biscayne Bay would pass through the plant and its works in less than a month.

X

Defendant Florida Power and Light Company is in the process of constructing a canal, 5½ miles long, to convey the effluent from the nuclear reactors referred to in Paragraph VIII above into Card Sound, a navigable water of the United States constituting a southerly extension of Biscayne Bay.

XI

The high water velocities resulting from the intake of the large quantities of water which will be withdrawn from Biscayne Bay for operation of the nuclear reactor will scour and disturb an extensive area of bay bottom. The removal of microlife from Biscayne Bay, which will occur with the passage of water to the plant, will destroy the existing ecological cycle. Not only will this loss occur throughout Biscayne Bay, including the area within the Biscayne National Monument, but as the water passes through the plant plankton and other small sea life will be cooked to death and, after the completion of the canal referred to in Paragraph IX above, will be discharged into Card Sound as organic refuse, causing therein massive enrichment and eutrophication. Since the waters of Card Sound and Biscayne Bay are interrelated, some of the waste and heated effluent will, in addition to causing severe damage in Card Sound, return to Biscayne Bay and to the Biscayne National Monument and continue the detrimental effect in that area. The flow of water from Card Sound to Biscayne Bay will be accelerated by the heavy withdrawals from Biscayne Bay to the plant. The withdrawals can also be expected to result in the movement toward the Monument of municipally and industrially polluted waters from northern Biscayne Bay and conceivably induce other damage to the water and marine resources of the Monument.

FIRST COUNT

XII

The operations of the defendant . . . destroy the sea life and existing ecology within the Biscayne National Monument, alter and degrade the scenery of the Biscayne National Monument, and impair, if not utterly defeat, the possibility of the Monument being a source of enjoyment for future generations.

SECOND COUNT

XIII

The operations of the defendant . . . are harmful to, and constitute a nuisance with respect to, the property now owned and hereafter to be acquired by the United States within the Biscayne National Monument.

THIRD COUNT

XIV

The discharge and the continuation thereof by the defendant of heated water, saturated with dead organisms, into the waters of Biscayne Bay, as described in Paragraphs VI and VIII above, is in violation of the Rivers and Harbors Act of 1899, 33 U.S.C. 407.

•   •   •

WHEREFORE, the United States prays:

(1) That defendant be permanently enjoined against so operating its presently existing fossil-fuel power plants and its nuclear reactors now under construction as to increase the temperature or otherwise adversely affect the quality of the waters of Biscayne Bay or to adversely affect marine life of the Biscayne National Monument and the lands therein;

(2) That a preliminary injunction issue enjoining the defendant pending the trial of this case:

    (a) Immediately to cease all activities in the operation of its existing fossil-fuel plants which result in the discharge into Biscayne Bay of waters of such temperature or quality as to adversely affect the marine life of the Biscayne National Monument and the lands therein to the extent such can be done consistently with the public interest in the continued operation of such plants;

    (b) To submit to this court, within 45 days, a plan for the operation of its existing fossil-fuel plants at Turkey Point, Florida, in such a way as to eliminate the destruction of the plankton and other marine life in the waters of Biscayne Bay and the discharge into the Bay of water of a temperature higher than the temperature of those waters under natural conditions, together with a schedule of the time within which such plan can be put into operation.

•   •   •

(b) Affidavit of L. Lee Purkerson, Marine Biologist

L. Lee Purkerson, being first duly sworn, deposes and says:

I have acquired a B.S. degree in Bacteriology and an M.S. degree in Microbiology from Oregon State University. In addition, I have attended the University of Miami, School for Marine and Atmospheric Sciences, for advanced training in Marine Biology. . . .

An underwater search of an area 500 yards offshore from the mouth of Grand Canal showed that few living plants remained and that none of the usual invertebrate animals populating "grass bed" environments remained. A zone of nearly complete destruction of the plant and animal life extended from the mouth of Grand Canal into the bay for 500 to 700 yards, affecting an overall area of about 100 acres. Beyond the limits of the area grossly affected by the heated effluents, extending to between 700 and 1000 offshore from Grand Canal, there was a transition zone characterized by varying degrees of damage.

During July and August 1968 near the mouth of Grand Canal, I noted a barren, lifeless zone of denuded sediments extending several hundred yards into the bay. Closer inspection revealed that the denuded sediments were covered with what appeared to be irregular mats of green or blue-green microalgae. There were, however none of the rooted plants or attached benthic algae that dominate the subtidal aquatic vegetation common to similar areas of the bay where sediments or sufficient depth exist. The area of barren sediment extended from 200 to 300 yards into the bay in the shape of a lopsided fan, covering an area estimated at 8 to 10 acres.

By late November 1968, an extension of the desolate area and marked erosion of exposed, unconsolidated bay sediments had occurred.

I commenced biological studies on May 1, 1969. A transect was established extending from the mouth of Grand Canal, E-NE (approximately 75° magnetic) into Biscayne Bay, a distance of 1500 yards. . . .

Ten acres near the mouth of Grand Canal remain devoid of the characteristic near-shore benthic communities common to South Biscayne Bay. Aerial photographs I had taken during mid-June 1969 clearly show the stark, barren sediments, pockets of mangrove peat and *Thalassia* rhizomes, the calcareous, sands washed from Grand Canal, and patches of *Diplanthera* at the fringes of the bald area. These observations were verified by underwater examination of the area. Underwater exploration also revealed a rock rubble habitat at the mouth of the canal where stone crabs and blue crabs had taken up residence.

By June 19, 1969, other species were disappearing, particularly at the inshore stations. The *Thalassia* bed at 600 yards had begun to lose its green color and was being coated by a brown gelatinous material. Some of the macroalgae had died at 800 yards; fifty to seventy percent of the corals were dead; the *Thalassia* was coated and epiphytized. At 100 yards, an increasingly large percentage of the *Thalassia* blades were losing color and vigor.

On June 27, I personally searched the bay bottom along the transect and found numerous dead pistol shrimp, blue crabs, spider crabs, dead algae, stone crabs, and molluscs. Dead animals were particularly numerous shoreward from the 1000-yard marker. On June 28, the bay bottom from 1500 yards along the transect to the mouth of Grand Canal was thoroughly searched by me. The bay bottom was littered with dead plants and animals, including sponges, spider crabs, blue crabs, corals, pistol shrimp, clams, snails, mussel, and several varieties of fish, in addition to the wilted and browned green algae.

I conducted a thorough underwater examination during July 1969 and found severe damage to benthic plant and animal populations, including corals, sponges, and sessile green plants.

The June 25 kill affected an area of Biscayne Bay totaling at least 570 acres. Observations conducted during mid- and late-July revealed that additional damage had occurred south from the mouth of Grand Canal which encompassed an additional 100 or more acres. Thus, the total estimated area of damage in Biscayne Bay, occurring during the summer months of 1969, based solely on the lethal effects of overheating, amounted to about 670 acres of bay bottom.

Excessive temperatures recorded on June 25—and for several days thereafter—killed all of the crabs that had taken residence within the rock pile at the mouth of Grand Canal. The hardier plants occupying the fringe zone outside the denuded sediments off the mouth of Grand Canal were again eliminated.

At sampling sites located 1500 yards north and 1500 yards south from the mouth of Grand Canal and 1000 yards from shore, the skeletal remains of killed invertebrates were evidence of earlier damage. In some instances, however, there was partial regrowth of new living sponge tissue upon the skeletal remains. Some genera of sessile green macroalgae had initiated new growth during late August and early September, whereas others were sparse, rare, or totally absent.

There was progressively less evidence of damage at stations 1500 yards east from the mouth of Grand Canal and at stations north and south from that point. Only the green macroalgae, the most sensitive sponges, the corals, and certain common molluscs were among those constituting the most dependable indicators of thermal stress and damage. Stations outside the area of thermal stress were inhabited by spiny lobsters, a large variety of swimming crabs, stone crabs, spider crabs, pistol shrimp, brittle stars, tiny starfish, a host of molluscs, sea anemonae, gorgonids, and all the other life forms comprising the normal flora and fauna of an undisturbed habitat common to Lower Biscayne Bay.

(c) Affidavit of George B. Hartzog, jr., Director of National Park Service

George B. Hartzog, jr., being first duly sworn, deposes and says:

I am the Director of the National Park Service of the Department of the Interior, an agency of the United States government, duly appointed to this office on January 6, 1964.

In my opinion, there is no other area in this country

exhibiting the unique characteristics of this natural monument. The fauna of this monument area include the rare American crocodile, several equally rare species of sea turtle, shrimp, sponge, spring lobster, and approximately 32 varieties of starfish, the sea horse and sea cucumber, and sharks and barracuda. The monument area also includes plant life that is unknown or rarely found anywhere else in this country.

(d) Affidavit of John R. Thoman, Director of Southeast Region of Federal Water Pollution Control Administration

John R. Thoman, being first duly sworn, deposes and says:

I am Director, Southeast Region, Federal Water Pollution Control Administration, U. S. Department of the Interior, 1421 Peachtree Street, Atlanta, Georgia. I have a Bachelor of Science degree in Sanitary Engineering from the Case Institute of Technology and have had advanced training at the Army Chemical Corps School and the Harvard School of Public Health. I am a Diplomate, American Academy of Environmental Engineers.

The studies being coordinated by the FWPCA in Biscayne Bay, Florida, are under my general supervision.

I first became aware of the Turkey Point Plant of the Florida Power and Light Company in the fall of 1967 when the company applied for a permit from the Army Corps of Engineers to dredge a canal outlet into Biscayne Bay from its property at Turkey Point. At my request, a visit to the plant and the dredging operations was arranged by the company for the various federal and state agencies involved in early February 1968. I participated in this tour and a subsequent meeting at which I orally informed company officials that the proposed discharge of cooling water through the canal system was not a satisfactory solution and that, in all probability, I would recommend to the Corps of Engineers that a permit be denied.

On a subsequent visit to the plant I was shown the results of the dredging on company property. The dredging was entirely on company property and did not extend to the bed of Biscayne Bay. The southerly most canal, known also as Grand Canal, had been dug to the bulkhead line, and cooling water was entering Biscayne Bay over a low ledge or shelf at the bulkhead line.

I am thoroughly familiar with the Turkey Point Plant of the Florida Power and Light Company, having visited the plant site and toured the surrounding areas on several occasions. I have approved the various study plans for the FWPCA work in Biscayne Bay and had a direct involvement in planning and organizing the initial work in 1968.

In my opinion, *various alternative solutions exist for the control of waste heat discharges at the existing fossil-fuel generating units at the Turkey Point Plant* of the Florida Power and Light Company. Among the various alternatives available, either singly or in combination, are several types of cooling towers, ponds with or without spraying devices, the use of cooler condenser water from deep artesian salt water aquifers, discharge into the Gulf Stream, conversion to a fresh water closed system, and a salt water closed system embodying one or several of the primary cooling methods listed above.

The best solution can be selected only through detailed engineering studies which I have not performed and which my staff is not prepared to do. These are detailed design studies normally performed by a consulting engineer or by a client, in this case Florida Power and Light Company. In my opinion, the company has not studied the available alternate cooling systems in sufficient depth to permit the selection of their present system as the best solution.

(e) Affidavit of John E. Hagan, III, Technical Director of Lower Florida Estuary Study

John E. Hagan, III, being first duly sworn, deposes and says:

I hold a Bachelor of Civil Engineering degree from the University of Florida and a Master of Science in Engineering degree from the University of Florida, 1960. I have been employed by the Federal Water Pollution Control Administration and its predecessor agency, the United States Public Health Service, Division of Water Supply and Pollution Control, since February 1960. I am presently a Technical Director of the Lower Florida Estuary Study and in this capacity have been in direct supervision of all activities of the project relating to Biscayne Bay, Florida, since April, 1969.

I supervised and participated in water quality studies in Lower Biscayne Bay, Florida, between September 30 and October 2, 1969, and on January 17, 18, and 19, 1970. Water samples were collected from near the surface and near the bottom at five locations adjacent to Turkey Point and east of Grand Canal at two-hour intervals for a period of 48 hours. A recording temperature monitor is located on the southwest side of Arsenicker Key outside the influence of the elevating temperatures.

During the September survey, temperatures at the monitor station ranged from 84°F to 85°F. At a station 500 yards east of Grand Canal at the surface temperatures ranged from 84° to 93.5°F and averaged 89.2°F. The increase in temperature was due to the cooling water discharge and averaged 4.7°F; the maximum increase was 9°F above background. Near the bottom of this station temperatures ranged from 84° to 89°F, and averaged 86.2°F.

Temperatures at a station 1500 yards east of Grand Canal averaged 84.5° and 84.7°F at top and bottom, respectively. At a station 3000 yards east of Grand Canal, both top and bottom temperatures averaged 84.3°F.

A dye tracer study was conducted in Biscayne Bay in the vicinity of Turkey Point January 12–13, 1970. The specific purpose of this study was to determine the distribution of the Florida Power and Light power plant condenser cooling water discharge in Biscayne Bay.

After exiting from the canal, the dye moved northeastward on the ebbing tide. Peak concentrations were found just east of Turkey Point, between high-water and low-water slack conditions. Approximately 1¼ hours before HWS (at 2:38 on 1/13/70), the dye patch began moving south; two hours and 22 minutes after the HWS, the dye patch was located approximately 1.1 miles northeast of the mouth of Grand Canal.

The dye, and hence heated water from Federal Power

Light effluent canal, moves northeastward from the canal, spreading over the area of Biscayne Bay adjacent to Turkey Point, and is persistent in concentration. The effluent from the canal is slowly dispersed and is *not* readily flushed from the area. Thus, any cooling of water in the bay primarily occurs through exchange with the atmosphere rather than by mixing and dilution.

Temperature monitoring on a limited scale was conducted through the spring and summer of 1968–69. In the late summer of 1969, full-scale temperature monitoring studies were undertaken.

Temperature monitoring began in May 1969 along a transect approximately 75° magnetic from the mouth of Grand Canal. A critical temperature condition occurred in June 1969. At 300 yards, the maximum daily temperature equaled or exceeded 90°F on all days. The maximum daily temperature observed *was 103°F. At 1200 yards off Grand Canal,* the maximum daily temperature exceeded 90°F on 43 percent of the days and reached a maximum of 97°F.

The first full month for which data are available from the present temperature-monitoring program is August 1969. Temperatures as high as 95°F occurred up to 1000 yards east and 1500 yards north of Grand Canal. The isotherms of the monthly mean of the daily maximum temperature indicate that the 90°F isotherm extends 1000 yards east, 1000 yards south, and to the shores of Turkey Point on the north, or an area of at least 620 acres.

The isotherm field of temperatures which were equaled or exceeded 10 percent of the time during August 1969 indicates that a temperature of 90°F was exceeded throughout an area of over 620 acres.

Cooling water effluent from the Florida Power and Light Turkey Point facility increased the monthly average of the maximum daily temperatures of at least 620 acres of Lower Biscayne Bay by more than 4°F. At the mouth of Grand Canal, the mean of the maximum daily temperature of 94°F during August 1969 was 8°F greater than intake temperature.

(f) Affidavit of Clarence M. Tarzwell, Director of National Marine Water Quality Laboratory

Clarence M. Tarzwell, being first duly sworn, deposes and says:

I have had over forty years of experience as an aquatic biologist in studies, surveys, investigations, and research.

I am presently Director of the National Marine Water Quality Laboratory which is located at West Kingston, Rhode Island.

The larva of several important fishes of the area are stressed by temperatures in excess of 86°F, the amount of stress depending, of course, upon the species. The consensus seems to be that temperatures above 90° even in the summer seasons will stress many of the organisms in the Biscayne Bay area. Studies and observations to date indicate that the area between 90° and 92°F. is quite critical, with stress increasing rapidly in this temperature area, and that temperatures over 92° F. become lethal to many species. Temperatures between 92° and 95°F. are drastically harmful and only a few species can survive temperatures above 95° F. for any period of time. However, we cannot consider temperature alone. Since the aquatic animals are coldblooded, their metabolism is dependent upon the temperature of the surrounding water. Thus, as temperatures rise their metabolism increases and their need for oxygen increases rapidly. For any contemplated increase in water temperatures we must consider the dissolved oxygen content of the water. These two factors are interdependent and must be considered together. At the higher allowable or favorable temperature levels dissolved oxygen concentrations should be at or near saturation if the normal life activities are to be carried on. High oxygen levels are specially important and necessary for the development of the larval forms of the fishes and the benthic invertebrates.

Phytoplankton and zooplankton are basic foods for many organisms. The estuaries are nursery areas where the young or larva stages of many important game and commercial species develop. The larva of the molluscs (mussels, clams, and oysters), the trochophore stages of the worms, and the zoea of the arthropods are all plankton forms in the estuarine water.

The Florida Power and Light Company has indicated that, with the proposed additions to the plant, 4240 cfs will be passed through their condensers. The company has further indicated that they intend to mix with this cooling water an additional 150 percent of this volume which will be discharged through their canal. This means that the total removal of water from Biscayne Bay will be 10,625 cfs. This is a tremendous volume of water. Lower Biscayne Bay has been stated to have an area of 100 square miles and an average depth of seven feet. At this rate of removal, this 100 square miles of water would be put down the ditch in 21 and a fraction days and the volume of water in Card Sound would be displaced in 6 and a fraction days. This means that the water from these estuarine areas, which are the nursery areas for the important food and game fishes, and their contained plankton plus the planktonic stages of the important benthic invertebrates plus the larva fishes would be put through the canal and pass down to Card Sound, the volume of which would be displaced every 6 and a fraction days. Totally disregarding the effects of heat, this removal of the water from Biscayne Bay and the rapid displacement of the water in Card Sound would effectively remove the organisms being produced in the estuary and *nullify it as nursery areas*. Such continuous removal of this water would result in its displacement by sea water which does not contain such concentrations of these larval stages. Further, the water removed from the estuary which contains the organisms produced in these nursery areas would be discharged in such volume that they would pass through Card Sound and out to sea. Because as stated above the volume of water in Card Sound would be displaced in six and a fraction days, these organisms must go out to sea or further south. Such change in water volumes would change the whole character of Biscayne Bay and Card Sound and result in a change in the aquatic biota which would be detrimental, as it would destroy their value as nursery areas:

The company has stated that it is their plan to mix the water from the condensors with enough water from Biscayne Bay to lower temperatures in the canal to 95°F. This temperature is lethal to many organisms. While some might survive the short-term exposure through the condensors, the long exposure of 95°F in the discharged channel would result in ensuring lethal conditions to many species.

(g) Motion for Preliminary Injunction

The United States of America, by its undersigned attorneys, by the authority of the attorney general, and acting at the request of the secretary of the interior, moves that this court, in order to prevent irreparable and continuing injury to the United States and to the public interest, immediately, on the basis of the affidavits attached to the accompanying memorandum in support of this motion, enjoin the defendant, Florida Power and Light Company:

(1) To cease all activities in the operation of its existing fossel-fuel plants which result in the discharge into Biscayne Bay of waters of such temperature or quality as to adversely affect the marine life of the Biscayne National Monument and the lands therein to the extent such can be done consistently with the public interest in the continued operation of such plants;

(2) To submit to this court, within 45 days, a plan for the operation of its existing fossil-fuel plants at Turkey Point, Florida, in such a way as to eliminate the destruction of the plankton and other marine life in the waters of Biscayne Bay and the discharge into the Bay of water of a temperature higher than the temperature of those waters under natural conditions, together with a schedule of the time within which such plan can be put into operation;

(3) To cease construction of any canal or other new facility which is designed to be operated or used for the discharge into Biscayne Bay or Card Sound of water of temperature higher than the temperature of those waters under natural conditions or which otherwise cannot be operated in accordance with the designed purpose thereof without adversely affecting the quality of the waters of

Biscayne Bay or the marine life of Biscayne National Monument and the lands therein.

(Signed) Shiro Kashiwa
Assistant Attorney General

(h) Memorandum in Support of Motion for Preliminary Injunction

On October 18, 1968, Congress enacted Public Law 90-606, 16 U.S.C. 450 qq, which authorized the secretary of the interior to establish in the state of Florida the Biscayne National Monument, "in order to preserve and protect for the education, inspiration, recreation, and enjoyment of present and future generations a rare combination of terrestrial, marine, and amphibious life in a tropical setting of great natural beauty . . ." The Senate Committee which reported on the bill that eventually became the Act of October 18, 1968, stated with respect to the then proposed Monument:

> The fauna of the area include the rare American crocodile, several equally rare species of sea turtle, shrimp, sponge, spring lobster, thirty-two varieties of starfish, the sea horse and sea cucumber, and sharks and barracudas that are less than eight inches long. Among the invertebrates, 116 different kinds have been identified, only fifteen of which are also found in the Everglades National Park notwithstanding the proximity of the two areas. The national monument also includes plant life that is unknown or rarely found anywhere else [114 Congr., Rec. 29628].

Section 4 of the Act of October 18, 1968, directed the secretary of the interior to preserve and administer the Biscayne National Monument in accordance with the provisions of 16 U.S.C. 1, which charges the secretary with the duty "to conserve the scenery and the natural and historic objects and the wildlife therein and to provide for the enjoyment of the same in such manner and by such means as will leave them unimpaired for the enjoyment of future generations." That is what, in this suit, the government, at the urgent behest of the secretary of the interior, is attempting to do, for the fragile ecology which supports this rare and precious sea life is in dire, immediate danger, and its destruction, if not prevented here and now, will be an incalculable loss and irreparable injury to all mankind, here and yet to be, and to the United States government, which by an Act of Congress undertook the responsibility of preserving "for the enjoyment of future generations" the infinite variety and delicate beauty of the creation which infuses the waters of Biscayne Bay.

The injury here sought to be enjoined results from an activity of the Florida Power and Light Company which began in 1967, and which, with increasingly manifest destruction of the ecology and marine life of the area, continues today, and is threatened by the company to be continued at an accelerated rate. This activity is the withdrawal from Biscayne Bay of large quantities of salt water—including such marine life as that water might contain and which is small enough to pass through the intake screens—and the use of that water for cooling purposes in connection with the company's fossil-fuel operated power plants adjacent to Biscayne Bay. The plankton and marine life in the water are boiled to death in the heat exchange and cooling process, and are then, along with the now heated water, discharged back into Biscayne Bay. The heated water has a visible, destructive effect on fish, sponges, mollusks, crabs, and aquatic vegetation; the richly nutrient cooked organic matter discharged into the bay not only discolors the water but may also eventually result in the eutrophication of Biscayne Bay.

In addition to this present activity, the Florida Power and Light Company plans to aggravate immeasurably the situation by increasing considerably its withdrawal of water and marine life from Biscayne Bay and by discharging the additional amounts of heated water resulting from this increased withdrawal into Card Sound, a branch of Biscayne Bay. The adverse effects upon the Biscayne National Monument authorized by Congress, both of the present practice of the Florida Power and Light Company as well as of the proposed practice of that company, are described in detail in the attached affidavits and establish conclusively the genuine harm which is now being done,

and which is threatened to be done, to the area designated
by the secretary of the interior to be within the Biscayne
National Monument. Because the continued existence of an
ecological system not found elsewhere in the world, and,
consequently, the continued existence of entire species of
plants, animals, and marine life, is jeopardized by the
defendant's activities, it is clear that the injury being
suffered and threatened is irreparable.

Because the activity inflicting this injury effects destruction of scenery, natural objects, and wild life which Congress has authorized to be preserved, because this activity
injures federally owned property and constitutes a nuisance
which the law will abate, and because this activity is in
violation of the Rivers and Harbors Act of 1899, 33
U.S.C. 407, this court has the jurisdiction and the responsibility to enter an order immediately enjoining the
defendant to take all possible steps which can be taken to
eliminate, or at least minimize, the damage which is being
done presently and which is threatened.

> Respectfully submitted,
> (Signed) SHIRO KASHIWA
> Assistant Attorney General
> State of Florida

(i) Postscript

The *Miami Herald*, April 17, 1970:

Federal Judge C. Clyde Atkins declined Thursday
to order a halt to the dumping of hot water into lower
Biscayne Bay by Florida Power and Light Company's
Turkey Point electrical generating plant.

Atkins held that U.S. Justice Department attorneys
and Interior Department witnesses had simply failed to
prove that the hot water discharge into the bay was
causing any "irreparable harm."

The judge denied requests by the federal government
to order the so-called thermal pollution stopped or
reduced and also declined to order the utility company
to produce a plan for immediate reduction of the hot
water discharge.

"It is my conclusion that the government has not
carried the burden of showing that the present opera-

tion of the Turkey Point plant is causing irreparable damage to lower Biscayne Bay," Atkins said.

"I do find that the present warm water discharge causes some damage, but it is minimal and retrievable," he added.

The *Miami Herald*, April 22, 1970:

The dredging of the main hot water discharge ditch from Florida Power and Light Company's Turkey Point plant is under consideration for possible criminal prosecution, U.S. Attorney Robert Rust said Tuesday.

Rust said he was seeking the advice of U.S. Attorney General John Mitchell on whether to prosecute FP&L for violating the 1899 Rivers and Harbors Act because it did not obtain a permit before digging the so-called Grand Canal from its plant into Biscayne Bay.

Violators of the act may be punished by fines of up to $2500, a year in prison, or both.

The court refused to grant the United States government the relief it sued for in this case. An appeal is being taken. No permit can be found enabling Florida Power and Light Corporation to build its partly finished canal and a criminal investigation may follow.

5.2 Heating Up Lake Michigan: UAW Brings Action Against Prospective Thermal Pollution

"The United Automobile Workers (UAW) and its members in Illinois intend to prevent the destruction or contamination of Lake Michigan by thoughtless or reckless construction of nuclear reactors using lake waters," said Robert Johnston, regional director of the one and one-half million member United Automobile Workers Union. Johnston announced that the Union's attorneys have filed suit in the Circuit Court of Cook County against Commonwealth Edison Company, which has been building a nuclear reactor near Zion, Illinois, on Lake Michigan. The UAW's suit charges that the Commonwealth Edison plant as now designed would discharge heated water in huge quantities resulting in massive destruction of fish life and hastening the development of other conditions which would rapidly cause the deterioration of the lake for drinking water and recreational use. Johnston stated further that there is serious danger that radioactive wastes (tritium) will be discharged into the lake with the threat of harmful consequences to all who use the lake.

Joining in the suit are numerous owners of property located on or near Lake Michigan, who fear the loss of substantial property values as a result of increased pollution of the lake and possible radioactive contamination.

Johnston stated that the UAW is calling upon the state of Illinois and all communities located on Lake Michigan to join in this suit. Noting that the attorney general is empowered by newly enacted legislation to act against water pollution, he said, "If the state of Illinois acts at all, it must act now. Lake Michigan is already showing serious signs of deterioration because of massive industrial and domestic pollution. Many beaches have already been closed and the few remaining beaches are threatened with being closed soon. Under these circumstances, it would be utterly reckless to add systematic thermal pollution from billions of gallons a day of heated water that will be discharged from the projected Commonwealth Edison Plant at Zion, Illinois. The plants are already under construction at Zion, Illinois, with completion of the first plant set for 1972 and the second in 1973. There are scientific methods by which the risks of thermal pollution and radioactive contamination can be avoided. We are asking the court to see that these are utilized to protect the public."

Harold A. Katz and Irving M. Friedman, chief counsel for the plaintiff, said that it was their intention to seek an injunction to prevent the Commonwealth Edison Company from utilizing Lake Michigan water unless it is returned to the lake at its natural temperature by the use of appropriate cooling devices. They said that six nuclear reactors are now under construction in the Lake Michigan area—three in Wisconsin and one in Michigan, in addition to the two under construction at Zion, Illinois. Two more have been planned for southern Michigan. This is the first lawsuit that has been filed growing out of the Lake Michigan nuclear reactors. The billions of gallons of water per day recirculated into Lake Michigan would be 18° to 20°F hotter than the ambient water temperature. This constitutes thermal pollution. This heating-up phenomenon has an adverse effect on oxygen which is essential to all aquatic life. It would increase the toxicity of existing pollutants and accelerate the activity of aquatic plant nuisances and accelerate Lake Michigan's becoming like her sister, Lake Erie, a huge dormant cesspool.

Robert Johnston (UAW) v. Commonwealth Edison Company

IN THE CIRCUIT COURT OF COOK COUNTY, ILLINOIS
COUNTY DEPARTMENT—LAW DIVISION

ROBERT JOHNSTON,
individually, and on behalf of
all others similarly situated as
members of UNITED
AUTOMOBILE, AEROSPACE,
AND AGRICULTURAL
IMPLEMENT WORKERS OF
AMERICA, Region Four,
Plaintiffs

v.

COMMONWEALTH EDISON
COMPANY, a corporation,
Defendant

COMPLAINT FOR DECLARATORY JUDGMENT
AND FOR OTHER RELIEF

Now comes Robert Johnston individually, and as Regional Director of the United Automobile, Aerospace, and Agricultural Implement Workers of America, who work and reside in close proximity to Lake Michigan (hereinafter sometimes referred to as "the Lake") in the state of Illinois.

The United Automobile, Aerospace, and Agricultural Implement Workers of America is an international labor organization; an unincorporated voluntary association composed of over 1.5 million workers. In excess of 100,-000 of these members are in Region Four (UAW) and they are residents and citizens of the state of Illinois who live and work in areas directly adjacent to Lake Michigan. They constitute a class who have a special and direct interest in the conservation of the Lake. All of the members of this class obtain their drinking water from Lake Michigan and the industries in which they are employed obtain water for industrial purposes directly or indirectly from the Lake; further, the members of the class use and depend upon the recreational facilities of the Lake's waters and beaches and surrounding environment, including Illinois Beach State Park, and other similar facilities located in or around Chicago, Waukegan, Zion, Lake Forest, Highland Park, Glencoe, Kenilworth, Wilmette, and Evanston, in the state of Illinois.

The members of the class are so numerous that it is impracticable to bring them all before the court. Plaintiff Johnston will fairly insure the adequate representation of all members of the class. There are common questions of law and fact . . .

• • •

4. Defendant generates and furnishes substantially all the electrical power used in the city of Chicago and other areas within the state of Illinois.

5. Defendant Commonwealth Edison has initiated construction of two nuclear power plants near the city of Zion in the state of Illinois. (These plants will hereinafter sometimes be referred to as the "Zion Nuclear Complex." A map detailing the location of these plants is appended hereto and labeled Appendix A. [See p. 247.] The first Zion Nuclear Plant is scheduled for completion in 1972, the companion plant in 1973. Upon completion, this nuclear facility will furnish electrical power to portions of the northern part of Illinois.

6. The Zion Nuclear Complex abuts directly on the shores of Lake Michigan. Upon completion, as an integral part of its day-to-day operation, the Zion Nuclear Complex will withdraw from and then discharge into Lake

Michigan approximately 3,000,000,000 gallons of water a day.

7. Because of heat wastage in the Zion Nuclear Complex, the three billion gallons of water a day which is to be discharged into Lake Michigan will be a minimum of 18° to 20° hotter than the ambient water temperature. This phenomenon, of discharging heated water into water which exists in its natural state at a cooler temperature is generally termed "thermal pollution."

8(a) Prior to initiating construction of the Zion Nuclear Complex and at all times thereafter, Defendant Commonwealth Edison knew, or should have known, that the discharge of heated effluents into a body of water will decrease the capacity of the water to dissolve oxygen which is essential to the existence of all aquatic life; further, that it will accelerate the metabolic rates of fish and other organisms living in the aquatic environment, increase the toxicity of existing pollutants, and, in combination with nutrients already present in the water, it will accelerate the activity of aquatic plant nuisances.

(b) The water quality of the Lake in recent years has significantly declined. The criteria by which the quality of a body of water is measured, applied to the Lake, demonstrate unmistakably that the Lake has deteriorated and is continuing to deteriorate and that the entire future of the Lake as the source of municipal and industrial water and as the major recreational area of northern Illinois is in jeopardy. The introduction on a systematic, massive, and constantly recurring basis of a new major source of pollution into the Lake, which is already in a desperate struggle for survival, constitute a public nuisance.

9. Prior to initiating construction of the Zion Nuclear Complex and at all times thereafter, Defendant Commonwealth Edison further knew, or should have known, the following facts:

(a) The thermal discharge from the Lake Nuclear Complex will accelerate eutrophication, or aging, of Lake Michigan which will be immediately manifested by a substantial increase of algae. Such algal development will destroy the usefulness of beaches and will greatly increase the cost of purifying water for domestic and industrial use. The development of such algae can ultimately destroy the existence of the Lake through rapid acceleration of the normal aging process of the Lake as a result of the eutrophic process.

(*b*) Because of the thermal discharge of the Zion Nuclear Complex, Lake Michigan in and around the city of Zion will be rendered uninhabitable during the summer months for certain species of cold water game fish such as Lake Trout, Coho Salmon, and Atlantic Salmon. As a consequence, all plaintiffs will be deprived of an important fishing ground, further curtailing their leisure time activities.

(*c*) The thermal discharge of the Zion Nuclear Complex in combination with the thermal pollution resulting from discharges by other power plants abutting on the shores of Lake Michigan will kill off and eventually eradicate the trout and salmon fishery in the Southern Basin of Lake Michigan, and hence completely deprive all plaintiffs of an important source of sport fishing.

(*d*) The thermal discharge of the Zion Nuclear Complex will increase the collective, or synergistic, toxicity of other pollutants, such as domestic sewage, refinery wastes, oils, tars, insecticides, detergents, synthetic fibers, and fertilizers. This will compound the already critical, pervasive, and egregious problem of pollution of the Lake, endangering the health and welfare of all persons utilizing the waters of Lake Michigan for any purposes, including drinking said waters, swimming, fishing, and industrial usage.

(*e*) The thermal discharge of the Zion Nuclear Complex will create an environment which will encourage the propagation and growth of a deadly fish disease known as *Columnaris*. This disease attacks both trout and salmon. Should such a disease flourish, all plaintiffs would be deprived of sport fishing; further, trash fish such as alewives would proliferate and, consequently, foul the beaches and shores of the Lake.

(*f*) The thermal discharge of the Zion Nuclear Complex will render the water immediately adjacent to the plant too hot for swimming and other water sports, thus depriving all plaintiffs of the use of this area for recreation.

10. The plaintiffs have the right to use and enjoy the facilities of the Illinois Beach State Park, including the use of the Lake. This park represents a substantial investment on behalf of all of the taxpayers of the state of Illinois, including the plaintiffs, which investment will be jeopardized by the activities of the defendant described herein.

11. Prior to initiating construction of the Zion Nuclear Complex, and at all times thereafter, Defendant Commonwealth Edison knew, or should have known, that the Zion Nuclear Complex will periodically discharge into Lake Michigan radioactive waste products and that the amount of this radioactive waste so discharged will increase on a yearly basis. Further, said defendant knew, or should have known, that there is a serious possibility that the radioactive waste product so deposited will contaminate the water of Lake Michigan rendering them unfit for human consumption.

12. Prior to initiating construction of the Zion Nuclear Complex, and all times thereafter, Defendant Commonwealth Edison knew, or should have known, that the deleterious affects to Lake Michigan and its adjoining parks and beaches, as more fully described in Paragraph 9 and 11, resulting from the discharge of heated effluents and radioactive waste products could be avoided by the construction of cooling towers and other safety devices.

13. Nevertheless, despite the defendant's knowledge that the thermal discharge of the Zion Nuclear Complex will result in algae littering and fouling both public and private beaches, increasing costs for domestic and industrial water purification, a massive decline in the game fish population, and an increase in the toxicity of pollutants already in Lake Michigan, leading to conditions dangerous to the health and well-being of all persons utilizing the Lake in whatever way, and despite defendant's knowledge that there is a serious possibility that radioactive wastes discharged from the Zion Nuclear Complex will irreparably

contaminate Lake Michigan, defendant has refused and continues to refuse to provide for the installation of a suitably safe system for the protection of the Lake and the protection of the public.

14. Upon completion of the Zion Nuclear Complex in 1973, defendant Commonwealth Edison will discharge into Lake Michigan 3,000,000,000 gallons of heated effluents as well as significant amounts of radioactive waste products. As a result, all plaintiffs will suffer irreparable harm through resulting substantially increased cost for water treatment for domestic and industrial usage and through the serious interference with and the possible destruction of the recreational facilities now afforded them by Lake Michigan. Further, the resultant depletion and destruction of the Lake's recreational facilities will substantially lower the property values of the residences and other building structures either abutting on or in close proximity to Lake Michigan, as well as depriving the owners of these structures of unique recreational opportunities.

15. The loss of Lake Michigan to the people of northern Illinois as the source of quality water for domestic, industrial, and recreational purposes would constitute irreparable harm for which there is no adequate remedy at law. No monetary damages could rectify the loss or deterioration of the Lake to the Chicago metropolitan area. Since millions of citizens of Illinois would be adversely affected by such a catastrophe, any remedy at law would require a multiplicity of parties; the computation of individual damages would impose insuperable problems on the court; damages could not be assessed for those yet unborn; and the defendant could not respond adequately in damages to compensate for the losses suffered.

WHEREFORE, plaintiffs respectfully pray on behalf of themselves and all others similarly situated that this court:

1. Enter a declaratory judgment declaring that:

(*a*) Defendant Commonwealth Edison is under a duty to the plaintiffs to build and to use the facility referred to in this Complaint as the Zion Nuclear Complex in a safe and reasonable manner; and that the discharge of heated effluents and radioactive wastes from said Complex into the waters of Lake Michigan by defendant would be unwarranted and unreasonable conduct in breach of this duty; and,

(b) Should defendant Commonwealth Edison breach its duty to plaintiffs and discharge heated effluents and radioactive wastes into Lake Michigan, all plaintiffs would be irreparably harmed in that such conduct would adversely affect domestic and industrial water usage from Lake Michigan and substantially impair or destroy many recreational opportunities now afforded plaintiffs by the Lake, and irreparably damage plaintiffs and all others similarly situated by substantially lessening the value of their property abutting on or near Lake Michigan, as well as depriving these plaintiffs of unique recreational opportunities.

2. Enter a preliminary and permanent injunction restraining defendant Commonwealth Edison from discharging heated effluents and radioactive wastes into Lake Michigan from the structures referred to in this Complaint as the Zion Nuclear Complex.

3. Enter judgment in favor of plaintiffs and against defendant Commonwealth Edison for the cost of this action.

4. Grant such other and future relief as this honorable court may deem just and proper.

> (Signed) Katz and Friedman
> Attorneys for the Plaintiffs

Postscript: As of March 1971 this case is still pending. It is of interest to note that Michigan has enacted a new law prohibiting return of water to the Great Lakes that is 1°F. higher than ambient (natural) temperature of the water.

5.3 Mrs. Heck against the Beryllium Corporation

Edward L. Wolf of Philadelphia represented the plaintiff in this landmark air pollution case. The facts, the pleadings, and the first two witnesses are summarized in this section and additional reference is made to this case

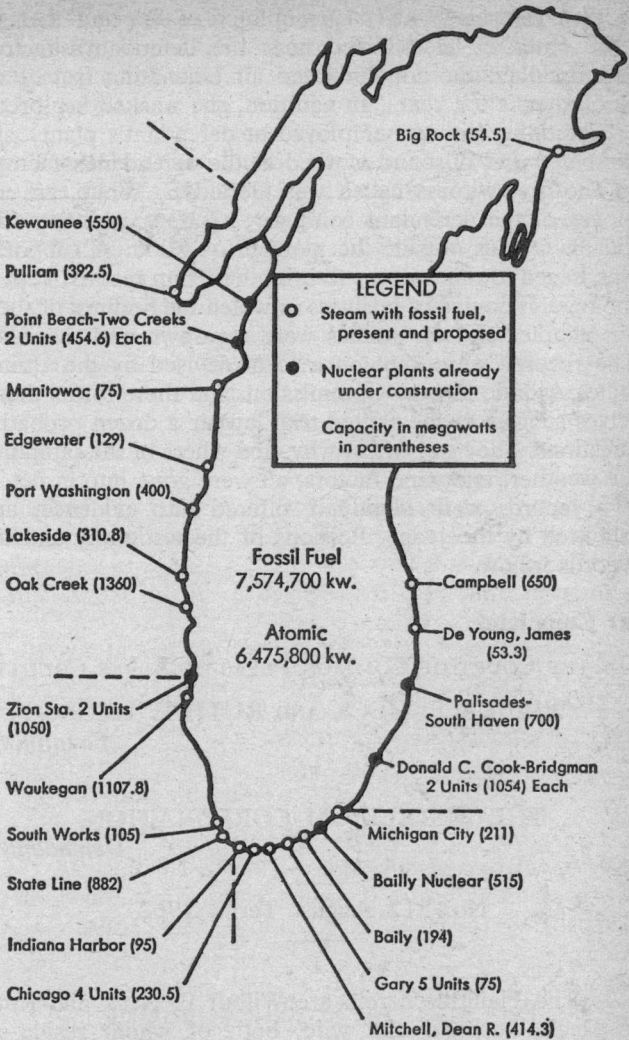

Big Rock (54.5)

Kewaunee (550)

Pulliam (392.5)

Point Beach-Two Creeks
2 Units (454.6) Each

Manitowoc (75)

Edgewater (129)

Port Washington (400)

Lakeside (310.8)

Oak Creek (1360)

LEGEND
○ Steam with fossil fuel,
   present and proposed
● Nuclear plants already
   under construction
   Capacity in megawatts
   in parentheses

Fossil Fuel
7,574,700 kw.

Atomic
6,475,800 kw.

Campbell (650)

De Young, James
(53.3)

Palisades-
South Haven (700)

Zion Sta. 2 Units
(1050)

Donald C. Cook-Bridgman
2 Units (1054) Each

Waukegan (1107.8)

Michigan City (211)

South Works (105)

Bailly Nuclear (515)

State Line (882)

Indiana Harbor (95)

Baily (194)

Chicago 4 Units (230.5)

Gary 5 Units (75)

Mitchell, Dean R. (414.3)

MAP OF LAKE
MICHIGAN AND
PROPOSED ATOMIC
PLANTS

in §7.2. [See also §4.8(*b*) for opinion of Appellate Court.] Mrs. Ruth E. Heck lived near the defendant's factory and breathed the contaminated air emanating from their smokestacks for years. In addition, she washed her brother's clothing (he was employed at defendant's plant) and thereafter her husband worked at the defendant's factory.

The first witness called was Gerald E. White, an employee of the defendant company, a safety engineer, who did air studies outside the plant in question. A subpoena was issued to this witness to bring with him records kept in the regular course of business in which the findings of these air samples and air studies were set down and recorded. The records were kept on a form devised by the United States Atomic Energy Commission, and these forms themselves suggest to the skilled trial lawyer a dozen probative questions. The how, when, why, and where of the sampling, the weather, and wind factors, all were gone into in detail. The records were identified, offered into evidence, and admitted by the judge. Portions of the testimony and the records follow.

(a) Complaint

IN THE COURT OF COMMON PLEAS OF BERKS COUNTY

WILBUR F. HECK AND RUTH E. HECK,
Plaintiff(s)

v.

THE BERYLLIUM CORPORATION,
Defendant(s)

No. 312 August Term, 1962

1. The Plaintiffs herein are Wilbur F. Heck and Ruth E. Heck, husband and wife, both of whom reside at Antietam Road, R. D. #1, Temple, Berks County, Pennsylvania.

2. The Defendant, the Beryllium Corporation, is a corporation organized and existing under and by virtue of

the laws of the state of Delaware and is a citizen thereof, engaged in the business of manufacturing and processing beryllium, with a place of business located in Muhlenberg Township, Temple, Berks County, Pennsylvania.

3. At all times hereinafter set forth, the defendant company did manufacture and sell to the public in general a product known as beryllium or a derivative thereof.

4. Beryllium is a harmful, dangerous, poisonous, and deleterious substance, which, if introduced into the human body, causes serious, permanent, and grievous personal injuries.

5. At the times relevant to the allegations of this complaint, and for a long time prior thereto, the defendant company owned and operated a factory situated in Temple, Berks County, Pennsylvania, which factory was operated by its agents, servants, and employees who were then and there acting in the course and scope of their employment with and under the direct and exclusive control of the defendant, the Beryllium Corporation.

6. The wife Plaintiff, Ruth E. Heck, resided in Berks County in close proximity to defendant company's factory in Temple, Berks County, Pennsylvania, during the period relevant to the allegations in this complaint.

First Cause of Action

7. The defendant company negligently allowed beryllium to escape from its factory located in Temple, Berks County, Pennsylvania, and to permeate and otherwise mix with the air and atmosphere of the surrounding area so as to expose the wife plaintiff to the effects of beryllium.

8. On or about November 25, 1960, and subsequently thereto, as a result of exposure to beryllium, which the defendant company negligently allowed to escape into the atmosphere in and around the wife plaintiff thereby allowing such beryllium to be introduced into her system, the wife plaintiff became disabled and suffered severe, personal, and permanent injury and illness.

9. The aforesaid injuries were occasioned solely as a result of negligence on the part of the defendant in the manufacture of beryllium and its products and the main-

tenance of its plant situated in Temple, Berks County, Pennsylvania, without any negligence on the part of either of the plaintiffs contributing thereto.

SECOND CAUSE OF ACTION

10. Plaintiffs incorporate herein by reference the allegations contained in paragraphs 1 thru 6, inclusive, as fully as though the same were here set forth at length.

11. The defendant company has, at all times relevant to the allegations of this complaint, allowed beryllium to escape from its factory located in Temple, Berks County, Pennsylvania, and to permeate and otherwise mix with the air and atmosphere of the surrounding area so as to expose the wife plaintiff to the effects of beryllium.

12. The manufacture and processing of beryllium creates an extraordinary risk to persons such as the wife plaintiff who are within the area of danger.

13. The manufacture and processing of beryllium is an ultrahazardous activity, and, therefore, the defendant is absolutely liable for the resulting injury sustained by the wife plaintiff, Ruth E. Heck, as aforesaid.

THIRD CAUSE OF ACTION

14. Plaintiffs incorporate herein by reference the allegations contained in paragraphs 1 thru 6, inclusive, as fully as though the same were here set forth at length.

15. The activities of the defendant company as aforesaid constituted a nuisance to the plaintiffs and their property, and they are, therefore, liable for injuries which have resulted therefrom.

(b) Defendant's Safety Engineer Testifying for Plaintiff

GERALD E. WHITE, direct testimony:

Q: Mr. White, what is your full name and address?

A: My name is Gerald Eugene White. I reside at 311 Sycamore Road, West Reading, Pennsylvania.

Q: By whom are you presently employed?

A: Beryllium Company.

Q: In what capacity?

A: Safety engineer.

Q: How long have you been safety engineer?

A: Since 1949.

Q: How long have you been an employee of the defendant, the Beryllium Corporation?

A: Since the fall of 1947.

Q: Sir, in the course of your employment and regular course of your business, did you do any air studies of the outside of the plant in Temple (Pennsylvania)?

A: Yes, I have done some.

Q: Do you have them with you?

A: I have.

Q: For what period of time do they cover?

A: The samples were taken over a period from 1950 to 1957.

Q: Will you give to the reporter as plaintiff's Exhibit 1 the samplings which you said were outside samplings, samples of the outside atmosphere of the environs of your plant here in Reading, Pennsylvania, between 1950 and 1955.

A: They are not in chronological order but they are in this one folder.

Q: Now Mr. White, these air samples appear on a form entitled "United States Atomic Energy Commission, New York Operations Office, Medical Division." Who made these studies?

A: I've taken the air samples.

Q: And the Atomic Energy Commission had nothing to do with these samples, did they?

A: No, I just used their forms.

Q: Mr. White, you conducted these studies for the Beryllium Corporation. In what capacity was it that you did it?

A: My position was safety engineer.

Q: What would the sample number indicate?

A: The sample number indicates the location at which the sample was taken.

Q: The next is the date it was taken?

A: Yes, sir.

Q: Will it state the hour it was taken?

A: Yes, sir.

Q: And the sample description, what was that?

A: The sample designation was the location and it could be where at the given time the sample was taken.

Q: What would the rate and time indicate?

A: The rate indicates the amount of cubic feet per microgram of air that was the rate of the sample.

Q: It then indicates the time the sample was on?

A: The length of time the sample was operating.

Q: Then you have "analyzed for 'Be'?"

A: "Be." This is the chemical symbol for beryllium.

Q: Now we have quantity. What's that?

A: Well quantity would have been the total amount of material collected that the sample was analyzed for.

Q: The total amount of beryllium found on the pad or filter?

A: Yes. It would have been a quantitative amount.

Q: You determined this by metric volume, by taking the total amount of beryllium on the pad or filter at the time of the sample and the amount of air that went through the sample and you come out with an answer beryllium present or not present and, if present, it's so much per cubic meter, is that right?

A: It was generally reported out as the quantity per cubic meter of air.

Mr. Wolfe: With permission of defense counsel, I would like to put a map here of the city of Reading. Mr. Bowers, will you put the map up here, please. While the map is being put up it is to designate certain areas as stations.

Q: Did you take air samplings at the Daniels' house?

A: Yes.

Q: Did you take samplings at Dr. Kirvels' house?

A: Yes.

Q: And you also sampled from the roof and yard of the Beryllium Corporation in Reading, Pennsylvania?

A: Yes, on the exhibit I gave you.

In this manner, Mr. Wolfe, counsel for the plaintiff, was able to get into evidence as part of plaintiff's case the samples taken by the defendant's safety engineer which showed noncompliance with the recommendations of the Atomic Energy Commission as to air purity around beryllium plants.

(c) Defendant's Laboratory Director Testifying for Plaintiff

The second witness at the trial was Mr. Stoudt from the W. B. Coleman and Company, director and general manager of the laboratory which supervised the analysis of beryllium for the plaintiffs as metallurgists and chemical analysts. The testimony permitted by the court took the following form.

ROBERT F. STOUDT, direct:

Q: Mr. Stoudt, where do you live?

A: Medford, New Jersey.

Q: By whom are you presently employed?

A: W. B. Coleman and Company.

Q: Could I have the address of W. B. Coleman and Company?

A: Ninth Street and Rising Sun Avenue, Philadelphia.

Q: How long have you been employed by Coleman and Company?

A: Thirteen years.

Q: In what capacity?

A: As laboratory director and general manager.

Q: Mr. Stoudt, what is the business of W. B. Coleman and Company?

A: We are chemists, metallurgists, and engineers.

Q: Does your company make analysis of beryllium?

A: Yes, their samples and also other metal alloys.

Q: Was your company in that business in 1949 and 1948?

A: Yes.

Q: Did all these samples that you analyzed come from the Beryllium Corporation?

A: Yes.

Q: Mr. Stoudt, were you the director of the laboratory at the time these reports were completed?

A: Yes.

Q: Were you familiar with procedures which were employed during the period of time in terms of analysis of beryllium?

A: Yes.

Q: How was the analysis done?

A: This determination is by spectrograph which is an instrument used for measurement of various metallic elements. Beryllium is one. Actually I am familiar with the metal inasmuch as the sample is received at the laboratories and is put into a solution. This solution is introduced into carbon electrodes which are then, through high voltage, exposed to photographic film. The spectrum which is produced on the film will include any of the metallic elements. In this case, for instance, it is only the beryllium content, as this film is processed and is introduced into an instrument known as a densilometer, and from this instrument the operator can take certain electronic measurements of the intensity—again, in this case, of beryllium content—and from that reading, this electronic reading, convert from certain working graphs the actual beryllium content.

Q: Is the spectograph making a film, is that right?

A: That's right.

Q: The film is put into the densilometer and the film is read by the densilometer and the operator merely reads the number?

A: That's right, and electronic machines.

At this point, attorney Edward Wolfe offered the records as part of the plaintiff's case under the Business Records Act of Pennsylvania and on a second ground that the exhibits were records with which Mr. Stoudt had personal knowledge. These records indicated that the recommendations of the Atomic Energy Commission as to the limitation of beryllium in the atmosphere was exceeded by the defendant corporation.

(d) Examples of Defendant's Records Used for Plaintiff

W. B. COLEMAN & CO.
METALLURGISTS—CHEMISTS—ENGINEERS
9TH ST. AND RISING SUN AVE.
PHILADELPHIA 40, PA.

No. 701324/26   **Date** January 11, 1955

ANALYSIS OF   Air Samples

RECEIVED FROM   Beryllium Corporation
                             Reading, Pennsylvania
                             Attn: Mr. G. White

SAMPLE MARKED
REMARKS   P. O. # 45924

The submitted dust samples were examined spectrographically to determine the beryllium content and to establish a possible lower limit of detection of 0.01 micrograms.

Analysis of prepared standards indicated that the lowest value detected under ideal conditions is 0.05 micrograms. Further analysis of the submitted samples showed the beryllium content of each to be less than our limit of detection.

                             (Signed) R. J. Stoudt

W. B. COLEMAN & CO.
METALLURGISTS—CHEMISTS—ENGINEERS
9TH ST. AND RISING SUN AVE.
PHILADELPHIA 40, PA.

Date   July 30, 1953

LABORATORY NO.   667949/59

ANALYSIS OF   Beryllium

RECEIVED FROM   The Beryllium Corp.
                             Reading, Penna.

SAMPLE MARKED
REMARKS

Sample No.	Beryllium (micrograms)
E-872	1.22*
E-873	7.45*
E-874	3.10*
E-875	0.68*
E-877	5.15*
E-880	0.25
E-881	0.57*
E-882	0.40*
E-946	0.75*
E-947	8.25*
E-948	0.95*

(Signed) R. J. Stoudt

(e) Postscript

A verdict for the plaintiffs was appealed, a new trial was ordered, and the case was settled thereafter.

5.4 Scholar Smites Smokestacks

The Puget Sound Air Pollution Control Agency forbids the emission of sulfur dioxide from any premises which will result in "concentrations and frequencies at ground level in excess of one part per million over an average in time of five minutes once in any eight-hour period." According to the agency's records, the American Smelting and Refining Company (Asarco) has been cited for 226 violations of regulations during the period of January 1, 1969, to January 1, 1970. A total of sixteen $250 civil penalties have been assessed and paid under protest. Asarco applied formally for a variance from existing regulations and requested a permit for the construction of a taller stack, 1,100 feet in height, 435 feet higher than the stack now in use, as the only known available means by which the company might be able to comply with the regulations of the agency.

* The Atomic Energy Commission set 0.25 micrograms per cubic meter of air as the maximum allowable concentration, exceeded by 10 of 11 samples taken.

William Rodgers, assistant professor at law at the University of Washington and volunteer legal counsel for Clean Air for Washington stated: "We ask only that the smelter make use of available technology for removing dangerous pollutants from its smokestack emissions rather than seeking to disperse these air pollutants over a wide area." Professor Rodgers feels that if the smelter is allowed to solve its air pollution problem by building an 1100-foot stack, communities distant from the plant which have not previously been bothered by its emissions may suddenly be beset by new and damaging air pollutants. On February 5, 1970, Professor Rodgers served the papers [§5.4(a)] opposing Asarco's application before the Puget Sound Air Pollution Control Agency in the Superior Court of the State of Washington in the county of King. Professor Rodgers used the testimony of authorities such as Dr. Clarence Gordon, professor of botany at the University of Montana; Dr. Warren Winkelstein, chairman of the department of epidemiology of the California School of Public Health, who has studied the effects of sulfur dioxide on human health; Richard Stroupe, professor of economics at Montana State University, who has analyzed the economics of the Tacoma Smelter operation, as well as six University of Washington staff members, Dr. Franklin Badgley, professor of atmospheric sciences; Robert Charlson, professor of atmospheric chemistry; Dr. C. Beat Meyer, associate professor of chemistry; Dr. James Crutchfield, professor of economics in public affairs; Michael Pilat, research professor of civil engineering; Dr. Richard Walker, chairman of the Department of Botany; and Peter E. Breysse, research assistant professor in the Department of Preventive Medicine. Professor Rodgers argued that other control methods are available and that every type and concentration of gaseous emission from a copper smelter can be controlled. He cited both the McKee report and the experiences of other smelters which have converted the pollutant material to liquid sulfur dioxide, elemental sulfur, and sulfuric acid, and in some cases made these by-products profitable. Professor Rodgers concluded that "to grant a variance sanctioning the construction of a tall stack would be greatly damaging to the public interest and flatly inconsistent with the proclaimed mission of the Puget Sound Air Pollution Control Agency." The agency agreed, and Professor Rodgers won an important test case. The application by Asarco for an 1100-foot smokestack construction was turned down on March 25, 1970.

(a) Answer and Complaint in Intervention

COUNTY OF KING

AMERICAN SMELTING AND REFINING COMPANY, a corporation,

Plaintiff   No. 702001

v.

PUGET SOUND AIR POLLUTION CONTROL AGENCY, a multicounty authority,

Defendant   ANSWER AND
                   COMPLAINT IN
and   INTERVENTION

CLEAN AIR FOR WASHINGTON and the WASHINGTON ENVIRONMENTAL COUNCIL, nonprofit corporations,

Intervening defendants
in behalf of themselves
and all other persons
similarly situated

COME NOW the intervening defendants, Clean Air for Washington and the Washington Environmental Council, and in answer to plaintiff's petition for Declaratory Judgment and Injunction:

BY WAY OF FURTHER ANSWER AND AS A CROSS-COMPLAINT AGAINST THE PLAINTIFF, INTERVENING DEFENDANTS ALLEGE AS FOLLOWS:

I
Identity of Defendant Intervenors

The Washington Environmental Council is a nonprofit Washington corporation with offices at 119 S. Main, Seattle, Washington, 98104. Clean Air for Washington is a nonprofit Washington corporation with offices at 306 W. Republican, Seattle, Washington, 98119.

II
Interest of Defendant Intervenors

By their by-laws, membership, activities, and conduct, the Washington Environmental Council and Clean Air for Washington have exhibited a special interest in the aesthetic, conservational, health, and recreational aspects of the air environment of the state, and in all aspects of air pollution control designed to protect the public, their property, and the environment from the ravages of pollution.

• • •

IV
Laws Involved

That plaintiff, in operating its business of smelting and refining ores and concentrates, is subject to the following provisions of law:

1. RCW 70.94, the "Washington Clean Air Act."
2. RCW 7.48, "Nuisances."
3. RCW 9.66, "Nuisances."
4. Public Law No. 91-190, 83 Stat. 852, "National Environmental Policy Act of 1969."
5. Regulation I, Puget Sound Air Pollution Control Agency. And especially:
6. RCW 7.48.140(7), reading as follows:

Public nuisances enumerated. It is a public nuisance . . . To erect, continue, or use any building, or other place, for the exercise of any trade, employment, or manufacture, which, by occasioning obnoxious exhalations, offensive smells, or otherwise, is offensive or dangerous to the health of individuals or of the public.

7. RCW 9.66.050, reading as follows:

Deposit of unwholesome substance. Every person who shall deposit, leave, or keep, on or near a highway or route

of public travel, on land or water, any unwholesome substance, or who shall establish, maintain, or carry on, upon
or near a highway or route of public travel, on land or
water, any business, trade, or manufacture which is noi-
some or detrimental to the public health; or who shall
deposit or cast into any lake, creek, or river, wholly or
partly in this state, the offal from or the dead body of any
animal, shall be guilty of a gross misdemeanor.

8. Section 101 (c), Environmental Policy Act of 1969,
reading as follows:
The Congress recognizes that each person should enjoy
a healthful environment and that each person has a responsibility to contribute to the preservation and enhancement of the environment.

V
Claimed Violations: State Law

That plaintiff presently is violating the law in the following particulars:

1. It is maintaining a nuisance in violation of RCW 7.48
and 9.66.

2. It is operating its business in repeated violation of
Regulation I Answer and Complaint in Intervention–4
of the Puget Sound Air Pollution Control Agency and, on
this separate ground, is maintaining a nuisance.

3. It is committing repeated criminal violations of RCW
9.66.010 and is maintaining a nuisance.

VI
Claimed Violations: Federal Law

That plaintiff presently is depriving members of the
community of the federal statutory right to a healthful
environment created by the National Environmental Policy
Act of 1969.

VII
Facts on Violations: Sulphur Dioxide Emissions

During the period January 1, 1969 to January 1, 1970,
the plaintiff has committed a total of 226 violations of
Regulation I of the Puget Sound Air Pollution Control
Agency which prescribes maximum allowable sulphur

dioxide concentrations. On a monthly basis, the violations are as follows: January, 1; February, 7; March, 21; April, 5; May, 28; June, 5; July, 24; August, 29; September, 22; October, 6; November, 31; December, 47.

VIII
Facts on Violations: Other Emissions

That the plaintiff, in operating its business, releases many chemicals into the atmosphere, including sulphur dioxide, sulphur trioxide, sulfuric acid, arsenic, lead and cadmium compounds, and other forms of particulates and gases. That these emissions have invaded the property and have been absorbed into the bodies of members of the community.

IX
Dangerous Properties of Emissions

That the gaseous and particulate emissions from the operation of plaintiff's business have highly dangerous biological and chemical properties which have been demonstrated in toxicological studies on human beings and test animals. That the arsenic compounds emitted in the opereration of plaintiff's business are proven carcinogens in animal tests. That the sulfuric acid emitted in the operation of plaintiff's business has been proven to be highly injurious to plants, property, animals, and human beings in toxicological studies.

X
Effects of Emissions

That the plaintiff, in operating its business, has caused great harm and damage to the community to the extent of many millions of dollars annually in the following respects:

1. Vegetation, including grasses and trees of many varieties, has been damaged and destroyed.

2. Property, building materials, and furnishings have been damaged and property values reduced.

3. Individuals have suffered extreme discomfort, annoyance, and inconvenience.

4. Individuals have suffered temporary or permanent

damage to their health, including sinusitis, rhinitis, bronchitis, emphysema, dermatitis, and other diseases.

5. The community has suffered an increased mortality rate.

XI
Danger to the Community

That the membership of the intervening defendants and other members of the community fear for their personal comfort, repose, health, and safety by reason of the operation of plaintiff's business as a nuisance.

XII
Complaints from the Community

That the defendant agency, during the period April 1968 to August 1969, has received a total of 1476 complaints from inhabitants of the community complaining about the operating of plaintiff's business and, in particular, the taste of sulphur, the odors of sulphur, damage to their plants, property, and health caused by sulphur compounds, and difficulty in breathing the polluted air.

XIII
Ability To Control Harmful Emissions

That plaintiff presently has the ability to eliminate or reduce greatly the release of harmful emissions into the atmosphere and among the members of the community but refuses to do so.

• • •

XV
No Remedy at Law

That intervening defendants have no adequate remedy at law.

PRAYER

Wherefore defendant intervenors pray:

1. That this court hold that Regulation I, and specifically Section 9.07 thereof, is not in violation of either the Constitution of the state of Washington or of the United States and that all acts and activities of the defendant agency are done pursuant to the lawfully dele-

gated *police power* of the state and in furtherance of the
health, safety, and welfare of the inhabitants of the state
and the tricounty areas of King, Pierce, and Snohomish
Counties.

2. That the court enter a permanent injunction restraining plaintiff from further operating its Tacoma Smelter so
that ground-level concentrations of sulphur dioxide exceed
the maximum allowable concentrations established by the
defendant agency's regulations.

3. That the court enter a permanent injunction restraining plaintiff from further operating its Tacoma Smelter
so as to create a nuisance and to violate the right to a
healthful environment.

4. That this court appoint a receiver to operate the
Tacoma Smelter in accordance with law.

5. That this court appoint a referee to observe the operation of plaintiff's smelter, record information about its
emissions, and report fully to the court.

6. That intervening defendants have such other and
further relief as may seem meet and proper in the
premises.

> (Signed) *William H. Rogers, Jr.*
> Attorney for Defendant Intervenors
> 267 Condon Hall
> University of Washington

(b) Findings and Decision of the Board of Directors of the Puget Sound Air Pollution Control Agency

WHEREAS, American Smelting and Refining Company
requested a variance from Section 9.07 of Regulation I
during a twenty-six-month period of construction of an
1,100-foot smokestack at the Tacoma Smelter Plant of
the American Smelting & Refining Company, and

WHEREAS, the Variance Application set forth that the
new tall stack would replace the existing 560-foot stack,
and

WHEREAS, the Board of Directors of the Puget Sound
Air Pollution Control Agency set a public hearing on the
variance application for March 11 and 12, 1970, and due

and proper notice of said hearing was given according to law, and

WHEREAS, the matter came on for hearing on March 11 and 12, 1970, at Tacoma Community College, Tacoma, Pierce County, Washington, and testimony was heard for and on behalf of the applicants and the opponents to the variance application, and

WHEREAS, the Board continued the matter until the twenty-fifth day of March, 1970, at which time the Board will render its findings and decisions regarding the variance application of American Smelting and Refining Company, and

WHEREAS, the recess meeting coming on for hearing on this twenty-fifth day of March, 1970, the Board makes the following Findings of Fact on the questions raised by the variance application:

1. Would the tall stack enable American Smelting and Refining Company to lower ground-level concentrations of sulfur dioxide so as to comply with Section 9.07 of Regulation I upon completion?

Finding of Fact: Based upon the testimony of Mr. Paul Humphrey and Dr. Franklin Badgley and the testimony of the American Smelting and Refining Company's witnesses, there is ample evidence that, while the tall stack can cause a reduction in ground-level concentration of sulfur dioxide (SO_2), the capability of the tall stack to reduce ground-level concentrations sufficiently to comply with Section 9.07 of Regulation I is impossible. The meteorological conditions peculiar to the area around the Tacoma Smelter site creates a convection cell which brings the smelter plume down to ground level and the plume from the proposed tall stack would be subject to the same phenomena. There was not sufficient evidence presented that under all meteorological conditions the tall stack would reduce the ground-level concentrations of SO_2.

2. Will the proposed curtailment program be sufficient to minimize violations of Section 9.07 during the variance construction period and after the tall stack is constructed?

Finding of Fact: The Board finds that from the testimony of American Smelting and Refining Company and the testimony of witnesses from the Agency, the present and proposed personnel procedures and equipment are lacking at the Tacoma Smelter to conduct an effective curtailment program with the existing stack. Evidence was sufficient to show that some improvement could be expected with a total meteorological curtailment program, but that additional time and equipment and personnel would be required to make it an effective program, and then still the program would not be sufficient in and of itself to reduce the ground-level concentrations of SO_2.

3. Are there any processes which could control all or most of the sulfur dioxide (SO_2) generated?

Finding of Fact: There are presently two known and used processes to reduce sulfur dioxide emissions and they are the production of sulfuric acid and the production of elemental sulfur in one form or the other. There were no facts presented by the applicant that there was any intention on the part of the applicant to install facilities to reduce emissions other than a general statement indicating such a program in six to eight years. The tall stack proposed does not reduce the amount of emission of SO_2.

4. Is the proposed variance request compatible with new sulfur dioxide (SO_2) standards which the Board will be required to consider for adoption in order to comply with Air Quality Standards soon to be adopted by the State Air Pollution Control Board?

Finding of Fact: The granting of a variance from Section 9.07 of Regulation I at this time would necessitate a reapplication for variance after the adoption of new SO_2 ground-level or new emission standards. Further, since the Board has found in Finding of Fact No. 1 that the tall stack would not meet present standards, the Board finds that the tall stack would not meet future stricter standards regarding sulfur dioxide.

5.   Has American Smelting and Refining Company presented a program for reduction of emissions during the requested variance period?

Finding of Fact: The Board finds no adequate program for reduction of emissions or ground-level concentrations during the requested variance period has been presented either through curtailment or other means.

Based upon the Findings of Facts, the Board does hereby make the following two necessary findings pursuant to Section 7.01 entitled "Variance" of Regulation I:

1.   The applicant, American Smelting and Refining Company, has not established that the emissions of sulfur dioxide (SO_2) to occur or proposed to occur during the variance period would not endanger public health or safety; and

2.   The applicant, American Smelting and Refining Company, has made no showing that compliance with Section 9.07 of Regulation I from which the variances sought would produce serious hardship to the applicant without equal or greater benefit to the public.

BASIS: The Board heard testimony for and against the variance application on the bases of health, but the applicant did not produce any evidence or testimony that the tall stack would not be injurious to the health or safety of the inhabitants within the jurisdiction of the Agency. In regard to the hardship question, the only hardship claimed by American Smelting and Refining Company was a lack of a market for by-products of the emission control processes.

Based upon the Findings of Fact and the Findings of the Board, the Board of Directors of the Puget Sound Air Pollution Control Agency hereby enters its decision on the

variance application of American Smelting and Refining
Company, No. 70-1:

> THE VARIANCE APPLICATION OF THE AMERI-
> CAN SMELTING AND REFINING COMPANY BE
> AND THE SAME IS HEREBY DENIED.

Passed by the Board at the recessed hearing of the variance application this 25th day of March, 1970.

5.5 Asarco Violates City Air Regulations

(a) Petition

Following the lead of Richard Marshall, Esq., the trail-
blazing attorney from El Paso, the City of El Paso has
commenced litigation against the American Smelting and
Refining Company for multiple air pollution violations.
The conditions complained of violated the standards of the
Texas Air Control Board. Portions of the city's petition
and complaint follow:

IN THE DISTRICT COURT OF EL PASO COUNTY,
TEXAS

FORTY-FIRST JUDICIAL DISTRICT

THE CITY OF EL PASO,
Plaintiff

v.

No. 70-1701

AMERICAN SMELTING and
REFINING COMPANY *et al.*,
Defendants

TO THE HONORABLE COURT:

Now comes the city of El Paso, a municipal corporation,
hereinafter sometimes referred to as plaintiff, and acting
pursuant to a formal resolution of the City Council, and
complaining of the American Smelting and Refining Company, a corporation organized under the laws of New
Jersey and authorized to do business in the state of Texas,
herein sometimes referred to as defendant, and joining
herein as third party defendant, the Texas Air Control

Board, an agency of the state of Texas organized and existing under the Clean Air Act of Texas, 1967, codified as Vernon's Annotated Civil Statutes, Art. 4477-5 as amended by the 61st Legislature, hereinafter sometimes referred to as Board, and for cause of action would show the court as follows:

I

Defendant American Smelting and Refining Company is a corporation organized under the laws of the State of New Jersey, doing business in El Paso County, Texas.

II

The occurrences herein complained of all occurred and are occurring in El Paso County, Texas.

III

American Smelting and Refining Company owns or claims and occupies a certain tract of land containing approximately 747.12 acres, more or less, in the J. Baker Survey No. 10, Abstract No. 7, in the city of El Paso.

IV

There is located on the land above referred to a copper, lead, and zinc smelting plant which is owned, operated, and used by the defendant American Smelting and Refining Company for the purpose of recovering the above metals from raw or concentrated ores.

V

To produce and obtain copper, lead, and zinc from raw ore or concentrated ore the defendant American Smelting and Refining Company causes said raw ore or concentrated ore to be processed in such a manner as to produce and release into the atmosphere, in, about, and around the property occupied by defendant's plant, dust and particulate matters which circulate through the air on, over, and across neighboring lands.

VI

From time to time, as the result of the above-described processes at defendant's plant location above referred to, the described dust and particulates resulting from defendant's operation circulate through the atmosphere and carry on the winds beyond the boundary of defendant's land and on, over, and across the lands of others, in such concentrations and for such durations, both singularly and in combination, as to be injurious to or adversely affect human beings, animal life, vegetation, and property, and are of such nature both singularly and in combination and are from time to time present on such neighboring lands, for such duration, and in such concentration, both singularly and in combination, as to be harmful to humans, animal life, vegetation, and property, and to interfere with the normal use and enjoyment of animal life, vegetation, and property.

VII

By acts of the 60th Legislature, Regular Session, 1967, Chapter 727, codified as Vernon's Annotated Civil Statutes, Article 4477-5 as amended by the 61st Legislature (1969), the present Texas Air Control Board was created as the principal authority in this state on matters relating to the quality of the air resources in the state of Texas and for setting standards, criteria, levels, and emission limits for air content and pollution control. The present Air Control Board is the agency now empowered to administer and enforce the provisions of Article 4477-5 as amended, subject to the provisions of Section 4.03 of Article 4477-5 as amended, which authorizes the local governments, including plaintiff, to perform certain functions necessary to the administration and enforcement of such law.

VIII

Effective January 23, 1968, the Texas Air Control Board, in compliance with the provisions of Article 4477-5, revised and amended the General Provisions and Regulation I of the Rules and Regulations of said Board. The Texas Air Control Board further revised Regulation I of said Rules on July 30, 1969, which revised Regulation I was effective at all times material to this petition.

Paragraph IV(C) of Regulation I of the Rules and Regulations of the Texas Air Control Board, revised July 30, 1969, and effective as of the date of the filing of this petition, reads as follows:

C. Emission Limits for Suspended Particulate Matter. To assist in meeting the ambient air quality standards specified in Paragraph IV (B) of this Regulation, the Board hereby establishes limits on the emission of suspended particulate matter which may be made from any property. The contribution of suspended particulate matter by a single property to an affected land use area shall be measured by the difference between the upwind level and the downwind level of air contaminants for the property as outlined in Appendix B, or by stack sampling calculated to a downwind concentration, in accordance with Paragraph IV (D) below and as outlined in Appendix C. If the contribution from the property, determined in accordance with the procedure in Appendix B or C, exceeds the emission limits set forth below, the property is in violation of this Regulation. A property is in compliance if the contribution from such property does not exceed the applicable limits specified in the schedule.

Micrograms of suspended particulate matter per cubic meter of air sampled:

Land Use Area Affected	Property Emission Limits
Type A	100
Type B	125
Type C	150
Type D	175

The revised General Provisions of the Rules and Regulations of the Texas Air Control Board, including the portions above-quoted in this petition, became effective on the twenty-third day of January, 1968, and are still the current General Provisions promulgated by the Texas Air Control Board. Regulation I of the Rules and Regulations of the Texas Air Control Board, including the provisions above-quoted, was revised on July 30, 1969, and was in effect at all times material to the allegations contained in this petition.

IX

Plaintiff would show that the defendant American Smelting and Refining Company has its smelting plant located in an area primarily industrial in character and should be classified as Type C Industrial Area under ¶IV of the General Provisions above set forth in this petition. The defendant's plant is located in close proximity to an area in which property is being used for single- and multiple-family residences, which would be classified as a Type A Residence or Recreation Area under ¶IV of the General Provisions of the Rules and Regulations of the Texas Air Control Board herein before set forth in this petition. Defendant's plant is also located in close proximity to an uninhabited area of land which would be classified as Type D usage under the Rules and Regulations of the Texas Air Control Board above-quoted. Therefore, under Regulation I, as set forth in this petition, defendant American Smelting and Refining Company is prohibited from contributing airborne particulates to air over and across neighboring lands classified as Type A lands in excess of 100 micrograms per cubic meter of air. Defendant American Smelting and Refining Company is further prohibited from contributing airborne particulates into the air over and across neighboring lands classified as Type D in excess of 175 micrograms per cubic meter of air.

X

Plaintiff would show that from time to time defendant American Smelting and Refining Company, in the operation of its plant and facilities, has repeatedly caused emission of particulate matter into the atmosphere in concentrations well in excess of 100 micrograms per cubic meter of air and also in concentrations well in excess of 175 micrograms per cubic meter of air, and that such particulate matter in such concentrations has crossed on, over, and across the properties of others in violation of the above-quoted Rules and Regulations of the Texas Air

Control Board in violation of Article 4477-5 Vernon's Annotated Civil Statutes.

XI

Plaintiff would show that in addition to defendant being in violation of Regulation I, as herein set forth by virtue of its failure to control emission of particulate matter to a level consistent with the requirements of such Regulation, defendant, by failure to control the emission of particulate matter, has caused and is causing the particulate matter to disseminate into the atmosphere and contaminate the air, and such particulate matter carried in the air, on, over, and across neighboring lands, both singularly and in combination and in such concentrations, and for such duration which tends to be injurious to and adversely affect humans, animal life, vegetation, and property, and further such particulate matter impairs the normal use and enjoyment of surrounding land by the people who own and occupy such surrounding land, as well as interferes with normal use and enjoyment of animal life, vegetation, and property of people on such neighboring lands.

XII

This action by plaintiff is authorized by Article 4477-5, Section 5.03, and in compliance with said section, and attached to this petition as Exhibit A, and incorporated in this petition for all intents and purposes is a formal resolution by the City Council of the city of El Paso authorizing the exercise of the power conferred by the above article.

XIII

Plaintiff would further show the court that the defendant American Smelting and Refining Company has violated Regulation I of the Rules and Regulations of the Texas Air Control Board in the following particular instances:

1. March 26, 1970, defendant discharged into the atmosphere 803.512 micrograms per cubic meter of particulate matter, said particulate matter being carried over and onto Type A land.

2. On March 30, 1970, defendant discharged into the

atmosphere 311 micrograms per cubic meter of particulate matter which carried over and onto Type D land.

3. On April 2, 1970, defendant discharged into the atmosphere 213 micrograms per cubic meter of particulate matter which carried over and onto Type D land.

4. On April 6, 1970, defendant discharged into the atmosphere 342 micrograms per cubic meter of particulate matter which carried over and onto Type A land.

5. On April 21, 1970, defendant discharged into the atmosphere 267 micrograms per cubic meter of particulate matter which carried over and onto Type D land.

Plaintiff would show the court that all of the above violations violate Regulation I of the Rules and Regulations of the Texas Air Control Board as above set forth in this petition.

WHEREFORE, PREMISES CONSIDERED, plaintiff prays that defendant American Smelting and Refining Company be cited as required by law and ordered to appear and answer herein and that the Texas Air Control Board be cited as a third party defendant and ordered to appear and answer herein, and further that defendant American Smelting and Refining Company be ordered to appear and show cause why a temporary injunction should not issue enjoining it from the further emission of particulates into the atmosphere and across neighboring lands in excess of limits specified in Regulation I of the Rules and Regulations of the Texas Air Control Board, and that defendant American Smelting and Refining Company be ordered to show cause why it should not be enjoined from further emission of dust and particulates across neighboring lands in such concentrations and for such durations as tend to be harmful to human, animal life, vegetation, and property or as to interfere with normal use and enjoyment of animal life, vegetation, and property, and on final trial hereof plaintiff prays that defendant be assessed penalties over to and in favor of the state of Texas in the amount of $5000, being the statutory maximum of $1000 per day for each day that defendant has violated the Clean Air Act of Texas and the Rules and Regulations lawfully promulgated under such Act, and further that additional penalties in the amount of $1000 per day, as provided in said Act, be assessed against defendant for each and every day hereafter that defendant violates the Clean Air Act of Texas after the date of filing of this petition, as the court may find, and as the court may deem proper, and further, on final trial hereof, Plaintiff prays that defendant be permanently enjoined from causing the emission of particulates into the atmosphere and across neighboring lands in excess of those amounts provided in Regulation I of the Rules and Regulations of the Texas Air Control Board. Further, plaintiff prays that it have its cost and all other relief both at law and in equity to which it may be entitled.

> TRAVIS WHITE, City Attorney
> JOHN C. ROSS, JR., Assistant City Attorney
> WADE ADKINS, Assistant City Attorney
>
> Room 203 City-County Building
> El Paso, Texas, 79901

(b) Texas District Court Order

On this the 28th day of May, 1970 came the parties to the above styled and numbered suit, for a hearing on Plaintiff's application for temporary injunction, and both parties having announced ready the Court proceeded to review the pleadings, including the exceptions and motions filed herein, and having heard the testimony and arguments of counsel relating to the motions, the Court is of the opinion that the following Order should be entered:

IT IS HEREBY ORDERED that ASARCO shall install an afterburner on the copper anode furnace and shall complete upon receipt of equipment now on order, the installation of this item by not later than June 30, 1970; said company is further Ordered to erect a baghouse on the zinc holding furnace and to complete the installation of such baghouse by not later than October 15, 1970; IT IS FURTHER ORDERED that ASARCO will make weekly tests of its low level particulate emissions and to this end endeavor to keep it within the guide lines of Regulation I, Rules and Regulations of the Texas Air Control Board, and that they will further coordinate these testing efforts through counsel of record, with the City-County Health

Unit, with the results of these tests to be submitted to the Court by the 15th of October, 1970; and this matter shall be set over for hearing until October 29, 1970.

SIGNED and ENTERED this 2nd day of June, 1970.

(c) Postscript

Status as of March 30th, 1971: A twenty-seven months' stay has been granted on an order directing compliance, pending the results of the new plant construction which will include:

1. $15 million for plant to recapture emissions and convert them to sulfuric acid.

2. $1.9 million for plant for research to return the effluent to basic sulfur.

3. Six Cottrell Pollution Control Devices have been installed at the stacks and an I.B.M. Computer is monitoring the stacks and twenty-one (21) fallout zones.

5.6 Airlines Agree To Cut Pollution

One of the most obnoxious sources of air pollution comes from planes taking off and landing at airports. New Jersey's Department of Health brought suit last year against Eastern Airlines, alleging violation of the state's Air Pollution Control Code. The basis of the complaint was proof that the Ringelmann smoke chart standards had been violated. Theodore A. Schwartz, then deputy state attorney general, maintained the action on the part of the state successfully.

As a result of the New Jersey suit, a stipulation was entered into in 1970 which barred excessive pollution not only by Eastern but by eight other airlines as well. Each airline had to make extensive equipment changes to meet the state anti-pollution standards. We set forth below a copy of the complaint served by Mr. Schwartz, the affidavit of an industrial hygienist for the Department of Health, and the stipulation entered into by the parties.

(a) Complaint in Department of Health, State of New Jersey v. Eastern Airlines, Inc.

DEPARTMENT OF HEALTH, STATE OF NEW JERSEY, *Plaintiff* v. EASTERN AIRLINES, INC., **a** corporation of the state of Delaware,	Civil Action VERIFIED COMPLAINT

Defendant

FIRST COUNT

The Department of Health, state of New Jersey, plaintiff, with offices located at John Fitch Plaza, city of Trenton, county of Mercer, state of New Jersey, hereinafter designated as "Department," says:

1. The Department is authorized, empowered, and obligated to protect and preserve the health of the public in the state of New Jersey and is empowered by law to enforce the provisions of the New Jersey Air Pollution Control Act, N.J.S.A. 26:2C-1 *et seq.*, and is empowered by law to enforce the provisions of the New Jersey Air Pollution Control Code, hereinafter referred to as "Code," which by the terms of the aforementioned Act has the force and effect of law.

2. The defendant Eastern Airlines, Inc. (hereinafter referred to as "Eastern") is a corporation of the state of Delaware with offices located at Newark Airport, city of Newark, county of Essex, state of New Jersey.

3. Eastern operates commercial aircraft for the transportation of passengers and freight.

4. Eastern uses the airport facilities of Newark Airport for a passenger terminal and other operations including the departure and arrival of its aircraft.

5. The department conducted investigations at Newark Airport on April 11, 1969, April 28, 1969, and May 27, 1969, to observe the operations of Eastern in regard to the dark smoke discharged into the open air by its aircraft departing and arriving at Newark Airport as set forth in the affidavit of David Shotwell which is attached hereto

and made a part hereto.

6. The said investigations indicated that smoke from certain of Eastern's aircraft and engines upon takeoff and landing at Newark Airport was being discharged into the open air, the shade or appearance of which was darker than No. 3 of the Ringelmann Smoke Chart, in violation of Chapter IV, Section 2.1, of the New Jersey Air Pollution Control Code.

7. The said investigations indicated that Eastern's aircraft bearing the Nos. N9333 and N9324E, upon taking off from Newark Airport on April 11, 1969, discharged smoke into the open air from their engines the shade or appearance of which was darker than No. 3 of the Ringelmann Smoke Chart in violation of Chapter IV, Section 2.1, of the Code.

* * *

Eastern's aircraft bearing the Nos. N8961E, N8926E, and N8132E, upon landing at the Newark Airport on May 27, 1969, discharged smoke into the open air from their engines the shade or appearance of which was darker than No. 3 of the Ringelmann Smoke Chart, in violation of Chapter IV, Section 2.1, of the Code.

11. The Department pursuant to the provisions of N.J.S.A. 26: 2C-19 is empowered and authorized to institute this action for injunctive relief to prohibit and prevent further violation of Chapter IV, Section 2.1, of the New Jersey Air Pollution Control Code.

WHEREFORE, the Department demands judgment against Eastern for temporary and permanent injunctive relief,

(a) Ordering Eastern to forthwith cease and desist from causing, suffering, allowing, permitting, or emitting smoke into the open air from its aircraft departing and arriving at Newark Airport the shade or appearance of which is darker than No. 2 of the Ringelmann Smoke Chart, in violation of Chapter IV, Section 2.1, of the Code.

(b) Ordering Eastern to install such devices or mechanisms or make such modifications to its engines on its aircraft arriving or departing at Newark Airport in order that smoke will not be discharged or emitted into the open air from its aircraft engines, the shade or appearance of which is darker than No. 2 of the Ringelmann Smoke Chart, in violation of Chapter IV, Section 2.1, of the Code.

(c) Ordering Eastern to submit to this court and the Department, on a date to be fixed by this court, a complete report setting forth in detail a time schedule for the implementation of steps taken by Eastern to abate the discharge of smoke from its aircraft engines into the open air the shade or appearance of which is darker than No. 2 of the Ringelmann Smoke Chart, in violation of Chapter IV, Section 2.1, of the Code.

(d) Such other relief as the court may deem just and proper.

SECOND COUNT

1. The Department repeats the allegations set forth in the First Count of the complaint.

2. The Department pursuant to the provisions of N.J.S.A. 26:2C-19 is empowered and authorized to institute this action to recover the maximum penalty of $2500 for each violation of Chapter IV, Section 2.1, of the Code.

WHEREFORE, the Department demands that this court impose the penalty as provided by the N.J.S.A. 26:2C-19,

(a) Ordering Eastern to pay a penalty of $2500 for each violation of Chapter IV, Section 2.1, of the Code which occurred on April 11, 1969, April 28, 1969, and May 27, 1969, making a total penalty demand of $22,500.

> ARTHUR J. SILLS
> Attorney General of New Jersey
> Attorney for Plaintiff
> (Signed) Theodore A. Schwartz
> Deputy Attorney General
> State of New Jersey

(b) Affidavit of David J. Shotwell, Principal Industrial Hygienist

DAVID J. SHOTWELL, of full age, being duly sworn according to law upon his oath, deposes and says:

1. I am employed by the Division of Clean Air and

Water in the State Department of Health as a Principal
Industrial Hygienist.

2. On April 11, 1969, I conducted an investigation at
Newark Airport, city of Newark, county of Essex, regarding the emission of black smoke from the defendant's aircraft engines during takeoff.

3. During the course of my inspection I observed the
defendant's aircraft bearing numbers N9333 and N9324E
taking off from Newark Airport.

4. I also observed at this time that black smoke was
being emitted into the open air from the engines of these
aircraft, the shade or appearance of which was darker
than No. 3 of the Ringelmann Smoke Chart in violation
of Chapter IV, Section 2.1, of the New Jersey Air Pollution Control Code. I observed these violations for a
period of seven minutes on each aircraft.

5. On April 28, 1969, I conducted another investigation at Newark Airport regarding the emission of black
smoke from the defendant's aircraft engines during landing.

6. During the course of my inspection I observed the
defendant's aircraft bearing number N8972E landing at
Newark Airport.

7. I also observed at this time that black smoke was
being emitted into the open air from the engines of this
aircraft, the shade or appearance of which was darker
than No. 3 of the Ringelmann Smoke Chart in violation
of Chapter IV, Section 2.1, of the Code. I observed this
violation for a period of five minutes.

8. On May 27, 1969, I conducted another investigation
at Newark Airport regarding the emission of black smoke
from the defendant's aircraft engines during takeoff and
landing.

9. During the course of my inspection I observed the
defendant's aircraft bearing numbers N8931E, N811N,
and N8919E taking off from Newark Airport.

-10. I also observed at this time that black smoke was
being emitted into the open air from the engines of these
aircraft, the shade or appearance of which was darker than
No. 3 of the Ringelmann Smoke Chart in violation of
Chapter IV, Section 2.1, of the Code. I observed these

violations for a period of five minutes on each aircraft.

11. During the course of this inspection I also observed the defendant's aircraft bearing numers N8132N, N8926E, and N8961E landing at Newark Airport.

12. I also observed at this time that black smoke was being emitted into the open air from the engines of these aircraft, the shade or appearance of which was darker than No. 3 of the Ringelmann Smoke Chart in violation of Chapter IV, Section 2.1, of the Code. I observed these violations for a period of five minutes on each aircraft.

13. During all of my inspections the weather was clear.

(Signed) David J. Shotwell

(c) Stipulation of Settlement with Time Schedule for Abatement

DEPARTMENT OF HEALTH, STATE OF NEW JERSEY,	SUPERIOR COURT OF NEW JERSEY,
Plaintiff	CHANCERY DIVISION,
v.	ESSEX COUNTY
AMERICAN AIRLINES, INC., a corporation of the state of Delaware, NORTHEAST AIRLINES, INC., a corporation of the commonwealth of Massachusetts, PIEDMONT AIRLINES, INC., a corporation of the state of North Carolina, TRANS WORLD AIRLINES, INC., a corporation of the state of Delaware, NATIONAL AIRLINES, INC., a corporation of the state of Florida, EASTERN AIRLINES, INC., a corporation of the state of Delaware, UNITED AIRLINES, INC., a corporation of the state of Delaware, BRANIFF AIRWAYS, INC., a corporation of the state of Nevada, and DELTA AIRLINES, INC., a corporation of the state of Delaware,	Docket No. C 3330-68
	STIPULATION
Defendants	

WHEREAS, seven different actions were commenced by order to show cause, each dated August 12, 1969, against the defendants American Airlines, Inc., Northeast Airlines, Inc., and others; and

WHEREAS, by the complaints herein the plaintiff, Department of Health, state of New Jersey, sought, *inter alia*, orders requiring each of the nine airline defendants to submit to the court and to the Department, on a date to be fixed by the court, a complete report setting forth in detail a time schedule for the implementation and completion of the steps and procedures necessary to be taken by each such airline to abate the discharge into the open air of smoke from its engines, the shade and appearance of which is darker than No. 2 of the Ringelmann Smoke Chart, in violation of Chapter IV, Section 2.1, of the New Jersey Air Pollution Control Code; and

WHEREAS, answers were filed herein by each of the nine defendant airlines, which answers alleged, *inter alia*, in substance, that the only jet aircraft operated by the nine defendants as to which a means was presently known for reducing the smoke from its engines to a shade or appearance which would enable it to comply without doubt with the said Code are those powered by the JT8D engine manufactured by the Pratt & Whitney Division of United Aircraft Corporation, which JT8D engine is used by the nine defendant airlines on the aircraft known as the Boeing 727, the Boeing 737, and the McDonnell Douglas DC-9; and

WHEREAS, the said JT8D engines in use upon the said jet aircraft, by reason of the smokiness of such engines and the number of such aircraft in use, produce approximately seventy percent of the total smoke emission from jet aircraft; and

WHEREAS, at a meeting convened in Washington, D. C., on January 20, 1970, by the Secretary of Transportation and the Secretary of Health, Education, and Welfare of the United States, which was attended by representatives of thirty-one airlines (including representatives of each of the nine defendants herein), and was also attended by Deputy Attorney General Theodore A. Schwartz of the state of New Jersey, a voluntary agreement was reached by and between the said thirty-one airlines and the two federal departments calling same, with respect to a program for sharply reducing the smoke emission from all JT8D engines in use on the jet aircraft operated by such airlines; and

WHEREAS, since that time a further hearing has been held between the undersigned attorneys for the nine defendant airlines herein and the Department of Health of the state of New Jersey and the Office of the Attorney General of the state of New Jersey, at which a basis for the settlement of this action was agreed to which is compatible with the agreement reached at the meeting in Washington on January 20, 1970; and

WHEREAS, all of the parties hereto are anxious to implement that settlement;

NOW, THEREFORE, IT IS HEREBY STIPULATED AND AGREED by and between the undersigned, the attorneys for the respective parties hereto, as follows:

1. Depending upon the availability from the Pratt and Whitney Division of United Aircraft Corporation of new or modified reduced smoke combustor cans for replacement purposes on existing JT8D engines (and the availability of any necessary associated hardware), the defendant airlines herein agree that:

(a) Within ninety days from January 20, 1970, they will have begun the ordering of such reduced smoke combustor cans for installation on the JT8D engines in use upon their jet aircraft.

(b) During the next scheduled major engine overhaul of the JT8D engines used by the said airlines in connection with the operation of jet aircraft, the present combustor cans in use on the engines will be replaced by such reduced smoke combustor cans.

(c) The program of installing such reduced smoke combustor cans on all of the JT8D engines in all aircraft operated by them will be substantially completed by December 31, 1972.

2. Within thirty days of the date of this stipulation, each of the nine defendant airlines will provide the Department of Health of the state of New Jersey with the number of the JT8D engines which it has on hand, as of the date of this stipulation, for use on the jet aircraft operated by it.

3. Semiannually, beginning on July 1, 1970, until completion of the program, each of the nine defendant airlines will submit to the Department of Health of the state of New Jersey a progress report on the installation of the aforesaid reduced smoke combustor cans on the JT8D engines owned by such airline. Each such report shall include a statement of the number of JT8D engines on hand, the number of such engines which have been equipped with such reduced smoke combustor cans, the number of such reduced smoke combustor cans on hand available for installation in JT8D engines, the number of such reduced smoke combustor cans on order from Pratt & Whitney Division of United Aircraft Corporation but not yet delivered, and the number of major engine overhauls on JT8D engines used by the said airline in connection with the operation of jet aircraft during the preceding six-month period.

4. The defendant airlines agree that all new Boeing 727, Boeing 737, and Douglas DC-9 aircraft hereafter delivered to them from and after the date hereof, which shall be equipped with JT8D engines manufactured after March 1, 1970, will have the aforesaid reduced smoke combustor cans on all engines, and further agree that all new technology aircraft, such as the Boeing 747, the McDonnell Douglas DC-10, and the Lockheed 1011, which shall be used by the said airlines shall be designed so as to be virtually smokeless.

5. In the event that the companies which manufacture and supply jet engines to the defendant airlines develop combustor cans which will substantially reduce the smoke from jet engines presently in use by the defendant airlines other than the JT8D engines, the defendant airlines agree that when such improved combustor cans have been ap-

proved and adequately tested for those engines they will consult with the Department of Health of the state of New Jersey regarding a replacement program for them.

•   •   •

7. The plaintiff, Department of Health, agrees that it will take no action to collect any fines for any violations of Chapter IV of the New Jersey Air Pollution Control Code by the aircraft operated by any of the nine defendant airlines, whether prior to or subsequent to this stipulation, if such airline has met the terms and conditions of this stipulation.

5.7 Lawyer Sues 200 Air Polluters on Behalf of the People of Los Angeles

School children in Los Angeles have not been able to exercise outside on certain days because of toxic air conditions. This shocking fact of life has existed for several years and the problem has not yet been solved. The young courageous lawyer, Roger J. Diamond, attempted to do something about it. Attorney Diamond served a fifty-page complaint against 200 polluters including General Motors, filing the action in Superior Court of the State of California for the County of Los Angeles, docket number 947429.

This is a class action in behalf of the population of Los Angeles County (7,119,184 persons). In fourteen separate causes of action, the plaintiff seeks to do battle with the makers of 3,369,198 motor vehicles which are making the air unfit to breathe in and around Los Angeles. Defendants immediately moved to dismiss the complaint and on the day the motion was heard the courtroom looked like the meeting place of a large bar association.

Among the 200 defendants are thirty-two metal refining or smelting plants; four cast iron foundries; nineteen plants doing metal smelting and secondary smelting; seven brass foundries; three aluminum foundries; five rubber tire manufacturing or rubber reclaiming plants; three automobile assembly and automobile body plants (General Motors, Chrysler, and Ford); seven glass manufacturing plants; two frit manufacturing plants; thirteen bulk gasoline loading facilities. Plaintiff also sued the U.S. Gypsum Company, a Rockwell manufacturing plant; fifteen asphalt manufacturing plants; seven asphalt saturators; seventeen petroleum refineries; twenty-nine chemical plants; eleven asphalt paving hot plants; thirty-one paint, enamel, lacquer, or varnish manufacturing plants; the Southern California Edison Company at three locations; as well as six airlines.

Defendants in this action are discharging enormous quantities of pollutants sufficient to constitute a continuing public nuisance. Said pollutants are poisons, noxious gases and chemicals, particulates, lead, fumes, carbon monoxide, hydrocarbons, oxides, nitrogen oxides of sulfur and other noxious and harmful substances and odors, and they are continuing to discharge the dangerous gases and particulates into the atmosphere of the county of Los Angeles.

Request is made for special administrator to facilitate the retrofitting of each motor vehicle registered in the county of Los Angeles with a device to reduce the pollution from motor vehicles. A restraining order is asked for injunctive relief restraining defendants from emitting and discharging pollutants into the atmosphere of the county of Los Angeles. This action asked the court to declare "that the air and atmosphere belong to each member of the public for the public benefit, that no private person may destroy or use any part or all the air and atmosphere to the detriment of the public, the plaintiff, and members of the represented class."

Defendants demurrer was sustained.

(a) Complaint

SUPERIOR COURT OF THE STATE OF CALIFORNIA FOR THE COUNTY OF LOS ANGELES

> ROGER J. DIAMOND, possessor
> of real property in and resident of
> the county of Los Angeles, in
> behalf of himself and all other
> possessors and residents,
> ROGER J. DIAMOND, inhabitant
> of the county of Los Angeles, in

                        behalf of himself and all other
                        inhabitants,
                                            Plaintiffs
                v.

                GENERAL MOTORS CORPO-
                RATION and approximately
                200 others,
                                            Defendants

                        • • •

9. As a direct and proximate result of the carelessness and negligence of the defendants . . . plaintiff and all others similarly situated on behalf of whom the plaintiff has brought this suit has suffered the following injuries and damages: shortening of life span; increased chances of suffering heart attacks; emphysema; lung cancer; damage to and destruction of body tissue; eye irritation; brain damage; exhaustion due to lack of oxygen; fatigue; and many other injuries. . . .

10. Defendants have threatened to, and will unless restrained by this court, continue to design their motor vehicles so as to emit enormous amounts of pollutants as heretofore alleged when operated as intended within and throughout this county.

11. At the present time there are at least 3,369,198 motor vehicles registered in the county of Los Angeles, all of which were designed and manufactured by said defendants. The identity of the particular defendant which designed and manufactured each particular motor vehicle now registered in the county of Los Angeles is ascertainable by examining the particular motor vehicle or by examining official public records maintained by the State of California, Department of Motor Vehicles.

12. The reasonable cost of retrofitting each said motor vehicle designed and manufactured by the defendants and registered in the county of Los Angeles so as to substantially reduce the pollutants emitted and thereby cease the injuries and damages to plaintiff and those similarly situated as alleged is $200 each.

                        • • •

26. Defendants have created "a continuing public nuisance in that enormous quantities of pollutants, poisons, noxious gases and chemicals, particulates, lead, fumes, carbon monoxide, hydrocarbons, oxides of nitrogen, oxides of sulphur, and other noxious and harmful substances and odors have been, are, and continue to be emitted and discharged by each named defendant into the atmosphere in the county of Los Angeles.

27. Said pollution has been and is proximately caused by the employment of unnecessary and injurious methods of operation by each said defendant.

28. Said occupation, use, and maintenance of defendants' property constitutes a nuisance within the meaning of Civil Code, §3479, in that said pollution has injured and is injuring the health of plaintiff and all persons on behalf of whom plaintiff has brought this law suit, has been and is indecent and offensive to the defenses of plaintiff and all persons on behalf of whom plaintiff has brought this suit.

Page 27, ¶10: "There are 7,119,184 persons in the class represented by plaintiff."

Page 29: Defendant oil companies have "maintained each such station in such a manner as to constitute a continuing public nuisance in that enormous quantities of unburned gasoline and gasoline vapors have been, are, and continue to be emitted and discharged and have been and are evaporating and continue to evaporate into the atmosphere of the county of Los Angeles upon the pumping of gasoline from station pumps into the fuel tanks of each motor vehicle receiving gasoline at each such station."

Said unburned gasoline and gasoline vapors have constituted and do constitute a form of pollution.

Page 35 of the complaint, ¶3: "As a proximate result of said smoke pollutant and other said materials being deposited on said property and carried into the air space, plaintiff and said class numbers have been and are being damaged in that the value of their property has been diminished and their enjoyment of said property has been and is being impaired and destroyed."

The above-described trespasses have been and are

proximately caused by the employment of unnecessary and injurious methods of operation by each of said defendants.

Page 49 of the complaint, on eleventh cause of action:

"1. For an injunction permanently restraining defendants from emitting and discharging pollutants into the atmosphere of the County of Los Angeles.

"2. For an injunction permanently restraining defendants from selling, distributing or transferring into the County of Los Angeles pollution creating motor vehicles and from authorizing and permitting certain dealers, agents, and representatives to do what defendants shall have been enjoined from doing;

"3. For a declaration that the air and atmosphere belong to each member of the public for the public benefit; that no private person may destroy or use any or all of the air and atmosphere to the detriment of the public plaintiff and members of the represented class."

• • •

Dated: April 15, 1969

               ROGER J. DIAMOND
               Attorney for plaintiffs and for those similarly situated

(b) Plaintiff's Memorandum of Law

The plaintiff candidly admits that the purpose of the suit is to return the air of the county of Los Angeles to a livable condition and make the area a desirable place to live for the plaintiff and the class he represents. This is not a very difficult task. If it can be accomplished by the judicial branch of government, with long-established legal principles, then the pollution-plagued populace will be eternally grateful to those judges who possess the courage and wisdom to grant the relief prayed for.

It is not only the view of plaintiff that the judiciary can and must solve the pollution crisis. More and more legal scholars are arriving at the same conclusion [see, for example, Rheingold, "Civil Cause of Action for Lung Damage Due to Pollution of Urban Atmosphere," 33 *Brooklyn Law Review* 17 (1967); Note, "The Cost-Internalization Case for Class Actions," 21 *Stanford Law Review* 383

(1969), Juergensmeyer, "Control of Air Pollution through the Assertion of Private Rights," 1967 *Duke Law Journal* 1126]. Plaintiff respectfully suggests that the court read the "Class Action," *Stanford Law Review* article, for it deals primarily with the utility and desirability of employing the class action device against those dumping their garbage into the atmosphere. "Air pollution imposes on outsiders an uncompensated cost that is not subjected to any pricing mechanism. Many of those who are presently using the atmosphere for waste disposal are not required to pay for the privilege; conversely, there is no effective means whereby other air users may offer payment to stop the pollution" (*Stanford Law Review* at 385). "A means of coping with externalities that involves a minimum of official interference with the operation of the free market is by creating, or redefining, private rights" (21 *Stanford Law Review* at 401). It should be noted that plaintiff is not even asking the court to create or redefine rights. He is merely asking the court to recognize *existing* private rights.

Since defendants do not appear to argue that the individual, traditional lawsuit for nuisance or product liability (i.e., one plaintiff versus one defendant) has been "pre-empted" by federal, state, and county statutes, rules, regulations, ordinances, agencies, and officials, it is evident that their basic cry is that, while one industrial defendant might be liable for polluting one neighboring family, such defendant, properly joined with other defendants, may not be held accountable if their conduct produces massive pollution of an entire county.

This Alice-in-Wonderland reasoning is as absurd as and similar to the reasoning of the polluting defendant properly rejected by the Court of Appeal in *People v. Union Oil Company,* 268 A.C.A. 616 (2d Dist. 1968). In that case, defendant's oil refinery was continuously dumping its filthy, disgusting waste into the harbor. Defendant, in attempting to secure appellate approval of the lower court's sustaining of its demurrer, argues that the statute under which it was prosecuted prohibited *only occasional pollution.* In response, the court stated, 268 A.C.A. at 622,

"Defendant's interpretation would mean that criminal prosecution is reserved for the occasional violator, but immunity is conferred upon one who continuously, willfully, and inexcusably dumps any quantity of pollutants into the waters of this state." Defendants' arguments are strikingly similar, unless they assert that all private causes of action against single defendants for trespass, nuisance, strict liability, and negligence have also been eliminated by federal, state, and local preemption.

Defendants do not maintain that this suit would impede the effective enforcement of the existing governmental pollution scheme and thus result in a prolongation of our polluted air which is being inhaled into our lungs 18,000 times a day. If that were their argument it would have to be seriously considered by this court. Of course, if plaintiff thought this were true, this suit would not have been filed on behalf of the represented class, nor would it have been sponsored by the Clean Air Council, a nonprofit corporation.

It appears to be defendants' contention that the mere existence of an elaborate scheme of laws concerning air pollution somehow precludes private litigation. This cannot be so. There is extensive regulation of drugs by the Federal Food, Drug, and Cosmetic Act, 52 Stat. 1040, as amended, 21 U.S.C. §301 *et seq*. No drug may be introduced into interstate commerce without prior approval of the Secretary of Health, Education, and Welfare. The statutory format encompasses the Secretary of Health, Education and Welfare, the Food and Drug Administration, and other agencies. Regulations are promulgated pursuant to the Act. The United States is authorized to bring civil injunctive suits against various violators of the Act and regulations established pursuant to the Act. Criminal sanctions are also imposed. Yet private lawsuits have been brought against various drug companies in state courts based on state causes of action (e.g., negligence, breach of warranty, etc.) [See *Gottsdanker v. Cutter Laboratories* 182 Cal.App.2d 602 (1960); *Toole v. Richardson-Merrel, Inc.*, 251 Cal.App.2d 785 (1967)].

Defendants' real argument must be that the various tiers

of government have established standards for air pollution which, if met by the defendants preclude this lawsuit. The question then becomes one of legislative intent: Did the legislature or Congress intend to protect the polluters by enacting a "shield"? In other words, has the government told industry, "You may pollute and poison the people up to a certain level, without recourse on the part of the people. However, if you exceed our standards, we will attempt to prevent it"? This interpretation of legislative intent is certainly not to be favored, for it directly opposes the obvious and stated purpose of the legislation: to facilitate the elimination of poison from the lungs of the people.

The better interpretation, and the one obviously intended, is that the government will use its force and might if a polluter exceeds governmental standards imposed on it. If the polluter conducts its factory or builds its motor vehicle so as to comply with governmental standards, it might still be subjected to a civil suit by one who could establish that he was proximately harmed by unlawful conduct (i.e., conduct for which the law imposes liability—nuisance, negligence, strict liability, etc.). . . .

[Mr. Diamond then cited recent newspaper headlines showing awareness of pollution:]

1. FREEWAY FUMES MAY REDUCE DRIVER ABILITY, OFFICIAL SAYS
2. LUNG CANCER DEATH RATE INCREASE TOLD
3. MORE EMPHYSEMA
4. TIE X-RAY DANGER BREATHING SMOG
5. TESTS SHOW SMOG CAN BE LETHAL TO ELDERLY
6. PARK HEAD PREDICTS 10,000 A DAY DEATH RATE FROM SMOG
7. SMOG SHORTENED LIVES, SICKENED AND FRIGHTENED MILLIONS IN THE LOS ANGELES BASIN AS NEVER BEFORE DURING 1967, AND ITS INCREASING INTENSITY INDICATED THAT 1968 WOULD BE WORSE
8. LEAVE SMOG AREA, SAY 60 ON U.C.L.A. MEDICAL FACULTY

9. POLLUTED AIR FACTOR IN COMMON COLDS
10. EMOTIONAL, PHYSICAL CHANGES CAUSED BY SMOG, TESTS SHOW
11. SCIENTISTS WARN OF THREAT TO OXYGEN SUPPLY
12. MANKIND IS STANDING TRIAL AS A MASS POISONER
13. "SILO POISONING" CHEMICAL NOW CITY AIR PROBLEM, DOCTOR SAYS
14. POSSIBILITY OF SMOG CAUSING MUTATIONS RAISED BY SCIENTIST
15. MAN COULD BE BURNING HIMSELF OUT OF EXISTENCE
16. MAN'S TOLERANCE FOR SMOG IS NEARING LIMIT, SCIENTIST SAYS
17. BREATHING CAN KILL YOU
18. TROJANS WIN DUEL IN SMOG AND FOG, 28-16 . . .

Evidence in the case at bar will show that medical authorities urge that people stay in their houses during smoggy days. Thus, the smog prevents people from going out to their backyards. This certainly constitutes an interference with the possession of a portion of real property.

The causes of action in negligent design and strict liability are well stated. Plaintiff has clearly alleged that the motor vehicles manufactured, distributed, and sold by defendants are defective because their exhaust emissions are proximately injuring the members of the class who are within the foreseeable risk of harm. That is, one who resides in the county of Los Angeles can be reasonably expected to be injured by the exhaust emissions caused by defective automobiles. In *Elmore v. American Motors Corporation,* 70 A.C. 615 (1969), the Supreme Court held that "the doctrine of strict liability in tort is available in an action for personal injuries by a bystander against the manufacturer and the retailer" (70 A.C. at 624–625). Specifically, the case permitted recovery by a third party against the manufacturer and retailer of a motor vehicle with a defectively connected drive shaft. The court stated

that such an automobile constitutes a substantial hazard
to other persons. . . .

Whether air is considered a public resource or is considered to be "owned" by the state, the state cannot convey
it away. *People v. Gold Run D. and M. Company,* 66 Cal.
138 (1884) involved the pollution of public rivers, but its
principles and language are relevant and persuasive:

> As we have already said, the rights of the people in the
> navigable rivers of the state are paramount and con-
> trolling. The state holds the absolute right to all
> navigable waters and the soils under them. . . . The soil
> she holds as trustee of a public trust for the benefit of
> the people; and she may, by her legislature, grant it to
> an individual; but she cannot grant the rights of the
> people to the use of the navigable waters flowing over
> it; these are inalienable. Any grant of the soil, there-
> fore, would be subject to the paramount rights of the
> people to the use of the highway. And such was the
> doctrine of the common law. "The *jus privatum*," says
> Lord Hale, in De Jure Maris, p. 22, "must not prej-
> udice the *jus publicum,* wherewith public rivers and
> arms of the sea are affected to public use." It is, there-
> fore, beyond the power of legislatures to destroy or
> abridge such rights, or to authorize their impairment
> (66 Cal. at 151–52).

The court affirmed an injunction against defendant permanently enjoining it from polluting a river.

The court recognized that it was a long-standing custom
for hydraulic miners to dump wastes into the river. In this
connection, it stated (66 Cal. at 151):

> [A] legitimate private business, founded upon a local
> custom, may grow into a force to threaten the safety
> of the people, and destruction to public and private
> rights; and when it develops into that condition, the
> custom upon which it is founded becomes unreason-
> able, because dangerous to public and private rights,
> and cannot be invoked to justify the continuance of the
> business in an unlawful manner.

What the court said in 1884 with respect to the pollution
of public waterways is true today with respect to massive

air pollution. That is, many years ago, during our industrialization period, air pollution might have been an acceptable cost of building the economy. The times have changed. The plaintiff and the represented class are literally facing agonizing death. The entire county will be uninhabitable in a few years unless the court takes action. The state having no power to give away the inalienable right to use the navigable waterways, a fortiori it has no power to give away the public air.

The law has recognized that navigable water is a scarce resource (*People v. Gold Run D. and M. Company,* supra). It should now recognize what all mankind knows, that the earth is a self-contained unit and that the atmosphere is scarce. The oxygen we breathe is generated by plant life, most of it from the ocean (which is also being polluted by many of the defendants in this case). The air we breathe is certainly as important if not more important than our navigable water. The state may not "give away" our breathable air in the guise of pollution laws which authorize pollution. . . .

"Smog control is a problem requiring continuous study, research, and supervision." So long as this is the attitude of defendants and government, the situation will get worse. The evidence will show that there has been enough study and research. *What we need is clean air!!!* The technology and knowledge and expertise exist now. What is lacking is the will and determination.

The elaborate history of air pollution and the futile attempts to control it are summarized by the defense. The frightening thing about the history is the time span. The Director of Air Pollution was established in 1945. More laws, agencies, boards, etc., have come and gone. Politicians have been elected on the issue. But the air gets filthier. Time is running out.

5.8 Saving the Estuaries—Putting Teeth in the "Trust Doctrine"

There is presently pending in the Eastern District of Virginia a unique case under a "trust doctrine" which is

attempting to defeat the sale of lands abutting the Hunting
Creek Estuary of the Potomac River. Bernard Cohen, attorney for the plaintiffs, has defined and found precedent
in the law for a trust doctrine holding that the sale of this
kind of land to a private developer would be a loss to the
people of Virginia of their natural and beautiful riverfront,
as well as an illegal act by the general assembly of Virginia.
It is the plaintiff's contention in that suit that the Commonwealth of Virginia holds all subaqueous land of navigable waters in trust for all the people and may not dispose of said land except in aid of navigation. Counsel for
the plaintiffs holds that any attempt by the state legislature
to breach that trust is illegal on various constitutional
grounds. The complaint and pretrial statement, as well as
the summary of the witnesses' statements which have been
filed in court, are all set forth in the excellent set of papers
that follow.

(a) Complaint in Fairfax County Federation of Citizens Associations v. Hunting Towers Operating Company, Inc.

The plaintiff, Fairfax County Federation of Citizens
Associations, Inc., is a nonprofit federation of approximately 120 citizens' associations having approximately
30,000 members in its component groups. The Federation is concerned with the preservation and conservation
of natural resources, particularly as they affect the urban
and suburban environments, and acts to protect the interests of its members in case of any improper or illegal
exercise of public power affecting its interests.

● ● ●

There are common questions of law and fact affecting
the several rights of all citizens of the State of Virginia.

6. This is a class action to declare Chapter 546 of the
Acts of Assembly of 1964 unconstitutional because it is
in violation of the constitutional rights of the plaintiffs
and all others similarly situated. Plaintiffs additionally
seek a declaration of their rights pursuant to §2201 of
Title 28 in that the defendants, their officers, agents, employees or attorneys, and those persons in active concert
or participation with them have stated their intentions to

proceed with the fill of subaqueous public lands of the Potomac River in violation of Article IV, §2, and the Fourteenth Amendment of the United States Constitution and the laws of the United States made pursuant thereto and in violation of the constitution of the state of Virginia and in particular §§1, 11, 63, and 185.

NATURE OF THE ACTION

7. On March 31, 1964, the General Assembly of Virginia enacted House Bill 591 as Chapter 546 of the Acts of the Assembly.

8. Chapter 546 authorizes the conveyance to Francis T. Murtha, Trustee, of all of the Commonwealth's rights, title, and interest in and to certain subaqueous public lands lying in the Potomac River.

• • •

11. Howard P. Hoffman Associates, Inc., and Francis T. Murtha, Trustee, have applied for and received a permit from the U.S. Corps of Engineers to fill approximately 9.4 acres of the total of 36.5 acres authorized to be conveyed under Chapter 546.

• • •

13. All of the area included in Chapter 546 lies in Hunting Creek Estuary of the Potomac River.

14. Said estuary and the Potomac River are "navigable waters" as that term is used as a legal word of art.

• • •

19. The area known as Duke Marsh forms the southern border of Hunting Creek Estuary and has been for many years a wildlife preserve for gulls, terns, and diving ducks, and other waterfowl.

20. The northern border of Hunting Creek Estuary is Jones Point which is being developed by the National Park Service as a fifty-acre recreation park.

COUNT ONE
• • •

21. The Commonwealth of Virginia holds subaqueous land of navigable waters in trust for all of the people and may not dispose of said land except in aid of navigation.

22. The attempted transfer of said land by the state legislature is in breach of said trust.

WHEREFORE, plaintiffs pray for the following relief,

(*a*) That pursuant to title 28, USC. 2281 and 2284, a three-judge federal district court be immediately convened to hear and determine this proceeding;

(*b*) That Chapter 546 of the Acts of Assembly of 1964 be declared unconstitutional and that any deed heretofore or hereafter granted by the Commonwealth of Virginia be declared null and void; and

(*c*) Further that a temporary restraining order be issued, followed by a permanent injunction restraining and enjoining defendants Hunting Towers Operating Company, Inc., Murtha and Hoffman from filling any of the land described in Chapter 546.

COUNT TWO
• • •

25. There was no debate nor were there more than perfunctory, deminimus committee hearings.

26. The stated purpose and findings of the Act are arbitrary and capricious and bear no resemblance to actual fact.

27. The action of the Virginia Legislature in enacting Chapter 546 lacked due process and equal protection of the law.

• • •

WHEREFORE, plaintiffs pray that Chapter 546 of the Acts of Assembly of 1964 be declared unconstitutional and that any deed heretofore or hereafter granted by the Commonwealth of Virginia be declared null and void.

COUNT THREE
• • •

29. The consideration called for by Chapter 546 of the Acts of Assembly, 1964, is not less than $30,000.

30. The value of the land in question is considerably more than $30,000.

31. Plaintiffs are denied equal protection of the law

in that the arbitrary minimum price is offered only to specified private parties.

32. Plaintiffs are denied their property rights in the subject property without due process of law because the sum realized from the authorized private sale will be substantially less than would have been realized had the land been put up for public sale and other potential purchasers not excluded.

33. The effect of this "giveaway" is to indirectly place the credit of the state of Virginia behind this private venture, in the form of a donation, which is in violation of §185 of the Virginia Constitution.

WHEREFORE, plaintiffs pray that Chapter 546 of the Acts of Assembly, 1964, be declared unconstitutional and of no force and effect and that any deed heretofore or hereafter granted by the Commonwealth of Virginia be declared null and void.

34. The proposed fill of land by defendants Murtha and Hoffman will:

(a) permanently change the shoreline of the Potomac to the irreparable harm of the plaintiffs;

(b) seriously and permanently injure and destroy nearby Jones Point Park which is currently being developed by the National Park Service as a public recreational area;

(c) seriously and permanently injure and destroy nearby areas as a wildlife preserve;

(d) adversely affect the navigability of Hunting Creek Estuary of the Potomac River.

WHEREFORE, plaintiffs pray that a temporary restraining order be issued, followed by a permanent injunction, restraining and enjoining defendants Hunting Towers Operating Company, Inc., Murtha and Hoffman from filling any of the land described in Chapter 546.

> FAIRFAX COUNTY FEDERATION OF
> CITIZENS ASSOCIATIONS, INC.
> NORTHERN VIRGINIA CONSERVATION
> COUNCIL, INC.
> CITIZENS COUNCIL FOR A CLEAN
> POTOMAC, INC.

Counsel for Plaintiffs:

COHEN, HIRSCHKOP & HALL
110 North Royal Street
P. O. Box 234
Alexandria, Virginia 22313

(b) Pretrial Statement of Plaintiffs

The plaintiffs submit the following issues and statement of positions as well as an outline of witnesses and their testimony on those issues, in accordance with the pretrial order of this honorable court:

I. *ISSUES*

A. Who owns the property to be conveyed by Chapter 546 of the Virginia Acts of Assembly of 1964?

1. The plaintiffs maintain that the Commonwealth of Virginia owns all of the land described in Chapter 546 and that the nature and quality of the ownership is a trust for the benefit of all of the citizens of the United States.

2. The plaintiffs maintain that in addition to the trust ownership of the subject land the riparian owners have a legal interest, but differ with the defendants on what that interest is. Plaintiffs say the riparian owners' interest is not absolute, fee simple but are mere usufructuary rights, and are subservient to the paramount rights of the public.

3. Plaintiffs say the public rights are property rights and other rights protected by the 9th and 14th Amendments of the Constitution as well as the Virginia Constitution.

    (a) In addition to the property rights in the submerged land itself, there is a property right in the ecosystem, which is very valuable.

B. Is the conveyance by the state a breach of the trust? Plaintiffs emphatically say "yes," because:

1. land is unique; especially land under navigable waters;

2. the total *cost* to the public of the giveaway monumentally exceeds any public benefits;

3. there is no dollar value payable to the state which can compensate for the permanent loss of thirty-six

acres of the Potomac River, a valuable national, natural resource;

4. the damage to the plaintiffs' rights in the ecosystem are an injury to valuable constitutionally protected rights.

II. *WITNESSES AND THEIR STATEMENTS*

In order to understand the significant magnitude of the loss to the public (the beneficiaries of the trust) it will be necessary to understand to some extent the subject of "ecology" and the "ecosystem." Ecology deals with the interrelationship between all living things and the environment. (For example—algae and protozoa, animal and man, vis-à-vis air, soil, and water.)

A. Dr. William O. Negherbom. One expert witness for the plaintiffs (Dr. William O. Negherbom, 109 Center Street, N., Vienna, Virginia) will testify as to the definition of ecology and the ecosystem; the great significance of the Potomac River and its relationship to the unique characteristics of Chesapeake Bay; the relationship of all estuaries to the Potomac River and the specific importance of Hunting Creek Estuary to the Potomac and Chesapeake Bay; the detrimental and irreversible, significant damage to the ecology of the Potomac River and Chesapeake Bay if 36.5 acres of land under the estuary are filled. Dr. Negherbom will state that the loss can and must be measured relatively against any purported benefit and that in this case there will be a serious net loss to the public if the fill is allowed to proceed.

B. Dr. Roland C. Clement. Another expert witness (Dr. Roland C. Clement, Weed Avenue, Norfolk, Connecticut) will testify that there has been a lack of ecological awareness regarding the value of estuaries which would be compounded were 36.5 acres of Hunting Creek Estuary deeded away and filled. He will state that:

1. The Potomac River is a valuable natural resource in and of itself, measurable in several ways, including but not necessarily limited to navigation, recreation, esthetics, wildlife habitat, and as part of the ecosystem.

2. Society has failed to conceive of our resources holis-

tically (i.e., that they have an existence other than as
the mere sum of their parts) as part of a process or
ecosystem.

3. Removals from the ecosystem are not a mere subtrac-
tion process but can cause collapse of the whole system. That is because the processes in the estuary are
synergistic: the behavior of the whole is not predictable
from the behavior of its parts.

4. There are alternatives available for correcting the hor-
rendous damage to this watershed.

5. Landfilling is not a correction but will result in a net
social and economic loss.

> FAIRFAX COUNTY FEDERATION OF
> CITIZENS ASSOCIATIONS, INC., *et al.*
> Plaintiffs

(c) Memorandum to Court by Plaintiffs

The defendants have misinterpreted the position of the
plaintiffs and the trust doctrine and its applicability to the
case at bar. First, they have used the confusion in the case
law to label the trust doctrine as insubstantial; second, they
imply a rigidity in plaintiffs' position. Neither conclusion is
correct.

The plaintiffs candidly stated that the trust doctrine was
not a rigid, inflexible rule of law, but rather a standard
which must be followed if the state is to meet its fiduciary
responsibility in protecting the public interest. The trust
doctrine also procedurally aids plaintiffs' position in that
certain presumptions in its favor are established. Plaintiff
reiterates its conclusion contained in the original brief that
public lands may not be alienated except in extraordinary
circumstances and then only for promoting public benefit.

What Are the Criteria and Indicia the Courts Look to in Applying the Trust Doctrine?

Plaintiffs assert that a thorough reading of the trust
doctrine cases from the states which have had to deal extensively with the problem shows that the courts have
carved out standards and criteria for applying the trust
doctrine to individual cases. The most significant standard

gathered from reading all of the cases is that the transfer is *necessary* for the promotion and benefit of the public beneficiaries of the trust. One consideration in determining necessity is whether or not there is an alternative to the transfer of the trust property. In further considering the necessity of the proposed transfer the courts consider certain indicia in determining whether or not the public interest will be promoted. The indicia of promoting the public interest will include:

1. public control;
2. public use and purpose;
3. will the resource be changed (e.g., will a lake remain a lake or will an estuary remain an estuary);
4. will other uses of the resource be greatly impaired;
5. will the change offer greater convenience to the public at large.

The trust doctrine evolved as an answer to a very important and complex problem: Under what circumstances can the object of a public trust be alienated?

If after applying all of the above criteria the decision is made in favor of the transfer, then one additional factor is examined and that is the question of fair consideration. The public must not be cheated in the transfer. This requires consideration of monies involved and also whether or not there can be *any* fair consideration for the transfer where a very unique natural resource is involved.

Let us examine the application of the established criteria to the Hunting Creek Estuary case.

1. Is the project necessary?

No—there has been no showing of necessity to build a residential apartment project at the subject location. There has been no showing by the defendant that this is a needed project and that there is no alternative. There has been no showing that the claimed objectionable features of the estuary (odor and pollution) cannot be alternatively treated.

2. Will a public body control the use of the transferred area?

No—the grant is an outright grant to a private developer, and there will be no public control.

3. Will the transferred area be for public purposes and public use?

No—a private apartment project is planned; this represents the most private type of use.

4. Will the estuary be changed?

Yes—Dr. Clement and Dr. Negherbom both predict that the value of the estuary and its place in the food chain will be permanently and irreparable damaged.

5. Will the public use of the estuary as an estuary be destroyed or greatly impaired?

Yes—the major public interest in the estuary is as a wildlife habitat and for its value in the ecological food chain. The testimony of Drs. Negherbom and Clement as to the adverse effect on the estuary is uncontradicted.

6. Will any great benefit accrue to the public at large as a result of the transfer and landfill?

No—the project will be of great benefit only to a private entrepreneur and the few people who by virtue of their financial circumstances will be able to take advantage of the superior residential qualities of the development. The claimed benefit of increased taxes flowing to the city of Alexandria is more than offset by the destruction of the estuary as an important element in the ecosystem of the entire geographical area involved.

While certain transfers of trust property may be held to be proper, it is clear that the attempted transfer of Hunting Creek Estuary is so far over the line as to be a prime example of a constitutionally prohibited transfer.

What Are the Public Rights, Privileges, and Immunities Protected Under the State Trust and Has There Been a Breach of the Trust?

In two centuries of case law on the subject, "the protection of the rights of the public, whatever those may be" still lacks clear enumeration. Instead, the courts have dealt with the problem of public rights in and to navigable waters and its subaqueous lands on a case by case basis, raising the trust theory and the concept of the public interest on some occasions and ignoring it or claiming to distinguish it on others.

Recognizing, however, the indisputable fact that these rights do exist, it is completely within the power and jurisdiction of this court, and more importantly is the obligation of this court, to recognize and protect these rights with precision when called upon to do so. Drawing on existing statutory and case law, and from the literal language and intent of the Fifth, Ninth, and Fourteenth Amendments of the Constitution protecting life, liberty, and property, the court must determine whether the rights asserted by the plaintiffs to free navigation, unique property rights in submerged land, natural resources, scenic beauty, ecological integrity, and fish and wildlife reserves are public rights protected by the Constitution and its Amendments; and whether the state, by the attempted sale of part of Hunting Creek Estuary to the defendants, with knowledge of defendant's intention to drain and fill this land and erect structures not in aid of navigation, has denied to the plaintiffs, and the class they represent, public rights, privileges and immunities fully protected by the Constitution.

In *Scenic Hudson Preservation Conference v. Federal Power Commission,* 354 F.2d 608 (1965), the Second Circuit Court of Appeals was confronted with just such a question. Plaintiffs seeking to set aside orders of the Federal Power Commission granting Consolidated Edison a license to construct a hydroelectric project asserted successfully that the Commission had failed to compile a record sufficient to support its decision and, more importantly, that certain relevant factors, such as the public interest in scenic beauty and the conservation of natural resources, were ignored.

In this case, the court clearly recognized the responsibility of the Federal Power Commission in the "conservation of natural resources, the maintenance of natural beauty, and the preservation of historic sites" (354 F.2d at 614). While this responsibility was defined in the Federal Power Act, 16 U.S.C. §803(*a*), the existence of these rights are not limited by the presence of such a statute. They are rights of free men and exist without benefit of government. Free men create government to protect these rights from infringement by other men; they do not abdicate to the government they create the power to abrogate the very rights which the government was created to protect.

Congress, in an effort to protect the public's right to the conservation of the nation's natural resources and related environment, including fish and wildlife and recreational values therein, has on numerous occasions passed legislation on the subject (see Federal Water Pollution Control Act, 33 U.S.C. 466, *et. seq.*: Fish and Wildlife Coordination Act, 16 U.S.C. 661–66c: Fish and Wildlife Act of 1956, 16 U.S.C. 742*a, et seq.*). On this point it is useful to quote from Senate Report 1981, 85th Congress, 2d Session, accompanying the amendment Bill, H.R. 13118 to the Fish and Wildlife Coordination Act, cited *supra*:

> The dredging of these bays and estuaries along the coastlines to aid navigation and also to provide landfills for real estate and similar developments, both by federal agencies or other agencies under permit from the Corps of Engineers, has increased tremendously in the last five years. Obviously, dredging activity of this sort has a profound disturbing effect on aquatic life, including shrimp and other species, of tremendous significance to the commercial fishing industry. The bays, estuaries, and related marsh areas are highly important as spawning and nursery grounds for many commercial species of fish and shellfish. . . .

These acts are an acknowledgment of the existence of some of the very rights plaintiffs herein assert.

Plaintiffs will demonstrate to this court (in this brief and by evidence at trial), the gross, overwhelming, cumulative effect of depletion of natural resources, ecological imbalance, elimination of scenic beauty, and the destruction of fish and wildlife reserves and recreational areas caused by landfill projects. We believe this will clarify the nature of the public trust in submerged land and help to crystallize and articulate all of the public rights subject to constitutional safeguards which fall within the penumbra of rights protected by emanations from a number of constitutional amendments including the Fifth, Ninth, and Fourteenth Amendments.

The Ninth Amendment of the United States Constitution states that "the enumeration in the Constitution, of certain rights, shall not *be* construed to deny or disparage others retained by the people."

(d) Postscript

The "Trust Doctrine" was effective in keeping the land in the public domain, and as of July 10, 1970, the builders gave up on this project.

5.9 Lead Pollution from Automotive Exhausts—Get the Lead Out

On May 5, 1970, the Environmental Defense Fund (EDF) submitted a petition to the Department of Health, Education, and Welfare (HEW) seeking remedies for the lead pollution caused by the presence of lead in automotive exhausts. The petition detailed the probable health hazard, primarily to urban children, from this atmospheric lead. The petition and portions of the memorandum follow.

(a) Petition for Action Under the Clean Air Act Directed at Eliminating Automotive Lead Pollution from the Atmosphere

UNITED STATES DEPARTMENT OF
HEALTH, EDUCATION AND WELFARE
In re

ENVIRONMENTAL DEFENSE FUND, INC.
Individually and on behalf of all the people
of the United States of America
Petitioner

The Environmental Defense Fund, Incorporated (EDF), is a non-profit, public benefit membership corporation organized under the laws of the State of New York. It is comprised of scientists, lawyers and other citizens dedicated to the protection of man's environment from harmful and unnecessary intrusions. Because it is concerned that automotive lead emissions constitute a dangerous health problem threatening man with serious physiological effects including the retardation of full mental development, EDF hereby petitions the Secretary for the following action on behalf of its membership and the public generally:

1. The immediate formulation and announcement of atmospheric lead air quality criteria;
2. The establishment of an automotive lead emission standard that makes it unlawful to emit lead from automotive exhausts;
3. The immediate issuance of a directive to automobile manufacturers instructing them to disclose prominently to the consuming public the octane requirements of new and old automobiles and the disadvantageous environmental and economic consequences of using excessively high octane gasoline.
4. The immediate prohibition of the use of leaded gasoline in vehicles owned or operated by federal departments and agencies; and
5. The immediate implementation of the Fuel Additives Registration provision of the Air Quality Act.

In view of the high atmospheric concentrations of automotive lead emissions and the urgency of the human health problem, we request that action on this petition be taken immediately. A memorandum in support of the petition is attached.

> Respectfully submitted,
> BERLIN, ROISMAN AND KESSLER
> 1910 N Street, N. W.
> Washington D. C. 20036

May 5, 1970

(b) Memorandum in Support of EDF Petition

Blood lead concentrations in average Americans today exceed one fourth of those considered diagnostic for lead poisoning in adults. Americans are unusual among the world's peoples in that they accumulate lead throughout their entire lives. Lead poisoning can produce liver, kidney and brain damage and deterioration of the central nervous and reproductive systems. Children are especially susceptible to lead poisoning, mental retardation being one of many possible effects.

The health implications of lead are not confined to the

effects of acute exposure. Chronic exposure at levels typical of urban environments is known to produce biochemical changes in healthy adults. In animal experiments, injury has been observed at lead exposure levels typical of those experienced by urban Americans. Decreased longevity was found in chromium deficient mice with lead body burdens typical of Americans. Americans are thought to be chromium deficient.

At least one third of the lead body burden of urban dwelling Americans is attributable to lead emitted from automotive exhausts. It is therefore imperative that this wholly unnecessary source of atmospheric lead pollution be eliminated. The detrimental effects of lead in the biosphere have long been recognized.

A. THE HEALTH PROBLEM

Lead poisoning (plumbism, saturnism) is one of man's earliest self-inflicted diseases. The extent of the problem has been recognized in a report prepared under the sponsorship of the Department of Commerce (Morse 1967):

> Lead has been known to be toxic for over two thousand years and in spite of its recognition as an industrial poison, it continues to be the cause of numerous outbreaks of chemical intoxication of industrial or accidental origin . . . Lead is so widely used in modern technology that occupational health and public health authorities must always be alert to controlling the hazard.

Lead poisoning first became a major problem in Roman times, when lead became widely available as a byproduct of silver smelting. The Roman difficulties stemmed from the custom of using lead as a lining material for containers of food, water and wine and from its use as an actual ingredient of wine and medicines. It has been suggested that lead poisoning was a major factor in the decline of the Roman Empire (Gilfillan 1965).

During the early years of the twentieth century, lead was widely used in paint. In 1918, it was estimated that 40% of all painters showed evidence of lead poisoning (Sollman 1967).

Today obvious symptoms of lead poisoning are most frequently found in ghetto children, who ingest peeling paint and putty and are exposed to especially high concentrations of atmospheric lead from automotive emissions.

Almost all of the increase in lead concentration occurred within the last 50 years. The sharp rise in lead level corresponds closely with the introduction of tetraethyl lead into gasoline in 1923.

Lead is now used as an additive in 90% of all motor gasoline made in the United States. In 1968 in the United States about 300,000 tons of lead were used as gasoline additives, which is about 25% of the total lead used in the United States.

In 1966 motor vehicles discharged 190,000 tons of lead into the atmosphere (Morse 1967). Recently, it was estimated that the removal of lead from automotive fuel would "eliminate(s) the 500 million pounds of lead which is currently being emitted from the exhaust pipe of the nation's automotive fleet. A substantial portion of the lead in humans is attributable to automotive emissions.

The average person breathes about 20 m³ of air daily and the efficiency at which the body absorbs inhaled lead approximates 40%, whereas only 10% of ingested lead is absorbed by the body. (Patterson 1965; Kehoe 1959; 1960; 1964a; 1964b.)

The amount of lead that is absorbed from the atmosphere is a function of the size of the lead particle inhaled. Lead emitted from automobile exhausts is particularly suited for retention in the atmosphere and eventual absorption by the body. About 75 percent of particulate lead from automobile gasoline combustion is less than 0.90 microns in mean diameter, a size that easily reaches the alveoli of the lungs.

Analysis of measured blood lead levels in Americans shows a direct correlation with exposure to atmospheric lead (Goldsmith 1967; Craig 1970). At least one-third of the lead in urban dwelling Americans is directly attributable to automotive emissions. Additionally, an appreciable portion of the lead in food may originate from fallout of lead introduced into the atmosphere by automobiles. Lead concentrations in plants along highways often exceed 100 ppm. Americans, in contrast to citizens of foreign countries, are not in lead balance.

B. LEAD EMISSIONS AGGRAVATE OTHER AUTOMOTIVE POLLUTION PROBLEMS

Automotive lead emissions not only pose a serious health threat in their own right, but they also aggravate other automotive pollution problems. As stated by Assistant Commissioner Megonnel of NAPCA, "to add insult to injury, lead in gasoline tends to build up in the internal combusion engine with the result that hydrocarbon emissions are increased."

The testimony of Standard Oil Company of Indiana was most persuasive. That company "tested more than 200 catalysts, particularly those useful in reducing emissions of nitrogen oxides, and found none that performed satisfactorily with leaded fuels. [It] did find a number of catalysts that work effectively for extended periods of time, but only with unleaded gasoline."

Nevertheless, oil companies have resisted developing the refining capability needed to produce unleaded gasoline allegedly because of the economic cost to the consumer. The economics, however, are open to question. Assistant Commissioner Megonnel has observed:

> . . . it is a well advertised fact that leaded gasoline shortens the life of the spark plugs, and that the halogens added to gasoline to scavenge the lead, shorten the life of tailpipes and mufflers. It poisons catalysts which hold promise in achieving very low emissions. When we compare what the American Petroleum Institute has established as the additional cost of lead-free gasoline, with what we estimate the consumer would save in spark plug and exhaust system replacements, we figure the consumer would be out of pocket about $1.50 per year for lead-free gasoline, and lead-free lungs.

C. SEVERAL DECISIVE ACTIONS ARE REQUIRED WITHOUT DELAY

All scientific work is incomplete—whether it be observational or experimental. All scientific work is liable to be upset or modified by advancing knowledge. That does not confer upon us a freedom to ignore the knowledge we already have, or to postpone the action that it appears to demand at a given time (Hill, 1965).

At best, knowledge of the scientific and medical realities of atmospheric lead pollution is incomplete. Existing knowledge demands decisive, expeditious action, however, for it compels but one conclusion: atmospheric lead, at levels now common in urban areas, is a human health hazard and serves no necessary purpose. This being the case it is incumbent upon the Secretary to do the following:

1. Atmospheric Lead Air Quality Criteria Must Be Formulated and Announced.

Air quality criteria are, as characterized by the House Committee on Interstate and Foreign Commerce, "The *sine qua non* to effective air pollution control . . . the issuance of such criteria is among the prerequisites for the development of air quality standards by the States. . . .

Congress was particularly concerned that criteria be promulgated expeditiously for the "subtler, less dramatic long-range effects of air pollution [which] are of much more serious consequence to the population as a whole than the occasional major tragedy."

Atmospheric lead represents such a threat. Children are particularly vulnerable to its metabolic and biological effects and large segments of the population have already accumulated body lead levels approaching one-half the generally accepted level of industrial toxicity. The promulgation of atmospheric lead criteria must not be postponed; more than three years ago the Congress was assured that they would be forthcoming.

2. Automotive Lead Emission Standards Must Be Established Which Make It Unlawful to Emit Lead from Automotive Exhausts.

Section 202(a) of the Air Quality Act directs the Secretary to

. . . by regulation, giving appropriate consideration to technological feasibility and economic costs, prescribe *as soon as practicable* standards, applicable to the emission of any kind of substance, from any class or classes of new motor vehicles or new motor vehicle engines, which in his judgment cause or contribute to, or are likely to cause or contribute to, air pollution which endangers the health or welfare of any persons, *and such standards shall apply to such vehicles or engines whether they are designed as complete systems or incorporate other devices to prevent or control such pollution.*

The underscored language, which represents the amendment made to the provision by the 1967 legislation, emphasizes that the Secretary is under a mandate to establish standards expeditiously, including lead emission standards.

3. Automobile Manufacturers Must be Directed to Disclose Engine Octane Requirements.

Since the higher octane gasolines generally contain increased amounts of lead it is important that the demand for and utilization of those grades be reduced. The consumer gains no benefit by using a higher octane gasoline than is required in his automobile. Indeed, such use exacerbates our air pollution problem and wastes consumers' money. Most owners, however, do not know the octane requirements of their vehicles.

The automotive industry should be directed 1) to disclose prominently (for example both in some appropriate place on the vehicle and in the owner's manual), the octane requirement of each new automobile, the absence of any benefit resulting from the use of a higher octane gasoline and the adverse consequences (environmental and economic) of utilizing gasoline with excessively high octane and 2) to suitably convey similar information to the owners of existing automobiles. The Federal Trade Commission presently is considering promulgation of a rule which would require service stations to prominently display the octane number for all gasoline which they market. Although this is desirable it can accomplish its intended objective only if the consumer is aware of his automobile's octane needs.

4. The Secretary Must Prohibit the Use of Leaded Gasoline in Vehicles Owned or Operated by Federal Departments or Agencies.

The National Environmental Policy Act imposes upon federal departments and agencies the responsibility for taking the leadership in pollution abatement. This responsibility was underscored by the President on March 5 when he affirmed that: "The Federal Government shall provide leadership in protecting and enhancing the quality of the Nation's environment to sustain and enrich human life" and instructed federal agencies to "initiate measures needed to direct their policies, plans and programs so as to meet national environmental goals." (Executive Order 11514.)

If this objective is to be realized the Secretary must prohibit the use of leaded gasoline in vehicles owned or operated by federal departments or agencies. The Clear Air Act authorizes the Secretary to take such action. Congress, distressed over the failure of the Federal Government to take the leadership in cleaning up its own pollution, authorized the Secretary in 1963 to "establish classes of potential pollution sources for which any Federal department or agency having jurisdiction over any building, installation, *or other property shall, before discharging any matter into the air of the United States, obtain a permit from the Secretary for such discharge,* such permits to be issued for a specified period of time to be determined by the Secretary and subject to revocation if the Secretary finds pollution is endangering the health and welfare of any persons."

It is incumbent upon the Secretary to declare automotive lead emissions a pollution source and to prohibit their discharge by any vehicle under federal control without the prior issuance of a permit. Federal agencies have the capability of converting to alternative, cleaner fuels—such as unleaded gasoline, compressed natural gas, liquified natural gas, liquified petroleum gas and propane. They must be required to do so.

5. The Registration of Fuel Additives Provision of the Air Quality Act Must Be Implemented Without Delay.

Section 210 of the Air Quality Act authorizes the Secretary to collect information about automotive fuel additives. To date no effort has been made to implement that section. It is incumbent upon the Secretary to immediately initiate a program for the expeditious collection of that necessary information so that public health and welfare can be protected as envisioned by the Congress.

Respectfully submitted,
BERLIN, ROISMAN AND KESSLER
1910 N Street, N. W.
Washington, D. C. 20036

CHAPTER 6

SUITS AGAINST THE GOVERNMENT—RADIATION, PESTICIDES, AND CONSERVATION

SUITS AGAINST THE GOVERNMENT— RADIATION, PESTICIDES, NOISE AND CONSERVATION

The concept of protecting the environmental equities demands that projects like the SST (supersonic transport plane) be fully tested before production starts.

The Government should not set standards for air and noise pollution after the fact. The argument that billions have been spent on developing the SST, and that its production should not be curtailed just because it is loud on takeoff, spews out vapor and smoke that does not look or smell good and sticks in the lungs—such arguments have been all too often successful. Petitions have been served on the Federal Aviation Administration to set these critical environmental standards for the SST *NOW*—before this sonic boomer shatters the sanctuary of the few remaining places of silence left to man and beast.

The proliferation of DDT before its permanent and nondegradable properties were fully tested or understood underscores the need for holding up production and distribution until scientific testing has been completed. Government must place the burden on industry to establish by competent means that the product will do the job as advertised with no serious harmful effects on our environment. The failure to follow this procedure, and the dangers that follow, are clearly delineated in the DDT fiasco.

The nuclear blast in Colorado known as "Project Rulison" forced the Atomic Energy Commission to publicly state why it was important to allow the blast, and how it would be a useful and safe venture. The brief on "Project Rulison" describes the unsuccessful fight to stop the blast.

The Department of Transportation considered paving over the great swamp alongside the Everglades National Park, to use it as a huge airport to land the upcoming SSTs. (You see how the problem feeds on itself.) The Sierra Club was successful in thwarting this potentially disastrous insult to the wildlife that remains in southern Florida.

The Army Corps of Engineers' attempt to dam up and straighten out with concrete the Oklawaha River are all described in this chapter, as well as the attempt to put the South Carolina Hilton Head Island fishermen out of business.

All of these insults to the environment and ecology are *interrelated*. Through the cycle of water pollution, evaporation of polluted water up through acrid smoke and air, and through factory fumes, and cooling condensation with precipitation coming down now as dirty rain or snow, the problem is escalating. And for those that smirk at the concept of dirty rain, please recall the instance of the "Lucky Dragon," those innocent Japanese fishermen who were struck by rain falling through a radiation belt—with devastating results.

All of us are in the unbreakable habits of breathing and drinking, and the great equalizer is that the owner of the polluting factory breathes the same air and drinks the same water as do his workmen. It is the only air and water in town to use, and that fact dawning on the polluter, along with litigation making pollution more expensive than controlling it, might turn the tide and make the water we drink taste like it used to, and the air that we breathe sweet like it used to be.

6.1 Project Rulison: The Atomic Energy Commission on Trial

Ever since the spectacular explosion of July 16, 1945, man has attempted to harness the vast potential of atomic energy for peaceful purposes. A relatively small amount of atomic fuel can produce a tremendous amount of power, and an atomic reactor does not need oxygen to operate.

However, many problems remain to be solved before atomic power use becomes practical. Dangerous side effects of thermal pollution, and difficulty in disposing of atomic wastes, in addition to the possibility of nuclear explosion and the resulting fallout, are problems which must be solved before atomic power plants can be put into operation.

Since fossil fuels with their high sulfur content give off carbon dioxide when used to produce energy, they are a serious source of air pollution. And since these conventional fuels will become exorbitantly expensive as their limited supply diminishes, atomic energy for power is of vital importance.

Nuclear energy plants in the United States use boiling water reactors and pressurized water reactors. Water is converted to steam, which drives the turbine and produces power and electricity. We have discussed the thermal pollution problems in the Michigan (§5.2) and Florida (§5.1) cases, and with the Rulison case we now tackle the problem of an actual bomb blast for the purpose of stimulating gas production.

Project Rulison is a joint experiment sponsored by the Atomic Energy Commission, the Department of Interior and Austral Oil Company, Inc. The program manager is CER Geonuclear Corporation. Rulison is part of the "plowshare program" of the AEC, which is designed to develop peaceful uses of nuclear explosive technology. The scientific purpose of the project is to study the economic and technical feasibility of nuclear stimulation of the low-permeability, gas-bearing Mesa Verde sandstone formation in the Rulison field of Colorado.

"Nuclear stimulation" entails the detonation of a nuclear device which will create a cavity and attendant fracture system, resulting in the production of natural gas in the formation. The Mesa Verde site, because of its low permeability, does not produce natural gas in commercial quantities, although it does have a significant gas reserve.

The original action to enjoin Project Rulison brought by the American Civil Liberties Union was summarily dismissed by the federal district court. Following the dismissal, a second action was brought on behalf of the Colorado Open Space Coordinating Council (COSC). Although the court refused to enjoin the nuclear blast, a preliminary restraining order was entered prohibiting the release of the radioactive gases trapped underground following the blast. The ACLU action was then revived, and consolidated with the COSC action. Ultimately, however, the district court allowed the release of the gas. The Project Rulison case was no complete victory for the plaintiffs. The lawsuit, however, for the first time caused the *Atomic Energy Commission* to stand trial on the issue of *radiation safety standards,* a matter traditionally considered to be within the AEC's exclusive domain. The brief, prepared mainly by Victor John Yannacone, jr., argues that "persuading courts to transform academic theories into remedies for legal protection of the environment is ultimately the task of the practicing attorney. James Moorman is quoted in the brief as saying: "The problems facing the lawyer can be formidable. The law may be new, unfamiliar and technically astute. Again, it may be a vast collection of miscellaneous, unfamiliar precedence. Worst of all, it may be nonexistent. . . ."

The first and perhaps the greatest hurdle in a suit with the federal government is a motion to dismiss for lack of reviewability. The brief which follows touches on that point and four others. It concludes with a request for a restraining order until such time as defendants, the AEC and others, can show by substantial evidence that such detonation of a nuclear bomb will not cause contamination of the permanent biogeochemical cycles of the biosphere with radioactive materials, and that such detonation of a nuclear bomb will not release any ionizing radiation into the environment.

Because the government puts so much of its litigation effort into such motions, he who defeats one may consider himself to have won a major victory. In fact, establishing the right of the citizen to sue to protect the environment by defeating such motions is of the first priority. Precedents in the field are trophies to be sought after.

(a) Plaintiffs' Brief—Complaint

COLORADO OPEN SPACE COORDINATING COUNCIL, on behalf of all those entitled to the protection of their health and safety and of the health and safety of those generations yet unborn, from the hazards of ionizing radiation resulting from the distribution of radioactive materials through the permanent biogeochemical cycles of the biosphere as a result of the defendants' conduct of *Project Rulison,* and on behalf of all those entitled to the full benefit, use, and enjoyment of the national natural resource treasures of the State of Colorado without degradation resulting from contamination with radioactive material released as a result of the defendants' conduct of *Project Rulison,* and all others similarly situated,

Plaintiffs,

—against—

AUSTRAL OIL COMPANY, INCORPORATED

and

CER GEONUCLEAR CORPORATION,

Defendants

U.S. ATOMIC ENERGY COMMISSION, BUREAU OF MINES, U.S. DEPARTMENT OF INTERIOR, and LOS ALAMOS SCIENTIFIC LABORATORY,

as their several interests may appear.

POINT 1   Actions of the Atomic Energy Commission are subject to judicial review under the provisions of the Administrative Procedure Act.

The Atomic Energy Commission was established under the Atomic Energy Act of 1946, ch. 724, §2, 60 Stat. 756 (1946), *as amended* 42 U.S.C. §2031 (1964). The original bill provided for "Government control over atomic energy and for Government programs of information, production, research, and development." S. Rep. No. 1211, 79th Cong., 2d Sess. 9 (1946). The Atomic Energy Commission was to be "responsible for administering domestic controls over atomic energy, for carrying on production, research and . . . development." There was to be "an absolute Government monopoly of production of fissionable materials," and the Commission was to be "the exclusive producer of atomic weapons." However, the private sector, under supervision of the Commission, was to be allowed to participate in industrial research in the field of atomic energy, and in the ownership, mining, and refining of source materials from which fissionable materials are produced. The Commission was empowered to license the manufacture and use of atomic energy devices, but only after the prior approval of Congress, since "devices utilizing atomic energy, if widely used, would so multiply potential hazards to national health and safety that even careful Government regulation would fail to provide adequate safeguards." The Act, however, did "not permit the Commission to license the use of devices which produce fissionable material in the course of utilizing atomic energy."

Section 12(a)(2) of the 1946 Act gave the Commission the authority to "[e]stablish safety and health regulations for the possession and use of fissionable and byproduct materials to minimize the danger from explosion, radioactivity, and other harmful or toxic effects incident to the presence of such materials." S. REP. No. 1211, 79th Cong., 2d Sess. 28 (1946).

Section 14 of the Atomic Energy Act of 1946 clearly provided for judicial review of any agency action under the Act pursuant to the Administrative Procedure Act:

> SEC. 14. (a) [S]ection 10 of [the Administrative Procedure] Act [presently codified as 5 U.S.C. §§701-06 (Supp. IV, 1968)] (relating to judicial review) shall be applicable, upon the enactment of this Act, to any agency action under the authority of this Act . . . .
>
> (b) Except as provided in subsection (a), no provision of this Act shall be held to supersede or modify the provisions of the Administrative Procedure Act.
>
> (c) As used in this section the terms "agency action" and "agency" shall have the same meaning as is assigned to such terms in the Administrative Procedure Act.

POINT 2 The plaintiffs have sufficient standing to sue under the Administrative Procedure Act.

Plaintiff Richard T. Crowther

Plaintiff Crowther, as a property owner who would sus-

tain property damage from the unsafe release of radioactive material into the atmosphere and as a human being
whose body would suffer damage from exposure to ionizing radiation is a "person suffering legal wrong because
of agency action," and "is entitled to judicial review
thereof."

"Legal wrong," as the term is used in 5 U.S.C. §702
(Supp. IV, 1969), "is the invasion of a legally protected
right." Pennsylvania R.R. v. Dillon, 335 F.2d 292.

Plaintiff Colorado Open Space
Coordinating Council, Inc. (COSC)

Plaintiff COSC, as a non-profit public service corporation whose purposes include the preservation of the environment and protection of human beings from pollution,
is a person "adversely affected or aggrieved" within the
meaning of the Atomic Energy Act and Administrative
Procedure Act. Nashville I-40 Steering Comm. v. Elling-
ton, 387 F.2d 179 (6th Cir. 1967), *cert. denied,* 390 U.S.
921 (1968); Scenic Hudson Preservation Conf. v. FPC,
354 F.2d 608 (2 Cir. 1965), *cert. denied,* 384 U.S. 941
(1966); Sierra Club v. Volpe, — F. Supp. — (N.D. Cal.
1969); Citizens Comm. for the Hudson Valley v. Volpe,
302 F. Supp. 1083 (S.D.N.Y. 1969); Powelton Civic
Home Owners Ass'n. v. HUD, 284 F. Supp. 809 (E.D.
Pa. 1968); Road Review League, Town of Bedford v.
Boyd, 270 F. Supp. 650 (S.D.N.Y. 1967); International
Chem. Workers v. Planters Mfg. Co., 259 F. Supp. 365
(N.D. Miss. 1966). The court in *International Chemical
Workers* stated:

> [R]ecent court decisions have recognized the standing
> of group plaintiffs as a "person aggrieved" where the
> group, *qua* group, has an interest in the outcome of the
> administrative agency's determination although it
> might, incidentally, represent broader community in-
> terests as well.

259 F. Supp. at 367.
A non-profit, civic organization representing citizens
who were to be displaced by a proposed urban redevelop-

ment project had standing as "persons aggrieved" under the Administrative Procedure Act to seek judicial review of agency action allegedly disregarding these citizens' interests, though the "relevant statute," the National Housing Act, did not specifically provide for judicial review. The court stated that

> neither economic injury nor a specific individual legal right are necessary adjuncts to standing. A plaintiff need only demonstrate that he is an appropriate person to question the agency's alleged failure to protect a value specifically recognized by federal law as "in the public interest"; he may then invoke judicial scrutinization of the agency's performance in protecting—or in failing to protect—that specific value. He has standing to ask whether the agency action is violative of the public interest.
>
> . . . .
>
> The Administrative Procedure Act (5 U.S.C. §702) entitled a person who is "aggrieved by agency action within the meaning of a relevant statute" to obtain judicial review of that action. . . . [A] party must be considered "aggrieved" if, by his conduct and activities, he has demonstrated "special interest" in the values recognized and protected by the relevant statute. . . . The plaintiff . . . [a]ssociation is certainly an adequate and appropriate representative of those citizens' interests. If the public interest in these values is to be protected, the voices of those most dramatically affected by disregard of the values must be heard. If the residents in the project site have no standing to raise these issues "in the public interest," then, for all practical purposes, no one has standing, and the Secretary's determinations would be virtually immune from judicial review. . . . [S]uch result would neither be consistent with the presumption of judicial review by the Administrative Procedure Act, 5 U.S.C. §704, nor specifically authorized by the National Housing Act.

The court concluded that

> the provisions of the National Housing Act recognizing and protecting the values of rehabilitation, relocation and integrated local planning manifest a congressional

intent that non-profit civic organizations representing the citizens *who will be displaced by the proposed project are to be considered "aggrieved"* by agency action allegedly disregarding their interests.

POINT 3   The scope of review of agency action is governed by 5 U.S.C. §706 (Supp. IV, 1969):

To the extent necessary to decision and when presented, the reviewing court shall decide all relevant questions of law, interpret constitutional and statutory provisions, and determine the meaning or applicability of the terms of an agency action. The reviewing court shall—

. . . .

(2) hold unlawful and set aside agency action, findings, and conclusions found to be—

(A) arbitrary, capricious, an abuse of discretion, or otherwise not in accordance with law;

(B) contrary to constitutional right, power, privilege, or immunity;

(C) in excess of statutory jurisdiction, authority, or limitations, or short of statutory rights;

. . . .

(F) unwarranted by the facts to the extent that the facts are subject to trial de novo by the reviewing court.

The "hospitable interpretation" of the Administrative Procedure Act required by Abbott Laboratories v. Gardner, 387 U.S. 136 (1967), "applied not only where a specific statute is claimed to preclude judicial review, but also where it is invoked as delimiting the scope of judicial review." Phillips Petroleum Co. v. Brenner, 383 F.2d 514, 517-18 n.8 (D.C. Cir. 1967), *cert. denied*, 389 U.S. 1042 (1968).

POINT 4   The doctrine of sovereign immunity may no longer be raised by a federal administrative agency, even in the absence of a statute waiving such alleged immunity.

The general doctrine of the immunity of the United States from suit without consent of Congress is a rule conceived by the federal judiciary. There is no basis for this rule either in the Constitution itself or in any specific statute of Congress, but rather sovereign immunity is a rule adopted by the United States Supreme Court.

Apparently the first assertion of the sovereign immunity of the federal government was the following dictum by Chief Justice John Marshall in Cohens v. Virginia, 19 U.S. (6 Wheat.) 264, 411-12 (1821): "The universally received opinion is, that no suit can be commenced or prosecuted against the United States; that the Judiciary Act does not authorize such suits."

POINT 5   In those actions where the right of judicial review is available under the Administrative Procedure Act, sovereign immunity is waived.

> This express authorization of judicial review in this case [under the Administrative Procedure Act] disposes of the argument that the suit is in substance one against the United States where the United States has not given its consent to be sued. The United States has consented to this review. The fact that the United States has some interest in the controversy does not provide an exception to the grant of a right of review.

Adams v. Witmer, 271 F.2d 29, 34 (9th Cir. 1958).

> We are of the opinion that the reasons given by the trial court for lack of jurisdiction are not sound. Title 5 U.S.C. Sec. 1009 [presently codified as 5 U.S.C. §§701-06 (Supp. IV, 1969)] expressly provides for review of administrative or agency action at the instance of "any person suffering legal wrong" because of such action "or adversely affected or aggrieved by such action" subject to certain exceptions stated in that section. Instead of reaching a conclusion that the action was "in effect one brought against the United States without its consent," the court should have made inquiry whether the action was one authorized by the section referred to above. If so, the necessary consent of the United States will be found to exist.

Mulry v. Driver, 366 F.2d 544, 547 (9th Cir. 1966).

In Brennan v. Udall, 251 F. Supp. 12 (D. Colo. 1966), the appellant owned 160 acres of land which was in 1917 patented to one Baxter, reserving to the United States "all

the nitrate, oil, and gas in the lands," as required by 30
U.S.C. §§121-23 (1964). Brennan and Humble Oil Company, holder of an option to purchase the land, petitioned
the Director of Land Management for a decision that oil
shale was not included in the patent. The Director, with
the approval of the Secretary of the Interior, held that oil
shale was included in the patent. Appellant filed suit against
the Secretary of the Interior, challenging his decision. Jurisdiction was alleged under the Administrative Procedure
Act. The District Court (Doyle, J.) held:

> [T]he Administrative Procedure Act authorizes bring-
> ing of the suit and the granting of the relief de-
> manded . . . .
>   The defendant maintains that this suit is one that
> seeks to quiet title and as such is an unconsented suit
> against the sovereign. . . .
>   Cases relied on by defendant in support of his posi-
> tion that this Court lacks jurisdiction do not involve the
> issue of excess of administrative authority, but rather
> concern only challenges to the correctness of a decision
> committed by law to administrative discretion.

CONCLUSION

WHEREFORE, the Plaintiffs demand judgment of the
defendants:

DECLARING

The rights of the people of the State of Colorado to the
protection of their personal health and safety and the
health and safety of those generations yet unborn from the
hazards of ionizing radiation resulting from the distribution of radioactive materials through the Colorado Regional Ecosystem as a result of *Project Rulison.*

The rights of the people of the State of Colorado to the
full benefit, use, and enjoyment of the national natural resource treasures of the State of Colorado without degradation resulting from contamination with radioactive material
released by *Project Rulison.*

The rights of the people of the State of Colorado to a
full disclosure by the defendants of the facts, if any, supporting the claims that:

Safety of the public is a prime consideration of all Project Rulison participants. All factors that affect safety will be investigated thoroughly, reviewed by a panel of safety consultants, and evaluated on the basis of the knowledge gained from the extensive experience of previous nuclear detonations.

AEC experience with more than 270 underground nuclear detonations indicates that escape of radioactivity into the atmosphere is highly unlikely to result from Project Rulison.

Ground motion has been carefully calculated and no significant damage is predicted.

Ground waters in the Rulison site area have been evaluated by numerous engineers and scientists, who are convinced that there will be no contamination of the ground water.

Extensive operational safety measures have been undertaken to protect the public.

RESTRAINING

the defendants, jointly or severally, individually or in concert with others from any act which will result in the contamination of the permanent biological, geological, and chemical cycles of the Biosphere with radioactive material or the release of any ionizing radiation into the environment.

RESTRAINING

the defendants from proceeding with the detonation of any nuclear bomb in the State of Colorado, until such time as the defendants have showed good cause supported by substantial evidence that such detonation of a nuclear bomb will not cause contamination of the permanent biogeochemical cycles of the Biosphere with radioactive materials, and that such detonation of a nuclear bomb will not release any ionizing radiation into the environment.

TOGETHER

with such other and further relief shall seem just and proper to the Court under the circumstances.

6.2 Izaak Walton League Stops DDT Use in Wisconsin

(a) DDT: After the Sound and Fury by William H. Rodgers, jr.*

Pesticides are in the news. Mackerel fishing has been suspended in Los Angeles harbor due to high concentrations of DDT in the marine environment. The United States Department of Agriculture (USDA) recently seized thousands of turkeys bound for the nation's Thanksgiving tables because they contained traces of heptachlor in excess of established tolerance levels. The federal government and several of the states have acted to impose severe restrictions on the use of DDT and related chlorinated hydrocarbon pesticides amidst widespread controversy over environmental contamination and possible human health hazards.

• • •

The action by the federal government was the release, by Secretary Finch of HEW on November 12, 1969, of the recommendations of the secretary's Commission on Pesticides and Their Relationship to Environmental Health. This commission, which was made up of a large cross-section of governmental officials, representatives of the pesticides industry, and university scientists, confirmed what many people had been saying about DDT for years: the chemical has created a worldwide pollution problem almost without parallel.

A lethal combination of qualities—persistence, mobility, solubility in fat, and toxicity—distinguish DDT as a pollutant par excellence. It has been estimated that one billion pounds of DDT are circulating through the world's water and air supply. Traces of the chemical have been found in penguins in the Antarctic, Eskimos in the Arctic, and tuna in the mid-Pacific. Residues have been detected in the body tissues of people throughout the world.

* William H. Rodgers, jr., Assistant Professor of Law, University of Washington. Mr. Rodgers was the volunteer attorney representing the Washington Environmental Council in the Washington DDT hearings. He is the petitioner in a proceeding before the Food and Drug Administration requesting an order establishing zero-tolerance levels for DDT on agricultural commodities.

The toxicity of this widely disseminated pesticide upon nontarget organisms has been thoroughly documented. Numerous species of birds have suffered significant reproductive setbacks. Many marine biologists consider the chlorinated hydrocarbon pesticides to be the most serious form of water pollution. One reputable study concludes that DDT slows down photosynthesis in marine plant life, thus interfering with the fundamental chemical process by which green plants absorb the sun's energy and make it available to all living things.

Whether the persistent pesticides pose a threat to human health is still an open question. The secretary's Commission concedes, however, that high residues of DDT have been associated with certain diseases in human beings such as cancer, hypertension, and liver disease. And recently conducted animal experiments have produced disturbing findings. Only last year a study sponsored by the American Cancer Institute disclosed that DDT and other pesticides caused tumors in mice. This research, which was ridiculed by industry spokesmen at the Washington hearings, was termed "impressive" by the Commission, which concluded, "with the evidence now in, DDT can be regarded neither as a proven danger as a carcinogen for man nor as an assuredly safe pesticide; suspicion has been aroused and it should be confirmed or dispelled."

Against this background, the action in Washington takes on a new perspective. What has happened looks a bit like the habitual response of the beleagured public official: when in difficulty, appoint a commission.

For all practical purposes, complete bans have been imposed in Michigan and Wisconsin. A one-year moratorium is in effect in Arizona. In New York and California use restrictions have been imposed on many crops.

What is incredible about the DDT controversy is not that we confronted the risk but that we permitted the licensing and sale of DDT before the long-range dangers were fully understood. For the future, at the federal level it is essential that points of view other than the pest-control orientation of USDA be represented in the process of registering chemical pesticides where irrevocable decisions are made. Unquestionably, HEW and Interior deserve a role in the decision-making because of the invariable human health and environmental issues implicated by a decision to register. Legislative proposals to implement this objective are presently pending before Congress.

DDT is but the rhetorical peak of a pollution issue that includes many types of chemicals that are widely distributed in the environment. Of immediate interest are related chlorinated hydrocarbons which share DDT's toxic qualities—dieldrin, aldrin, endrin, heptachlor, and others. The herbicide 2,4-d, which is used in Washington in quantities several times in excess of our current DDT usage, also has been implicated as a health hazard in recent scientific studies. Numerous other compounds deserve careful scrutiny.

Enforcing legal controls over startling technological developments is an issue with consequences challenging the ultimate survival of mankind. The DDT controversy has demonstrated that Washington is not immune from the risks nor secure from the consequences of failure.

(b) Petitioners' Brief in Wisconsin DDT Case
Yannacone v. the Pesticide Industry

The defeat of the use of DDT in Wisconsin was planned and executed in the petition of Citizens Natural Resources Association, Inc., Wisconsin Division, Izaak Walton League of America, Inc., bringing a petition before the Department of Natural Resources of the state of Wisconsin represented by Yannacone & Yannacone.

The dangers of DDT, its persistent qualities and dangers, are clearly set forth in the first 3 pages of the brief and the summation appearing at the end. Coming at the conclusion of a logical exposition of the problem and quoting from the men recognized as experts in the field, the research scientists in the laboratory, researches all lead to one valid conclusion which was persuasively argued in Wisconsin that "if the waters of the state are to be used for fish or wildlife as well as human beings there can be no question but that they must be safe for the fish and wildlife as well as the human beings. There can be no further reasonable scientific doubt that DDT is causing damage to populations of fish and wildlife at levels now present in the Wisconsin Regional Ecosystem. Wherefore the petitioners pray that DDT be declared a pollutant under the provisions of the laws of the state of Wisconsin."

The petition was successful and the proliferation of DDT with its attendant dangers have been stopped in Wisconsin.

DEPARTMENT OF NATURAL RESOURCES STATE OF WISCONSIN

Petition of
CITIZENS NATURAL RESOURCES ASSOCIATION, INC., WISCONSIN DIVISION, IZAAK WALTON LEAGUE OF AMERICA, INC.

For a declaratory ruling on the use of dichloro-diphenyl-trichloro-ethane, commonly known as DDT, in the state of Wisconsin.

YANNACONE & YANNACONE
Attorneys for Petitioners

TABLE OF CONTENTS

by numerous transport mechanisms involving air and water.

Point   4

Because of the very low water solubility and very high lipid solubility of DDT and its principal environmental metabolite DDE, DDT residues are preferentially accumulated by living organisms.

Point   5

DDT manifests broad biological activity in a wide variety of living organisms.

Point   6

DDT and its principal environmental metabolite, DDE, are already present in the waters of the Wisconsin Regional Ecosystem in amounts which indicate acute or chronic levels harmful to animal, plant, or aquatic life.

Point   7

The continued use of DDT in the Wisconsin Regional Ecosystem will be deleterious to fish.

Point   8

The continued use of DDT in the Wisconsin Regional Ecosystem will be deleterious to birds.

Point   9

Great raptor population crashes have followed the contamination of the world's ecosystems with DDE. In the past two decades, peregrine falcons are being subjected to the processs of extinction on two continents. Bald eagles are also being extirpated in some regions.

Point   10

The substantial preponderance of the credible scientific evidence presented at the hearing indicates that the eggshell changes marking reproductive failures in major bird populations on two continents were due to environmental residues of DDT.

Point 11

The enzyme induction effects of DDT in birds, animals, and man together with the demonstrated absence of any scientifically credible "no effect level for DDT or DDE, demonstrate the manifest need to discontinue use of DDT under any circumstances where it can enter the environment.

Point 12

DDT is a nerve toxin, manifesting direct lethal effects as well as only recently understood sublethal effects on the nervous system of all animals.

Point 13

The continued use of DDT in American agriculture, particularly in areas where diversity of argo-ecosystems are encouraged, is no longer scientifically justified.

The matter before the department is a petition for a declaratory ruling seeking to determine the applicability of a departmental "rule or statute enforced by it" *(227.06, Stats.).*

THE STATUTES

The petition seeks a ruling declaring that DDT and its several environmental metabolites are pollutants under the provision of certain statutes.

144.01   Definitions. The following terms as used in this chapter mean:
. . . (11) "Pollution" includes contaminating or rendering unclean or impure the waters of the state, or making the same injurious to public health, harmful for commercial or recreational use, or deleterious to fish, bird, animal, or plant life.
RD   2.01   Guidelines for application of standards.
. . . (2) Where two or more uses are designated in one water sector, the more exacting standard will apply. As an example, if the maximum permissible concentration of a substance in a water used for public supply is higher than allowable for fish and other

aquatic life, and both of these uses are involved in one
sector, then the allowable concentration cannot exceed
that for fish and aquatic life.

RD 2.02 Categories of standards. To preserve
and enhance the quality of waters the following standards are established to govern water management decisions. It should be recognized that these standards will
be revised as new information or advancing technology
indicate that revisions are in the public interest.

(1) Minimum Standards. Regardless of the water
quality standards and water use, untreated or inadequately treated wastes may not impair a designated
use nor may standards be interpreted to permit a lower
quality within a water sector than that now existing or
required by outstanding orders. As a result of municipal, industrial, commercial, domestic, agricultural, land
development, or other activities, conditions may arise
which will be controlled by the following standards:
. . .

(*d*) Substances in concentrations or combinations
which are toxic or harmful to humans shall not be
present in amounts found to be of public health significance, nor shall substances be present in amounts
which, by bioassay and other appropriate tests, indicate
acute or chronic levels harmful to animal, plant, or
aquatic life. . . .

(3) For Fish and Other Aquatic Life. (*a*) The
following standards are applicable to surface waters
where maintenance of fish reproduction is of primary
importance in the public interest and natural conditions
permit: . . .

(*c*) Unauthorized concentrations of substances are
not permitted that alone or in combination with other
materials present are toxic to fish or other aquatic life.

POINT 1

Residues of DDT and its principal environmental metabolite DDE, are a unique environmental hazard because
of their physical, chemical, and biological properties.

An *ideal insecticide* might be described as one that
substantially reduces the pest population while at the same
time having its action restricted to the target organism and
the site of application (*Transcript, 220, 221*). Unfortun-

ately, certain chlorinated hydrocarbon insecticides, especially DDT, affect many species of nontarget organisms, even at distances remote from the site of application, and must be considered as anything but ideal insecticides.

The behavior of DDT residues in the environment can only be understood by a consideration of their physical, chemical, and biological properties (*Transcript, 226*). Dr. Charles Wurster testified early in the hearing that DDT and its metabolites have a combination of four properties that explain their environmental effects (*Transcript, 225, 226*). The four properties that make DDT a unique environmental problem are its great chemical stability or persistence; its mobility; its combination of low water solubility with high lipid solubility; and its broad biological activity.

POINT 2

Residues of DDT and its principal environmental metabolite, DDE, are very stable persistent compounds and remain in the permanent ecological cycles of the biosphere for many years.

Dr. Wurster discussed a paper by Nash and Wolson (Transcript, 234) in which thirty-nine percent of the DDT applied to a field in Maryland and was still present seventeen years later. While this would imply a half-life of about ten years if all that disappeared had decomposed or been degraded, this assumption cannot be made because there was no measurement of the amount lost by environmental transfer without decomposition or degradation. Thus it appears that the half-life in the world ecosystem could be far greater than ten years. The ubiquitous presence of DDT and its principal environmental metabolite, DDE, indicate that great quantities are transferred to untreated areas rather than being decomposed.

Dr. Paul Edward Porter, manager of the Physical and Analytical Chemistry Department in the Agricultural Research Division of the Shell Development Company, a division of the Shell Oil Company, called as a witness on behalf of the Task Force of DDT of the National Agricultural Chemicals Association (*Transcript, 2202, 2240*), confirmed the fact that DDT residues remained in the environment for many years by pointing out that, on the average, approximately twenty percent disappears from the soil each year, and that the disappearance consists of both decomposition and loss from the site of application.

Dr. Porter:

A: Well when DDT is applied to crops, it undergoes a period of rapid decline, which is believed to be the result of evaporation. After the initial rapid decline, it generally degrades further at a rate that is logarithmic in time and in this period the exact mechanism of its disappearance is not known. A part of the loss is caused by wash off by rain, a part of it perhaps by evaporation, a part of it could be by metabolic processes in the plant. But . . .

• • •

The decline in residues of the DDT, DDE, and DDD are roughly logarithmic in time. And the half-lives reported corresponding to these logarithmic decreases that have been reported on crop materials range from as little as two days to on the order of forty days. My feeling, from looking at the data, is that the longer time is more appropriate. . . . So that the half-lives that are pertinent to actual loss of DDT and its metabolites would be more on the order forty days, thirty to forty days. . . .

• • •

Well, I think that as far as the continued survival of this DDT and its metabolites in a plant phase, this is certainly limited by the survival of the plant. And when the plant is harvested, why the residue goes with the harvested material. Any plant material that dies has a finite lifetime and moves on into some other phase at the time the plant dies. . . .

Part of the DDT that's agriculturally applied certainly reaches the soil, and so DDT is actually applied to the soil. It is very tightly sorbed to the soil particles. . . . "Sorbed," in order not to specify either way. I don't think it is known whether its absorption or adsorption.

It is very tightly bound to the soil particles, and it is not readily moved by water. If it is moved, it is essentially by a process of physical dislodgement of the soil particles carrying them down into the deeper layers. A certain amount is moved down by cultivation. In the soil, DDT is relatively stable, it does degrade, it does disappear from the soil, and— . . . Available data on the rate of disappearance of DDT and its metabolites from soil had been reviewed. . . . The decline is roughly logarithmic again. There are very broad limits on the half-lives that are associated with it. But on the average approximately twenty percent of the content disappears per year; twenty percent of the amount present at any time disappears each year.

• • •

POINT 3

DDT is mobile and with the passage of time it leaves the site of application and is transported throughout the world by numerous transport mechanisms involving air and water.

While DDT has one of the lowest water solubilities known for an organic chemical, the value is still finite and because of the vast quantities of available water in the biosphere even the low solubility of 1.2 parts per billion in water is still significant. DDT residues are reached by water from the sites of application and can be carried in in solution wherever flowing water goes, eventually reaching the oceans of the world.

DDT has a strong tendency to form suspensions in water and this greatly increases the DDT-carrying capacity of water, since larger amounts can be suspended in the water than can be carried in solution.

DDT tends to sorb to particulate matter which is eroded by water and carried downstream in river systems, eventually reaching the world's oceans.

While DDT is essentially a nonviolate material, it has a very low—but nevertheless finite—vapor pressure and slowly but steadily and predictability escapes into the air.

DDT has a tendency to suspend not only in water but in air, and the application procedures which emphasize the production of tiny particles or droplets create airborne suspensions of DDT which travel great distances from the site of application.

DDT residues sorbed to particulates travel with these particles when they are picked up as dust by the winds and enter the worldwide patterns of atmospheric circulation.

DDT also enters the atmosphere by the process of co-distillation with water—as the water evaporates it carries the DDT with it.

The physical and chemical properties of DDT explain the capacity of water to carry DDT residues away from treated areas and the mechanisms whereby DDT passes into the air and is transported about the world within the normal circulation patterns of the atmosphere.

To put the matter finally at rest, Dr. Lucille S. Stickel, Pesticide Research Coordinator, Patuxent Wildlife Research Center of the United States Department of Interior, reported an experiment in which mallard ducks were fed controlled amounts of DDT at environmental levels. She summarized her findings and indicated that each group of DDT-dosed mallards broke twenty-four percent of its eggs while the controls broke only four percent, and the egg-shells of DDT-dosed mallards were 13.5 percent thinner than those of the controls. She also indicated that the eggs laid and incubated by the DDT-dosed mallards produced half or less than half as many healthy ducklings than the controls. Dr. Stickel concluded:

> . . . It is evident that small amounts of DDE in the diet of mallards affect their reproduction adversely in two important ways: first, eggs are cracked and broken; second, even eggs that begin development fail to produce a normal number of healthy ducklings. It is also evident that thickness of egg shells is associated with these events and is a strong indicator of serious problems *(Transcript, 1216–20)*.

Dr. Stickel also described her unique experiments with kestrels, commonly called sparrow hawks, of the genus *Falco*. These experiments were unique in that no predatory bird had previously been reared in captivity with enough success to permit experiments. By 1967, Dr. Stickel had solved the problem of rearing kestrels in captivity and an experiment similar to that done with the mallard ducks was performed. The kestrels, however, received food containing mixtures of DDT and deldrin, both at environmental levels, and Dr. Stickel reported:

> . . . Shells of eggs laid by dosed birds were approximately fifteen percent thinner than those of controls. Shells of the second generation fed the diet of their parent were also approximately fifteen percent thinner than those of their controls. These results speak for themselves and are in harmony with the results with mallards.
>
> From these studies it is evident that DDT in minute amounts can cause marked impairment of the reproductive success among at least two major bird groups *(Transcript, 1220, 1221).*

> Q: But it is a fact, isn't it, Doctor, that modern insect control, especially with the use of broad-spectrum chemicals of long persistence, such as DDT, requires some extensive systems analysis in order to comprehend all the effects on a given system?
>
> A.   Yes, sir. All effects.
>
> MR. YANNACONE: Thank you very much, Doctor.

SUMMATION

The issue is clear. All the evidence available to environmental scientists and the manufacturers of DDT concerning the safety, toxic effects, and justifications for the continued use of the broad-spectrum, persistent chemical biocide, 1,1,1-tricholro-2,2-bis(chlorophenyl)ethane, more commonly referred to as dichloro-diphenyl-trichloroethane —DDT, have been tested in the crucible of cross-examination.

The Industry Task Force for DDT of the National Agricultural Chemicals Association raises the issue of benefit versus risk. The rules under which the hearing was conducted have decided that matter on behalf of the people of the state of Wisconsin. If the waters of the state are to be used for fish or wildlife as well as human beings, there can be no question but that they must be safe for the fish and wildlife as well as the human beings. There can be no further reasonable scientific doubt that DDT is causing damage to populations of fish and wildlife at levels now present in the Wisconsin Regional Ecosystem.

Wherefore, the petitioners pray that DDT be declared a pollutant under the provisions of the laws of the state of Wisconsin.

> Respectfully submitted,
> YANNACONE & YANNACONE
> *Attorneys for petitioners*

6.3 SST—Supersonic Transport Planes

The topic of supersonic transport planes (SSTs) has caused heated debate in Congress, and rightfully so. Problems of emergency landings, and the potential disaster in a midair collision and trailing wind turbulence are awesome. The future supersonic jets will fly in the stratosphere, 60,000 to 70,000 feet above the earth, leaving a water vapor trail for 18 months. Further study is necessary to better determine the effects of supersonic jet transports in the stratosphere before they are mass produced.

There is also evidence that jets contribute to high clouds. Observations at Denver indicate that from 1950 to 1958, on the average about 8% of the sky was covered by high clouds when there were no lower cloud layers. From 1965 to 1969, about twice that portion of the sky was covered by high clouds. Similar observations have been recorded at Salt Lake City. Although there may be other contributing factors to the cloud increase, both cities are on heavily traveled air routes.

It seems abundantly clear that the dangers of midair collision, emergency landings, and the possibilities of climate and weather changes by the future supersonic transport plane mandates increased investigation before the world is committed to mass-producing them—separate and apart from the problem of the sonic boom.

William A. Shurcliff has written a 153-page treatise on this problem which was published by Ballantine Books. He is director of the Citizens League Against the Sonic Boom. On page 85 of this excellent book he noted:

"The Boeing SST would burn about 1 ton of fuel each

minute at takeoff, far more than the subsonic jets burn. The amount of toxic pollution inflicted on the nearby downwind communities would be large. The director of the Atmospheric Sciences Research Center at Albany, New York, Dr. V. J. Schaefer, world-famous atmospheric physicist, foresees the possibility of SSTs discharging approximately 150,000 tons of water vapor daily into the upper atmosphere and producing 'global gloom.' "

C. Edward Graves, naturalist and writer, commented: "Imagine a hike or a pack trip into the wildest part of the country in order to enjoy its peculiar characteristics, only to have the quiet of an evening campfire shattered by cannonading booms from the sky! Their unexpectedness is one of the worst features. Tranquility would no longer exist. The nerve-shattering impact upon man, and the harassment to wild life through constant exposure to the sonic boom are incalculable."

The resourceful, youthful attorney handling the appeal in *Nelms* v. *Melvin Laird* in the United States Court of Appeals for the Fourth Circuit is 86-year-old George E. Allen, Sr., of Richmond, Va. This remarkable trial lawyer has handled Supreme Court cases for 60 years, and the excitement and success of his life in court is reflected in the book entitled *The Law as a Way of Life*. A digest of his appellate brief, which in its entirety runs 40 pages, plus citations, follows along with portions of the brief submitted to the Federal Aviation Administration by the Environmental Defense Fund.

(a) Appellants' Brief for Compensation for Sonic Boom Damage

UNITED STATES COURT OF APPEALS FOR THE FOURTH CIRCUIT

No. 14,568

JIM NICK NELMS, et al

Appellants

VS.

MELVIN LAIRD, Secretary of Defense, et al

Appellees.

Geo. E. Allen
Richmond, Virginia
Counsel for appellants.

ISSUES PRESENTED FOR REVIEW

(a) Whether the discretionary function exception in the Federal Tort Claims Act is applicable and,

(b) Whether this issue can be properly resolved on *ex parte* affidavits, pro and con, involving disputed questions of fact.

STATEMENT OF THE CASE

This is a suit against the United States for compensation in damages resulting from the phenomenon known to the non-expert as "sonic boom," which occurs when the speed of an aircraft exceeds that of sound.

The Government filed a motion for summary judgment based upon affidavits. The trial court granted the motion upon the ground that the actions were barred by the discretionary function exception to the Federal Tort Claims Act as set forth in 28 U.S.C.A., §2680(*a*). Clerk's Record, p. 89. Plaintiffs appealed. The ground of the appeal was that "when a civilian area has been affected by Air Force aircraft, the Air Force must accept responsibility for restitution and payment of just claims."

Plaintiffs allege that their home was damaged by "sonic boom" generated by United States Air Force aircraft travelling over their home at supersonic speeds. Damages are claimed in the sum of $16,000.00. The affidavits on behalf of appellants show that when the plane passed over their home, the house "shook all over, the clock came off the wall, the glass fell over the table." "The walls were cracked all over in every room of the house and outside. Plaster was all over the house and had to be swept up." "The glass came out of the door and in the kitchen window. Walls were cracked in every room. Plastering was on the floors."

The home of neighbors who live across the highway

from plaintiffs' home was damaged and window lights broken out from the sonic boom at the same time.

"Our house was damaged at the same time****. The plane came over nearly every day at that time."

" ****when that sonic boom came over approximately 2:30 p.m. I saw fish jump out of the pond. A day or two before that, I was at the store, about 100 yards from there, when another sonic boom came over, and items shook on the shelves and bottles rattled out on the floor****."

According to the building contractor, "the blocks were laid right, and the footing was poured according to specifications. As far as I know, the soil was in good condition."

"On December 17, 1968, the walls were cracked in every room, and the floors had dropped in the center of the house **** with it cracking up like it did I would hate to live in it because I think it is danger of falling in."

"All material used by the plaintiffs in building their home met the specifications of the State Law and the requirements of the North Carolina Concrete Masonry Association."

According to a general contractor, it is "impossible to fix whole house. Must build from start. Cost of building estimated at $13,500.00." Exhibit B.

"The buildings were left in such poor condition that the only value Nelms had left was the plot of ground, well, trees, etc."

Defendants conceded that there was damage, but contended that the damage was not caused by "sonic booms." The defense, as summed up by General Holloday, of the Air Force, was that: "My superior and I have determined, in the exercise of the authority and discretion vested in us, that these training flights in supersonic aircraft over land areas of the United States are essential to the security of the United States."

ARGUMENT

Summary

A. The discretionary function exception in the Federal Tort Claims Act is inapplicable for the following reasons:

(1) The flights complained of constitute an invasion of the property of complainants under the Fifth Amendment to the Constitution of the United States and the North Carolina law to such an extent as to amount to a taking or damaging of property without compensation.

(2) The activity involved in the operation of supersonic aircraft is of such a nature as to come within the classification of ultrahazardous activities, making the operators strictly liable.

(3) The Government, in directing supersonic flights, is under a mandatory duty to make them at such heights as to avoid damage to property owners on the ground beneath the flights.

B. The affidavits, pro and con, raise an issue of fact to be determined by trial instead of upon exparte affidavits.

Relevant Constitution and Statutory Provisions

28 U.S.C.A. §1346(*b*) provides that the District Courts of the United States shall have jurisdiction of claims for damages for loss of property caused by the negligent or wrongful act or omission of any employee of the Government while acting within the scope of his office or employment, under circumstances where the United States, if a private person, would be liable to the claimant in accordance with the law of the place where the act or omission occurred.

28 U.S.C.A. §2680 excepts from the act any claim based upon the exercise or performance or failure to exercise or perform a discretionary function or duty on the part of a federal agency or an employee of the Government.

The Constitution of the United States, Amendment V provides in part " *** nor shall private property be taken for public use, without just compensation."

The Constitution of North Carolina, where this cause of action arose, provides, Art. I, §17, "No person ought to be taken, imprisoned or disseized of his freehold, liberties or privileges or outlawed or exiled or in any manner deprived of his life, liberty or property, but by the law of the land."

The Bill of Rights, Art. I, §35 of the Constitution of North Carolina declares:

> "All courts shall be open, and every person for injury done him in his lands, goods, person, or reputation, shall have remedy by due court of law and right and justice administered without sale, denial or delay."

The General Statutes of North Carolina, Vol. 2C Replacement 1965, §63-11 provide:

> "Sovereignty in space above the lands and waters of this state is declared to rest in the State, except where granted to and assumed by the United States."

This Section was cited by the U.S. Supreme Court in the Causby case, p. 1068 of 66, S. Ct. Reporter.

Section 63-12 of the North Carolina Statutes is as follows:

> "The ownership of the space above the lands and waters of this state is declared to be vested in the several owners of the surface beneath subject to the right of flight described in 63-13."

Section 63-13 provides:

> "Flight in aircraft over lands and waters of this state is lawful unless at such a low altitude as to interfere with the then existing use which the land or water, or space over the land or water, is put by the owner, or unless so conducted as to be injurious to the health and happiness, or eminently dangerous to persons or property lawfully on the land or water beneath."

Section 63-13 of the North Carolina Statute was cited with approval in the Causby case, p. 1068 of the S. Ct. Reporter, the Court saying:

> " **** Our holding that there was an invasion of respondents' property is thus not inconsistent with the local law governing a landowner's claim to the immediate reaches of the superadjacent airspace."

A-(1). *The Flights Complained of Constitute an Invasion of the Property of Complainants Under the Fifth Amendment to the Constitution of the*

*United States and the North Carolina law to
Such an Extent as to Amount to a Taking or
Damaging of Property Without Compensation.*

In *United States v. Causby,* 328 U.S. 256, 66 S. Ct.
1062, decided May 27, 1946, an action was brought by
Causby and his wife against the United States to recover
for the alleged taking by the defendant of plaintiffs' home
and chicken farm which was adjacent to a municipal airport leased by the defendant in the State of North Carolina.

Mr. Justice Douglas, in delivering the opinion of the
Court, said the case was one of first impression. The problem presented, he said, is whether respondents' property
was taken within the meaning of the Fifth Amendment by
frequent and regular flights of army and navy aircraft over
respondents' property. After discussing the question at
some length and referring to the ancient doctrine that the
common law ownership of land extended to the periphery
of the universe; but that such a doctrine has no place in
the modern world, Mr. Justice Douglas continues:

" **** [2, 3] But that general principle does not control
the present case. For the United States conceded on
oral argument that if the flights over respondents' property rendered it uninhabitable, there would be a taking
compensable under the Fifth Amendment. It is the
owner's loss, not the taker's gain, which is the measure
of the value of the property taken. United States v.
Miller, 317 U. S. 369, 63 S.Ct. 276, 87 L.Ed. 336, 147
A.L.R. 55. Market value fairly determined is the normal measure of the recovery. Id. And that value may
reflect the use to which the land could readily be converted, as well as the existing use. United States v.
Powelson, 319 U.S. 266, 275, 63 S.Ct. 1047, 1053, 87
L.Ed. 1390, and cases cited. If, by reason of the frequency and altitude of the flights, respondents could
not use this land for any purpose, their loss would be
complete.

**** [7, 8] We said in *United States v. Powelson,* supra,
319 U.S. at page 279, 63 S.Ct. at page 1054, 87 L.Ed.
1390, that while the meaning of 'property' as used in
the Fifth Amendment was a federal question, 'it will

normally obtain its content by reference to local law.'
If we look to North Carolina law, we reach the same
result. Sovereignty in the airspace rests in the State
'except where granted to and assumed by the United
States.' Gen.Stats., 1943, §63-11.

The flight of aircraft is lawful 'unless at such a low
altitude as to interfere with the then existing use to
which the land or water, or the space over the land or
water, is put by the owner, or unless so conducted as
to be imminently dangerous to persons or property lawfully on the land or water beneath.' Id., §63-13. Subject to that right of flight, 'ownership of the space
above the lands and waters of this State is declared to
be vested in the several owners of the surface beneath.'
Id. §63-12. Our holding that there was an invasion of
respondents' property is thus not inconsistent with the
local law governing a landowner's claim to the immediate reaches of the superadjacent airspace.

[9] The airplane is part of the modern environment of
life, and the inconveniences which it causes are normally not compensable under the Fifth Amendment.
The airspace, apart from the immediate reaches above
the land, is part of the public domain. We need not
determine at this time what those precise limits are.
Flights over private land are not a taking, unless they
are so low and so frequent as to be a direct and immediate interference with the enjoyment and use of the
land. We need not speculate on that phase of the present case. For the findings of the Court of Claims plainly
establish that there was a diminution in value of the
property and that the frequent, low-level flights were
the direct and immediate cause. We agree with the
Court of Claims that a servitude has been imposed
upon the land."

Causby has been cited with approval many times by
subsequent cases.

In *American Airlines, Inc., et al v. Town of Hempstead*,
272 F. Supp. 226, June 30, 1967, the Court said, citing
Causby:

"So far as landowners are concerned, they are constitutionally entitled to just compensation if overflights are such in nature, proximity and frequency as to amount to a taking of the property for public purposes."

In *Creel, etc. v. City of Atlanta,* U.S. Ct. of Appeals, Fifth Circuit, 399 F.2d 777, August 20, 1968, the Court said:

" **** Moreover, at least two cases clearly demonstrate that allegations of such repeated flights directly overhead would make out a Federal cause of action."

In *Town of East Haven, et al v. Eastern Airlines,* 282 F. Supp. 507 the Court said, citing *Causby*:

" **** If Government aircraft or a public airport cause 'a direct and immediate interference *with the enjoyment and use*' of private property, then there has been a 'taking.' "

In *U.S. v. Peat, et al,* 305 F. Supp. 83, the Court said,

" **** Causby involved a suit in the Court of Claims against the United States to recover for an alleged taking by the Government of plaintiffs' home and chicken farm which was adjacent to a municipal airport leased to the Government. **** As many as 150 chickens were killed when they flew into walls from *fright*. The value of the property was significantly depreciated.

In *U.S. v. Gravalle,* 407 F.2d 964, 968, the Government undertook an extensive series of supersonic flights over Oklahoma City for the purpose of determining what, if any, damage would result to property and persons from sonic booms, and homeowners established that their homes did in fact sustain damage. The Court termed the test a deliberate tort for which the government would be held liable under the Tort Claims Act.

If a private person, whose property has been taken or damaged by the Government for public purposes cannot sue the Government for compensation, the framers of the 5th Amendment to the Constitution were engaged in an exercise of futility. This cannot be. Courts are always jealous of the rights of private citizens when such rights clash with the power of the State.

A-(2). *The Activity Involved in the Operation of Super-Sonic Aircraft is of Such a Nature as to Come Within the Classification of Ultrahazardous Activities, Making the Operators Strictly Liable.*

This seems to be the theory of the Department of the Air Force. The regulation issued October 6, 1967, Clerk's Record, p. 31, states at p. 33 of the Clerk's Record, p. 3 of the Regulation:

> "When a civilian area has been affected by Air Force aircraft, the Air Force must accept responsibility for restitution and payment of just claims."

This practice is followed by the Air Force, according to a well written article in the Journal of Air Law and Commerce, Vol. 32, pp. 597 to 606, published by the Southern Methodist Law School.

The author says at p. 597:

> "In order to establish that a particular sonic boom was the proximate cause of the damage in any given case, it is necessary to consider the extent of damage that a boom can cause."

With reference to recovery, under the Federal Tort Claims Act, the author says:

> "In most instances where government or military aircraft have caused sonic boom damage, the Government has paid for any property damage (mostly broken windows and cracked plaster) without the necessity of the claimant's bringing any legal action. Where there have been large scale experiments or exercises, the Government has agreed before the flights took place to pay for any sonic damage actually caused by such flights."

The author says in a footnote on p. 597 that these assertions are still made in the form of letters sent out by the Air Force in response to sonic boom complaints.

Continuing, the author says:

"When the Government receives a complaint, it first sends out a letter indicating its position that the possibility of boom damage in any case is extremely remote. This eliminates approximately 83% of the claims. If the property owner persists, a check is made to determine if a sonic boom occurred near the time and place of the alleged damage. If not, no further steps are taken. If so, investigators are sent to inspect the damaged property, and if all that is found is minor glass and bric a brac damage, the Government will normally satisfy the claim.

"However, the Government is extremely reluctant to pay for structural damage to property, and according to Government experience, large plaster cracks do not ordinarily occur in the absence of accompanying glass damage. If suit is brought, the common practice is for the Government to admit liability for damage caused by the boom, but to question the extent of damage proximately caused."

The author says in a footnote on p. 598 that the foregoing information was obtained from officers in the claims section of the Judge Advocate General's Office, Carswell Air Force Base, Ft. Worth, Texas.

Continuing, the author says:

"If it is necessary to bring an action against the Government, either of two basic approaches can be pursued. Claims brought under the Federal Tort Claims Act, 28 U.S.C. 2672, are determined adminstratively while actions brought under 28 U.S.C. 1346 are pursued in the Federal Courts. §1346 gives the District Court concurrent jurisdiction with the Court of Claims over claims for money damages for injury to or loss of property or personal injury or death caused by the negligence or wrongful act or omission of any employee of the Government acting within the scope of his employment.

"There are two similar theories as to the nature of sonic booms. One group whose theory is more widely accepted explains the phenomena in terms of waves; a second group adheres to a theory based upon the movement of air particles. There is, however, uniform agreement among both groups of experts that *the sonic boom is a pressure wave accompanied by noise*. Thus the scientific definition of an explosion seems to coincide with the general definition of the word explosion. Both definitions include a violent expansion accompanied by noise which follows the sudden production of great pressure. Moreover, the varied occurrences already held to have been explosions indicate the judicial tendency against an extremely limited or rigid classification." (P. 600.)

Under the title, Strict Liability, the author writes:

"According to the Restatement of Torts, §520, Comment (c) 1938. Comment (b) declares that an activity may be ultra hazardous because of the condition which it creates. Comment (a) goes on to say that the rule is applicable to an activity which is of such utility that the risk unavoidably involved in carrying it on, cannot be regarded as so unreasonable as to make it negligence to carry it on.

"An activity is ultra hazardous if it (a) necessarily involves any risk of serious harm to the person, land or chattels of others which cannot be eliminated by the exercise of utmost care, and (b) is not a matter of common knowledge. Even if flight regulations are such as will keep over pressures within a non damage range, the Oklahoma City tests indicate that boom scatter or violation (due to wind velocity, temperature, terrain features, humidity, boundary layer turbulence and other meteorological parameters causes one boom in a thousand—at every point in the boom carpet which will be 50 to 80 miles wide, to be twice as strong as the mean strength on the flight tract for a series of flights. Moreover, specifically if flights are planned so that boom caused over pressures will be only 1.5 pounds per square foot during the flight and two pounds per square foot on take-off, the over pressures from one flight in a thousand will be three or four pounds per square foot which, as noted previously, will cause considerable damage to glass and plaster as well as minor structural damage to frames and walls. Therefore, the operation of super-sonic transport aircraft will involve a risk of serious hazard to property which cannot be eliminated

by the exercise of utmost care and since flying supersonic is not a matter of common usage, such operations
should be classified as ultra hazardous activities.

"Previously, both the courts and the law looked upon
aviation from the viewpoint expressed by the American
Law Institute in 1938 that aviation is an ultrahazardous
activity. The Uniform Aeronautic Act adopted in 23
states, imposed absolute liability on the owners, operators and lessees of aircraft for any damage caused by
their operation, so long as there was no contributory
negligence on the part of the person harmed. However,
this view has been rejected since aircraft operation has
become safer, and the trend of decisions has established
the general rule that an airplane is not an inherently
dangerous instrument when properly handled by a competent pilot exercising reasonable care, and that the ordinary rules of negligence apply. (P. 603.) However, in
the case of sonic booms, this point has not yet been
reached, but if technology and procedures should advance to the point where all damage can be eliminated
by the exercise of due care, only then should the courts
refuse to find strict liability for boom damage. (P.
604.)

"The analogy between 'explosions' and sonic booms
may be of use to the landowner in establishing strict
liability, as well as in recovering under an insurance
policy. Almost all American jurisdictions have held the
defendant absolutely liable for injury caused by rocks
and debris thrown by blasting. This is true whether the
injury is to persons or to property. The majority of
states also finds absolute liability for concussion damages resulting from blasting. However, a minority of
states does make a distinction and require proof of
negligence in concussion cases, unless a nuisance is
shown. Sonic booms are very similar to concussion
shock waves in that both, being shock waves, involve
abnormal pressure zones emanating from outside the
premises affected. (P. 605.)

"The Courts have relied primarily on two grounds to
impose strict liability in blasting cases. Trespass is
commonly agreed to have been committed when debris
or rock are thrown onto plaintiff's property. *Asheville*

Construction Co. v. Southern Ry., 19 F.2d 32 (4th Cir.).

"The majority of states have refused to distinguish cases in which the damage is caused by the concussion or vibration effects of blasting. Such courts find trespass in both situations. While this theory is still sound, the trend has been to hold the defendant strictly liable because he is engaged in an ultrahazardous activity. Regardless of the theory applied, though, in most jurisdictions, the defendant is held strictly liable for all damages caused by his blasting operations. (P. 604.) *Fairfax Inn, Inc. v. Sunnyhill Mining Co.*, 97 F.Supp. 991 (N.D. W.Va. 1951).

"It is therefore submitted that strict liability should be found applicable against the airlines in the case of damaging sonic booms for two reasons. First, the operation of supersonic aircraft will cause some damage which cannot be eliminated by the exercise of the utmost care, and it therefore should be treated as an ultrahazardous activity. Secondly, sonic booms involve the same phenomena and effects as do concussions from blasting; therefore, the blasting laws should apply. (P. 605.)

"The statutory standard is no more than a minimum, and does not necessarily preclude a finding that the actor was negligent in failing to take additional precautions. *** the wholly innocent landowner should be allowed to recover from the airlines, which should be held strictly liable on public policy grounds. Since supersonic transports will cause certain inevitable damage, the airlines should be required to pay their own way. Since the traveling public is demanding supersonic aircraft it should bear the ultimate cost for the actual physical damage to property, which inevitably follows, through the increased fares which the airlines will be forced to charge on supersonic flights." (P. 606.)

In *D'Anna v. U.S., Thompson v. U.S., Klaus v. U.S.*, 181 F.2d 335, at page 337, Judge Parker, speaking for the Court, said:

"One who flies an aeroplane is opposing mechanical forces to the force of gravity and is engaged in an undertaking which is fraught with the gravest danger to persons and property beneath if it is not carefully operated or if the mechanism of the plane and its attachments are not in first class condition. At common law, the hazardous nature of the enterprise subjected the operator of the plane to a rule of absolute liability to one upon the ground who was injured or whose property was damaged as a result of the operation. A.L.I. Restatement Torts secs. 519, 520, d; Prosser on Torts, p. 452."

"In 45 Words and Phrases, p. 627, many cases are cited in which the phrase 'wrongful' has been interpreted to mean any act which in the ordinary course of events infringes on the right of another to his damage. . . . To say that a tort giving rise to absolute liability is not a 'wrongful act' would be a technical refinement of language incompatible with that liberal interpretation of the sovereign's waiver of immunity which the highest court in the land has admonished us to employ. . . ." (104 F.Supp. at 116.)

Whether aviation is treated as an extra hazardous activity or classified as a trespass, there is ample authority that strict liability ensues from ground damage caused by airplanes.

In *Dahlstrom v. U.S.*, 129 F. Supp. 772, the trial court stated that there is persuasive authority to the effect that where the law of the state where the accident occurred makes the injurious flight of aircraft a trespass and therefore imposes liability even in the absence of negligence, then the flight is wrongful within the meaning of the Federal Tort Claims Act.

A-(3). *The Government, in Directing Supersonic Flights, is Under a Mandatory Duty to Make Them at Such Heights as to Avoid Damage to Property Owners on the Ground Beneath the Flights.*

The great boast of the common law is that it has a remedy for every wrong, excepting cases of *damnum ab-*

scue injuria. In order to have a remedy for changed conditions, the common law amends itself to meet the changing conditions of society. As the late Judge Parker so well said in *Barnes Coal Corporation v. Retail Coal Merchants Asso.*, et al, 128 F.2d 645, at p. 648:

> "It must be remembered, in this connection, that the common law is not a static but a dynamic and growing thing. Its rules arise from the application of reason to the changing conditions of society. It inheres in the life of society, not in the decisions interpreting that life; and, while decisions are looked to as evidence of the rules, they are not to be construed as limitations upon the growth of the law but as landmarks evidencing its development. As was said in *Hurtado v. California,* 110 U.S. 516, 530, 4 S.Ct. 292, 28 L.Ed. 232, 'Flexibility and capacity for growth and adaptation is the peculiar boast and excellence of the common law'; and, in the recent case of *Funk v. United States,* 290 U.S 371, 54 S.Ct. 212, 216, 78 L.Ed. 369, 93 A.L.R. 1136, wherein the ancient rule that the wife was not a competent witness for the husband in a criminal trial was repudiated on the ground that it was no longer in harmony with the spirit of the common law as it had developed, the Court quoted this statement from *Hurtado v. California* as to the flexibility and capacity for growth of the common law, and went on to say: 'To concede this capacity for growth and change in the common law by drawing its inspiration from every fountain of justice,' and at the same time to say that the courts of this country are forever bound to perpetuate such of its rules as, by every reasonable test, are found to be neither wise nor just, because we have once adopted them as suited to our situation and institutions at a particular time, is to deny to the common law in the place of its adoption a 'flexibility and capacity for growth and adaptation' which was 'the peculiar boast and excellence' of the system in the place of its origin."

In this case the Government was under a *duty* at common law, as well as by virtue of the constitutional and statutory provisions of the State of North Carolina, to fly its planes at a height that would avoid damage to land owners.

(b) Petition by Environmental Defense Fund, to the Federal Aviation Administration for Environmental Standards on SSTs

FEDERAL AVIATION ADMINISTRATION

In re

ENVIRONMENTAL DEFENSE FUND, INC.
Individually and on Behalf of
All the People of the United
States of America,
                    Petitioner.

PETITION UNDER THE FEDERAL AVIATION ACT REQUESTING THE IMMEDIATE PROMULGATION OF THE ENVIRONMENTAL STANDARDS THAT WILL GOVERN CERTIFICATION OF THE SUPERSONIC TRANSPORT

The Environmental Defense Fund, Incorporated (EDF), is a non-profit public benefit membership corporation organized under the laws of the State of New York. It is comprised of scientists and other citizens dedicated to the protection of man's environment from harmful and unnecessary intrusions. EDF is convinced that the civilian supersonic transport will present numerous substantial environmental and human health hazards.

Before the supersonic transport will be permitted to enter commercial service certificates of airworthiness will have to be issued. At that time the FAA will have to explore fully those hazards and determine whether certification will be in the public interest. However, if the formulation and announcement of standards is delayed until the certification stage is imminent, economic and technological investments will impose unfortunate restraints on the decision-making process to the prejudice of the public.

When the United States launched its supersonic transport programs in the early 1960s, the public was assured that the Government investment would not exceed $750 million. To date, Government expenditures approximate $700 million and, according to the proponents of the program, we are still at least two years away from prototype testing and eight years away from commercial production. The Government investment alone is now placed at several billion dollars.

Accordingly, EDF, on behalf of itself, its membership and the public generally, hereby petitions for the following action:

1. An immediate determination that the noise standards applicable to subsonic aircraft will be applied to supersonic aircraft, without any reduction of those standards, and

2. The immediate initiation of a public rulemaking proceeding to consider the minimum environmental standards that will govern certification of the supersonic transport and the formulation and publication of those standards at the earliest feasible date.

Respectfully submitted,
BERLIN, ROISMAN and KESSLER
1910 N Street, N. W.
Washington, D. C. 20036

May 15, 1970

(c) Memorandum by Petitioners

On January 1, 1970, with the signing into law of the National Environmental Policy Act (NEPA), the President formally launched the decade which, it is heralded, will be one of unprecedented environmental concern. The puproses of the Act, as stated in Section 2, are:

> To declare a national policy which will encourage productive and enjoyable harmony between man and his environment; to promote efforts which will prevent or eliminate damage to the environment and biosphere and stimulate the health and welfare of man; to enrich the understanding of the ecological systems and natural resources important to the Nation; and to establish a Council on Environmental Quality.

As will be shown, the legislation seeks the realization of two overriding objectives: The reexamination of national priorities particularly as they relate to federal spending programs which have adverse environmental consequences and the analysis of environmental factors at the earliest possible time so as to minimize adverse effects, preclude irreparable damage and permit an inquiry which is unimpeded by economic exigencies.

There is no program to which the legislation appears more directed than the supersonic transport program. It involves unprecedented governmental assistance, poses serious ecological problems, including human health effects not occasioned by proven alternatives, and the feasibility of conducting a meaningful environmental inquiry becomes more difficult each day it is deferred.

Interest in a United States SST program began building in 1960. The following year the Congress appropriated $11 million for a two year research program. In 1963, having been assured by the Administration that the Government investment would never exceed $750 million, Congress appropriated an additional $60 million. To date the Government investment is approaching $700 million with the experts agreeing that several billion may be required before commercial operation is possible. The anticipated in-service date has now been postponed from the mid-1970's until at least 1978.

Before the supersonic transport will be able to be utilized in commercial aviation, certificates of airworthiness will have to be issued. At that time it will have to be established that the aircraft can be certified consistent with NEPA and the noise abatement provision of the Federal Aviation Act. But if the environmental inquiry and the promulgation of standards are postponed until commercial operation is imminent, the Federal Aviation Administration will find itself in precisely the dilemma that each of those Congressional directives are designed to avoid: the need to temper environmental interests by the already accomplished commitment of economic resources.

At a minimum, in fairness to the taxpaying public, the Congress, the private developers of the SST and the Federal Aviation Administration itself, the FAA should immediately promulgate the environmental standards that will be applicable to the certification of the supersonic transport. If the airport noise limits already promulgated for subsonic aircraft apply to the SST—and there would not appear to be any justification for failing to apply them— it is clear that the presently contemplated aircraft could not be certificated for entry into commercial service.

I.

THE FAA SHOULD DETERMINE IMMEDIATELY THAT THE NOISE STANDARDS APPLICABLE TO SUBSONIC AIRCRAFT WILL BE APPLIED TO SUPERSONIC AIRCRAFT

A. The FAA Has a Statutory Duty to Do All That Is Feasible to Abate and Control Noise Pollution

Aircraft noise has become a problem of serious proportions to many people in many locales. It represents an intrusion on the pattern of their lives and a disruption of the environment which cannot go unattended. It can, and must, be alleviated. Aircraft noise is a burgeoning national problem, which can only become worse if action is not taken.

In that statement the Senate Committee on Commerce succinctly summarized the intention underlying enactment, in 1968, of the noise and sonic boom abatement section of the Federal Aviation Act. "The purpose of *** [the] bill is to authorize and require the Federal Government to establish and apply noise reduction standards to the issuance of certificates [by the FAA] and to prescribe and amend such rules and regulations as are necessary to provide for the control and abatement of aircraft noise."

Under the legislation the FAA is charged with actively carrying forth a noise reduction program. It is a mandatory duty. As stated by the House Committee on Interstate and Foreign Commerce:

B. Airport Noise Associated With the SST and Its Implications

The SST airport noise problem was most recently summarized by Russell E. Train, Chairman, Council on Environmental Quality:

At present the most significant unresolved environmental problem I see for the supersonic transport is the high level of noise in the vicinity of airports . . . In terms of the measures used by the Federal Aviation Administration to assess annoyance, the SST would be three to four times louder than current FAA sideline noise standards and four to five times louder than the 747. In terms of noise pressure, the sideline noise level would also be substantially higher than that of subsonic jets meeting the FAA requirements.

In addition, prolonged high level noise can incite fear and anxiety, create a loss of equilibrium and cause mental fatigue. "For example, astronauts, upon being exposed to 145-dB sounds from a jet engine at full thrust, experienced difficulty in carrying out simple arithmetical operations and tended to put down any answer in order to end the experiment quickly * * *." Speaking directly of the new projected SST airport noise levels, the Presidential Environmental Panel has reported:

Land use planning in the vicinity of airports is the only satisfactory solution to [the noise] problem at the present time. Airport personnel and airline passengers, however, will be exposed to very high noise levels regardless of land use planning. Prolonged exposure to intense noise produces permanent hearing loss and may also disrupt job performance by interfering with speech communication, distracting attention, and otherwise complicating the demands of the task. *Noise-induced hearing loss looms as a major health hazard in American industry.* However, a national hearing conservation standard governing allowable or safe exposures remains to be established.

*The SST will produce as much noise as the simultaneous takeoff of 50 jumbo jets * * *.*

C. The Subsonic Airport Noise Limits Must Apply as Well to the SST

In summarizing the report of the Presidential Environmental Panel, the Department of Transportation states:

The "airport noise" problem should be based on what people near airports will accept, and design requirements established accordingly, not in reverse order. *We should not wait for the aircraft to be built, and then set standards based on what has been accomplished.*

Therefore, in November, 1969, the FAA promulgated approach and sideline noise limits after considering factors relative to human health and comfort. There is no logical basis for drawing a distinction between subsonic and supersonic aircraft.

II.

THE FAA SHOULD PROMULGATE THE ENVIRONMENTAL STANDARDS THAT WILL GOVERN CERTIFICATION OF THE SST

A. Under the National Environmental Policy Act the FAA Will Have to Consider Fully the Environmental Effects of the SST Before It Can Be Certified

The 1968 amendment to the Federal Aviation Act requires that one environmental intrusion of air travel be considered—noise. The National Environmental Policy Act requires that all environmental intrusions be considered. Before any federal action is taken which "significantly affect[s] the quality of the human environment" the federal agency must consider:

(*i*) the environmental impact of the proposed action,
(*ii*) any adverse environmental effects which cannot be avoided should the proposal be implemented,
(*iii*) alternatives to the proposed action,
(*iv*) the relationship between local short-term uses of man's environment and the maintenance and enhancement of long-term productivity, and
(*v*) any irreversible and irretrievable commitments of resources which would be involved in the proposed action should it be implemented.

That is the real thrust of the legislation. As the Senate report states:

As a result of this failure to formulate a comprehensive national policy, environmental decisionmaking

largely continues to proceed as it has in the past.
Policy is established by default and inaction. Environmental problems are only dealt with when they reach
crisis proportions. Public desires and aspirations
are seldom consulted. Important decisions concerning the
use and the shape of man's future environment continue to be made in small but steady increments which
perpetuate rather than avoid the recognized mistakes
of previous decades.

* * * *

Past neglect and carelessness are now costing us
dearly, not merely in opportunities foregone, in impairment of health, and in discomfort and inconvenience,
but also in a demand upon tax dollars upon personal
incomes, and upon corporate earnings. The longer we
delay meeting our environmental responsibilities, the
longer the growing list of "interest charges" in environmental deterioration will run. The cost of remedial
action and of getting on to a sound basis for the future
will never again be less than it is today.

"[P]eople differ greatly in their vulnerability to startle."
Undoubtedly, this explains why a report prepared for the
Surgeon General recommends "serious study" of "the possible health effects of sonic boom exposures on sick and
disabled populations." According to Cohen "one cannot
rule out the possibility that the *startle quality of the boom
may trigger attacks in cardiac patients, induce seizures in
epileptic sufferers,* or generally aggravate those illnesses
for which rest and absence of excitement are believed essential to recovery."

Apart from these human health implications the sonic
boom poses threats to fish and wildlife. (It has already inflicted serious and irreparable damage upon unique natural areas.) The migratory patterns of birdlife undoubtedly
will be affected as will be the normal routine of oceanic
island wildlife. There is also a possibility that the ocean
may resonate the boom at certain depths with unknown
consequences to marine life.

With all of the unknowns about the sonic boom, one
thing at least is clear at this time: As Shurcliff has docu-

mented, the experts agree there is no "cure" for the boom even vaguely in sight.

Atmospheric Intrusions

The Department of Transportation summary of the Presidential Environmental Report on the SST states:

> Increased water vapor released into the atmosphere from combusion of aircraft fuel could be a problem, in terms of local climates and changes in atmospheric circulation and must be further examined.

On May 12, 1970, in testimony before the Joint Economic Committee, the Chairman of the Council on Environmental Quality gave some indication of the magnitude and seriousness of the SST's atmospheric problems:

> I now turn to a potential problem which has not received the attention it deserves. The supersonic transport will fly at an altitude between 60,000 to 70,000 feet. It will place into this part of the atmosphere large quantities of water, carbon dioxide, nitrogen oxides and particulate matter. This part of the atmosphere is to a substantial extent, isolated from the rest of the atmosphere. For example, on the average, 18 months are required for a water molecule introduced into the atmosphere at 65,000 feet to find its way to the lower atmosphere. A fleet of 500 American SSTs and Concordes flying in this region of the atmosphere could, over a period of years, increase the water content by as much as 50 to 100 percent. This could be very significant because observations indicate that the water vapor content of the stratosphere has already increased about 50 percent over the last five years due presumably to natural processes, although there is a possibility which should be researched that subsonic jets have been contributing to this increase.
> Water in this part of the atmosphere can have two effects of practical significance. First, it would affect the balance of heat in the entire atmosphere leading to a warmer average surface temperature. Calculations on the magnitude of this increased temperature are most uncertain but probably it would be on the order of .2 to .3°F. Secondly, water vapor would react so as to

destroy some fraction of the ozone that is resident in this part of the atmosphere. The practical consequences of such a destruction could be that the shielding capacity of the atmosphere to penetrating and potentially highly dangerous ultraviolet rays would be lost.

Hazards to Passengers and Crew

The Presidential Environmental Panel has concluded that:

> There is an urgent need to carefully evaluate the inherent operational and environmental hazards that will be encountered while accelerating from zero to Mach 3 and cruising at supersonic speeds in a hostile environment. Passengers and crew will be vulnerable to a number of potentially serious physical, physiological, and psychological stresses associated with rapid acceleration, gravitational changes, reduced barometric pressure, increased ionizing radiation, temperature changes, and aircraft noise and vibration.

> Men cannot tolerate acceleration loads above 4 to 5g. Visual disturbances occur between 3 and 4g. At 5g loss of consciousness occurs. Turbulent flight may cause brief, linear acceleration of 10 to 12g which could cause fractures in unrestrained persons. Angular accelerations in turns and linear-angular accelerations during turbulent flight are important causes of motion sickness.

The danger of sudden and exaggerated aircraft movement is a real one. "At altitudes of about 55,000 to 65,000 feet, where SSTs will cruise, CAT [clear air turbulence] regions have been found to be surprisingly numerous, according to investigations made with military supersonic planes."

A sudden loss of cabin pressure—caused for example by an explosion resulting in a small air frame rupture or the breakage of several windows—would also prove fatal in moments according to the Presidential Environmental Panel:

> *A loss of pressure at 65,000 feet would result in all aboard losing consciousness within fifteen seconds.*

In addition, the SST will have manueverability problems, may well have stability problems, and will be particularly susceptible to *hail, lightning and fire*. The latter is a result of its unprecedented fuel consumption. *"The fuel load of the Boeing SST at take-off will be almost 200 tons."*

CONCLUSION

In summarizing the report of the Presidential Environmental Panel, that "we should not wait for the aircraft to be built, and then set standards based on what has been accomplished," the Department of Transportation had specific reference to the problem of aircraft noise. However that conclusion applies with no less force to the full range of environmental considerations.

The early announcement of standards responsive to environmental problems is particularly essential in the case of the SST. As already stated, when the United States launched its own SST program we were assured that the public commitment would never exceed $750 million; it is already approaching $700 million and there is ample evidence to suggest that it will amount to several billion.

What is particularly shocking is the fact that it is impossible to point to any advantage flowing to the public in return for this unprecedented allocation of public resources in support of a private business venture. The experts have concluded that the SST will have a negative effect on this country's balance of payments, it offers little, if any, increased employment opportunities or potential for technological fallout, it has no national defense implications and its foreign policy effects are adverse.

Moreover, the economics of the SST have been called into serious question both in terms of the aircraft sale price and the estimated number of sales. The airlines themselves are skeptical as to whether the SST will make economic sense. At best, it is extremely doubtful that the United States Government will recoup any part of its investment.

What is not at all the subject of doubt is that the SST —an aircraft which will serve at most 1% of the population—presents grave environmental and human health problems which the Departments of Health, Education and Welfare, Interior and Labor and the President's Science Adviser agree must be considered without further delay.

It follows that it is incumbent upon the FAA to now publish the environmental standards that will be applied when certificates of airworthiness are sought. Foreign policy considerations require that we now advise the British, French and Russians of what the applicable certification requirements will be as to noise and the other environmental and human health problems.

Accordingly, the following actions are required:

1. An immediate determination that the noise standards applicable to subsonic aircraft will be applied to supersonic aircraft without any reduction of those standards, and

2. The immediate initiation of a public rulemaking proceeding to consider the minimum environmental standards governing certification of the supersonic transport and the formulation and publication of those standards at the earliest feasible date.

> Respectfully submitted,
> BERLIN, ROISMAN and KESSLER
> 1910 N Street, N. W.
> Washington, D. C. 20036

6.4 Saving the Oklawaha

The Environmental Defense Fund brought an action to stop the construction of the Cross-Florida Barge Canal which the United States Army Corps of Engineers moved to dismiss on the grounds of government immunity. An ancient legal doctrine states that the king is the source of all law, can do no wrong, and therefore cannot be sued in the courts of law. Translated into the American judicial system, a citizen generally cannot sue the government. This was the major defense raised by the government in an effort to get the suit dismissed. Meanwhile, however, public controversy has exerted pressure in Florida against construction of the canal. The complaint of which excerpts follow, asks for an injunction and directions by the court to the defendant to drain the Rodman pool, to minimize the danger to it, and to allow nature to repair the damage already done to wildlife and fish habitat.

Pollution dangers are spelled out in the complaint specifying how they will adversely affect the Floridian aquifer in Silver Springs. The governor of Florida has called for reevaluation of the project; a Florida Congressman changed his mind concerning the project and several others are wavering; and [then] Secretary Hickel of the Department of the Interior sent a letter to the Corps of Engineers requesting a 15-month moratorium on construction of the canal while environmental costs and economic benefits can be reevaluated. Nevertheless, the Corps of Engineers, true to its traditions, continued to forge ahead, building a canal we didn't need and in the process destroying a wild river that we do need. The Florida Defenders of the Environment are assisting in the litigation, and David S. Anthony of the University of Florida has acted as chairman of the Scientists Advisory Committee.

On January 15, 1971, Judge Barrington Parker denied the government's motion to dismiss the complaint on the grounds of sovereign immunity and standing to sue. The judge granted a preliminary injunction stopping the construction of the canal by the United States Army Corps of Engineers. Immediately thereafter, President Nixon ordered the project abandoned.

(a) Complaint of the Environmental Defense Fund Against the Army Corps of Engineers

IN THE UNITED STATES DISTRICT COURT
FOR THE DISTRICT OF COLUMBIA

ENVIRONMENTAL DEFENSE FUND,
INCORPORATED, et al.,
   Plaintiffs,
 v.   Civil No. 2655-69

CORPS OF ENGINEERS OF THE
UNITED STATES ARMY, et al.,
   Defendants.

COMPLAINT

1. This is a civil suit seeking equitable relief which arises under:

The Fifth, Ninth, and Fourteenth Amendments to the Constitution of the United States.

The National Environmental Policy Act of 1969.

The Environmental Quality Improvement Act of 1970.

The Federal Water Pollution Control Act, as amended by the Water Quality Improvement Act of 1970.

The Refuse Act.

The Fish and Wildlife Coordination Act.

The Migratory Bird Act.

33 U.S.C. §540 providing that river development projects under Defendants' jurisdiction shall be carried out with due regard for wildlife conservation.

16 U.S.C. §§580m and 580n, providing that river development projects under Defendants' jurisdiction shall be carried out in such manner as to maximize conservational and recreation values of the areas involved.

The Anadromous Fish Act of 1965.

Act of August 25, 1950, providing for a study to develop and protect Atlantic Coast fishery resources.

Act of September 22, 1959, providing for the study of migratory game fish and game fish waters to develop wise conservation policies and practices.

Act of August 19, 1949, 16 U.S.C. §759, providing for a study of Atlantic Coast shad to recommend measures to arrest their decline and increase their abundance and best use.

Plaintiff, Environmental Defense Fund, Inc. (EDF), a non-profit, public-benefit membership corporation organized under the laws of the State of New York.

EDF brings this action on behalf of its members and all other citizens of the United States who have an interest in the protection and enhancement of our natural environment, including scenic rivers, wildlife and the quality of our water resources.

Plaintiff, Florida Defenders of the Environment (FDE), is a private voluntary unincorporated association whose members are citizens and/or residents of the State of Florida. Its office is at Room 210, 35 North Main Street, Gainesville, Florida 32601.

The individuals whose names and address are given below all join as individual plaintiffs in this action; each of them has hunted or fished and/or otherwise derived use and enjoyment from the Oklawaha River and its valley in their natural state. They bring this suit individually and, on behalf of all other persons, too numerous to be joined, who wish to *preserve and enhance the Oklawaha River, protect the fish in the river, the wildlife in its valley, and the quality of its waters.*

John H. Couse, P.O. Box 146, Ft. McCoy, Florida 32637, etc.

Defendant, Corps of Engineers, is a branch of the United States Army. It is charged by statute with the accomplishment of certain civil functions of the Department of the Army, such as the construction of canals, dikes and the like. Defendant Stanley R. Resor is Secretary of the Army of the United States. Defendants have been responsible for the illegal actions, including failures to perform duties owed to plaintiffs complained of herein. Relief is sought against these defendants in their official capacities to enjoin them from further illegal actions, and to compel them to fulfill their legal duties to plaintiffs.

General Allegations

The Oklawaha River is one of the principal rivers of Florida. A navigable river, it has its source in several large lakes of the central peninsula, including Lake Griffin, Lake Eustis, Lake Harris and Lake Dora. It flows northward for some sixty miles and enters the St. Johns River about eight miles below Lake George. The great flow of the water from Silver Springs, *one of the largest fresh-water springs in the world,* joins the Oklawaha through Silver Springs Run.

The Oklawaha is a sand-bottom river and its waters are clear, although stained tan by acids from the bark and leaves of the dense tree swamp through which it meanders. Throughout its course the river twists and doubles back and forth in a well-defined, heavily forested valley so that its actual length is a third again as long as its valley. Today, when so many of the diverse original Florida landscapes are threatened with obliteration, the Oklawaha, in its lower reaches, remains as it was, a dark, beautiful stream, clear and free-flowing. The resulting rich, fluctuating waters of the Oklawaha have created the dynamic conditions necessary for the maintainance of a productive sports fishery, and now as in past times, the river is noted for its fine fishing. Channel catfish, chain pickerel, and many species of sunfish including redbreast, shellcrackers, and speckled perch abound, and the river is famous for the exceptional size of its largemouth black bass. Another important species is the striped bass or rockfish, an anadromous game fish.

When the Oklawaha River runs high, as it does in the wet period of the climatic cycles, or in the annual rainy season, the water flows over its low banks and spreads out on the valley floor. During dry times the water recedes to within the river banks. The trees of the valley forest are adapted to these periodic floodings and recessions. They are for the most part deciduous, and include tupelo, water-locust, water-ash, swamp red bay, water oak, sweet gum, red maple, loblolly bay, Florida elm, water-hickory, cabbage palm and the magnificent bald cypress. On higher ground, along the edges of the valley, the typical hammock hardwoods such as magnolia, blue beech, hop-hornbeam and laurel oak make up the forest.

This hydric hammock (or tree swamp) supports a much more abundant and varied fauna than the adjacent pine islands. The delicately balanced conglomerate of diverse plant communities provides ideal conditions for the survival of many wildlife species. Wood ducks, herons, limpkins, gallinules and rails feed along the river's edge; snakes, turtles, and alligators sun themselves on downed tree trunks, and still present also are white-tailed deer, wild turkey, raccoon, otter, bobcat, black bear, and panther. Indeed, the Oklawaha Valley provides habitat for a majority of all the different kinds of terrestrial vertebrate animals resident in peninsular Florida.

The project area of the St. Johns River supports an extremely valuable freshwater fishery. Its largemouth bass and anadromous shad fisheries enjoy national reputations. Striped bass are caught throughout the year. In addition, a valuable commercial fishery exists for freshwater catfish, blue crab and anadromous shads.

An Act of July 23, 1942, Public Law 675, 56 Stat. 703, authorized appropriations for the construction of a Cross-Florida Barge Canal, "to promote the national defense and to promptly facilitate and protect the transport of materials and supplies needful to the Military Establishment * * *." In the 87th Congress, Second Session (1962), monies were appropriated for a study of the feasibility of the construction of a Cross-Florida Barge Canal. Thereafter, at the request of the Corps of Engineers, Congress has annually appropriated funds for the construction of the canal.

Defendants' plans for the construction of the Cross-Florida Barge Canal include 5 locks, 3 dams, and a channel of approximately 107 miles from the St. Johns River at Palatka, Florida, to the Gulf of Mexico near Yankeetown, Florida. Thirty-three miles of this waterway will be along the Oklawaha River, *totally destroying its natural state*. The result will be to destroy the habitat of many of the more valuable species of wildlife and fish, and thereby greatly diminish, if not eliminate, many of these species in the Oklawaha ecosystem. The canal will also result in the degradation and pollution of the water of the Oklawaha River and of the Floridan aquifer, including the water of Silver Springs, one of the great fresh water springs of the world.

I

First Claim for Relief

The Defendant Corps of Engineers, as an agency of the Federal Government, is required under Section 102(1) of the National Environmental Act of 1969, to interpret and administer all relevant policies, regulations, and public laws including the congressional authorization of the Cross-Florida Barge Canal, in accordance with the policies of the N.E.P.A. to the fullest extent possible. Section 202 of the

Environmental Quality Improvement Act of 1970 similarly directs that the Corps of Engineers as a—"Federal * * * agency conducting * * * public works which *affect the environment*," that it "shall implement the policy established under existing law; * * *."

The policies of N.E.P.A.:

> To "attain the widest range of beneficial uses of the environment without degradation, risk to health or safety, or other undesirable and unintended consequences; * * * *to create and maintain conditions under which man and nature can exist in productive harmony, employ a systematic, interdisciplinary approach, insuring the integrated use of the natural and social sciences and environmental design arts in planning and in decision-making* * * *."
>
> *Develop procedures, in consultation with the Council on Environmental Quality which will insure that* "presently unquantified environmental amenities *and values may be given appropriate consideration in decisionmaking along with economic and technical considerations."*
>
> *Include* in their recommendations on the "major federal actions significantly affecting the quality of the human environment, a detailed statement * * * on—
>
> *the environmental impact of the proposed action,*
>
> *any adverse environmental effects which cannot* be avoided should the proposal be implemented,
>
> *alternatives to the proposed action,*
>
> the relationship between local *short-term uses of man's environment and the maintenance and enhancement of long-term productivity,* and
>
> any irreversible and irretrievable commitments of resources which would be involved in the proposed action should it be implemented."

Prior to making any detailed statement, the responsible Federal official shall consult with and obtain the comments of any Federal agency which has jurisdiction by law or special expertise with respect to *any environmental impact involved.*

Second Claim for Relief

The Rodman Pool is planned by defendants for recreation purposes including public fishing for bass, bream and all types of pan fish. The Rodman Pool is presently infested with aquatic vegetation. These include huge mats of water hyacinths and submersed plants, particularly hydrilla and milfoil. The conditions which have encouraged the growth of these plants are such that the plants create a constant and serious obstacle to both navigation and recreational uses of the Rodman Pool. The Corps of Engineers is engaged in a vigorous and expensive effort to eliminate these plants from Rodman Pool by repeatedly spraying them with the toxic chemical, 2,4-D (2,4-dichlorophenoxyacetic acid). Such spraying can, if sufficiently intensive and repeated, destroy the water hyacinths. Even intensive spraying, however, cannot totally eliminate submersed weeds such as hydrilla and milfoil. Indeed, removal of the water hyacinths encourages the growth of the submersed weeds by increasing the sunlight which is available to them.

All of this aquatic vegetation absorbs substantial oxygen from the water of the Rodman Pool. Similar conditions will prevail in the Eureka Pool if it is developed. In their destruction by chemical means as described herein, the decaying plants have been permitted to dissolve in the waters of Rodman Pool, creating a further serious demand for oxygen. Consequently, the Rodman Pool has not met and does not meet the water quality standards for dissolved oxygen—4 parts per million (ppm)—prescribed by the Florida Air and Water Pollution Control Commission. Defendants conduct, therefore, is in violation of Federal as well as State law. Defendants can comply with such standards, policy and law applicable to dissolved oxygen and with Executive Order 11507, only by physically removing the water hyacinths and other aquatic vegetation from the Rodman Pool.

In attempting to control the growth of water hyacinths and other aquatic vegetation by spraying, Defendants make abundant use of the toxic chemical 2,4-D (2,4-dichlorophenoxyacetic acid). Upon information and belief, Defendant's use of 2,4-D violates the Federal water quality standards established by the Florida Air and Water Pollution Control Commission which are applicable to the discharge of toxic substances into waters of the State of Florida.

The Federal water quality standards for the State of Florida provides that Class III waters, which include the Oklawaha River, shall be "free from substances attributable to municipal, industrial, agricultural or other discharges in concentrations or combinations which are toxic or harmful to human, animal or aquatic life."

The chemical sprays used by Defendants are harmful to aquatic plant life. That is the sole purpose for their use. In this respect alone, Defendants have violated the Federal water quality standards for the State of Florida.

Under present plans, the dredging of the upper portion of the Ocala limestone and other portions of the Floridian aquifer will create conditions under which the flow of water from the canal to the aquifer becomes inevitable. During a state of equilibrium between the waters of the canal, particularly in the Summit Pool area, and the natural ground water level, any *contaminants in the canal will move toward a zone of outflow and enter the aquifer with the water*.

Construction of the Cross-Florida Barge Canal pursuant to present plans would destroy delicately-balanced high quality swamp and upland hardwood habitats which support wood duck, heron, deer, wild turkey, raccoon, otter, snakes, turtles, alligators, bobcat, black bear, panther and squirrel. Planned impediments to the normal water flow and planned alterations of the character of the waterway of the Oklawaha will virtually destroy the striped bass fishery of the Oklawaha River and substantially reduce and adversely affect, if not destroy, certain of the other valuable game fisheries of the Oklawaha.

In failing to consider these and other deleterious effects on the fish and wildlife of the region in constructing the canal, the Defendants have failed to comply with the Fish and Wildlife Coordination Act, 16 U.S.C. §662. They have failed to consult adequately with the United States Fish and Wildlife Service, Department of the Interior, and the State of Florida Game and Fresh Water Fish Commission, to give full consideration to and act in accordance with findings and recommendations contained in reports issued by each of those agencies, and to include in the project plans such justifiable means and measures for wildlife and fish purposes as those agencies have found should be adopted to obtain maximum overall benefits for the project and to minimize the loss of or damage to wildlife and fish resources.

In the construction of the Cross-Florida Barge Canal, Defendants are bound by the Act of June 20, 1938, 33 U.S.C. §540, which provides that all river improvements shall include a due regard for wildlife conservation. Defendants have failed to consider adequately that provision and the law and policy set forth in the Migratory Bird Act, Anadromous Fish Act of 1965, the Act of August 25, 1950 (studies for the protection of fisheries near the Atlantic Coast), the Act of September 22, 1959 (development of wise conservation policies for migratory marine fish), and the Act of August 18, 1949 (studies for the preservation of Atlantic Coast shad), all of which are in *pari materia* with the legislative authorization for the canal, and in so doing Defendants have thereby violated their statutory duty to give due regard to the conservation and protection of fish and wildlife in the project area and the Oklawaha ecosystem.

The zone of hydric hammock along the Oklawaha serves as a wintering ground and migratory route for many bird species that breed elsewhere in North America. The swamp along the river is the late summer habitat of large numbers of water birds, including anhinga, ibises, and herons. The reach of the Oklawaha River through which the canal is to be cut supports an abundant population of anadromous fish including striped bass. The project area of the St. Johns River also supports an extremely valuable freshwater fishery. Its anadromous shad fishery enjoys a national reputation. Striped bass are caught throughout the year. In addition, a valuable commercial fishery exists in the area for anadromous shads.

The planned destruction of much of the swamp and forest along the river would adversely affect the status of migratory bird species in far removed areas of North

America and would be detrimental to the water birds which presently inhabit the area, ultimately destroying the life cycle and sport fishing industry of the striped bass in that area. The boat traffic will include oil and other fuel-carrying barges and other vessels carrying other cargoes, which, if spilled, will have deleterious effects upon water quality and aquatic life. Because of the size of the canal, and particularly the width of the channel during low water, there will be a substantial risk of cargo—including oil—spills through the collision and grounding of the barges and other vessels using the canal. Therefore, as a matter of design, as distinguished from substantially unavoidable accident, the water of the canal and of the Floridian aquifer will be polluted and degraded if the canal is built and operated as presently designed.

Defendants' continued construction of the canal and impoundment of water into shallow, stagnant pools would create conditions conducive to the breeding of mosquitos, the destruction of fish and wildlife habitat, and the general degradation of a healthful environment within the meaning of the N.E.P.A.

Further construction of the canal, destruction of timber and wildlife, impoundment and pollution of waters, or substantial alteration of the land, waters, flora or fauna of the Oklawaha ecosystem in connection therewith would be a deprivation of the rights of Plaintiffs under the Fifth, Ninth and Fourteenth Amendments to the United States Constitution, and would cause irreparable damage to plaintiffs, for which they have no adequate remedy at law.

WHEREFORE, Plaintiffs pray for an ORDER:

1. Enjoining Defendants from proceeding further with the construction of the Cross-Florida Barge Canal, and all components thereof, and from making any substantial alterations of the lands and waters through which the canal is to be built and of those which are to be substantially affected thereby.

2. Directing Defendants to drain Rodman Pool immediately to minimize the damage to, and allow the natural repair of, the wildlife and fish habitat that has been in-

undated or otherwise adversely affected by the filling of the Rodman Pool.

3. Granting such other interlocutory relief to Plaintiffs as may be necessary to prevent irreparable injury, pending final judgment herein.

4. Directing Defendants to cease immediately the chemical spraying of water hyacinths in the Rodman Pool, and directing Defendants that they devise and implement plans for the physical (mechanical and/or manual) harvesting of the hyacinths and any other aquatic vegetation that constitutes an obstacle or threat to the navigational and recreational qualities of the waters of the Oklawaha River within the Rodman Pool area, or which would otherwise degrade the quality of those waters.

5. Enjoining Defendants from proceeding further with construction of the canal unless and until Defendants modify their canal plans to provide for a different routing of the canal that will eliminate substantial risk of pollution to the Floridian aquifer and Silver Springs.

6. Enjoining Defendants from proceeding further with the construction of the canal project, including all of its component parts, and from making any substantial alterations of the lands and waters within the canal project area and of those to be substantially affected by the project unless and until Defendants comply with each of the laws, statutes, policies, and executive orders heretofore referred to and relied on in this complaint.

6.5 Save the National Parks!

The Everglades National Park is a unique and exciting place with alligators, turtles, and birds of unusual size, shape, and color as to delight the mind and imagination of its millions of yearly visitors. The state of Florida was considering a "Big Cypress Swamp Jet Port" which would have threatened the existence of all of these natural wonders, birds, alligators, turtles, and unique fish life found in this tropical national park. This threat to the park and the danger to the flora and fauna acted as a call to arms to Victor John Yannacone, jr., that most ubiquitous defender of the ecology, the prime defender of the nonspeaking animal world.

On March 10, 1970, a fifty-eight page complaint was served on John A. Volpe, Secretary of Transportation of the United States of America, and Dade County, Florida, Board of County Commissioners acting as Dade County Port Authority, at the County Courthouse in Miami, Florida. The table of contents in this complaint, unique in itself, offers some index into the depth and perception of the attorney who created it. After setting forth the venue and jurisdictional aspects of the case and its qualifications as a class action, the complaint in detail traces the history of the Everglades Regional Systems. Some of the unique features of the irreplaceable Everglades National Park are described as "the abundance and diversity of epiphytic plants that is unmatched outside the tropics." These "air plants" include some twenty-five species of orchard, three species of peperomia, twelve species of bromeliads (wild pineapples), and about fifteen species of epiphytic ferns. About ten orchards and several plants of other groups are species unknown in the United States outside the Big Cypress. . . . There are twelve birds included in the list of rare and endangered fish and wildlife of the United States which occur in the Big Cypress swamp. Most of them also occur in the park estuaries that receive drainage from this area. The Eastern Brown Pelican, Florida Great White Heron, Wood Ibis (stork), Roseate Spoonbill, Florida Everglades kite, Southern Bald Eagle, American Peregrine Falcon, Florida Sandhill Crane, Sparrow, Shorttailed Hawk, Red Cockaded Woodpecker, White Pollak Pelican, Anhinga, Swallow-Tailed Kite, Limpkin. Most of these birds are already hard-pressed and have small, generally declining populations in the United States. Continued reduction or degradation of their remaining habitat is certain to cause further population declines and ultimately extinction. "If development of the jet port and land around it causes significant damage through drainage eutrophication, pesticide pollution, or otherwise adverse change, heavy losses to birds that now depend upon habitat in the Big Cypress and its downstream estuaries are inevitable. The endangered species that seem most precariously situated are the Cape Sable Sparrow and the Wood Ibis. Four mammals found in the area, the Mango Fox, Squirrel, Manatee, and Everglades Mink, are considered rare and endangered species. A total of fifteen to twenty amphibians and fifty-five to sixty reptiles are present in the area. Little is known of the life history of the great majority of these species, but many of them due to their great numbers—frogs, box turtles, anoles, etc.,—and/or size,—alligators, snakes, etc.—are important members of food chains within the Everglades system. Modification or destruction of this ecosystem would likely have considerable effect on the distribution and numbers of most of these species—in particular the rare and endangered American alligator.

The bulldozing of the Everglades National Park and the Big Cypress home jet port has not yet begun. All people who enjoy the park and those who will in the future owe Victor John Yannacone, jr., a word of thanks. This victory, whether it be temporary or permanent, was not easily won. James C. Baggott acted as local counsel. Excerpts from the amended complaint are set forth below.

(a) Amended Complaint

DISTRICT COURT OF THE UNITED STATES
for the
DISTRICT OF SOUTHERN FLORIDA

VICTOR JOHN YANNACONE, JR.,

individually and on behalf of all those entitled to the full benefit, use, and enjoyment of the national, natural resource treasure that is the Everglades National Park without degradation or diminution in value resulting from operation or development of the *Big Cypress Swamp Jetport,* and all others similarly situated, not only of this generation but of those generations yet unborn,

Plaintiff

v.

JOHN A. VOLPE, Secretary of Transportation of the United States of America, and

DADE COUNTY, FLORIDA, Board of County Commissioners, Acting as Dade County Port Authority County Court House, Miami Florida,

Defendants

TABLE OF CONTENTS

    (*e*)   Noise
    (*f*)   Bird Strikes
    (*g*)   Indian Tribes
    (*h*)   Fire and Smoke
11.   Plaintiffs Complain
12.   Equitable Jurisdiction

• • •

4. Jurisdiction

Jurisdiction of this court is invoked under Title 5, United States Code, §702(*a*):

> Any person suffering legal wrong because of agency action, or adversely affected or aggrieved by agency action within the meaning of a relevant statute, is entitled to judicial review thereof.

and the statutes relevant to this proceeding are Title 16, United States Code, §§1, 410, 410c, 410n and Title 49, United States Code, §§1651, 1633(*f*).

5. Class Action

This action is brought by the plaintiff on behalf of all those entitled to the full benefit, use, and enjoyment of the national, natural resource treasure that is the Everglades National Park.

The members of this class are so numerous as to make it impracticable to bring them all before this court. There are substantial questions of law and fact common to the class and common relief on behalf of all members of the class is sought.

The claims of the representative are typical of the claims of the members of the class, and the defendants' actions have substantial effect upon all members of the class, and thereby make appropriate final injunctive and corresponding declaratory relief with respect to the class as a whole, as a proper class action under Rule 23 (*b*) (2), Federal Rules of Civil Procedure.

The prosecution of separate actions by individual members of the class would create the risk of inconsistent or varying adjudications with respect to individual members of the class which would establish incompatible standards of conduct for the defendants, so that this action is a proper class action under Rule 23(*b*)(1)(A).

Adjudications with respect to individual members of the class would, as a practical matter, be dispositive of the interests of the other members of the class not party to this litigation so that this action is a proper class action under Rule 23(*b*) (1) (B).

The members of the class are fairly and adequately represented by this plaintiff and the plaintiff has no interest adverse to that of any individual who might be entitled to the relief sought herein.

6.   Declaratory Judgment

This is a proceeding for a judgment declaring the rights and legal relations of the parties to the matter in controversy, under Title 28, United States Code, §§2201, 2202, specifically,

(*a*) *Declaring*

the rights of the people of the United States in and to the full benefit, use, and enjoyment of the Everglades National Park without degradation and diminution in value from the acts of the defendants.

(*b*)   *Declaring*

that the defendants' actions violate the rights of the plaintiff and all the people of the United States, not only of this generation but of those generations yet unborn, similarly guaranteed under the Ninth Amendment of the Constitution of the United States and protected by the *due process* clause of the Fifth Amendment of the Constitution of the United States and by the *due process* and *equal protection* clauses of the Fourteenth Amendment of the Constitution of the United States.

•   •   •

10.   Effects of Defendants' Actions

(*a*) *Water Pollution.* Upon information and belief the development of the Big Cypress Swamp area will require drainage. The area will be latticed with a system of secondary canals leading to large, long primary canals which will rapidly remove water during rainfall periods. Unless some of this water is impounded for later use, it will all have to be vented directly into the coastal area of the park.

Removal of surface waters will result in greatly reduced ground water levels in the Big Cypress Swamp during the dry season. This, together with withdrawal for water supply purposes, will reduce water levels to a point where much of the rainfall will be required just for ground water recharge—thus greatly reducing the total volume of water available to the park.

Drainage of the Big Cypress Swamp then will result in a complete alteration of the regional systems. Overland sheet flow normally flowing into the park from the Big Cypress will cease. Drainage facilities to prevent flooding will remove excess rainfall when it occurs and unnaturally dump it into the park's estuaries. The hydroperiod of the system will be shortened from the present eight or nine months to four or five months, thus destroying the ecosystem of both the Big Cypress Swamp and its coastal zone.

A complete discussion of water quality in the Big Cypress requires data on seasonal variations in water quantity, water temperature, plant and animal communities, land use, and other parameters for which there is presently a dearth of knowledge. Many intricate and sensitive inter-relationships between the various components of the Big Cypress ecosystem are largely unknown, but they are integrated around a common need for quality water. Defendants' actions pose obvious threats to good quality water. Of primary concern are the threats posed by: (1) waste treatment practices; (2) pesticides; and (3) fallout from jet exhausts.

Waste effluents containing nitrogen and phosphorus compounds are usually not treated for removal of dissolved materials. When such effluents are released into lakes and swamps the nutrients become readily available, frequently causing large and usually detrimental algal blooms, a process referred to as eutrophication.

Without special treatment to remove nitrogen and phosphorus from any domestic and industrial waste reaching the Big Cypress–Everglades area, eutrophication will ensue. The extent of this will depend on the size of the airport and adjacent developments and the waste treatment received. As a result of eutrophication the less desirable planktonic algae will increase in relation to the more desirable epiphytic algae. These will form large blooms that will tend to deoxygenate the water at night, and, over an extended period of time, will silt over the bottom substrata. Alteration of water quality and microflora will, in turn, result in changes in the animal life, and, if the increase in eutrophication is not limited, will seriously damage the ecosystem in the Everglades and Big Cypress Swamp.

(b) *Pesticide Contamination.* In considering the threat from pesticides to the Big Cypress–Everglades area, the concentration of DDT and other persistent pesticides in the environmental transport systems must be examined. Biological magnification has been demonstrated by the U.S. Geological Survey in the aquatic ecosystems of south Florida. Persistent pesticides, such as DDT, are introduced into the aquatic transport system of the region by rainfall and runoff from agricultural and urban regions. The atmospheric transport of pesticides is now worldwide but, in the immediate region of agricultural or urban use, the fallout is heavier.

Pesticides are incorporated from the water into the algal mats that form the base of the food chains for many aquatic animals. These toxicants move through the food chains and become highly concentrated in the terminal organisms of each chain. Residues in the eggs of such birds as the Bald Eagle and Everglades Kite are only slightly lower than those that have been shown experimentally to discourage reproductive success. This biological magnification of pesticides has been known to be a threat to marsh ecosystems and to the aquatic life and birds of large lake systems for some time, but only recently has the threat to the south Florida regional system been called to public attention.

The relatively high concentration of DDT and its metabolites in the animals of south Florida represents an accumulative threat for years to come. For some species in the wild, the tissue level of certain pesticides is near the critical point of their survival.

The use of pesticides in Florida for agriculture, in homes, on lawns, gardens, and turf, and in mosquito control exceeds forty million pounds per year. This total includes chlorinated hydrocarbons such as DDT, organophosphates such as parathion, and carbamates such as Sevin. In Dade County, with a population of 1.5 million people, approximately five million pounds of these pesticides are used annually, including one million pounds of DDT and other persistent pesticides. The amount used annually is increasing as urbanization and agriculture increase.

A population of 150,000 people settling into communities in the vicinity of the jetport will affect an increase in the amounts of pesticides used in south Florida. The urban-industrial-agricultural development of the Big Cypress–Everglades region will use about 500,000 pounds of these toxicants. This would create an important addition to what is now reaching the ecosystem by aerial drift and terrestrial runoff. The additional pesticide burden will likely prove disastrous to some species, especially among terminal food chain animals.

Even at present rates of pesticide application in Florida, components of the Big Cypress–Everglades regional system will, in time, be irreparably damaged.

(c) *Air Pollution.* Not until the late 1950s was attention focused on aircraft as a source of air pollution. This coincided with the introduction of turbojet aircraft with their highly visible exhaust plumes during arrival and departure movements. Blankets of jet airplane exhaust became common at large airports. The odor of fuel permeated the surrounding area at ground level. Exhaust trails followed jets high into the air.

Emissions from aircraft consist primarily of carbon monoxide, nitrogen oxides, hydrocarbons, aldehydes, and particulates. Nearly 8000 tons per year of such aircraft pollutants were estimated to have been emitted over the New York metropolitan area in 1967.

As a maximum operating training facility, the Everglades Airport is expected to accommodate about 350,000 annual aircraft. Emissions upon the environment, according to the Department of Transportation, should approximate 3400 tons of emittants.

The Department of Transportation explains that:

> Over ninety-nine percent of the weight of the kerosene-type fuel consumed by a jet engine is exhausted in the form of invisible, nonpollutant gaseous products such as carbon dioxide, water vapor, oxygen, nitrogen, and excess air, all normal atmospheric constituents. Less than one percent consists of visible particulate and invisible gaseous pollutants. About one-half of one percent is visible particulate material (smoke) which consists of pure carbon and organic compounds. The invisible gaseous pollutants include unburned hydrocarbons, carbon monoxide, aldehydes, and nitrogen oxides which are present only in trace quantities.

In the nearly pristine conditions of the Big Cypress–Everglades area, such pollution tonnage would suddenly comprise a very high percentage of the total air pollutants.

Fallout material from jet emissions would blanket many square miles of the aquatic environment surrounding the jetport and fall out in the rainfall.

Certain hydrocarbons and their derivatives, particularly the phenols, are known to be highly toxic to aquatic organisms, and under proper atmospheric conditions the pollutant concentrations in water areas near the landing and takeoff approaches at the jetport could reach lethal limits for many animal species.

Earlier this year the Federal Water Pollution Control Administration obtained water samples from open water areas adjacent to the Miami International Airport. Analyses of the samples, which were taken from areas within the takeoff and landing approach zone, showed that the chemical oxygen demand consistently exceeded 24 ppm and reached a high of 158 ppm near an aircraft taxi service area.

Air pollution will also increase in proportion to the number of automobiles using the jetport access road and the port area. Whether or not a high-speed transportation facility is built, the increase of automobile travel in the Big

Cypress area associated with the jetport would cause a significant increase in pollutant emissions.

(*d*)   Wildlife Danger. There are twelve birds included in the list of rare and endangered fish and wildlife of the United States which occur in the Big Cypress Swamp. Most of them also occur in the park estuaries that receive drainage from this area.

11.   Plaintiffs Complain

That the actions of the defendants will directly destroy at least 400 acres of natural habitat of the Big Cypress Swamp and cause serious, permanent, and irreparable damage to the Everglades–Big Cypress regional ecosystem.

That pollution of the air from the effluent of aircraft engines will cause serious, permanent, and irreparable degradation to the environment of the Everglades National Park.

That the Miccosukee Indians will be suddenly and involuntarily subjected to round-the-clock noise levels commonly experienced by urbanites who live very near airports in many cities. There will be frequent high-level noise intrusion on the wilderness character of the northern part of Everglades National Park and even more on the Big Cypress and Conservation Area No. 3.

That the defendants' activities will increase hazards to aviation from bird strikes within the airport boundaries, over Conservation Area No. 3, and in the quadrant southwest from the training strip. Such bird strikes would involve large water birds, including several rare and endangered species, at altitudes ranging from ground to 2000 feet. Small animals which seek refuge on the runways in flood periods will add to this problem when they are crushed and attract carrion-eating birds.

That the combination of bird strikes, pest insect problems, and incidence of small animals on runways will probably lead to drainage of at least part of the jetport property. This is the Federal Aviation Administration recommendation in wetland areas for control of bird strikes. The Dade County Port Authority has announced no such plans, but has the capability and authority to construct canals for drainage within and without the port boundary, and use eminent domain authority on exterior lands. To be effective, any drainage effort would have to cover a large area using a grid of drainage canals. Drainage would materially increase the occurrence of fires, and such drainage will substantially and irreparably alter the characteristics of the Everglade–Big Cypress regional ecosystem.

That construction and imminent operation of the first training strip have elevated surrounding land prices and increased sales. Economic and social pressures for further development within and without the port property will mount rapidly, the one encouraging the other. Such development for housing, trade, or industry will inexorably lead to land drainage outside the jetport property. Land development and drainage will be accompanied by increased nutrient levels in the water, will alter the hydroperiod, and will promote eutrophication. To the extent and at the rate these changes take place, the south Florida regional ecological system will sustain serious, permanent, and irreparable damage.

12.   Equitable Jurisdiction

This action is properly brought in equity before this court on the following grounds:

(*a*) The subject matter is equitable in nature.

This action is brought for the purpose of restraining the defendants from damaging the unique national, natural resource treasure—the Everglades National Park, and its supporting regional ecological system, and doing irreparable injury which cannot be adequately compensated in damages to the class represented by plaintiff. The declaratory judgment and injunction demanded by the plaintiff are equitable remedies and the substantive character of the rights sought to be enforced by the plaintiff are historically in the province of a court of equity.

(*b*) There is no adequate remedy at law.

The law does not afford any adequate remedy for the

contemplated wrong resulting from defendants' action. There is no plain, adequate, and complete remedy at law as practicable and efficient as the equitable relief sought herein, nor are the damages sustained by the class represented by plaintiff as a result of the defendants' actions capable of adequate determination in any action at law.

WHEREFORE, the plaintiff on behalf of all those entitled to the full benefit, use, and enjoyment of the national, natural resource treasure that is the Everglades National Park without degradation or diminution in value resulting from the development of the *Big Cypress Swamp Jetport,* and all others similarly situated, not only of this generation but of those generations yet unborn, demand judgment of the defendants.

(*a*) *Declaring*

the rights of the people of the United States in and to the full benefit, use, and enjoyment of the national, natural resource treasure, the Everglades National Park, without degradation or diminution in value from the operation and development of the *Big Cypress Swamp Jetport.*

(*b*)   *Declaring*

that the defendants' actions violate the rights of the plaintiff and all the people of the United States, not only of this generation but of those generations yet unborn, guaranteed under the Ninth Amendment of the Constitution of the United States and protected by the *due process* clause of the Fifth Amendment of the Constitution of the United States and by the *due process* and *equal protection* clauses of the Fourteenth Amendment of the Constitution of the United States.

(*c*) *Restraining*

the defendants jointly or severally, individually or in concert with others, from any operation or development of the *Big Cypress Swamp Jetport* that will cause serious, perma-

nent, or irreparable damage to the national, natural resource treasure, the Everglades National Park.

(*d*) *Restraining*

the defendants jointly or severally, individually or in concert with others, from continued use of the existing facilities
of the *Big Cypress Swamp Jetport* for aircraft operations,
training or otherwise, except in the case of extreme
emergency.

6.6 Citizens Slow Down Expressway Construction

David Sive, counsel for the Sierra Club and other conservation groups, is one of the outstanding leaders of the
environmental movement in the courts. He is attorney for
the plaintiffs in the Hudson River Expressway cases and
for fishing cooperatives and island developers in the efforts
to preserve Hilton Head Island, South Carolina, and the
waters around it from the pollution threatened by a proposed large chemical plant. We include portions of the
brief on the Expressway Cases (§6.6) as well as excerpts
from the "Hilton Head" complaint (§6.7).

(a) Brief for Plaintiffs

UNITED STATES COURT OF APPEALS

FOR THE SECOND CIRCUIT.

425 F 2d 97 1969

CITIZENS COMMITTEE FOR THE HUDSON VALLEY AND
SIERRA CLUB,

Appellees,

v.

JOHN VOLPE, Individually and as Secretary of Transportation of the United States, WALTER J. HICKEL, Individually and as Secretary of the Interior of the United
States, STANLEY S. RESOR, Individually and as Secretary of the Army of the United States, and WILLIAM F.

CASSIDY, Individually and as Chief of Engineers, Corps of Engineers of the U. S. Army,

Appellants,

J. BURCH MCMORRAN, Individually and as Commissioner of the Department of Transportation of the State of New York,

Intervenor-Appellant.

Statement of the Cases.

The Expressway is a six-lane truck and passenger car road project, planned to be built by the State DOT, of which McMorran has been Commissioner. The portion of the Expressway involved in these cases would be approximately ten miles in length and go along the eastern shore of and in the Hudson River, Westchester County, New York, from Tarrytown to Crotonville. In each of the four actions plaintiffs have sought a judgment declaring unlawful, and enjoining the defendants from proceeding with the construction of, the Expressway.

The Village is a municipal corporate body. It lies on the east bank of the Hudson River, at the southern end of the Expressway, and would be crossed by part of it and bounded on the river side by another part of it. The Citizens Committee and the Sierra Club are two citizen conservation groups, the former local and in the area of the Expressway and the latter national, with a local Atlantic Chapter and a large number of members in the area of the Expressway. The offices and capacities of the Federal Defendants and of McMorran are clear from the captions.

Three separate claims are pleaded in each of the Volpe Actions:

1. Claims (hereinafter sometimes the "Sec. 401 claims") that construction of the Expressway would be in violation of 33 U.S.C. §§401, 403 and 525, and 49 U.S.C. §§1651 and 1655;

2. Claims (hereinafter sometimes the "Arbitrary action claims") that the grant by Cassidy and Resor of the Expressway Permit, permitting construction of a four and one half mile long portion of the Expressway in the navi-

gable waters of the Hudson River, purportedly under 33 U.S.C. §403, and the approval of the Expressway by Hickel's predecessor in office, Stewart Udall, purportedly under Public Law 89-605, were *arbitrary, capricious* and *otherwise unlawful*; and

3. Claims (hereinafter sometimes the "Constitutional claims") that construction of the Expressway and the Expressway Law are unconstitutional, under the due process and equal protection clauses of the fourteenth amendment to the United States Constitution. The Constitutional claims are described hereinafter in some greater detail.

The Issues.

The issues presented for review in these appeals by plaintiffs are the following:

1. Whether the District Court was in error in dismissing the claims of plaintiffs based upon alleged violations of the plaintiffs' rights under the fifth and fourteenth amendments to the U. S. Constitution;

2. Whether the District Court was in error in granting, to the extent set forth in the Sovereign Immunity Decision, the motions by McMorran to dismiss the complaints.

POINT I.

The Expressway Law, together with other statutes, grants McMorran vast powers to change permanently and adversely the lives of thousands of persons, businesses and institutions, without providing any standards for the exercise of such powers.

A. The Expressway Law and related condemnation statutes.

The Expressway Law provides for the construction of an unnamed expressway (subsequently referred to as the Hudson River Expressway) in the following terms:

"Beginning at a point on interstate route 503 in the vicinity of Beacon or in the vicinity of Wiccopee, to be determined by the superintendent of public works,* thence in a generally southerly direction to the vicinity of Ossining and thence continuing southerly, west of U. S. route nine, along or near the Hudson River to a connection or connections with existing highways, as determined by the superintendent of public works, in the vicinity of the structure on the Governor Thomas E. Dewey Thruway known as 'The Tappan Zee Bridge.' "

Lying within the scope of the Commissioner's discretion to take for the Expressway is each and every parcel of land within the river communities of Beacon, Nelsonville, Cold Spring, Garrison, Manitou, Peekskill, Buchanan, Verplank, Ossining, Tarrytown, North Tarrytown, Scarborough, Briarcliff, Wiccopee, Shenandoah, Glenham, North Highland, Nelson Corners, Fahnstock Corners, Hortontown, Tompkins Corners, Shrub Oak, Mohegan Lake, Crompond, Sunnybrook, Graymoor, Continental Village, Forsonville, Teatown, Quaker Bridge, Van Cortlandtville, Denington, Christian Corners, and Yorktown, numerous historic sites, and approximately 40 miles of the eastern shore of the Hudson River.

Named above are mainly river communities. How many other communities may be included depends only, as far as the Expressway Law is concerned, upon how far (a) with respect to the portion between Wiccopee and Ossining, McMorran wishes to go east of the river or, indeed, whether he decides to cross the river and go south along a course west of the river and then recross the river to its eastern side somewhere near Ossining; and (b) with respect to the portion between Ossining and the Tappan Zee Bridge, how McMorran construes the undefined phrase "along or near the Hudson River." That looseness is the rule of construction is clear from the fact that the phrase *"along or near* the Hudson River" (italics supplied), has been deemed to mean *in* the Hudson with respect to 4½ linear

* The "superintendent of public works" is now the Commissioner of the State DOT.

miles, calling for approximately 10,000,000 cubic yards of fill.

B. There are no standards for the exercise of McMorran's powers.

Under the Highway Law the power to make all determinations with respect to the Expressway, including but not limited to its exact route, its width, the nature, size and number of motor vehicles to be accommodated, the homes, stores, schools, factories and open lands to be taken or adversedly affected, and the extent to which the shoreline of the Hudson River is to be changed and the river filled in, is thus vested solely in the Commissioner of Transportation. No standards are prescribed by statute to govern the making of any of the said determinations by the Commissioner, a non-elective official.

POINT II.

The condemnation power and its delegation are subject to federal constitutional limitations other than the requirement of just compensation.

There is now no doubt that the delegation and exercise by a state of its powers of eminent domain are subject to due process and other constitutional limitations, in addition to the requirement of just compensation.

The condemnation must be for a public use and its exercise is subject to the requirements of due process. Legislative findings and standards are required in connection with condemnations for redevelopment and slum clearance projects. Condemnation may not be made an instrument of racial discrimination.

"Nevertheless, the power of eminent domain, great as it is, is subject to constitutional limitations, and the courts may interpose their authority to prevent a clear abuse of the exercise of that right [citing Illinois cases].

"It is also well settled that State power cannot be used as an instrument to deprive any person of a right protected by the Federal constitution." *Gomillion v. Lightfoot,* 364 U. S. 339. The gargantuan urban, suburban and rural development plan called the Expressway is not exempt from such constitutional limitations.

POINT III.

The grant of powers to McMorran, without standards for their exercise, violates due process.

A. Undue delegation of power violates due process.

Due process is not subject to precise definition. In whatever context due process is discussed—the condemnation power, the police power, or some other power—the test has been, in the words of Mr. Justice Cardozo:

> ". . . differently phrased by different judges in different contexts. . . . From the very nature of the problem these phrases and others like them are approximate suggestions rather than scientific definitions. In the last resort the line of division is too subtle to be catalogued." *Roberts v. City of New York,* 295 U.S. 264 (1935).

That undue delegation of legislative power violates due process is undisputed. In *A.L.A. Schechter Poultry Corp. v. United States,* 295 U. S. 495 (1935), in holding that the National Industrial Recovery Act was unconstitutional, the Supreme Court ruled that Congress is not permitted by the Constitution to abdicate, or to transfer to others the essential legislative functions with which it is vested. Part of the opinion follows:

> "*Second. The question of the delegation of legislative power.* We recently had occasion to review the pertinent decisions and the general principles which govern the determination of this question. *Panama Refining Co. v. Ryan,* 293 U.S. 388. The Constitution provides that 'All legislative power herein granted shall be vested in a Congress of the United States, which shall consist of a Senate and House of Representatives.' Art. I, §1. And the Congress is authorized 'To make all laws which shall be necessary and proper for carrying into execution' its general powers. Art. I, §8, par. 18. The Congress is not permitted to abdicate or to trans-

fer to others the essential legislative functions with
which it is thus vested."

B. The Expressway Law and related statutes violate the limits of delegation of powers.

The due process requirement of standards for the exercise of the condemnation power is no less stringent than
that for the exercise of the police power, "the least limitable
of the powers of government." *District of Columbia v.
Brooke,* 214 U. S. 138, 149 (1909). The exercise and
effect of the police power and the condemnation power are,
indeed, often strikingly similar, as in the cases drawing
finely spun definitions of what constitutes a "taking."

In such cases persons claiming that property has been
taken seek to nullify exercises of what the governmental
authorities deem to be exercises of the police power. The
claimants would receive their "just compensation" if the
exercises of the power would be "takings."

The Citizens Committee and the Sierra Club, *per se,*
own no real property. With the exception of the Phillipse
Manor Improvement Association, a corporate member of
the Citizens Committee whose lands will evidently be
taken, the Citizens Committee and the Sierra Club did not
prove that the homes or other properties of any of their
members are in the direct path of the Expressway, in large
part because of the elusiveness of the State DOT and the
now-it's here, now-it's there nature of that path. Nor could
they, within the confines of time and means on a trial that
was of inordinate length without such proof, prove in
standard law-of-damages manner the reduced value of the
homes of many of them living adjacent to that ever shifting Expressway path. Moreover, the Citizens Committee
and the Sierra Club are admittedly suing both in personal
and quasi-representative capacities, in vindication at least
in part of public rights.

*Plaintiffs' basic claim is that the Expressway will have a
vast effect upon the nature and quality of the lives of all
who live, work or play anywhere near it.* This is undisputed, however forcefully and sincerely the Expressway's
proponents and opponents argue that the changes will be

for better or for worse, respectively. Nor can it be disputed that most of the rules involving the exercise of the condemnation power evolved in an age when public works projects—e. g., roads, bridges, canals—did not appreciably affect the lives of persons other than the owners of the lands or other property taken. Payment in dollars alone was deemed the just compensation, because (1) with the dollars received the owner could buy the equivalent of that which was taken, and (2) the law was little concerned with any damage or injury from governmental action not measurable in dollars.

The urbanization of the landscape renders it impossible, however, in many cases, for any amount of dollars to replace the lands or water which may be taken. This is particularly true in the case of lands in a unique geographical area such as the shoreline or near the shoreline of one of the most dramatic stretches of a great river. And the indirect effects of public works projects of the vastness and complexity of expressways, massively cutting through urban and suburban areas, upon the persons and institutions who cannot make a claim for any "taking" of property, are many times greater than those upon the persons whose property is taken.

The vastness and complexity and the effects of highways across the nation have been described in Mowbray, *Road to Ruin,* Lippincott (1968), at pages 12 and 13:

> "There are 3,600,000 square miles of land in the United States. There are 3,600,000 miles of roads and streets in the United States: one mile of road for every square mile of land. The land area covered by roads and their rights-of-way is estimated to be about 24,000 square miles—equal to the area of the state of West Virginia. But apparently we have only begun. California alone has completed 2,700 miles of freeways, but the master plan calls for an eventual 12,500 miles; every mile of freeway consumes about 24 acres of land; every interchange eats up about 80 acres. The 41,000-mile interstate system now under construction will gobble up more land than the state of Rhode Island.

* * *

"When completed the interstate system will be thirty times as long as the Great Wall of China. The Bureau of Public Roads has estimated the enormous wealth that we are pouring into that 41,000-mile system; 'The pavement area of the system, assembled into one huge parking lot, would be 20 miles square and could accommodate two thirds of all the motor vehicles in the United States. New right-of-way needed amounts to 1½ million acres. Total excavations will move enough material to bury Connecticut knee-deep in dirt.' "

The basic fact is that expressways are not simply roads from point A to point B; *they are remakings of landscapes and cityscapes,* the appreciation and meaning of the effects of which are far beyond the provincialism of mere highway builders, engineers or commissioners of transportation. This provincialism is described well in Marine, *America the Raped* (Simon & Schuster 1969) at page 16:

"There is an engineers' way of looking at problems, an engineering approach to public questions, to planning, even to correcting the malfunctions that were introduced by engineers in the first place. It is the simple, supposedly pragmatic approach of taking the problem as given, ignoring or ruthlessly excluding questions of side effects, working out 'solutions' that meet only the simplest definitions of the problem. It is an approach that never seeks out a larger context, that resents the raising of issues it regards as extraneous to the engineering problem involved."

The law has not been completely insensitive to the multiplication of the effects of public works projects. The law of eminent domain itself now grants damages for some injuries which a century or even only a few years ago were not compensable.

That environmental protections also have become, in recent years, an important legislative concern of governments at every level is beyond dispute. Directing attention at only the Hudson River and the Valley itself, major planning and resource statutes have been enacted by both Congress and the New York State Legislature, each in fact competing to some extent with the other for the right and honor of protecting the unique resources of that river and valley.

Congress, by Public Law 89-605, has found and declared:

> "That the Hudson River Basin contains resources of immense economic, natural, scenic, historic and recreational value to all the citizens of the United States. . . ."

Public Law 89-605 goes on to grant the consent of Congress to the states of New York and New Jersey and, if they wish to participate, the states of Vermont, Massachusetts and Connecticut.

> "to negotiate with each other and with the United States for the purpose of entering into a compact, relating to the preservation, restoration, utilization and development of the natural, scenic, historic and recreational resources of those portions of the Hudson River Basin which lie within the boundaries of the participating states."

The Act requires that any and all United States governmental agencies refer to the Secretary of the Interior any plan or project, which may affect the resources of the Hudson River ". . . before taking final action . . . on such plan, or project."

By Ch. 345, Laws of New York 1966, the New York State Legislature set up the Hudson River Valley Commission as a permanent agency, the purposes of which:

> ". . . shall be to encourage the preservation, enhancement and development of the scenic, historic, recreational and natural resources of the Hudson River valley, and to encourage the full development of the commercial, industrial, agricultural, residential and other resources which are vital to the continued progress of the Hudson River valley."

The people of New York State, less than one month ago, also approved a basic amendment of the New York State Constitution, popularly called the *"Conservation Bill of Rights,"* providing that:

"The policy of the state shall be to conserve and protect its natural resources and scenic beauty and encourage the development and improvement of its agricultural lands for the production of food and other
agricultural products. The legislature, in implementing
this policy, shall include adequate provision for the
abatement of air and water pollution and of excessive
and unnecessary noise, the protection of agricultural
lands, wetlands and shorelines, and the development
and regulation of water resources. The legislature shall
further provide for the acquisition of lands and waters,
including improvements thereon and any interest therein, outside the forest preserve counties, and the dedication of properties so acquired or now owned, which
because of their natural beauty, *wilderness character, or
geological, ecological or historical significance, shall
be preserved and administered for the use and enjoyment of the people.* Properties so dedicated shall constitute the state nature and historical preserve and they
shall not be taken or otherwise disposed of except by
law enacted by two successive regular sessions of the
legislature."

This court may take judicial cognizance of the fact that
in 1967 New York State held a Constitutional Convention,
which adopted a new state constitution and submitted it to
the voters for approval at the 1967 general election. The
proposed new constitution contained, in slightly different
form, the "Conservation Bill of Rights." The proposed new
Constitution was defeated, primarily because of basic
church-versus-state issues involved in it. Of the dozens of
major and minor new constitutional provisions and changes
of old provisions embodied in the proposed new constitution, the only one which has subsequently been passed by
the Legislature and approved by the people of the State,
and in that alternative manner been adopted as a constitutional amendment, is the "Conservation Bill of Rights."

"The Commission's renewed proceedings must include as a basic concern the preservation of natural
beauty and of national historic shrines, keeping in
mind that, in our affluent society, the cost of a project
is any one of several factors to be considered."

Scenic Hudson Preservation Conference v. Federal Power Commission, 354 F. 2d 608.

CONCLUSION.

The dismissal of the constitutional claims and of the McMorran Actions should be reversed.

Dated: November 24, 1969.

WINER, NEUBURGER & SIVE,
Attorneys for Plaintiffs.

DAVID SIVE,
ALFRED S. FORSYTH,
DAVID M. PERLMUTTER,
SIGMUND ANDERMAN,
    Of Counsel.

6.7 Fishing Coop Successfully Opposed Chemical Plant Expansion

South Carolina's Hilton Head Fishing Cooperative was threatened with extinction when the BASF Corporation attempted to build a chemical plant that would place a killing effluent into the estuarine waters.

Shrimp and young fish as well as other forms of shellfish are very sensitive to chemical changes in the water.

The waters around Hilton Head Island are exceptionally clear and unpolluted. The Complaint served in that case follows below. As a result of the lawsuit, the BASF Corporation abandoned the project.

IN THE DISTRICT COURT OF THE
UNITED STATES
FOR THE DISTRICT OF SOUTH CAROLINA
CHARLESTON DIVISION

HILTON HEAD FISHING COOPERATIVE, INC.,
THE BLUE CHANNEL CORP., AND OCEAN
LAKE AND RIVER FISH COMPANY,
                                                    Plaintiffs,

VS.

BASF CORPORATION AND BADISCHE

ANILIN-UND SODA FABRIK, A. G.,
                              Defendants.

This action arises under:
The Constitution of the United States, Amendments 5,
    9 and 14;
Commerce and anti-trust regulations;
National Environmental Policy;
Refuse Act;
Federal Water Pollution Control Act;
Oil Pollution Act, 1924;
Foreign Trade Zones;
Rivers and Harbors Act of 1899;
Fish and Wildlife Coordination Act;
Anadromous Fish Act;
Endangered Species;
Estuarine Areas.

3. A. Plaintiff Hilton Head Fishing Cooperative, Inc.,
(hereinafter sometimes the "Cooperative"), is a corporation organized and operating under the laws of the State
of South Carolina, with its principal office and place of
business at Hilton Head Island, South Carolina. The members and stockholders of the Cooperative fish and trawl for
shrimp in and about the waters of the Atlantic Ocean adjacent to Beaufort County, Port Royal Sound, which are
located on the copy of the U. S. Coast and Geodetic Survey
Chart #1240, a portion of which is annexed hereto as
Exhibit "A" and which is hereby incorporated by reference
herein.

B. The shrimp is processed and packed by the Cooperative and its members at a processing plant in which the
Cooperative has an investment of approximately $135,-
000.00 and which is owned and operated by the Cooperative and located on Skull Creek, Hilton Head Island,
South Carolina.
Blue Channel engages approximately 150 fishermen
whose principal means of livelihood is fishing for crabs in
the waters of Chechessee River, Colleton River, Broad
River, etc., as located on Exhibit "A" attached hereto.

Defendant BASF Corporation (hereinafter sometimes "BASF-US") is a corporation organized and operating under the laws of the State of New York.

The waters in which Plaintiffs and their members, stockholders and other persons retained by them fish, trawl and collect shrimp, crabs and oysters, are substantially clean, pure and unpolluted tidal waters.

Shrimp, crabs and oysters are particularly sensitive to impurities and pollution and the deposit or release into the Fishing Waters, directly or indirectly, of any industrial pollution, waste, effluent or other foreign matter, would destroy the life and fitness for human consumption of the shrimp, crabs and oysters in the Fishing Waters.

BASF-US and BASF-Germany and other persons, firms and corporations acting in their behalf, plan to have and have begun construction of dyestuff, polystyrene and petrochemical plants producing numerous products, such as expandable polystyrene, dyestuffs, chemicals, pigments, plastics, ethylene, propylene, butadienen, and benzene from such liquid raw products as styrene and naptha, involving, among other things, a daily discharge of 2.5 million to 5 million gallons of effluent and industrial waste into the waters of Port Royal Sound and other of the Fishing Waters.

Federal Agencies which must grant licenses, permits and subsidies to BASF-US and BASF-Germany in connection with the Chemical Works include the following:

A. The Oil Import Administration Office of the Assistant Secretary—Mineral Resources of the Department of the Interior.

B. The Foreign Trade Zone Board of the Bureau of International Commerce of the Department of Commerce.

C. The United States Army Corps of Engineers, under 33 U.S.C. Sec. 403, granting a permit or permits to build one or more structures or perform other works in navigable waters.

13. Each Federal Agency, in any and all agency action in connection with the Chemical Works, is and shall be

required under Public Law 91-190 (National Environmental Policy Act of 1969), to:

A. Interpret and administer all relevant laws, regulations and policies of the United States in accordance with the policies set forth in the said Act, including:

(1) A national policy which will encourage productive and enjoyable harmony between man and his environment;

(2) The promotion of efforts which will prevent or eliminate damage to the environment and biosphere and stimulate the health and welfare of man;

(3) The enrichment of the understanding of the ecological systems and natural resources important to the Nation;

(4) The critical importance of restoring and maintaining environmental quality to the overall welfare and development of man;

(5) The continuing policy of the Federal Government, in cooperation with State and local governments, and other concerned public and private organizations, to use all practicable means and measures, including financial and technical assistance, in a manner calculated to foster and promote the general welfare, to create and maintain conditions under which man and nature can exist in productive harmony, and fulfill the social, economic, and other requirements of present and future generations of Americans;

(6) The continuing responsibility of the Federal Government to use all practicable means, consistent with other essential considerations of national policy, to improve and coordinate Federal plans, functions, programs, and resources to the end that the Nation may—

(1) fulfill the responsibilities of each generation as trustee of the environment for succeeding generations;

(2) assure for all Americans safe, healthful, productive, and esthetically and culturally pleasing surroundings;

(3) attain the widest range of beneficial uses of the environment without degradation, risk to

health or safety, or other undesirable and unintended consequences;

(4) preserve important historic, cultural, and natural aspects of our national heritage, and maintain, wherever possible, an environment which supports diversity and variety of individual choice;

(5) achieve a balance between population and resource use which will permit high standards of living and a wide sharing of life's amenities; and

(6) enhance the quality of renewable resources and approach the maximum attainable recycling of depletable resources.

B. Utilize a systematic, interdisciplinary approach which will insure the integrated use of natural and social sciences and the environmental design arts in planning and in decisionmaking which may have an impact on man's environment;

C. Identify and develop methods and procedures, in consulation with the Council on Environmental Quality established by title II of the Act, which will insure that presently unquantified environmental amenities and values may be given appropriate consideration in decisionmaking along with economic and technical considerations;

D. Include in every recommendation or report on proposals for legislation and other major Federal actions significantly affecting the quality of the human environment, a detailed statement by the responsible official on—

(i) the environmental impact of the proposed action,

(ii) any adverse environmental effects which cannot be avoided should the proposal be implemented,

(iii) alternatives to the proposed action,

(iv) the relationship between local short-term uses of man's environment and the maintenance and enhancement of long-term productivity, and

(v) any irreversible and irretrievable commitments of the resources which would be involved in the proposed action should it be implemented.

E. Study, develop, and describe appropriate alternatives to recommended courses of action in any proposal which involves unresolved conflicts concerning alternative uses of available resources.

15. All of the Fishing Waters are navigable waters of the United States within the meaning of that term as used in (Rivers and Harbors Act of 1899) and (Refuse Act); and interstate and navigable waters within the meanings of those terms are used in (Federal Water Pollution Control Act and Water Quality Act of 1965); and estuarine waters within the meaning of that term as used in 16 U.S.C. Secs. 1221-1226 (Estuarine Waters).

The Chemical Works would necessarily and unavoidably and because of, among other things, the intrinsic nature of the manufacturing processes and the waste products therefrom:

A. involve violation of 33 U.S.C. Sec. 407 (Refuse Act);

B. involve pollution of the Fishing Waters, in violation of the standards system hereinbefore described in Paragraph 8C of this Complaint and of the policy and provisions of 33 U.S.C. 446 *et seq.* (Federal Water Pollution Control Act: Water Quality Act of 1965);

C. involve serious hazards of oil pollution and spillage in violation of 33 U.S.C. Secs. 431-437 (Oil Pollution Act, 1946); and

D. violate the policy of 16 U.S.C. Secs. 661-665 (Fish and Wildlife Coordination Act) and of 16 U.S.C. Secs. 1221-1226 (Estuarine Areas).

17. Upon information and belief, the Chemical Works will necessarily and unavoidably and because of, among other things, the intrinsic nature of the manufacturing processes and the waste products therefrom:

(a) Seriously pollute the Fishing Waters;

(b) Kill or render unfit for human consumption the shrimp, crabs and oysters in the Fishing Waters;

(c) Destroy the business of each of the Plaintiffs and the means of livelihood of the members and stockholders, processing plant employees and the other persons who fish and trawl for the shrimp, crabs and oysters as hereinbefore described, and destroy the investments of the said persons in their boats and other equipment and supplies.

18. By virtue of the foregoing:

A. construction of the Chemical Works by Defendants BASF-US and BASF-Germany is unlawful and in violation of the rights of Plaintiffs and Plaintiffs would suffer therefrom irreparable injury;

B. substantial alteration of any of the lands or waters upon which the Chemical Works are to be built, or which are to be substantially affected thereby, for purposes of construction of the Chemical Works, in advance of final determination by each and every Federal Agency to which any applications or petitions are made or to be made, for any licenses, permits or subsidies, in connection with the Chemical Works, is unlawful and in violation of the rights of Plaintiffs, and Plaintiffs would suffer therefrom irreparable injury.

19. Plaintiffs have no adequate remedy at law.

AS AND FOR PLAINTIFFS' SECOND CLAIM

20. Plaintiffs repeat and reallege each and every allegation set forth in Paragraphs "1" through "18" with the same effect as though herein fully set forth and repeated.

21. Construction of the Chemical Works, and any substantial alteration of the lands and waters upon which the Chemical Works are to be built, or which are to be substantially affected thereby, in advance of final determination by each and every Federal Agency to which any applications or petitions are made or to be made, for any licenses, permits or subsidies, in connection with the Chemical Works, would be a deprivation of the rights of Plaintiffs under the Fifth, Ninth and Fourteenth Amendments to the United States Constitution, and a deprivation under color of laws, statutes, ordinances, regulations, customs and usages of the State of South Carolina of rights, privileges and immunities secured by the United States Constitution and by Acts of Congress, from which Plaintiffs would suffer irreparable injury.

22. Plaintiffs have no adequate remedy at law.

AS AND FOR PLAINTIFFS' THIRD CLAIM

24. Construction of the Chemical Works, and any substantial alteration of the lands and waters upon which the Chemical Works are to be built, or which are to be substantially affected thereby, in advance of final determination by each and every Federal Agency to which any applications or petitions are made or to be made, for any licenses, permits or subsidies, in connection with the Chemical Works, would be an unlawful nuisance from which Plaintiffs would suffer irreparable injury.

WHEREFORE, Plaintiffs respectfully pray for judgment:

1. Declaring the construction of the Chemical Works by Defendants BASF-US and BASF-Germany, and any substantial alteration of the lands or waters upon which the Chemical Works are to be built or which are to be substantially affected thereby in advance of final determination by each and every Federal Agency to which any applications or petitions are made or to be made for any licenses, permits or subsidies in connection with the Chemical Works, unlawful and in violation of the constitutional and other rights of Plaintiffs.

2. Permanently enjoining Defendants, BASF-US and BASF-Germany, and any agents or other persons, firms or corporations engaged or retained by them, from construction of the Chemical Works.

3. Permanently enjoining Defendants, BASF-US and BASF-Germany, and any agents or other persons, firms or corporations engaged or retained by them, from causing or effecting any substantial alteration of the lands and waters on which the Chemical Works are to be built or which are to be substantially affected thereby, in advance of final determination by each and every Federal Agency to which any applications or petitions are made or to be made for any licenses, permits or subsidies in connection with the Chemical Works.

4. Granting such interlocutory relief to Plaintiffs, pending final judgment in this action, as may be necessary to prevent irreparable injury pending final judgment herein.

DOWLING, DOWLING, SANDERS & DUKES, P. A.
AND WINER, NEUBURGER & SIVE

William H. Bowen of Dowling, Dowling,
Sanders & Dukes, P. A.
ATTORNEYS FOR PLAINTIFFS
P. O. Drawer 1027, Beaufort, S. C.
Beaufort, South Carolina
February 10, 1970

Postscript: As of November, 1970 the Company has
withdrawn its plans to construct a factory at Hilton Head.

CHAPTER 7

METHODS OF PROOF IN ENVIRONMENTAL LITIGATION

METHODS OF PROOF IN ENVIRONMENTAL LITIGATION

The methods of proof in environmental litigation are as varied, new and ingenious as the subject itself. Demonstrative evidence, of course, is standard procedure now. Pictures of the smoke and foul air, the swarms of dead fish immediately adjacent to the offending outfall or source of effluent have been used. Samples of the water which contain human waste don't have to be scientifically described to court or jury. They come, all too frequently, from municipal waste treatment plants that are overtaxed by a booming population. Perhaps the most dramatic pictures obtained in this field were conceived and executed by the office of Harry H. Lipsig in New York. Under cover of night, a helicopter, armed with spotlights and a professional photographer on board, came down dangerously close to a certain power company's smokestack. Suddenly the lights flashed on; the cameramen hung on, suspended from their aircraft and clicking away, making a permanent record of the black, offending emissions coming from the smokestack. The night watchman surely thought Martians were at work. Unique? Certainly; and singularly effective with both court and jury. (It is well known that violators will often let their air pollutants go up the stack under cover of darkness or on a foggy day.)

Many companies are now creating environmental departments which keep daily and hourly records of solid waste, liquid emissions and test samples of what is passing up through the smokestack. By use of subpoenas *duces tecum,* trial lawyers for many years have required defendants to bring to court records which give one a different picture than the one the public has been seeing from the advertising agencies and press releases.

In addition to the records, employees of the offending polluter can be subpoenaed, brought to court, and questioned about the findings relative to the required standards. This, however, should be done with great care as you cannot expect an employee to be a cooperative witness when you are suing his boss. We have set forth in this chapter the critical testimony of an expert in a water pollution case as well as an air pollution case, both of whom were employed by the defendant polluter.

The state and county health departments are now monitoring the water and air emissions around the major factories and public utilities. They, as well as the interstate sanitation commissioners in all of the states should make their records available; they can, if properly used, be a source of "impartial expertise." If conference and persuasion cannot settle the environmental dispute and a lawsuit must be commenced, then, hopefully, this chapter will help you to win it.

7.1 Securing, Examining, and Cross-examining Expert Witnesses in Environmental Cases*

by David Sive

It is a known lawyer's joke, kept carefully from laymen, that if a lawyer does a particular job once, he may deem himself an expert. This observation is even more applicable to the litigation of environmental matters than it is to matters such as chapter XI arrangement proceedings, Securities and Exchange Commission registration statements, or most other fields of acknowledged legal expertise. The reason is self-evident: The field is so new. The number of cases from which to draw one's experience is small, and the variety of fora and consequently of applicable procedural codes is large. The present situation may not be different from that existing in other fields of law which

* Reprinted by permission of *The Michigan Law Review*, May 1970, p.1175. (footnotes omitted.)

are currently in an evolutionary stage: midway between, at the one extreme, the stage of borrowing most of their substantive and procedural doctrines from already delineated areas of law, and, at the other extreme, the stage when they are recognized as separate bodies of law, with their own doctrines, their own chapters in the encyclopedias, and their own law school courses.

In light of the newness of the field and the paucity of experience among its practitioners, it becomes apparent that the characterization of a lawyer as an expert in this area is often the result much less of talent than of a fondness for the wild woods. But despite the fact that few lawyers have had any extensive experience in environmental litigation, lawyers will be called on more and more frequently in the coming years to try cases involving environmental matters. One of the problems that these lawyers will face, particularly if they are inexperienced in this area, is that of making effective use of expert witnesses; indeed, the use of expert witnesses in environmental litigation involves problems which lawyers have seldom faced in other fields of litigation. Accordingly—recognizing that this author's expertise stems primarily from a fondness for nature—this Article will explore the practicalities involved in securing, examining, and cross-examining expert witnesses in "environmental litigation."

I. Apologia

A. *Scope of the Problem*

It is necessary at the outset to define the scope of the problem with which this Article will deal. Environmental cases are litigated in both judicial and administrative tribunals. The judicial proceedings include plenary actions and special proceedings and are heard in both federal and state courts. The administrative proceedings include licensing proceedings before federal agencies such as the Federal Power Commission and Atomic Energy Commission. Whether such administrative proceedings are deemed quasi-judicial or not, they are within the scope of this Article so long as they are adversary and involve testimony under oath, examination and cross-examination of witnesses, a formal record of testimonial and documentary evidence, and findings and conclusions based solely on that record. Of course, many legislative bodies and committees, as well as administrative agencies, conduct nonadversary "hearings" with formal records. Such hearings often involve the testimony and statements of large numbers of renowned experts, and a strong case can be made for urging that they are better instruments for ascertaining truth and wisdom than are adversary proceedings. The focus of this Article, however, is solely on proceedings which are adversary in nature and which involve the procedural aspects described above.

It is also necessary to examine the "environmental" nature of the litigation with which this Article is concerned. First, the Article deals with proceedings which determine the disposition or use of natural resources or aspects of our natural environment. Second, it is concerned only with the problems of, and it looks at the subject matter only through the eyes of, the conservationist who is attempting to protect the resource or environment from one special disposition, use, or claim. This limitation to the problems of the "protectors" is perhaps contrary to tradition as well as injudicious. Such limitation is absolutely necessary, however, because the problems of the two sides are as vastly different from one another as the refining of the pebbles in David's sling was different from the buildup of the might of Goliath's brawn.

The limitation to the problems of the "protectors" also delineates the party position of the client who is the focus of the discussion here. That delineation is important, for one's party position has significant procedural consequences in this area. In a plenary action, characteristically an action for a declaratory judgment and an injunction, the party position of the conservationist is generally that of the plaintiff. In an administrative proceeding, the relevant position is usually that of an opposing intervenor, that is, one opposing or seeking to condition the grant of a license to use a resource. Thus, the various procedural possibilities in these cases necessarily dictate that one's policy as to the use of expert witnesses be flexible in order to be effective.

B. *Necessity for Using Expert Witnesses*

It is essential, too, before dealing with the practical problems which are the primary focus of this Article, to examine briefly why expert witnesses should be used at all in environmental cases. The traditional role of the expert witness has been to assist adjudicatory bodies in finding out the "truth" in any given matter. The role has been molded by two primary factors: (1) the specific area about which the expert testifies is one in which he is in fact an expert, and (2) the area is beyond the average layman's scope of comprehension. The expert witness, then, provides knowledge which he, because of his training, has acquired and which would not be brought out or understood without his testimony. The lawyer for the conservationists in an environmental litigation should realize from the beginning that expert witnesses can be just as valuable in this type of case as in cases involving complex scientific data. The reasons for the importance of utilizing expert testimony in such cases are many. The expert witness usually knows far more about the type of case at hand than does the lawyer, who, as has been pointed out, generally has had little experience in this area. Thus, at the very least, the expert can quickly give the lawyer basic background knowledge about the specific problem; this knowledge will, of course, provide much of the theoretical framework within which the lawyer will prepare his practical legal strategy. It is fundamental that the more the lawyer really understands about various factors and problems present in any one case, the more able he will be to present as good a case as possible for his client.

In addition, in many cases, the expert witness can fulfill the traditional role of the expert—that of enlightening others on subjects which they could not fully grasp on their own. In this regard the expert may be crucial to the "protectors'" case. A court may not understand why, simply to "save the environment," it should enjoin the government from building a highway through a marsh or swamp. Indeed, to issue such an injunction on such vague grounds might well seem to a court to be a "step against progress." But the same court may at least weigh the competing considerations if an expert explains the fundamental theory of the delicate eco-system present in such a marsh. In some environmental cases, then, the expert, simply by fulfilling his traditional role, can make a vast difference in the outcome of the litigation.

The expert witness can also play a vital role in cases in which the question involved is more of aesthetics than of upsetting the balance of nature. In such cases, expert testimony is, by definition, far less precise because of the more subjective nature of his expertise. It is a much more difficult proposition, it seems, to produce expert testimony on the aesthetics of natural resources than it is to produce such testimony on the ecological balance present in a stream. Yet there are two reasons why such evidence should be introduced. First, any testimony, whether aesthetic or scientific, seems more influential if given by an "expert." Thus, as a matter of strategy, testimony as to aesthetics should be given by experts, for no matter how subjective their opinions in reality are, the very fact that the witnesses are introduced as experts would appear to imply objectivity in their critical standards. Second, such testimony may be helpful simply in articulating, in the best possible language, the "protectors'" position. A teacher of the fine arts, for example, is likely to be far more poetic, and thus, it is hoped, persuasive, in his description of aesthetic values than would someone who does not have his background, training, and interest in that field. For these reasons, the attorney for the "protectors" in any environmental litigation should secure and use expert witnesses at the earliest possible stage of the proceedings.

It is in light of the foregoing considerations that this Article will discuss the effective use of expert witnesses in environmental cases. Specifically, the Article will deal with five aspects of the problem: (1) selecting, securing, and compensating the expert witness; (2) the availability and conduct of discovery proceedings; (3) preparing the witness' direct testimony; (4) preparing the witness for cross-examination; and (5) the conduct of the examination and cross-examination at the hearing or trial.

II.   SELECTING, SECURING, AND COMPENSATING THE EXPERT

The initial problem in utilizing expert testimony is, of course, that of finding a competent expert witness. Since conservation groups are often concentrated very heavily in college and university communities, it is there that many good expert witnesses may be found. Thus, the conservationists' lawyer should open, and keep open, as many avenues of contact as possible with nearby academic communities. Other useful sources of expert witnesses are the various conservation societies which are rapidly multiplying. A catalogue of the various fields of expertise which members of these organizations may possess is of great help. Such a catalogue can be compiled and maintained through the use of questionnaires periodically sent to members. The conservationists' lawyer should continually be enlarging and updating these files of potential witnesses. He should also be in constant contact with other conservationist lawyers so that as large a pool of common knowledge as possible is built up. "Protectors" have a common cause and should assist one another as much as possible in the pooling of pertinent information.

Once a competent expert is found, the next problem is securing his services for trial. The primary problem in securing the services of an expert is often money. Protectors of resources and their lawyers, with very rare exceptions, simply cannot go out into the market and pay the arms' length fees of experts, since such experts generally receive from three hundred to seven hundred fifty dollars per day plus expenses. Fortunately, there are numerous experts who are willing to contribute their time without charge because they are dedicated to the cause of conservation. That dedication exists to an inspiring degree among surprisingly large numbers of expert physical and social scientists and others who are officers, employees, or merely members of major conservation organizations or citizens' groups which attempt to protect our nation's resources.* Thus, in many environmental cases, the conservationists are able to procure expert testimony without having to pay high fees, simply because the expert witnesses are themselves "protectors" and believe strongly enough in the cause they are advancing not to try to reap large personal gains from their efforts in the case.

Another helpful factor in persuading an expert witness to testify, even though he can be paid very little, is that environmental litigation is a matter of wide public importance and concern. Expert testimony in an important environmental litigation is a mark of prestige in almost anyone's curriculum vitae, although many persons who have rendered great service in such cases hardly need any such additional credentials. It is no derogation of the nobility and selflessness of those who have given many whole days and weeks, with no or ridiculously small compensation, to point out that such recognition may be helpful to the expert witnesses in intangible ways.

Balancing the advantages of dedication and evangelism against those of money, it appears that when the expert testimony is concerned with the resources or planning issue per se and thus requires less background data than does more technical testimony, the conservationist lawyer is fully as able to secure expert witnesses and testimony as is the opposition. When the testimony is more technical in nature, however, the conservationists' zeal cannot match the opposition's dollars.

In this connection, the conservationist lawyer should be aware of the tax consequences to the expert if that expert offers to testify. The question is often asked whether the expert may deduct the value of his services against income, as a charitable deduction. The answer is clearly that he may not. The explanation is simple: if the compensation

---

* In the *Storm King* proceedings, for example, several scientists, professors, and conservationists were willing to testify for the Scenic Hudson Preservation Conference and the Sierra Club without compensation, including Vincent Scully, Charles Callison, Richard Pough, David Brower, and Richard Edes Harrison.

were actually received, it would be ordinary income; and if the amount were then donated back to the organization, the net tax effect would be zero. In addition, when the testimony is given in the federal courts, statutory witness fees and mileage are taxable costs, but the amount of compensation of expert witnesses is generally not taxable.

III. THE AVAILABILITY AND CONDUCT OF DISCOVERY PROCEDURES

The conduct of an environmental litigation is governed, perhaps even more than is the conduct of most other litigations, by the availability of discovery proceedings—depositions on oral examination, inspection of documents and physical objects, and written interrogatories. The conservationists' lawyers should therefore make as efficient and effective use of the various discovery proceedings as is possible; the protectors, in other words, have a real need for the discovery procedures. This need for discovery is caused primarily by the tremendous inequality of knowledge, between the conservation organization and the governmental agency or other resource user or developer, concerning the project under examination. The mountains of studies, plans, and relevant files usually are all in possession of or controlled by the resource user. The hard evidentiary facts are often buried deep in the platitudinous gobbledygook in which bureaucrats specialize—a process in which the personnel of agencies dealing with resources seem to approach perfection.

Obtaining the hard evidence prior to trial is of special concern in connection with conservationists' expert testimony, because only with those facts can the experts' affirmative testimony be prepared. If the litigation is a plenary action, the conservationist group is typically the plaintiff, and its case must therefore be presented first. Without discovery proceedings, the very persons who would be examined on pre-trial depositions may have to be called as plaintiff's witnesses; and although under most present-day procedural codes one is not bound by the statements of one's own witness if that witness is hostile, nevertheless learning the facts by day and preparing the testimony of one's expert by night is not an efficient method of trial preparation. Therefore, at the very earliest point in preparing the case—even before the proceeding is brought, and as an important factor in determining whether the proceeding should be brought—the lawyer should ascertain the availability of discovery proceedings.

In a judicial proceeding, if there is a choice between some type of special proceeding and a plenary action, the general availability of discovery in the plenary action is almost enough, in and of itself, to dictate choosing that form of action. The rules governing proceedings before most federal agencies dealing with the regulation of resources do not permit discovery as a matter of right, although they do authorize applications for discovery. In such proceedings, however, discovery can often be obtained on an informal basis, encouraged by a hearing examiner who realizes the great savings in time. For example, in the proceedings involved in *Scenic Hudson Preservation Conference v. FPC* (the *Storm King* litigation), a vast amount of data was disclosed by the applicant outside of any formal discovery proceedings on a voluntary basis or under gentle prodding by the hearing examiner. In many cases the time factor may appreciably limit the use and value of discovery proceedings for the preparation of the testimony of expert witnesses. Whatever the disposition of the preliminary injunction motion that is usually made (because the injunction action is typically commenced in the very shadow of the bulldozer blades), the trial is generally expedited in environmental cases, and the time for discovery and all other trial preparation is severely abbreviated. In *Citizens Committee for the Hudson Valley v. Volpe* (the *Hudson River Expressway* cases), for instance, the rapid sequence of activity—preliminary-injunction motions, appeals from their denial, the court of appeals' affirmance with direction that a trial begin in four weeks, depositions on almost a day-to-day basis, pretrial hearings and motions, and trial itself—severely limited both the efficacy of the discovery proceedings and the use at trial of testimony elicited through discovery. The presentation of plaintiffs' case was to some extent a continuation of the discovery process, since some of plaintiffs' main witnesses were officials of the defendant governmental agency. Because judicial proceedings are generally expedited in environmental cases, then, the lawyer must be ready to prepare his case quickly and effectively. If he is not ready and has not prepared all of his strategy, the fast-moving sequence of judicial events will almost certainly cause his case to be presented in an incoherent and incomplete fashion.

In this connection, there are two useful techniques which plaintiffs' counsel can use in launching discovery almost simultaneously with the commencement of the action. Both are based on the Federal Rules of Civil Procedure. The first is to secure, ex parte, an order permitting the taking of depositions before the twentieth day after commencement of an action. The second is to make use of discovery by interrogatories to parties from and after the eleventh day after commencement of an action. Discovery for the purpose of determining the necessity of a preliminary-injunction motion may be permitted upon the institution of an action, and discovery to secure information to place before the court on such a motion would also seem proper.

In any event, the drastic shortening of the procedure does ease one problem of plaintiffs generally—the fact that under many codes of civil procedure defendants have priority in the taking of depositions. As a result of the shortened procedure in environmental cases, depositions are generally scheduled on the basis of the availability of witnesses and the convenience of counsel, rather than according to the priority gained by the first service of a notice.

The conservationist lawyer, in employing discovery techniques in order to gain the information necessary to prepare the testimony of his own experts may wish to conduct a pretrial examination of the opposition's experts. Such examination is very limited, since the usual rule in the federal courts requires a showing of good cause and special circumstances. However, the recent trend is toward liberalization of this rule, and what was said in a federal-condemnation case concerning the necessity of examining the government's expert witnesses should also apply to

environmental litigations in which the opposition's experts
are governmental officials or other witnesses testifying for
the government:

> I am inclined to think that such necessity or justifica-
> tion is implicit in every eminent domain case. There is
> nothing sacred about the rights of the government in
> eminent domain proceedings. The government ought to
> be as frank, fair and honest with its citizens as it re-
> quires its citizens to be with it.

In this regard, however, it has been held that only the
factual portions of the testimony or report of an adverse
party's expert may be discovered, and not his opinions or
conclusions per se. Nevertheless, the opinions or conclusions of the governmental agency's expert are frequently
embodied in the reports or brochures issued in promotion
of the project, and such reports are very handy outlines
for questioning. In general, it can safely be said that the
ordinary limitations on the pretrial discovery of an adverse
party's experts are much weaker in environmental litigation than they are in most commercial or tort actions. This
difference is in part based on the pressure of time, under
which the judge may find that the simplest means of expe-
dition is to rely on a liberal scope-of-discovery rule.

IV. PREPARING THE WITNESS'S DIRECT TESTIMONY

A. *The Conservationists' Own Expert*

To the extent that there are special problems in the
preparation of the direct testimony of experts in environmental litigation, those problems relate more to the substance of the litigation than to the procedure. The necessity that the attorney be as expert as, or more expert than,
the expert, the importance of the collection and ready
availability of the materials upon which the testimony is
based, the existence or nonexistence of a rule rendering it
necessary to elicit expert opinions by the traditional hypothetical question, and most of the other advice found in
trial practice guides, all apply to environmental litigations
just as they apply to other actions. The special problems

stem primarily from the fact that the subject matters of the expert testimony in environmental cases often involve questions of aesthetics.

A threshold problem in this area is that most expert witnesses testifying on behalf of conservationists in environmental cases are not professional witnesses, and for many it may be their first experience in an adversary litigation, although they may have frequently been "witnesses" at legislative hearings. Thus, a special effort must be made to explain to them the difference between the two types of hearings.

The *Storm King* litigation is perhaps the best example of the problems which the existence of aesthetic questions can cause in an environmental case. In that case, a citizens' conservation group opposed the grant of a license by the Federal Power Commission to the applicant, Consolidated Edison Company, to build a pumped-storage reservoir at Storm King Mountain. The United States Court of Appeals for the Second Circuit, in reversing the grant of the license, remanded the proceedings to the Commission. The nature of the proceedings to be held on remand was outlined in the now classic language of Circuit Judge Paul R. Hays:

> The Commission's renewed proceedings must include as a basic concern the preservation of natural beauty and of national historic shrines, keeping in mind that, in our affluent society, the cost of a project is only one of several factors to be considered.

The court's direction as to the nature of the renewed proceedings required an appraisal and analysis of the scenic beauty and of the place in history of Storm King Mountain and the surrounding area, for only by such an appraisal and analysis could the "basic concern" of "the preservation of natural beauty and of national historic shrines" be properly considered alongside the "cost of [the] project." Such measurement of natural beauty and the balancing of it against purely economic considerations has been, and probably will be, involved in most environmental cases. The primary duty of the expert witness, then, is to persuade the court that the aesthetic qualities of the natural resource in question are so great that any destruction of those qualities, for whatever practical or economic reason, will leave society worse off. The expert witness must convince the court that aesthetic values outweigh the practical economic reasons for any project which threatens the nation's natural resources.

In the *Storm King* litigation, for example, the scenic beauty could not be measured quantitatively. Nor, however, could it be claimed to be a purely subjective matter, for there would then be no standard by which the Commission or a court could hold Storm King Mountain to be more worthy of preservation than any other acreage which any person held particularly dear. Thus, it became the task of the two active intervenors opposing the project, the Scenic Hudson Preservation Conference and the Sierra Club, to prove, under the ordinary rules of evidence, the degree of natural beauty of Storm King. It required development of a theory and technique for which, so far as the attorneys for the two organizations could ascertain, there was no precedent; in no prior litigation known to them was there the problem of ascertaining the value to an "affluent society" of a landscape and the problem of weighing that value against cost factors.

Recognizing that a precise measurement was impossible, they attempted to develop a theory of proof which, they felt, did meet the demands of the court of appeals. The beginning point was a presumption of fact and of law that there do exist in this country some landscapes which are recognized as beyond any claims of use for power or other industrial purposes, except perhaps in some crisis not yet reached. Those landscapes are our national parks and national monuments. Absent some national emergency graver than any yet posed, no Federal Power Commission or court would hold that a power plant in the Yosemite Valley could satisfy the basic requirement of section $10(a)$ of the Federal Power Act that "the project adopted . . . shall be such as in the judgment of the Commission will be best adapted to a comprehensive plan for improving or developing a waterway or waterways. . . ."

The Hudson Highlands are not located within any national park and no serious proposal has been made to create a national park in that area. But proof that their beauty is as unique as that of areas such as Yosemite, the Olympic Mountains, and the Great Smokies did not seem too difficult, in light of some basic facts familiar to any moderately sophisticated geography student: that very few rivers cut through the main chain of the Appalachian Mountains from Georgia all the way to Maine; that the rivers which do so are the most spectacular at those very points, and that the only river which does so at sea level and is at that point wide and deep enough for oceangoing vessels is the Hudson.

The lawyers attempted to prove those facts primarily through the expert testimony of seven men: a leading planner and professor of planning, a professor of art history, a renowned cartographer, and four leaders in the conservation movement.* The testimony of those seven

* The planner was Professor Charles W. Eliot, 2d, of Harvard University; the professor of art history was Vincent J. Scully of Yale University; the cartographer was Richard Edes Harrison; and the conservation leaders were Charles Callison, David Brower, Richard Pough, and Anthony Wayne Smith, of the National Audubon Society, Sierra Club, Open Space Action Committee, and National Parks Association, respectively.

The clearest and most direct opinion was rendered by Mr. Callison:

"The Hudson River from its origin to the sea is a river of great beauty. Where it flows through the Highlands, from the breathtaking gateway at Storm King Mountain to Dunderberg downstream, the scenery from the river, or from either shore, is supreme. In my opinion this is the most beautiful stretch of river scenery in the United States."

Record I, at 4786. The supremacy of the scenic beauty of the Hudson at Storm King is directly related, said Mr. Callison, "to the dominant geological feature of eastern United States, the Appalachian Mountains." *Id*. The Hudson Gorge, he said, "is one of very few places where the main chain of the Appalachians is broken by a river."

Record I, at 4787. Finally, he compared the Hudson to the other rivers cutting through the Appalachian Mountains:

"Moreover none of the other rivers has the history, the drama of the Hudson. None has been as much the very waterway of history, the gateway to the north and west, the 'northwest passage' to an empire, if not to the Orient as Henry Hudson thought it might be.

experts was a mixture of eloquence and dry analysis, but it was all directed, in one way or another, toward the conclusion that the Hudson River at Storm King Mountain possesses sufficient scenic beauty that it should be protected against those who seek to use the area for an industrial enterprise. With a few minor portions of the prepared testimony being stricken on motion, the experts' testimony was admitted.

The preparation and introduction of such expert testimony, aimed at preserving aesthetic value by balancing aesthetic qualities against bare economic facts, poses some special problems under three traditional rules governing expert testimony. Although those rules have been subject to attack in recent years, they do have some ongoing vitality. But if there is one area in which they should be inapplicable, it is the area of environmental litigation.

One such rule is that expert testimony on the matter directly in issue is inadmissible, particularly if the issue is a mixed one of fact and law. In the *Storm King* litigation, the degree of scenic beauty of Storm King Mountain was a matter placed directly in issue by the court of appeals. Nevertheless, the testimony of the experts was received over objections based upon this traditional rule. An even more basic and ultimate issue of fact and of law in the Storm King litigation was whether the project "will be best adapted to a comprehensive plan for improving or developing . . ." the waterway—the Hudson River and Valley. Yet the expert testimony, both of the applicants' witnesses and of the opposing intervenors' witnesses, was received in the form of answers to almost that very question— whether the project "will be best adapted to [such] a comprehensive plan."

In short, the Highlands and Storm King Mountain are unique topographical and scenic features, not only in the East, but in the entire country. In the far West there are rivers that run through deeper gorges, the Colorado, the Snake, the Yellowstone, the Salmon, and the Columbia to name a few. But none of them, except perhaps the Columbia, is so great a river of history, of commerce, and of empire, connecting great mountains and wilderness with a great city and seaport at its mouth."

Record I, at 4789.

A second traditional rule is that expert testimony is not admissible if it deals with matters of common knowledge. It has been argued in environmental cases, including the *Storm King* and *Hudson River Expressway* cases, that the beauty of a mountain or a river, or of a highway, is a matter of common knowledge; and that any truck driver, as well as the foremost conservationist, is entitled to his opinion. Countering such arguments without the appearance of condescension or conceit is a problem. Moreover, the problem is not solved even when the testimony is received. Theories must be advanced under which that testimony will be granted due weight by the hearing examiner or by the trial judge. One such theory was advanced by Richard Pough, an expert for the opposing intervenors in the *Storm King* litigation, although that theory cannot at the present time be said to be accepted since the hearing examiner recommended the grant of Consolidated Edison's application. The theory is that beauty created by nature is equal in value to, and is to be accorded reverence equal to that of, the beauty of music, art, or poetry, and that experts should be available to testify to degrees of natural beauty just as they are able to testify to the quality of mortals' art. From this premise it follows that the traditional rule concerning expert evidence on matters of common knowledge should no more exclude the testimony of Professor Vincent Scully, an art history professor, concerning Storm King—or preclude attaching substantial weight to that testimony—than it should do so to the testimony of Leonard Bernstein on the value of a work of music, being litigated perhaps in an estate tax proceeding.

A third traditional rule governing expert testimony can hardly be fairly applied in environmental litigation. That rule is that the facts upon which an opinion is based must be established by evidence. This rule, of course, has several qualifications in ordinary nonenvironmental litigation. An expert surely may, for example, rely on any facts which are of such a nature that the court itself may take judicial cognizance of them, and he may also rely on reports not in evidence if such reliance is in accord with the practice of his profession. In environmental cases, however, none of the qualifications generally available really support the admissibility or weight of expert testimony. An example of such testimony is that of Richard Pough in the *Storm King* case. The issue involved arose out of literally hundreds of pages of expert testimony, adduced by both sides; and it concerned the precise degree of visibility of the project works from many different angles and locations, in all seasons, at all times of day and night, and in all weather. Mr. Pough testified that any such mathematical computations were not important. The issue, he said, was the "integrity of the Mountain" itself, that is, the integrity of the mountain to those who observe it. Was it to be interpreted as a demonstration of the scientific, judicial, and political prowess of the Consolidated Edison Company or as a uniquely beautiful creation of nature? If Mr. Pough was to testify on this issue, his testimony could hardly have been based on facts established by evidence.

The issue was summarized as follows in the brief submitted by this writer on behalf of the Sierra Club:

> It is this character and "integrity of the Mountain" and the surrounding areas, that must be borne in mind in determining the extent to which the Project, and all that goes with it, will mar the natural beauty of Storm King and its environs. If its meaning is changed, in the eyes of those who behold it, its supreme value as a preserver and embodiment of the spirit of the New World . . . to a whole nation, particularly the vast millions in its greatest metropolitan area, is forever lost. In that event, no combination of orders of this Commission, funds of the applicant, and skill of its eminent landscape architects, can be any more successful in putting the earth, rocks and trees of Storm King back together again, than were all the king's horses and all the king's men in the case of Humpty Dumpty. Painting concrete green cannot deceive its beholders into believing that it is the handkerchief of the Lord, and, if it can, this Commission should not, in the absence of some overwhelming economic necessity, direct such deception.

Brief for Intervenor, *In re* Consolidated Edison Co. of New York, Inc., Project No. 2338, at 26 (FPC, filed Aug. 14, 1967).

B. *The Adverse Party's Employee*

The preparation of the direct testimony of one's own expert is a cooperative process between expert and lawyer; and there is no problem of adversity of interest, although sometimes there are clashes of temperaments and techniques. The adverse party's expert, on the other hand, cannot generally be called for *direct* testimony, because an expert may not be compelled, against his will, to render expert testimony. Of course, an adverse party's expert may be subpoenaed, but again he cannot be compelled to give an expert opinion on direct examination. In the ordinary commercial or tort litigation in which expert testimony is needed, these rules cause little hardship, for each side secures its own expert, who is well able to study the subject matter. If that expert must inspect documents, physical objects, or lands, the discovery process is available. However, in environmental litigation in which the legality of a large public-works project is at issue, lack of finances, lack of time, and physical factors all generally prevent the plaintiffs from getting the materials or data for their experts to study. Yet in such cases experts who are employees of the governmental agency being sued have the requisite information and, in addition, frequently have opinions which, wrong or right, are at variance with the positions taken by the agency heads. Assuming that the knowledge and opinions of such experts are as much the property of the plaintiffs, whom we grace with the good name "taxpayers," as they are the property of the defendants, it seems that that knowledge and those opinions should be equally available to both parties. Accordingly, the conservationists' lawyers should be permitted not only to subpoena experts employed by the government, but to compel them to give expert testimony.

These problems, of course, may not arise if the government's expert is willing to give his opinion despite the fact that it might be used in opposition to positions taken by his employer; but such situations are understandably quite rare. Moreover, even if the situation does occur, the expert in an environmental case generally needs time to prepare his opinion, and yet it may be unethical for the plaintiffs' attorneys to confer with an adversary's employee prior to trial in order to inform him as to what he will be asked on direct examination. This problem, as well as the more usual one in which the government's expert is unwilling to give his opinion on direct examination, can be solved by allowing the plaintiffs' lawyers to examine the subpoenaed expert both before trial and on direct examination during trial.

V. PREPARING EXPERT WITNESSES FOR CROSS-EXAMINATION

It has already been pointed out that the expert witness, who may have testified many times before legislative bodies on matters involved in an environmental litigation, should be made aware of the exact nature of an adversary proceeding. It is also unnecessary to dwell at any length here on the instructions given to witnesses generally—to answer simply and truthfully, not to argue, not to regard cross-examination as a game of wits, not to attempt to figure out whether an answer will be helpful or harmful, and to leave strategy and tactics to the lawyers.

What remains, then, is to examine the special problems of the expert witness in environmental litigation. One of the most significant of those problems involves the degree to which opposing counsel will attempt to portray the witness as a composite of several objects of derision, among which are the feminized male, the unworldly sentimentalist, the professor who has never met a payroll, the enemy of the poor who need more kilowatts and hard goods, and the intellectual snob. For example, on cross-examination in the *Hudson River Expressway* cases, an expert cartographer was asked questions which were intended to show that he had been biased against the project in question before the litigation began, that he was a professional conservationist, that he was opposed to any interference whatsoever with nature, and that he was against all forms of indoor recreation. Similarly, in the *Storm King* litigation, an expert for the intervenors opposing the project was asked questions, and gave answers, which portrayed him as a professional conservationist. He was also referred to as a public-relations man on the basis of his answers to questions concerning his past. The extent to which the conservationists' experts may have to be cross-examined as to their opinions, backgrounds, and associations can be a definite deterrent to their willingness to testify, particularly because the appeal to testify is made generally with the equivalent of merit badges rather than with hard dollars. The expert witness must therefore be warned of the possible tacks of cross-examination to which he may be subjected and he must be reminded to keep calm no matter what direction the questioning takes.

Nevertheless, the probing into the opinions and past activities and associations of conservationists' experts is largely justified under ordinary rules of evidence. An expert's expertise may be impeached, and the bases of his opinion are a fair field for questioning. Moreover, when the subject matter of an expert opinion is the balancing of natural beauty against super-highways, rather than the permanency of a knee injury, the cross-examiner has far greater latitude than he normally does. The fact that this latitude poses tactical problems for the conservationists' counsel, and perhaps even civil liberties problems, is just one more of a whole new set of problems to be dealt with by conservationists' lawyers on a case-by-case basis.

Another special problem which almost all conservationists' experts must meet on cross-examination is what may be called the "wilderness problem." It involves defending a defense of Storm King Mountain, Mineral King, or Central Park, against charges that conservationists would turn Times Square itself into a rain forest or that they are hypocrites for riding automobiles or airplanes. On cross-examination by a good trial lawyer that defense is difficult. In the *Hudson River Expressway* cases, for example, plaintiffs' expert on the beauty of the Tappan Zee area of the Hudson, an eminent artist, found it difficult, under cross-examination which featured references to the admitted existing blight of the waterfront in some of the areas of the proposed road, to defend halting the construction of a roadway which would be much cleaner than some of the blighted areas. His answer involved subtle theories, psychological and artistic, on just when a scene may evoke feelings of nature's, rather than of man's, skill and intelligence.

There is no unique solution in environmental cases to the problem of such derision of an expert witness. The lawyer should simply try to have the expert well-prepared to present his subtle theories in as articulate and as concrete language as possible. The more vague and ethereal such testimony is, the more likely it is that the opposition's attempts at derision will be complemented and thus furthered, by the general psychological effect the witness has on the court. The witness, then, must have ready, in simple terms, basic theories of why and how man must remain a part of nature and nature a part of the life of man. A witness may be somewhat reassured by the fact that there have been, and will be, very few, if any, major environmental cases tried before a jury since the remedy sought in plenary actions generally includes an injunction. Nevertheless, it is important to instruct an expert witness not to be concerned if the cross-examining attorney indicates the deepest sadness or puzzlement at a statement the basic meaning of which is that man does not live by bread alone.

VI.   CONDUCT OF THE EXAMINATION AND CROSS-EXAMINATION

The direct testimony of the conservationists' expert witness may be prefiled in written form if the proceeding is before the Federal Power Commission or an agency with similar procedural rules. In such a case the first oral testimony of the witness is on cross-examination. If the expert's direct testimony is not prefiled and is given orally, it is best to have the questions written out beforehand, particularly the hypothetical questions when the rule prevailing in the jurisdiction requires that such form of questions be used in order to elicit expert opinions. In addition, although the expert should be instructed to answer questions fully and adequately, he must also be instructed not to add unnecessary detail or embellishments.

Frequently, in environmental litigation, as in other types

of litigation, far more can be accomplished on the cross-examination than on the direct. More often than not the attorney for the adverse party does not follow the instruction that most senior trial lawyers give to a young associate on his first case: in cross-examination ask questions only when you know what the answers will be. Indeed, as environmental cases increase in number, attorneys defending the resource-using agencies or companies will probably cross-examine less, as they discover that their cross-examinations uncover information which is more helpful than harmful to the protectors' cause.

On the other hand, the conservationists' lawyer's cross-examination of the expert witness of the resource-using agency or company can be fruitful. Such experts, particularly those engaged in planning or construction, still, by and large, do not understand the concept that some parts of the world cannot be improved or that sound public policy does not necessarily require that we have more of everything that we can build. This pursuit of bigness may not be as dramatically expressed as it was in the words of one of the company's planning experts on cross-examination in the *Storm King* litigation when he was comparing the proposed immense storage reservoir to the small pond now at its proposed site: "[a]ny large lake," he said, "is handsomer than a small lake." But the philosophy will, in most cases, be manifested in some why which clearly poses the issue of what the affluent society should seek.

Many of the experts cross-examined in environmental cases are, of course, physical scientists, economists, bridge builders, or others whose field does not embrace any of the broad issues involving the use of resources. In cross-examining such experts, there is no special technique peculiar to environmental litigations. A special problem does exist: money. The conservationists' attorney more often than not is unable to afford to have his expert with him either as the testimony is given or even that evening. The principal solution lies, again, in securing as much information as possible in the discovery proceedings. While the oral deposition of the expert himself may not be permitted, the conservationists' attorney can make use of interrogatories and inspection of documents to secure most of the factual information which will be given and discussed in the testimony. The task of the conservationists' attorney is not unlike that of the attorney for the stockholder-plaintiff in a stockholders' derivative action, and many of such attorneys' techniques may be borrowed for use in the even more uphill struggle against "progress."

VII. Conclusion

We are only at the threshold of the development of environmental law and of techniques in environmental litigation. Perhaps all that can be really set out with assurance is a summary of the task of the conservationists' lawyer in cases which have involved, and will involve, the weighing of the material against the aesthetic in the affluent society. The task may be simply stated as that of proving, without any revolutionary changes in the rules of evidence, what was said in the mid-nineteenth century by the conservationists' favorite nonlegal authority, Henry David Thoreau, in his *Walden*:

> Most of the luxuries, and many of the so called comforts of life, are not only indispensable, but positive hindrances to the elevation of mankind.

Many courts have now reached the stage of development at which they may permit litigation of the question of what does truly aid "the elevation of mankind."

7.2 Demonstration of Expert Testimony in Water Pollution Case

The expert who takes the stand in an environmental pollution case should know the practical as well as the academic problems involved. He should be fully familiar with the taking of samples, whether from air or water, the methods of analysis, and the standards. In addition, the expert should be able to answer the court's question concerning danger to the health of human beings, animals, and plant life. Such a man is the Director of the Interstate Sanitation Commission, Thomas Glenn, a professional engineer, a teacher, a member of the American Academy of Sanitary Engineers, and fully knowledgeable in the area of water and air pollution.

Examination of the expert should cover the following areas: (*a*) qualifications, academic background and standing in the field; (*b*) knowledge of the rules and regulations pertaining to the particular area in dispute; (*c*) a familiarity with the sampling of water and/or air in that particular locale; (*d*) the ability to determine whether the samples comply with the regulations and standards and/or whether a danger to health exists; (*e*) the ability to think on his seat in order to answer questions of the court which may not be anticipated; (*f*) the ability to stand up under cross-examination to answer leading questions in a form and manner that would be brief, candid, and helpful to his side of the case (he should be able to identify the samples, how, when, and where they were taken, how, when, and where they were tested, and have available in court not only the samples themselves but the bookkeeping entries proving their authenticity—oftentimes it is required that the engineer who actually obtained the samples be on hand to identify them); (*g*) the expert may be questioned about the methods of curing the problem and the time factor and costs involved. The court would be placed in a difficult position if it had to shut down a major power plant because there were no alternatives to the pollution problem. Therefore, the expert should be prepared to answer questions concerning alternative remedies for cutting down or abating pollution altogether. He should be familiar with the costs and the time factor for building substantial air and water treatment systems which would solve the particular problem. Often judgments are rendered setting forth a time schedule (such as ninety days to enter contracts, six months to commence construction, and eighteen months to comply with the standards of purity for air and water pollution) that the locality has established. Examples follow of each of the above procedures.

DIRECT EXAMINATION

(a) Qualifications

BY MR. LANDAU:

Q: Are you a licensed engineer, sir?

A: Yes, I am a licensed professional engineer.

Q: For how long have you been so licensed?

A: Over ten years, about fifteen, I think, now.

Q: Are you associated with the Interstate Sanitation Commission?

A: I am the director and chief engineer of the Interstate Sanitation Commission.

Q: Are there engineers that are associated with you, sir?

A: Yes.

Q: Have you done anything in the field of teaching in sanitary engineering, sir?

A: I have taught for about nine years in sanitary engineering at Rutgers University.

Q: Did you receive any degrees, sir?

A: I have a degree in Bachelor of Science in chemical engineering from the University of Texas. I have a Master of Science degree from New York University.

Q: Are you also a member of the Air Pollution Control Association?

A: Yes.

Q: Are you a member of any honorary societies having to do with the field we are discussing here today?

A: I am a diplomate of the American Academy of Sanitary Engineers. The Board I served on is the American Sanitary Engineering Intersociety Board.

(b) Knowledge of Rules and Regulations

Q: May I ask you, sir, in the association that you have with the Interstate Sanitation Commission, can you advise the court whether or not the village of Port Chester comes into the Interstate Sanitation Commission's area of responsibility?

A: Yes.

Q: Is the village of Port Chester located somewhere between Greenwich and Blind Brook, as appears on the map?

A: Yes.

Q: If Your Honor please, I have attached a copy of the map to the complaint indicating what the jurisdiction of the Interstate Sanitary Commission is.

Q: As part of the work of the Interstate Sanitary Commission, are certain standards set as to what sewage treatment should be given waters in different places?

A: Yes, they have two classifications and they have standards for each of the classifications.

Q: All right. Now, can you tell us, sir, whether the classes are Class A and Class B waters.

A: Yes. Class A and Class B waters.

Q: Tell us briefly, sir, what are Class A waters?

A: Class A waters are or may be used for recreational purposes such as swimming, bathing, shell fishing; Class B aren't intended for recreational purposes.

Q: Have these standards been in effect for some period of time?

A: Yes. The standards were set in 1936 but the waters were actually classified in 1937.

Q: Can you tell me, sir, whether or not the village of Port Chester, with particular reference to their water facilities, whether or not Class A and Class B waters pertain thereto.

A: They are Class A waters, what the waters that Port Chester discharges into have been classified as Class A. Our jurisdiction ends where the tidal waters of the Byram River ends. So that portion of the Byram River which is tidal is Class A itself, and also flows into waters classified as Class A.

Q: Can you advise whether or not, sir, the outflow or effluent from the area of Port Chester goes into the area known generally as the Long Island Sound?

A: Yes, after it has passed through the Byram River.

Q: From your experience and observation, can you tell us whether or not in the Long Island Sound there are any facilities for fishing, swimming, or shellfish cultures to be taken?

A: Yes.

(c) Familiarity with Testing and Sampling

Q: Have you done any sampling—just yes or no, for the moment—as to the condition of waters in the Port Chester area?

A: Yes.

Q: And when was the most recent sample study done?

A: As far as the waters themselves, as recent as this morning. As information, also, we have sampled for several days last week and we have made spot checks every Friday for twelve weeks.

Q: Can you tell me, sir, whether or not a twenty-four-hour test during the week or weekend has been performed— just yes or no.

A: Yes.

Q: When was a twenty-four-hour, around-the-clock test performed?

A: The latest one was on October 4, 1965.

Q: Within four days of today?

A: Last Thursday.

Q: That was around-the-clock, was it, sir?

A: Twenty-four hours.

Q: Can you tell me, sir, what are the requirements for treatment of sewage water in Class A areas, briefly, if you can.

A: Well, one of the requirements is to remove all floating solids, all oil, and also one of the requirements is to remove at least sixty percent of the suspended solids. Then it has a coli form content, during the bathing season, requirement.

Q: Now, Mr. Jones, prior to coming here, did you bring with you certain samples, sir, taken from the water of the Port Chester sewage system?

A: Yes.

Q: And I ask you, sir, to look at these four samples. Just look at them first, sir. (*Four jars showed solid waste in the water.*)

THE COURT: Don't open them up.

Q: I ask you to look at them and ask you if those are samples taken under the authority of the Interstate Sanitation Commission.

A: Yes.

Q: And where were those samples taken?

A: These came out of the Purdy Street sewer.

Q: Where is that located, sir?

A: This is out of Port Chester, and I would say it is roughly two or three blocks north of the treatment plant effluent.

Q: When were these samples taken?

A: These were taken last Saturday.

Q: Over what hourly period, sir?

A: Well, we have the start, the first one of these was found at one o'clock in the afternoon, one at two o'clock, one at one-thirty and one at two-thirty.

(d) Ability to Evaluate Samples and Test Results

Q: Can you say, sir, whether or not, from the last tests taken, and I am just talking now of the tests taken in the last couple of weeks, the last two or three weeks, can you tell whether or not in the Class A waters in the area of the village of Port Chester the removal of all floating solids, to the degree of sixty percent of suspended solids, has been performed?

A: Yes. We ran our twenty-four-hour survey, and on October 4 from eight o'clock in the morning to three-thirty, which is our normal sample day, the removal was forty-four percent. We sampled from sixteen hundred on to eleven-thirty that night, and the removal was forty percent. So, on both of these periods, they were well below the sixty percent requirement.

Q: Then in that particular category of removing floating solids—I mean suspended solids—did the village of Port Chester pass or fail the test laid down by the law?

A: They have failed.

MR. SMITH: I object to that.

THE COURT: I sustain the objection.

Q: The requirement, therefore, of sixty percent wasn't met by the various percentages you have told about. Can you tell us, sir, whether or not, in one of the tests, twenty percent less of the floating solids was removed than is required?

A: Yes. The one from four o'clock in the afternoon to

eleven-thirty that night, when they only had forty percent removal of the suspended solids.

Q: And the requirement of the Interstate Sanitation Commission is what?

A: Sixty percent removal.

Q: Can you tell us what the results of those tests were?

A: These are the ones that reported on the suspended solids, where they had the removal of forty-four percent between eight o'clock and three-thirty in the afternoon, and from four o'clock to eleven-thirty they had forty percent removal of suspended solids.

THE COURT: Are these solids that would settle out?

THE WITNESS: This would be solids that would settle out. This would be solid matter which would settle out and which would form sludge, and this test also failed to meet our requirements.

THE COURT: Where were those tests taken on Thursday, the fourth of October?

THE WITNESS: They take the samples of the effluent coming into the plant and then they sample the effluent before it goes out into the Byram River so they can see what the efficiency of the removal is.

THE COURT: That is at the disposal plant?

THE WITNESS: That's at the sewage disposal plant. This here is out of the storm sewer.

THE COURT: The four jars haven't been tested yet.

THE WITNESS: No.

Q: Can you tell us, Mr. Jones, whether or not there are some visual tests that can be applied to the four jars that are before you? Just yes or no.

A: We could tell by the consistency. It's a glazelike material.

Q: And can you tell by a visual test of examining those jars that stand before you now as to whether or not, from viewing them, these waters comply with the requirements of the Interstate Sanitation Commission? First of all, can you tell?

MR. SMITH: I object to that question, Your Honor. I can't see how he can tell by looking at that what the test is going to show unless it is tested.

MR. LANDAU: Can we have the witness testify to that, Your Honor?

THE COURT: Yes.

A: *No. Floating matter. You don't have to run a chemical test to determine that there is floating matter of this type here, sir.*

(e) Ability to Answer Questions Put by the Judge

THE COURT: Where were these tests made?

THE WITNESS: They were taken near the Purdy Street outfall.

THE COURT: In the harbor?

THE WITNESS: In the Byram River itself.

THE COURT: Does whether it's high or low tide have any effect upon your sampling and the result?

THE WITNESS: Yes. That's the reason, Judge, back during the summer months we sampled for four days, so that we would get the benefit of hitting all the tidal schedules, since it changes each day.

Q: Can you form an opinion, Mr. Jones, just yes or no, as to the cause of these violations?

A: Yes.

Q: Will you tell us in your opinion what the cause is?

A: One of the causes is that the treatment plant is not meeting our requirements, and another one is that the industrial wastes haven't been intercepted.

Q: And are you referring to the treatment plant and the industrial wastes of the village of Port Chester?

A: Yes.

THE COURT: Why isn't it meeting the test?

THE WITNESS: Well, primary treatment plants—

THE COURT: What is your opinion as to the reason why?

THE WITNESS: Primary treatment plants have difficulty meeting our requirements, and this is a primary treatment plant. That is one of the reasons that New York State has a new policy now, as of August of 1965, that all their treatment plants are going to have to go to secondary treatment in our water.

THE COURT: What do you mean by secondary treatment?

THE WITNESS: Primary, you slow down the flow so the heavier particles will settle out in a settling tank and are ready for disposal. In the secondary, you add a biological step. You take out some of the demand for oxygen. Also you get a better removal of the settleable solids. You go through a biological step after the primary settlement.

THE COURT: What sort of sewage plants do they have?

THE WITNESS: They have primary treatment.

(f) Ability to Stand Up under Cross-Examination

CROSS EXAMINATION

Q: Who determines whether the waters in the area of the village of Port Chester, such as the Byram River, is Class A or Class B?

A: This is determined by the Commission after holding public hearings.

Q: Was the village of Port Chester invited to the public hearings, sir?

A: Yes—I am sure they were invited and I would have to look up the record to see if any attended.

Q: When was this hearing held, sir, do you remember?

A: In 1937. It was held in the city of Rye.

Q: When this public hearing was held, was it determined at that time that the Byram River was a commercial, navigable water?

A: It was determined at that time, for best usage it should be classified as Class A.

Q: Has there been any human being that was made sick by the waters that you say are so contaminated?

A: I can't speak of anyone, but this type of water has caused disease in man, yes.

Q: I don't care about that. How about the waters in the Byram River right now? That is what we are concerned about, the Byram River. Has anyone been made sick by the Byram River that you know of?

A: I can't say.

Q: Did you see boats, pleasure boats, in the Byram River when you made your investigation?

A: Yes.

Q: And these pleasure boats go up and down the river

without any hindrance? How does the Byram River, the fact that the Byram River is as bad as you say it is, how does that affect boating?

A: Because it plates out on the sides of boats and they have to constantly repair the bottom and plate them because, also, I wouldn't dare fall overboard from a boat in that river.

MR. SMITH: I move that that be stricken out, Your Honor. That is not an answer to it.

THE COURT: No. Motion denied. You asked him how and he is telling you.

(Return to Direct Examination)

Q: You have seen youngsters sailing small sailboats in the area, have you?

A: Yes.

Q: And on some occasions you have seen these youngsters capsize and go into the water?

A: Yes, sir.

(g) Ability to Suggest Solutions

THE COURT: You say the new policy that went into effect in August—

THE WITNESS: All these plants are going to have to put in secondary treatment. They are helping to finance the communities on this, on this Proposition No. 1 in the November election which is a billion-dollar referendum.

THE COURT: You say that is a policy statement of theirs. It doesn't have the effect of law, does it, or statute?

THE WITNESS: Yes, right now they are—we have other treatment plants in our A waters where they are meeting now, setting up timetables to go to secondary treatment.

THE COURT: You don't think the Port Chester plant then can meet this test unless it has facilities for secondary treatment?

THE WITNESS: That's right. They haven't, and I don't expect them to.

7.3 Use of Expert in Air Pollution Case

When Ed Wolf of the Philadelphia Bar answered ready to the call of the Calendar in *Heck v. The Beryllium*

Corporation, 424 Pa. 140 (1966), he had done his home-work.

He knew that he had a good claim against the Beryllium Corporation in negligence and that his client had been seriously injured, but the case could not be proven by eyewitnesses or by any of the usual methods of proving an injury case; the poisonous particulate discharged by the Beryllium Corporation was not visible to the naked eye, and yet it plugged up the fine air holes of the lungs of the plaintiff and caused serious damage. New methods of proof, new terminology, and an innovative approach was required. Mr. Wolf proved himself up to this tremendous challenge, and all lawyers attempting to try an air pollution case should be fully familiar with *Heck v. The Beryllium Corporation.* An industrial hygienist was hired to do twenty-four-hour monitoring samples which were tested out in spectrographic analysis. Wind speed and problems of inversion are important when toxic material, alleged to have come from a smokestack and thereafter carried by winds to the area of the plaintiff's residence or usual shopping and working area, are in issue. The United States Weather Bureau records are helpful in this matter of proof. Their record center is in Nashville, North Carolina. Meteorological consulting firms are also useful when wind currents and direction are in dispute. Formulas for determining concentration of a contaminant have been determined by various mathematical dispersion formulas, one of which is seen in *Environmental Radioactivity,* by Merrill Eisenbud, McGraw-Hill, 1963 (see Hilsmeier & Gifford Formula). An atmospheric physicist with a background in dispersion principles should handle this portion of your case. Excellent demonstrative evidence was used by Ed Wolf in the Pennsylvania case; a map of the area was attached to the pleadings setting forth the relationship of the plaintiff's house and shopping center to the industrial plant charged with causing the air pollution, as well as the weather station which was monitoring same (see illustration). Topography plays an important part; valleys are likely to increase the heavy concentration of pollutants.

Mr. Wolf determined that "the quality of the pollutant

that is permitted to escape into the atmosphere will, of course, be directly proportionate to the production, capacity, and methods of production." Therefore, production schedults keyed into known air studies are unbeatable combinations and will show definite contamination ratios and "new kinds of torts require new methods of proof, require new mathematical formulas as well as imagination and resourcefulness." Pathological evaluation of a biopsy of the lung can establish a firm diagnosis and lays the groundwork for the hypothetical question. Medical proof ties up the negligence in a causal connection. "When a portion of the biopsy material is used in spectrographic analysis, results should confirm the presence within the lung of the toxicant to which it is contended the victim was exposed and which the defendant negligently put into the public airways."

Beryllium and lead patch tests, as well as urine analysis and blood studies, can help establish the presence of the toxicant within the body. It was determined in the Heck case that ten years before the trial the plaintiff had washed the clothes of a relative who worked for the Beryllium Corporation. This single fact of plaintiff's activities give some index into the depth of the questions asked and how careful the lawyer must be in getting a correct history to determine the source, areas, and frequency of contamination. The concentration of the pollutant is determined based on an average of thirty-day concentration. In the factory, maximum allowable concentration is determined on an eight-hour exposure to a healthy worker. An outdoor concentration figure is based on twenty-four-hour exposure to a cross-section of the population. The toxicant beryllium can be fatal. Acute beryllium poisoning which caused temporary lung changes as a result of exposure to high concentrations over a short period of time is curable and will not cause permanent disability; whereas chronic beryllium disease, which is the exposure to beryllium in small concentrations over long periods of time, will cause permanent disability or death. "Through litigation there is an answer that will both benefit the community at large and indemnify the victim." Justice Cardozo wrote: "The final cause of law is the welfare of society." Ed Wolf cautions the lawyer not to decline air contamination cases because they are difficult. He has led the way and made it easier. Excerpts from his excellent case follow.

Map of area to locate specific points of interest, together with topography of the area, can be used as demonstrative evidence in the courtroom.

LEGEND OF MAP
Plaintiff's house ◪
Plaintiff's shopping center ◩
Industrial plant (pollutant) ▦
Weather station ◼

(a) Tracing Air Pollution to Its Source by Use of Scientific Demonstrative Evidence

The Heck case rested heavily on the testimony of Merrill Eisenbud, professor of environmental medicine at New York University Medical School and industrial hygienist, a specialist in the field of preventive medicine. This witness was familiar with the United States Atomic Energy Commission's investigation into the dangers of beryllium manufacturing and the foreign particulate matter that is thrown off by reason of its production. He was also well acquainted with the health safety rules and regulations of companies producing these dangerous smokestack emissions and was conversant with the work *Recommendations for Control of Beryllium Hazards*. The Atomic Energy Commission had advised the company of the results of investigations concerning the beryllium content of the outside atmosphere as early as 1948 and that this information was imparted to Mr. Englehart, president of defendant corporation. Dr. Eisenbud had sufficient expertise to analyze and explain the defendant company's air studies and had, prior to the time of trial, examined all of the facts and figures. From this data, comprised of air samples taken, United States Department of Commerce Weather Bureau reports, and summaries of the Reading Municipal Airport, the expert witness made up a "wind rose" for the area involved in this lawsuit. By obtaining the defendant's air studies in advance of trial and allowing his expert to analyze them, he was able to formulate a hypothetical question as to proximate cause, incorporating the defendant's own records. Because the witness was the author of *Environmental Radioactivity* and had widespread expertise, he was able to define the words *plume diffusion-inversion,* and discuss dispersion factors with the court and jury in a way that impressed the jury and helped make his final conclusions persuasive. The exhaustive cross-examination of Merrill Eisenbud reviewed the biopsy and the method of securing same, as well as the biopsy material.

He was able to testify with authority that the average person inhales twenty cubic meters of air per day and that the mass of the lung is 1000 grams. He arrived at the fact that the amount of inhaled dust which deposits in the lung is twenty-five percent and the length of time it takes fifty percent of that deposited dust to be eliminated from the lung would be 120 days. Dr. Eisenbud was able to demonstrate how the conclusions of the biopsy data supported his own assumptions. The concentrations at a distance of four miles in a south-southeasterly direction from the plant confirmed and were consistent with his independent findings. Defendant in this case, as in other pollution cases, tried to demonstrate that the source of the "poison" was from another origin, i.e. coal burning, etc. However, Dr. Eisenbud was equal to that task, was familiar with the type of evasive defense, and labeled the contribution of coal and coal ash to the sick plaintiff's problem as insignificant. Defense counsel pressed the witness hard on "ground levels" and "stack height" and intervening hill formations between the defendant's offending smokestacks and the place where the injured plaintiff resided and shopped. Again Dr. Eisenbud was prepared for this line of questioning as he had previously studied the factors of the stack's height with relationship to sea level, the plaintiff's house, the intervening topography, and that of the area where she spent time shopping each week. All of that was programmed into the computer-type mind that Dr. Merrill Eisenbud brought to court, and his data, experience, conclusions, and opinions were unshakable. The applicability of the Hilsmeier & Gifford curve to the conditions of the defendant's plant prior to the commencement of the action was carefully explained along with the empirical and theoretical scientific methods resulting in the data being transformed to dotted lines on geometric graph paper forming a curve. Counsel tried to show that the witness based his conclusions on data with which he was not personally familiar and which he did not personally observe and therefore his conclusions were strictly hearsay and not worthy of consideration.

Not only was Dr. Eisenbud well acquainted with the manner in which the Hilsmeier & Gifford curve was created, but he was also familiar with the Pasquill refinement of that theory. All of this 100 pages of testimony culminated in the following questions and answers.

Q: Doctor, do you have an opinion, based upon your study of the company's air samples in evidence and the meteorological data which you have testified about, as to the concentrations, if any, in the environs of the defendant's plant, concentrations of beryllium in the environs of defendant's plant from 1951 to 1955 and the period of time covered by the air studies and area if only to what extent.

A: Yes I do.

Q: Will you tell us your opinion.

A: I find during that period the concentration of beryllium in the atmosphere in the vicinity of the plant was elevated above normal levels; that the source of the abnormally high concentrations of beryllium was defendant's plant; that the concentrations of beryllium frequently exceeded 0.01 micrograms per cubic meter as far as ten to twenty miles from the plant, and, on the average, exceeded 0.01 micrograms per cubic meter within five miles of the plant.

Q: Sir, do you have an opinion as to whether or not the concentrations which you testified to were more or less than an average of 0.01 for a thirty-day period during the period 1951 through 1955 at or around four miles?

A: I believe they were in excess of 0.01.

(b) Witnesses Appearing in the Case of Heck v. the Beryllium Corporation

Gerald E. White, safety engineer of the Beryllium Corporation

Albert F. Stoudt, chemical engineer and managing director of the W. B. Coleman Laboratory which conducts analyses of beryllium and carries out other work in the field of chemistry, metallurgy, and engineering.

Kenneth J. Betts, in charge of spectographic laboratory qualified by W. B. Coleman and Company, employed by them as well as by defendant corporation for spectographic analyses

Merrill Eisenbud, Professor of Environmental Medicine at the New York University Medical School, author, whose testimony comprises approximately 150 pages of trial testimony

Virginia Vought, Pennsylvania Department of Health, Occupational Health, a chemist who performed analysis of the biopsy taken from Ruth Heck and found beryllium in the tissues of the plaintiff

Dr. Arthur L. Koven, consultant to the defendant corporation, assigned to the investigation of the problem of beryllium and its toxicity

Dr. Harriet L. Hardy, a medical doctor and research scientist in the field of occupational medical problems associated with the Division of Occupational Hygiene of the Massachusetts Department of Labor, also associated with the Atomic Energy Commission at Los Alamos, who examined the plaintiff and found her suffering from beryllium poisoning

Dr. Harold L. Israel, physician specializing in pulmonary diseases

George P. Desjardins, pathologist

Jacob R. Bowers, Berks County Planning Commissioner (who interpreted and explained the map setting forth the location of the plant sample stations, plaintiff's home, shopping area, and other fixed areas important to the proof of proximate cause)

Herman Newstein, a physics professor and meteorologist.

In addition, counsel for plaintiff called past and present presidents of defendant corporation to indicate state of mind and/or notice concerning the dangerous poisons emanating from their stacks.

(c) Arthur L. Koven, Defense Witness

Dr. Arthur L. Koven was a witness employed by the Beryllium Corporation to evaluate the problem of beryllium and its toxicity to employees in the plant. He is an ophthalmologist and, in attempting to expedite his expertise in the beryllium toxicity field, contacted such people as Dr. Tebrock, medical director of Sylvania, Dr. Kehoe, director of the Kittering Laboratory, Dr. Choak, chemist at that laboratory, Doctors Tabershaw and Hardy, the first to recognize the entity of berylliosis, and Doctors Vorwald and VanAustin of the Cleveland Clinic. Dr.

Koven was called for multiple reasons, first to show that the defendant knew it had a serious problem. Further, Dr. Koven was subpoenaed to show that Dr. Eisenbud was recognized as an expert by the defendant company and, in fact, was contacted by them for consultation and recommendations. The witness did answer that he had contacted Dr. Eisenbud in reference to industrial hygiene control procedures, methods of analysis, and how to set up the proper programs as well as means of testing techniques. After establishing the preliminary factual information with the witness, Attorney Wolf asked the following questions:

Q: What did you recommend to the company with respect to a standard concerning the outplant emission of beryllium?

A: . . . In that time the Atomic Energy Commission had recommended a level of 0.01 micrograms per cubic meter of air and this would be a good recommendation to try to follow. . . .

Q: Did you do anything, Dr. Koven, to determine whether or not the possible emissions of beryllium into the outside atmosphere subsequent to your recommendations were maintained at any particular level?

A: That phase of the study was delegated to another consultant who was an expert on air pollution.

Q: Do you know whether or not any outside air studies were made by the company after 1955?

A: I believe so.

Q: Do you know whether air samples were made in 1956, '57, and '58 outside the plant by Mr. White?

A: I believe Mr. White would have them.

Q: If I told you that the company's air studies which have been brought into court here were from 1951 through 1955, that these were the only air studies which the company is alleged to have made or have the information concerning with respect to the outside content of beryllium outside the environs of the plant, does that refresh your recollection or does it assist you in remembering whether the fact is correct?

A: No.

Q: Can I ask you this, sir. Did you formulate an opinion as of 1953 or 1954 as to whether or not some person outside the plant can be hurt by the emission of beryllium unless it was controlled?

A: I was impressed with the work that was done in Ohio in that regard.

Q: You mean the number of cases they found?

A: By the fact that so-called community cases were found in that study. I discussed this with others. I found there were some who questioned such entity, others who believed very definitely in such an entity and the possibility of such an entity was realized at that time.

Q: I ask you what your impression was.

A: When I said the last statement I meant that I realized that such a possibility was real.

Q: Was it a fact that the Ohio cases occurred at the Beryllium Company refinery or alloid produced at such as the Reading plant?

A: Yes it was.

Q: Was that significant?

A: Yes.

Q: You said you made your recommendations to the company. Who in the company did you make your recommendations to?

A: At that time I believe the president of the company was a gentleman by the name of Donachie. I made the recommendation to him.

Q: The major hazard of the industry arises from the inhalation of beryllium and certain beryllium compounds. Is that a correct statement?

A: The statement is correct.

Q: Doctor, did you read an article appearing in the *American Industrial Hygiene Association Journal* in December of 1959 entitled "Air Pollution Studies of Community Surrounding a Beryllium Plant" by Dr. Jan Lieben of the division of occupational health, Commonwealth of Pennsylvania?

A: Yes, I know that article.

This testimony established knowledge and notice on the part of the defendant company as to the air hazards their company created.

(d) Harriet L. Hardy, Plaintiff Witness

Dr. Harriet L. Hardy works in the Department of Medicine at Massachusetts General Hospital in Boston and is chief of the Occupational Medical Clinic there, a department she created in 1946. She was the Assistant Medical Director of the Massachusetts Institute of Technology in Cambridge and has been teaching in this field at Harvard Medical School since 1949. In addition, she teaches at local hospitals, the Veterans Administration, Tufts Medical School, and M.I.T. The government has sought her advice on a number of important areas of expertise and she has been awarded numerous prizes for her work, most particularly on beryllium toxicity, which she has been researching and studying since 1945. Counsel for plaintiff was able to demonstrate that the defendant, Beryllium Corporation, had sought the advice and recommendations of Dr. Hardy who was now appearing on behalf of the plaintiff.

Q: What is the name of the condition or conditions which could occur by exposure to beryllium in the neighborhood?

A: Beryllium disease or beryllium poisoning is another way of speaking of it.

Q: Would you explain to the jury just what beryllium disease or beryllium poisoning is.

A: I do a lot of teaching and I have studied this matter since 1945, but from the actual study of cases the knowledge now seems to make it clear that this is a bodywide disease following the inhaling of significant amounts of toxic beryllium compounds. It appears correct to say that beryllium gets into the bloodstream and is carried around the body into the liver, spleen, the bones, the kidneys, as well as the lung, and that what is inhaled, a good proportion of it, goes out in the urine, and this is a very important point. Under circumstances of a sudden sharp high exposure and exposure over a short period of time the worker may develop an acute beryllium poisoning, meaning that he gets sick while he is in the beryllium plant or he gets sick within a week but he gets completely well. . . . The patient gets well from acute beryllium poisoning and this is usually a matter of affecting the lung. The chronic disease, by definition, is a disease that lasts a long period of time but, also, into this concept is a notion that it comes as a result of a series of exposures that are less than the ones that cause acute disease or acute effect in the lung, and it is the chronic disease we are dealing with in these discussions for the most part, indicating it lasts more than a year. It can affect the liver, spleen, kidneys, as well as the lung, and we have some evidence that it may actually cause some changes within the skull. It also brings about certain chemical changes in the body that result in such complications as kidney stones. I mention this to make this point that this is not just a lone disease. It's a bodywide disease. The truth is that it's like tuberculosis and the organ most frequently affected is the lung, so that the patient has an abnormal chest X-ray and a cough, has shortness of breath, has the usual signs and symptoms, but also on laboratory studies various abnormalities that we don't need to go into here.

Q: Doctor, what part if any does a biopsy play in determining whether or not a person has berylliosis or beryllium disease?

A: The biopsy is a confession of the physician that it is not judgment proof to make the diagnosis by looking at the chest X-ray and by listening to patient's complaints; and the important point to make is that beryllium disease mimics other diseases, especially a disease called carcoidosis for which there is no known cause; so the biopsy means the taking of bit of tissue, sometimes it's a node from the neck, sometimes a node under the skin, sometimes a bit of liver, sometimes a bit of the lung. In one way learning two things from this one: whether or not it has foreign material, in this instance beryllium poisoning, and whether or not the picture under the microscope may give the final diagnosis.

Q: Of what significance is the finding of beryllium in a biopsy?

A: The only significance is that the individual has been exposed to beryllium. It's quite impossible to make the diagnosis from the presence of beryllium alone.

Q: Now at my suggestion while consulting with Dr. Harold Israel, did you have an opportunity to examine Mrs. Ruth Heck?

A: I did.

Q: Have you had experience in examining persons who are alleged to have berylliosis?

A: I have.

Q: Are you the keeper of the Beryllium Registry?

A: Yes I am.

Q: What is the Beryllium Registry?

A: Well, there are at least three attempts between 1947 and '52 to bring into one place all the knowledge that exists to the cases of illness that appear to be due to inhaling toxic beryllium compounds. Finally in 1952 funds were given to me in my care at the Massachusetts General Hospital, and with the help of the secretary and a younger physician I directed the collection of as much of these materials as could reasonably be gained to go into a registry with the idea of discovering the relationships between exposure and illness and because, as you see, this is the disease that was new to us since 1945 in Massachusetts, to see what we might learn about this literally new disease.

Q: Are you the person who bears the responsibility for determining from clinical exposure whether or not a person has berylliosis as it may effect their entry in the registry?

A: Yes.

Q: As a clinician would you say, and I don't want you to be immodest, that you are an expert in the clinical aspect of diagnosing beryllium and beryllium disease?

A: Yes.

Q. And did you perform an unrestricted physical examination of Mrs. Heck?

A: Yes, I did.

Q: As a result of this physical examination did you arrive at a diagnosis?

A: I did.

Q: What is your diagnosis? Did you take a history as well and will you give it to us.

A: Mrs. Heck reported to me she was suffering from a cough and weakness beginning in 1959 following a chest cold, as she called it, which persisted. She reported that the first chest X-ray was then in November 1961 and her physician found her substantially confined to bed. She was worse in the morning and on any effort, when she is excited or has to go upstairs (since she gets short of breath). At the time of my taking of the history, she said that any effort produced shortness of breath whereas at the beginning of her complaints in '59 this was not true. She suffered considerably from exhausting coughing spells. Her weight at the time was 160 from her previous 180 (at the time she began to suffer from a cough in the winter of 1959). She does not smoke. Her appetite is good. Various other things were all right. One more bit of history. She suffers from time to time with what she calls chills and fever. She told me that she has had eleven pregnancies and nine normal children, the last one born in 1958. She had an operation in 1959 which she says was unrelated.

Q: Would you tell us your significant findings in your physical examination?

A: This woman became short of breath and began to cough while she was undressing and when I asked her to take a slightly deeper breath so that I could examine her chest with the stethoscope she had what is described as clubbing of her fingers, cyanosis of the nail beds. The heart rate was 110, the rhythm was regular; there were no murmurs but the second pulmonic sound was markedly accentuated and in examining her lung there were moist rales heard at both bases. Those are the salient points.

Q: Did you discuss treatment with Dr. Israel?

A: I did.

Q: What recommendations did you make concerning treatment?

A: I recommended sterosis: the dose of steroids that she was receiving be increased.

Q: As far as steroids is concerned, is the use of steroids a recommended medication for maintaining a person suffering from beryllium disease?

A: Yes.

Q: Dr. Hardy, would you tell us whether or not you arrived at a diagnosis with respect to Mrs. Heck's condition at that time?

A: I did.

Q: What was your diagnosis?

A: Chronic beryllium poisoning.

Q: Will you tell us the significance of the biopsy findings in this case?

A: The findings of beryllium in Mrs. Heck's lung biopsy is significant when correlated with her clinical history of illness: my findings on physical examination in September of 1962 plus the history of exposure to certain beryllium compounds because of where she lived plus the exposure due to her brother's workclothes.

Q: Is the Heck case included in the beryllium registry? (*This question was objected to and the objection was sustained.*)

Finally, counsel for plaintiff tried to introduce factual testimony in written material demonstrating that the witness had advised the defendant company through its president just how dangerous beryllium was and that she had diagnosed two cases in one local hospital and had notified the defendant corporation of these conditions and had spoken face to face with Dr. Koven and Dr. Denache, but this factual material to show "state of mind" of the defendant and actual notice on behalf of its president was objected to and that objection was sustained.

(e) Wind Sample and Laboratory Report

COMMONWEALTH OF PENNSYLVANIA

DEPARTMENT OF HEALTH
OCCUPATIONAL HEALTH

SAMPLE AND LABORATORY REPORT

REGION _____ Region VI _____

DATE COLLECTED _____

DATE SUBMITTED _____ 4/24/62

NAME OF COMPANY	ADDRESS		
Ruth Heck	Antietam Road, R.D. #1, Temple, Pa.	EX. NO.	PMC

PRODUCT MANUFACTURED	MATERIAL SAMPLED	APPARATUS

COLLECTED BY	COLLECTION MEDIUM	ANALYSIS DESIRED
Dr. Dattoli		Be

SUBSTANCES LIKELY TO INTERFERE AND LIKELY TO BE PRESENT   The specimen submitted is A lung biopsy
which we wish analyzed for Beryllium

COMMENTS

Spec.

REGION SAMPLE NUMBER	XXX SAMPLE NUMBER	SAMPLING LOCATION AND OPERATION	AIR VOLUME	LABORATORY RESULTS Micrograms Be/100 g. tissue
	4244	Ruth Heck — lung tissue — 3.15 g.		0.66
		sample		

REPORT OF ANALYSIS

ANALYSIS BY _____   DATE ___7/3/62___ _____

CHEMIST

FORM NY-89
REV. 6-1-59

UNITED STATES ATOMIC ENERGY COMMISSION
NEW YORK OPERATIONS OFFICE

HEALTH AND SAFETY LABORATORY
70 COLUMBUS AVENUE
NEW YORK 14, N. Y.

SAMPLE REQ.   **D**   4701

DATE SENT _____
DATE RECEIVED _____
DATE REPORTED _____

PLANT

MAILING ADDRESS

TYPE OF SAMPLE

ANALYZE FOR

METHOD OF DETERMINATION

ROUTE RESULTS TO

SAMPLE NO.	DATE	HOUR START	HOUR STOP	SAMPLE DESCRIPTION	SAMPLING RATE	TIME	Intensity	Quantity	RESULTS
0	9/18	9:30		#5 Wilshire & Los Vegas Blvd.	.14m	15 min	Bz	4.0	
1	9/18	3:00		#6 Mt. Laurel Rd. & 5th Ave	.14m	15 min	Bz	4.0	
2	9/18	3:30		#7 Euclid Ave. & 7th	.14m	15 min	Bz	4.0	
3	9/18	4:00		#8 Water & 8th	.14m	15 min	Bz	4.0	
4	9/16	2:00		#9 200 yds. E of Potsville W. on Little St.	.14m	15 min	Bz	4.0	
5									
6									
7									
8									
9									

COLLECTED BY **G. WHITE**   ANALYZED BY

SURVEYOR TO RETAIN LAST COPY—RETURN ALL OTHERS TO HEALTH AND SAFETY LABORATORY

(f) Recommendations for Control of Beryllium Hazards

UNITED STATES ATOMIC ENERGY COMMISSION
WASHINGTON 25, D.C.

TO: Those Listed Below   DATE: August 10,1951

FROM: M. W. Boyer, General Manager

SUBJ: RECOMMENDATIONS FOR CONTROL
            OF BERYLLIUM HAZARDS

SYMBOL: BMM:GAH

The following *tentative* recommendations for the control
of beryllium hazards supersede all previous memoranda
on this subject and are submitted for your information and
guidance. All AEC contractors using or producing beryllium or its compounds should be informed of these recommendations. (These recommendations, unless sooner
revised, will be effective until June 30, 1952).

1. The in-plant atmospheric concentration of beryllium
at beryllium operations should not exceed 2 micro-grams
per cubic meter as an average concentration throughout an
8-hour day.

2. Even though the daily average might be within the
limits of recommendation 1, no personnel should be exposed to a concentration greater than 25 micro-grams per
cubic meter for any period of time, however short.

3. In the neighborhood of an AEC plant handling beryllium compounds, the average monthly concentration at the
breathing zone level should not exceed 0.01 micro-gram
per cubic meter.

4. There should be an adequate medical program, supervised by a physician who is familiar with beryllium poisoning, to cover all workers exposed to beryllium and its
compounds.

5. If there is any evidence that an individual has chronic
beryllium poisoning, such an individual should be excluded
from any further exposure to beryllium compounds.

(g) Scientific Demonstrative Proof in Air Pollution Cases

Air Studies

by Edward M. Wolf*

How do you acquire information concerning the toxicant? This is achieved by air studies. Every air pollution case demands air studies. You must identify the toxicant, prove the concentration, and determine the exposure to which your client, the victim, has been subjected.

Air sampling requires the presence of an industrial hygienist with a sampling device, which is a vacuum cleaner. This air sampler is operated during a specifically measured period of time, at a precise geographic location. Random samplings can be made in this fashion at different locations downwind from the source of the contamination, and at selected times (night and day), or twenty-four hour monitoring devices can be employed in the backyard of the plaintiff's home, for instance.

Sampling is achieved by forcing air to flow through this vacuum cleaner-like device, through a filter pad. The filter pad is then analyzed to determine the identity of the residue left on it and to measure the quantity of these deposits. Since the sampling machines were operated over a specifically measured period of time and the quantity of air which was passed across the filter pad is known, the concentration of any particular material which is deposited on the pad can be measured with great scientific accuracy.

The next requirement is to have these pads analyzed. Several techniques are available but the most accurate is the spectrographic analysis.

Since we are working with the analysis of trace *materials,* this very sensitive procedure must be done at a laboratory which has qualified personnel and the proper equipment. Such laboratories are located at *Kettering Institute, Cincinnati, Ohio; University of Rochester, Rochester, New York; Massachusetts Institute of Technology, Cambridge,*

* From "Legal Approach to Industrial Pollution" by Isadore H. Bellis, Herbert F. Kolsby and Edward L. Wolf, in TRIAL Magazine (June/July, 1968). Reprinted by permission of the American Trial Lawyers Association.

*Massachusetts; and the Department of Industrial Hygiene,
Commonwealth of Pennsylvania, Harrisburg, Pennsylvania,
to mention only a few.*

It is important to employ experienced hygienists in the
air sampling procedure because the integrity of the samplings will depend in large measure upon the technique
employed in preserving the evidence and conducting the
tests.

To insure accuracy, a few measures to be taken are:

• Blank (or unused) sample pads from the same batch
must be included with the total pads to be analyzed so
that any material which is part of the pad itself can be
determined and subtracted from the total of the material
which is ultimately discovered.

• Each sample pad must be enclosed within an envelope
by use of a tweezer and sealed in that envelope after extrac-
tion from the machine. If this is not done, exposure to the
atmosphere will continue, and a valid sampling will not be
produced.

• Careful recording is necessary. Each sample must be
designated on the record with the following information:
the precise geographic location; the time commenced and
the time concluded; the weather conditions which existed
at the time; and the approximate wind direction.

To this record will ultimately be added the quantity
of the toxicant found from the analysis, measured in micrograms. Since we know the quantity of air which passed
through the filter and the duration of the filter's operation,
we can convert and express the concentration to which
our clients were exposed into micrograms per cubic meter
of air.

Climatological Survey

The pattern for the taking of samples must first be determined by a previously acquired climatological survey.

The toxicant to which our client is exposed or to which
he was exposed came from a source, whether a smokestack
or a group of smokestacks. It was then carried by the winds
to his or her home or job. It is essential to know the frequency of the occurrence of the particular winds—the

vehicles of contamination—flowing from the source to the victim's location. We will determine by the survey the dispersion of the contaminant.

Low-speed winds cause the damage by permitting the concentrations to remain intact. Higher-speed winds disperse the material and diffuse it, lowering the concentration and alleviating the danger. Wind speeds up to five miles per hour, when carrying contaminants, are extremely dangerous; wind speeds between five and ten miles per hour are moderately dangerous. It is essential, therefore, in an air sampling program to secure from the *United States Weather Bureau information concerning the frequency of occurrence of high- and low-speed winds in the area in question.*

The frequency and duration of inversions are also essential. Inversion is a meteorological condition. As altitudes increase, temperatures decrease. However, in an inversion situation, the air closest to the surface of the earth is cooler than the air above it. This air which is closest to the earth moves along parallel to the surface, contained by the air which exists above it, and is prevented from rising upward. Because it cannot rise and disperse its particulate matter into the upper atmosphere, it maintains high concentrations closer to the earth, i.e., the breathing zone.

The presence of low-speed winds and an inversion will effect an atmospheric condition that promotes the maintenance of heavy concentrations. *Weather information, such as that required for this type of survey, can be secured from the National Weather Records Center, Asheville, North Carolina, or any reputable meteorological consultant firm.*

Comparison of Data

It is also important not to overlook the location of the weather reporting centers in the area in question. For instance, if the particular location under survey is located close to an airport, but further away from the post office weather department which the city or town has as its reporting station, the two records must be compared to show the specific deviation of meteorological data from one location to the other.

In order to evaluate the air studies which we are taking
and those which may have been made in the past, we must
know the location of each sample, with respect to the prevailing winds on the day and time that the particular sample
was taken.

Wind is reported by the Weather Bureau by the sixteen
cardinal points of the compass of 360°. Each segment
encompasses 22½°. For instance, if a wind is from the
north, it would presumably cover 11¼° on each side of
north. In evaluating our air samples then we try to determine the quantity of material collected and its relationship
to the wind flow at that particular time. We can then
evaluate for that particular day the concentration and its
presence within the area of the total flow of contamination.

Once contamination has been determined through
analysis of the samples and the winds present at the time,
we can arrive at average concentration figures. These figures can be extrapolated to different points by virtue of
diffusion formulas.

The importance of the application of this information
to a factual situation can be illustrated. Suppose it is known
that, during a particular time period, a quarter of a mile
from the particular plant source of the contamination, the
concentration was x. For comparison, you want to know
what the concentration may have been at the same time
at other locations a half mile and a mile away. You may
extrapolate and determine concentrations by virtue of
mathematical dispersion formulas, one of which is the Hilsmeier and Gifford Formula. [See *Environmental Radioactivity* by Merrill Eisenbud (McGraw-Hill, 1963.)] *It is
essential that this portion of your case be handled by a
qualified atmospheric physicist or an industrial hygienist
with a background in dispersion principles.*

Demonstrative Evidence

This type of presentation demands the use of demonstrative evidence such as a map of the area, with the sampling
stations designated and a movable compass for wind direction. It is extremely important that the topographical conditions be investigated. This has a definite effect upon the

client's exposure. Those topographical conditions which increase the likelihood of heavy concentrations of pollutants are the existence of valleys and hillsides, unbroken by physical barriers between the source of pollution and the location of the plaintiff.

In evaluating the source of contamination, it is also necessary to learn the hours that the plant (or source) operates and how long these hours have been maintained. Is this a twelve- or twenty-four-hour contamination? The quantity of the pollutant that is permitted to escape into the atmosphere will, of course, be directly proportionate to the production capacity and methods of production. This is another area which must be evaluated. Production schedules keyed into known air studies are unbeatable combinations and will show definite contamination ratios.

Medical Diagnosis

Special techniques must be employed in establishing the medical aspects of air pollution cases. One of these techniques is biopsy with spectrographic analysis and pathological evaluation. In those cases where the pollutant causes a specific disease, a biopsy of the lung of the patient will establish a definite pathology which can be used to diagnose the condition.

When a portion of the biopsy material is used in spectrographic analysis, results should confirm the presence within the lung of the toxicant to which it is contended the victim was exposed.

Other types of tests are possible for proving diagnosis, such as the beryllium patch test and the lead patch test. These tests are less reliable, both in establishing the diagnosis and in establishing exposure. Lung function studies are a technique necessary to prove the disability in pulmonary cases. Blood studies and urinalysis are other studies useful in establishing a diagnosis and the presence of a toxicant within the body.

Frequently, *the proof of the medical aspects of the case will, in large measure, prove the liability aspects.* Certain types of toxicants have known maximum concentration figures, below which there have been no reported cases of disease occurrence, and above which all reported cases occurred. In many instances, the very fact that the diagnosis is made and the toxicant is identified within the lung of the victim alone can indicate that the victim was exposed to concentrations above a certain maximum figure.

In certain types of situations where there is no history of exposure to the toxicant from any other source but the one considered to be responsible, medical testimony stating the above could very well make out a prima facie case and eliminate the necessity of expensive and burdensome air studies. This is a gamble which someday a lawyer might take to establish a recognized shortcut to prove his case.

7.4 How the Defendant's Documentation Can Prove Your Case: The Subpoena Duces Tecum

Law schools should include, in the practice course, the proper way to draw subpoenas to help prove one's case. They should not be drawn on the eve of trial when there is not sufficient time to acquaint oneself with the essential records. Months before the trial date, a conference should be arranged with the expert witnesses to determine specifically which records covering what areas for what length of time will be necessary, as well as governmental documents which will overlap and check defendant's findings. Defendants in pollution cases can show two weeks of every year when the air and water samples comply with the standards and show no dangers to health. That is when the plant is shut down. A subpoena in depth will determine whether or not the plant was shut down for vacation or retooling during the times when they passed the air and/or water pollution tests. Therefore, the party bringing the action should test over a period before, during, and after the plant closes down for whatever reason, and in so doing the cause of the pollution can be further pinpointed.

A subpoena calling for the production of voluminous records which reveal the extent of defendant's pollution immediately sets the tone of the trial even before it begins and gives the offending party notice that he is in for a tough fight, for that is precisely what a full-blown trial is.

Most large corporations are starting to develop environmental departments, ecology centers, or public relations departments which gather information and try to give the impression that they are aware of the problem and are keeping records with a view toward correcting their operations. These records kept by defendants as well as state, county, local, and village health departments can be subpoenaed and, in the case of public records, "so ordered" by the trial judge; and they will be brought to court if they are material and relevant. The defense sometimes raised—that defendants had no knowledge of the pollution they cause—can be defeated by their own records when interoffice memoranda dated prior to the date of the lawsuit indicate a knowledge of the condition and a recommendation that the pollution be abated or modified. The optimum procedure would be to ask for the records to be delivered into court two or three days before the trial commences so that a review of those records with your expert can reveal weaknesses in your opponent's case and areas that should be gone into in detail on the direct case of the plaintiff. In those states that allow them, depositions or examinations before trial should be exercised to the fullest along with subpoenas requiring production of records at that time; thus, the issues can be narrowed and the chance of surprise in court decreased considerably. In short, the subpoena *duces tecum* is a powerful tool in the arsenal of the trial lawyer and affords the rare opportunity of proving the case with defendant's records kept in the regular course of business. A suggested form for such a subpoena follows:

(a) Example of Subpoena

THE PEOPLE OF THE STATE OF NEW YORK

TO: The Power House Energy Corporation
240 Broadway
New York City

GREETING: WE COMMAND YOU that, all business and excuses being laid aside, you appear and attend before the Honorable William S. Backer, Justice of the Supreme

Court, New York County, at the courthouse located at Foley Square, New York, New York, at Trial Term, Part V, on the twenty-second day of April, 1970, at ten o'clock in the forenoon and at any adjourned date to testify and give evidence in certain action now pending in the said court then and there to be tried between JOHN Q. PUBLIC, as plaintiff, and on behalf of himself and on behalf of all others similarly situated in the city of New York, and THE POWER HOUSE ENERGY CORPORATION, on the part of the said plaintiff, and that you bring with you and produce at the time and place aforesaid certain permits and/or licenses authorizing defendant under Public Service Law, provision 65 of the Consolidated Laws of the state of New York, to operate and provide safe and adequate electric service in and around the city of New York, and to further

PRODUCE all notifications received by the defendant over the period of the past twenty-four months from federal, state, county, local, and individual sources concerning pollution of the air and water, complaints pertaining thereto, and the names of any other cases presently pending involving the defendant in the field of pollution, and further

PRODUCE all pollution computer data obtained from the IBM quicktrain two time sharing terminal, as well as the IBM 1050 system and the IBM 744 data-processing system indicating the factors of air and water pollution over a period of twenty-four months past, as well as the accompanying computer analysis of both water and air pollution data, and further

PRODUCE all records of sample studies with the results, as well as the samples themselves, the time, place, and manner taken, along with the names of all persons involved in the sampling procedure, both as to air and water pollution and further

PRODUCE all maintenance manuals and logbooks for repairs and maintenance of all pollution control equipment as well as the cottrell synthesizer and all other pollution abatement and control equipment as well as the names of all persons involved with said maintenance and repair of said equipment, and further

PRODUCE all records of fuel consumption, coal, oil, gas, and all other fossil fuels and records of daily consumption over a period of twelve months past and produce all productions schedules as well as amount of production achieved, and further

PRODUCE all interoffice correspondence, memoranda, notes, and all other writings from and to the Environmental Control Department along with the findings, recommendations, work requests, and reports of the action taken as a result of these requests, and further

PRODUCE all company rules, regulations, and directions to the workmen in the plant as to pollution safety procedures to be followed as well as the method the company uses to oversee these procedures to enforce same, and further

PRODUCE reports determining the amount of water used by the plant and equipment over the past eighteen months, and further

PRODUCE analysis of the content of the water leaving the plant and entering the common sewer system, and further

PRODUCE records of the chemical purchases of the plant over the prior eighteen months, and further

PRODUCE a detailed map of the sewer system of said plant and produce samples of waters taken from said sewers and the point of sampling, and further

PRODUCE the analytical results of samples taken from the storm sewers, and further

PRODUCE records indicating the acidity of the wastes from the pickling operations, and further

PRODUCE records of purchase and use of detergent chemicals used in the defendant's washing equipment, and further

PRODUCE all records of the past eighteen months having to do with the cleaning of the detrex and ransohoff washers, and further

PRODUCE records indicating findings as to floating solids, settleable solids, and sludge deposits, and further

PRODUCE records indicating findings concerning garbage cinders, ashes, oil sledge, or other refuse, and further

PRODUCE findings as to dissolved oxygen content over the prior eighteen months on the twenty-four-hour tidal cycle covering the twelve-month period, and further

PRODUCE any and all reports concerning toxic waste, oil, deleterious substances, colored or other waste or heated liquids, and further

PRODUCE all notices of violations from state, federal, county, or village governments, and further

PRODUCE all private and/or complaints as to air and/or water pollution emanating from the plant, and further

PRODUCE records of purchase of chlorine for the period of eighteen months past, and further

PRODUCE reports of defendant's environmental department and sanitary engineers concerning the pollution problem and abatement procedures at defendants' plant for a period of eighteen months past, and further

PRODUCE any and all location plans indicating the location of defendant's plant relative to village sewer disposal unit, sewage treatment plant, the main sanitary interceptor, and the drainage area tributaries, and the harbor and swimming areas of the town defendant's plant is located in, and further

PRODUCE plans indicating locations of all sewers, sampling points, spent pickle liquor tanks, storm drain from village land, and diagram of defendant's plant and equipment, as well as the analytical results of the sampling of the storm sewers, and further

PRODUCE the maintenance manuals, logbooks, record entries of maintenance and repair, and all other records of operation for the electrostatic precipitators, baghouse and ventilating hoods, cottrell units, and furnace afterburners.

7.5 Sources of Further Information

Environmental pollution and conservation cases often turn on expert testimony. The scientific data is subject to various interpretations both as to the present toxicity or danger level, and to various prognostications as to the impact on the total environment. The Environmental Defense Fund early represented by Victor Yannacone, jr., was quick to understand the prime importance of obtaining a cross-section of the various sciences touching on the pollution field. In addition, he recruited men with courage and the ability to take the stand and make their positions known clearly, with sufficient expertise to withstand vigorous cross-examination. A list of the Environmental Defense Fund's experts gives a brief idea of the various fields and areas of study that can be helpful in shedding light on the mounting problem.

The college science departments are a great source of expert help. So are medical schools, hospitals, health departments and environmental protection agencies.

(a) Government Printing Lists of Interest

Any group wishing to build a library of excellent source material in the field of air and water pollution should obtain the list of publications available from the United States Government Printing Office entitled "Health and Medical Services, Air and Water Pollution, First Aid Industrial and Occupational Health and Sanitation," price list 51, 55th ed., Dec. 1969, Government Printing Office, Superintendent of Documents, Washington, D.C. 20402. Listed are forty-three publications dealing with air pollution as well as forty publications having to do with radioactivity; and under the heading of "Water Pollution" there are forty-three pieces of printed material available. These documents are accurate, contain scientific and medical citations with references for their conclusions, and are inexpensive.

(b) National Association of Counties Research Foundation List of Publications

An excellent set of publications can be obtained from the National Association of Counties Research Foundation, 1001 Connecticut Avenue N.W., Washington, D.C., 20036. A 182-page document entitled *Water Pollution*

Control can be obtained from that source for the sum of $1.00. Naco, as this county group is referred to, sells an eight-pamphlet packet called "Community Action Program for Air Pollution Control" which is well worth the $1.00 charge. The pamphlets are entitled as follows:

1. The areawide approach
2. Organization
3. Enabling legislation
4. Inspection and enforcement
5. Staffing and financing
6. Technical and financial assistance
7. Gaining community support
8. An action plan and bibliography

This material is recommended by the authors.

(c) How to Find Your State's Publications

Write to the Department of Health and Environmental Protection Agency at the state capitol for a list of publications and the names of other agencies with related responsibilities.

7.6 Future Weather Forecasting

Proposed legislation has already suggested that weather reports, both on the television and radio networks, include pollution data. The United States Department of Commerce and its environmental services administration publishes local climatological data which indicates, at the present, temperature, precipitation, and wind, as well as the normal means and extremes and the yearly averages. Since air and water pollution are continuously and completely involved one with the other, a polluted rain factor would be a useful part of the future weather program, as well as the air pollution contaminants and the results of water testing. Where phosphates are a particular problem, results of the Paap test could be included and, most important, a death rate chart indicating the number of deaths from emphysema and other respiratory diseases related to poisonous air. See pollution chart data following.

POLLUTION DATA

	JAN	MAR	MAY	JUL	SEP	NOV	TIME TO TOXICITY	TIME TO DANGER	TIME TO NONE SUPPORT OF LIFE
AIR POLLUTION									
PARTICULATE CONCENTRATIONS									
GASEOUS FUMES									
ODOR							6 MOS.	12 MOS.	18 MOS.
SMOKE									
WATER POLLUTION									
FLOATING SOLIDS									
SUSPENDED SOLIDS									
DISSOLVED OXYGEN CONTENT									
B COLIFORM							8 MOS.	12 MOS.	19 MOS.
POLLUTED RAIN FACTOR									

"PAAP TEST" (IMPACT OF PHOSPHATES AND CHEMICALS ON ALGAL GROWTH)

DEATH RATE RESPIRATORY DISEASES (MONTHLY)

Raymond Falconer set up a network of Gardner Small Particle Counters around New York State. There are twelve stations in all, three of them having continuous General Electric Condensation Nuclei Counters. Volunteer observers within the university and within the New York State Civil Defense Bureau have been obtained, and they are observing on a schedule of three times a day, five days a week. Personnel working in our weather room pick up this information and put it on punch cards. The cards are then forwarded to the computer center for processing. A program has been worked out whereby curves can be easily drawn through the printout values of the highest, lowest, and average particle counts each day, thus giving a quick survey of the variation in counts during the course of a month. In addition, for each month, the computer will print out a wind rose showing the direction from which the highest counts have been obtained. Another program attempts to draw automatically the air trajectory of particles starting upwind of certain cities six hours before noon and projecting the path to where it would go during the six hours after noon. The input is the hourly wind direction and velocity from all stations available in New York State. Information on the small particle count is included in Mr. Falconer's daily weather program.

Environmental or pollution weather forecasting should specify the concentration of the toxicant, i.e., sulfur dioxide parts per million. The present fad of reporting air conditions as acceptable, unacceptable, good, fair, or any other general adjective is of no specific value.

Pollution data can and should be specific, i.e., 311 micrograms per cubic meter of particulate matter in the atmosphere was discharged by the Asarco plant today. They should include specific findings, parts per million or micrograms per cubic meter of air with an indication of the length of time in which conditions will bring on sickness and loss of life if allowed to go unchecked.

7.7 Glossary

(a) Words Used in Water Pollution Control

Activated Sludge process removes organic matter from sewage by saturating it with air and biologically active sludge.

Adsorption is an advanced way of treating wastes in which carbon removes organic matter not responsive to clarification or biological treatment.

Aeration Tank serves as a chamber for injecting air into water.

Algae are plants which grow in sunlit waters. They are a food for fish and small aquatic animals and, like all plants, put oxygen in the water.

Bacteria are the smallest living organisms which literally eat the organic parts of sewage.

BOD, or biochemical oxygen demand, is the amount of oxygen necessary in the water for bacteria who consume the organic sewage. It is used as a measure in telling how well a sewage treatment plant is working.

Chlorinator is a device for adding chlorine gas to sewage to kill infectious germs.

Diffused Air is a technique by which air under pressure is forced into sewage in an aeration tank. The air is pumped down into the sewage through a pipe and escapes out through holes in the side of the pipe.

Digestion of sludge takes place in heated tanks where the material can decompose naturally and the odors can be controlled.

Distillation in waste treatment consists of heating the effluent and then removing the vapor or steam. When the steam is returned to a liquid it is almost pure water. The pollutants remain in the concentrated residue.

Effluent is the liquid that comes out of a treatment plant after completion of the treatment process.

Electrodialysis is a process by which electricity attracts or draws the mineral salts from sewage.

Incineration consists of burning the sludge to remove the water and reduce the remaining residues to a safe, nonburnable ash. The ash can then be disposed of safely on land, in some waters, or into caves or other underground locations.

Interceptor sewers in a combined system control the flow of the sewage to the treatment plant. In a storm, they allow some of the sewage to flow directly into a receiving stream. This protects the treatment plant from being overloaded in case of a sudden surge of water into the sewers. Interceptors are also used in separate sanitation systems to collect the flows from main and trunk sewers and carry them to the points of treatment.

Ion is an electrically charged atom or group of atoms which can be drawn from waste water during the electrodialysis process.

Lateral sewers are the pipes that run under the streets of a city and into which empty the sewers from homes or businesses.

Lagoons are scientifically constructed ponds in which sunlight, algae, and oxygen interact to restore water to a quality equal to effluent from a secondary treatment plant.

Mechanical Aeration begins by forcing the sewage up through a pipe in a tank. Then it is sprayed over the surface of tank, causing the waste stream to absorb oxygen from the atmosphere.

Microbes are minute living things, either plant or animal. In sewage, microbes may be germs that cause disease.

Mixed Liquor is the name given the effluent that comes from the aeration tank after the sewage has been mixed with activated sludge and air.

Molecule is the smallest particle of an element or compound that can remain in a free state and still keep the characteristics of the element or compound.

Organic Matter is the waste from homes or industry of plant or animal origin.

Oxidation is the consuming or breaking down of organic wastes or chemicals in sewage by bacteria and chemical oxidants.

Oxidation Pond is a manmade lake or body of water in which wastes are consumed by bacteria. It is used most frequently with other waste treatment processes. An oxidation pond is basically the same as a sewage lagoon.

tanks for the heavy matter to settle in.

Pollution results when something—animal, vegetable, or mineral—reaches water, making it more difficult or dangerous to use for drinking, recreation, agriculture, industry, or wildlife.

Polyelectrolytes are synthetic chemicals used to speed the removal of solids from sewage. The chemicals cause the solids to coagulate or clump together more rapidly than chemicals like alum or lime.

Receiving Waters are rivers, lakes, oceans, or other water courses that receive treated or untreated waste waters.

Salts are the minerals that water picks up as it passes through the air, over and under the ground, and through household and industrial uses.

Sand Filter removes the organic wastes from sewage. The waste water is trickled over the bed of sand. Air and bacteria decompose the wastes filtering through the sand. The clean water flows out through drains in the bottom of the bed. The sludge accumulating at the surface must be removed from the bed periodically.

Sanitary Sewers, in a separate system, are pipes in a city that carry only domestic waste water. The storm water runoff is taken care of by a separate system of pipes.

Secondary Treatment is the second step in most waste treatment systems in which bacteria consume the organic parts of the wastes. It is accomplished by bringing the

Primary Treatment removes the material that floats or will settle in sewage. It is accomplished by using screens to catch the floating objects and sewage and bacteria together in trickling filters or in the activated sludge process.

Sedimentation Tanks help remove solids from sewage. The waste water is pumped to the tanks where the solids settle to the bottom or float on top as scum. The scum is skimmed off the top, and solids on the bottom are pumped out to sludge digestion tanks.

Septic Tanks are used to treat domestic wastes. The underground tanks receive the waste water directly from the home. The bacteria in the sewage decomposes the organic waste and the sludge settles on the bottom of the tank. The effluent flows out of the tank into the ground through drains. The sludge is pumped out of the tanks, usually by commercial firms, at regular intervals.

Sewers are a system of pipes that collect and deliver waste water to treatment plants or receiving streams.

Sludge is the solid matter that settles to the bottom of sedimentation tanks and must be disposed of by digestion or other methods to complete waste treatment.

Storm Sewers are a separate system of pipes that carry only runoffs from buildings and land during a storm.

Suspended Solids are the wastes that will not sink or settle in sewage.

Trickling Filter is a bed of rocks or stones. The sewage is trickled over the bed so the bacteria can break down the organic wastes. The bacteria collect on the stones through repeated use of the filter.

Waste Treatment Plant is a series of tanks, screens, filters, and other processes by which pollutants are removed from water.

(b) Words Used in Air Pollution Control*

activated carbon: a highly adsorbent form of carbon, used to collect many gaseous pollutants. Used both for measurement and control.

activated water: a transient, chemically very reactive state created in water by absorbed *ionizing radiation*.

aerosol: particle of solid or liquid matter that can remain suspended in the air because of its small size. Particulates under 1 *micron* in diameter are generally called aerosols.

afterburner: a device that includes an auxiliary fuel burner and *combustion* chamber to get rid of combustible air contaminants.

air: so-called pure air is a mixture of gases containing about seventy-eight percent nitrogen; twenty-one percent oxygen; less than one percent carbon dioxide, argon, and other *inert* gases; and varying amounts of water vapor.

* Reprinted by permission of the National Tuberculosis and Respiratory Disease Association, from *Air Pollution Primer*, 1969.

air monitoring: the continuous sampling for and measuring of pollutants present in the atmosphere.

air pollution: manmade contamination of the *atmosphere*, beyond that which is natural and excluding the narrowly occupational, as the contaminated air that miners or asbestos workers breathe.

air quality control region: as the federal government uses the term, an area where two or more communities—either in the same or different states —share a common air pollution problem. Designated by the Secretary of Health, Education, and Welfare, these regions are required to set and enforce consistent air quality standards.

air quality criteria: as the federal government uses the term, the varying amounts of pollution and lengths of exposure at which specific adverse effects to health and welfare take place.

air quality standard: as the federal government uses the term, the prescribed level of a pollutant in the outside air that cannot legally be exceeded during a specified time in a specified geographical area.

airway resistance: the narrowing of the air passages of the respiratory system in response to the presence of irritating substances.

biosphere: all living things together with their environment.

bronchial asthma: abnormal responsiveness of the air passages to certain substances. An attack consists of a widespread narrowing of the bronchioles by muscle spasm, swelling of the mucous membrane, or thickening and increase of mucous secretions, accompanied by wheezing, gasping, and sometimes coughing.

bronchiole: small branch of the *bronchus.*

bronchus: a major airway of the respiratory system.

cancer: an abnormal, potentially unlimited, disorderly new cell growth.

carbon monoxide: a colorless, odorless, very toxic gas produced by any process that involves the incomplete combustion of carbon-containing substances. One of the major air pollutants, it is primarily emitted through the exhaust of gasoline-powered vehicles.

combustion: the production of heat and light *energy* through a chemical process—usually oxidation. One of the three basic contributing processes of air pollution, the others being *attrition* and *vaporization.*

centrifugal collector: any of several mechanical systems using centrifugal force to remove *aerosols* from a gas stream.

chromosome: a part of all cells of all organisms. Chromosomes are composed of genes and transmit characteristics from generation to generation.

cilia: hairlike cells that line the airways and by their sweeping movement propel the dirt- and germ-filled mucous out of the respiratory tract.

distillation: the removal of impurities from liquids by heating the liquids to the boiling point and then condensing the vapors.

dust: any solid particulate matter over 1 *micron* in size.

dust fall jar: an open-mouthed container used to collect large particles which fall out of the air in order to measure and analyze them.

ecology: the totality or pattern of the interrelationship of organisms and their environment and the science that is concerned with that interrelationship.

economic poisons: those chemicals used as insecticides, rodenticides, fungicides, herbicides, nematocides. Nematode is a class of parasitic worm or defoliant.

ecosphere: the layer of earth and troposphere inhabited by or suitable for the existence of living organisms.

emission factor: the statistical average of the amount of a specific pollutant emitted from each type of polluting source in relation to a unit quantity of material handled, processed, or burned; e.g., the emission factor of oxides of nitrogen in fuel oil combustion is 119 pounds per 1000 gallons of fuel oil used. By using the emission factor of a pollutant and specific data regarding quantities of material used by a given source, it is possible to compute emissions for that source—information necessary for an *emission inventory*.

emission inventory: a list of primary air pollutants emitted into a given community's atmosphere, in amounts (commonly tons) per day, by type of source. The emission inventory is basic to the establishment of *emission standards*. Also see *emission factor*.

emission standard: the maximum amount of a pollutant that is permitted to be discharged from a single polluting source; e.g., the number of pounds of fly ash per cubic foot of air that may be emitted from a coal-fired boiler.

environment: the aggregate of all the external conditions and influences affecting the life, development, and ultimately the survival of an organism.

epidemiology: the study of diseases as they affect populations rather than individuals, including the distribution and incidents of disease; mortality and morbidity rates; and the relationship with climate, age, sex, race, and other factors.

evaporation: the physical transformation of a liquid to a gas at a new temperature below its boiling point.

filter collector: a mechanical filtration system for a moving particulate matter from a gas stream, from measurement, analysis, or control. Also called bag collector. Filters are designed in a variety of sizes and material for specific purposes.

fluorides: gaseous or solid compounds containing fluorine, emitted into the air from a number of industrial processes; fluorides are a major cause of vegetation and—indirectly—livestock damage.

fly ash: the *particulate* impurities resulting from the burning of coal and other material, which are exhausted into the air from *stacks*.

fog: the condensation of water vapor in the air. Also see *smog*.

fossil fuels: coal, oil, and natural gas; so-called because they are the remains of ancient plant and animal life.

fume: solid particles under 1 *micron* in diameter, formed as vapors condense or as chemical reactions take place.

generator: a device that changes *mechanical energy* into *electrical energy*.

greenhouse effect: the phenomenon in which the sun's energy, in the form of light waves, passes through the air and is absorbed by the earth, which then reradiates the energy as heat waves that the air is able to absorb. The air thus behaves like glass in a greenhouse, allowing the passage of light but not heat.

half-life: the period of time required for half of the atoms of a given radioactive substance to decay.

heat island effect: the phenomenon of air circulation peculiar to cities, in which warm air builds up in the center, rises, spreads out over the town, and, as it cools, sinks at the edges; while cooler air from the outskirts flows in toward the city center to repeat the flow pattern. In this way a self-contained circulation system is put in motion that can be broken only by relatively strong winds.

hi-volume sampler: also called a Hi-Vol. A device used in the measurement and analysis of suspended *particulate* pollution.

hydrocarbon: any of a vast family of compounds containing carbon and hydrogen in various combinations; found especially in *fossil fuels*. Some of the hydrocarbon compounds are major air pollutants: they may be *carcinogenic* or active participants in the *photochemical process*.

incineration: the burning of household or industrial waste.

inertial separators: air pollution control equipment that uses the principle of inertia to remove *particulate* matter from a stream of air or gas.

inversion: the phenomenon of a layer of cool air trapped by a layer of warmer air above it so that the bottom layer cannot rise. A special problem in polluted areas because the contaminating substances cannot be dispersed.

nitrogen oxides: gases formed in great part from atmospheric nitrogen and oxygen when combustion takes place under conditions of high temperature and high pressure, e.g., in internal-combustion engines; considered major air pollutants.

particulate: a particle of solid or liquid matter.

photochemical process: the chemical changes brought about by the *radiant energy* of the sun acting upon various polluting substances. The products are known as photochemical *smog*.

ppm: parts per million; the number of parts of a given pollutant in a million parts of air.

precipitators: any of a number of devices using mechanical, electrical, or chemical means to collect particulates. Used for measurement, analysis, or control.

pulmonary emphysema: an anatomic change in the lungs characterized by breakdown of the walls of the alveoli, which can become enlarged, lose their resilience, and disintegrate.

pulmonary function: in medicine, a term used in describing the adequacy of the lung's performance.

Ringelmann chart: actually a series of charts, numbered from 0 to 5, that simulate various *smoke* densities, by presenting different percentages of black. A Ringelmann No. 1 is equivalent to twenty percent black; a Ringelmann No. 5 to 100 percent. They are used for measuring the opacity of smoke arising from *stacks* and other sources, by matching with the actual effluent the various numbers, or densities, indicated by the charts. Ringelmann numbers are sometimes used in setting emission standards.

scrubber: a device that uses a liquid spray to remove *aerosol* and gaseous pollutants from an air stream. The gases are removed either by *absorption* or chemical reaction. Solid and liquid *particulates* are removed through contact with the spray. Scrubbers are used for both the measurement and control of pollution.

smog: the irritating haze resulting from the sun's effect on certain pollutants in the air, notably those from automobile exhaust; see *photochemical process*. Also a mixture of *fog* and *smoke*.

smoke: solid or liquid particles under 1 *micron* in diameter.

soot: very finely divided carbon particles clustered together in long chains.

sorption: a term including both *adsorption* and *absorption*. Sorption is basic to many processes used to measure, analyze, and remove both gaseous and particulate pollutants.

spirometer: an instrument that measures the flow of air in and out of the lungs.

stomata: tiny opening upon the underside of the leaf, through which a plant takes in carbon dioxide and some polluting gases.

sulfur oxides: pungent, colorless gases formed primarily by the combustion of fossil fuels into major air pollutants; sulfur oxides may damage the respiratory tract as well as vegetation.

tape sampler: a device used in the measurement of both gases and fine particulates. It allows air sampling to be made automatically at predetermined times.

topography: the configuration of a surface including its relief and the position of its natural manmade features.

INDEX

FRIENDS OF THE EARTH, founded in 1969 by David Brower, is a non-profit membership organization streamlined for legislative activity in the United States and abroad aimed at restoring the environment misused by man and at preserving remaining wilderness where the life force continues to flow freely.

FRIENDS OF THE EARTH in order to fight without restrictions does not wish to be tax-deductible and for that reason has special need for and invites your participation.

Addresses:
FRIENDS OF THE EARTH

30 East 42nd Street
New York, N.Y. 10017

451 Pacific Avenue
San Francisco, California 94133

917 15th Street, N.W.
Washington, D.C. 20005

1372 Kapiolani Blvd.
Honolulu, Hawaii 96814

P.O. Box 1977
Anchorage, Alaska 99501

FRIENDS OF THE EARTH

☐ I enclose $_____for membership.
☐ I wish to participate actively from time to time.
  My special conservation interests are: _____
  _____
☐ My own field is: _____
☐ I enclose $_____as a contribution but do not want
  to join now.
☐ I should like to be kept informed of other books in the
  Survival Series.

NAME_____

ADDRESS_____

CITY_____STATE_____ZIP_____

*For four days the smog
held the city in its grip.*

KILLER SMOG

The True Story of the World's Worst
Air Pollution Disaster

William Wise

With an Introduction by Kenneth Watt

Considerable fog began to form late on a
Thursday evening. When it finally lifted four
days later, over 4,000 people were dead. Thousands of others were ill, many of them permanently affected. The scene was London, but
it could have been New York, Los Angeles,
or any one of a dozen major American cities.
The year was 1952, but it could be this year
or next.

"A distinct contribution to public understanding of the air pollution problem. A
thorough and fascinating job of inquiry."
—*Gladwin Hill*

"It takes only a few hours to read this chiller;
I recommend that you do so."
—*Medical Record News*

AN AUDUBON/BALLANTINE BOOK $1.25

For a complete list or to order by mail, send
to Dept. CS, Ballantine Books, 36 West 20th
Street, New York, N.Y. 10003

This is a plan to save spaceship Earth
by the author of the bestselling
THE POPULATION BOMB

HOW TO BE A SURVIVOR

Dr. Paul R. Ehrlich
with Richard L. Harriman

The 1970's is the decade of decision. In this decade, mankind will either take the necessary action to preserve his species or he will so erode, overtax and exploit his only habitat that he will destroy himself.

This is a plan to save the world, to keep it alive for the next thirty years. If we can do that, mankind will have a chance.

A Friends of the Earth/Ballantine Book $1.25

To order by mail, send $1.30 to Department CS, Ballantine Books, 36 West 20th St., New York, N.Y. 10003

PRAYING
WITH
CONFIDENCE

Praying with Confidence: Guided Prayers for Life's Moments

Scripture quotations marked AMP are taken from the Amplified® Bible (AMP), Copyright © 2015 by The Lockman Foundation. Used by permission. lockman.org

Scripture quotations marked ESV are taken from the ESV® Bible (The Holy Bible, English Standard Version®), Copyright © 2001 by Crossway, a publishing ministry of Good News Publishers. Used by permission. All rights reserved.

Scripture quotations marked MSG are taken from *The Message*, Copyright © 1993, 2002, 2018 by Eugene H. Peterson. Used by permission of NavPress, represented by Tyndale House Publishers.

Scripture quotations marked NIV are taken from the *Holy Bible*, New International Version®, NIV®, Copyright © 1973, 1978, 1984, 2011 by Biblica, Inc.™ Used by permission of Zondervan. All rights reserved worldwide. www.zondervan.com The "NIV" and "New International Version" are trademarks registered in the United States Patent and Trademark Office by Biblica, Inc.™

Scripture quotations marked NKJV are taken from the New King James Version®. Copyright © 1982 by Thomas Nelson. Used by permission. All rights reserved.

Scripture quotations marked NLT are taken from the *Holy Bible*, New Living Translation, Copyright © 1996, 2004, 2015 by Tyndale House Foundation. Used by permission of Tyndale House Publishers, Inc., Carol Stream, Illinois 60188. All rights reserved.

ISBN: 978-1-951701-45-1

Printed in China.

Created and assembled for Joel Osteen Ministries by
Breakfast for Seven
breakfastforseven.com

For additional resources by Joel Osteen, visit JoelOsteen.com

PRAYING WITH CONFIDENCE

Guided Prayers
for Life's Moments

Have you ever wondered if there's a better way to pray, a bold way to believe God for what you most need and desire? There is. It begins with knowing who you are and Whose you are as a child of the Most High God! I've heard people who spend their prayer time complaining to God, telling Him all of their problems, and that's ok.

God listens. He loves to hear from His children. I want you to pray boldly. In this powerful book, you'll find a compilation of heartfelt prayers from Lakewood through the years to guide you in praying with confidence.

"This is the confidence we have in approaching God: that if we ask anything according to His will, He hears us. And if we know that He hears us — whatever we ask — we know that we have what we asked of Him."
1 John 5:14–15, NIV

Whether you're dealing with a difficult situation, seeking guidance and direction, or simply looking for a way to deepen your relationship with God, this book has something for you. The more you understand how to release your faith and pray with confidence, the more you will see God move in your life . . . in your job, in your family, in your finances, in your health.

Now, if you're ready to start praying bold, confident prayers, let's begin this journey together. Let's do as the Scripture says: confidently approaching God, knowing *"that if we ask anything according to His will, He hears us . . ."* today, tomorrow, and every moment of our lives.

PRAY THIS

COME BACK TO GOD'S PEACE

Dear God,
This is the day You have made. I'm going to rejoice and be glad in it! Those things that are trying to weigh me down, things that I'm worried about, things that I'm struggling with, God, I'm turning all of it over to You. I know that You're on the throne. You're in control of my life. I trust You. I give You praise, not because everything is perfect in my life, but because You are in control. I'm coming back to that place of faith, that place of gratefulness, that place of peace. I've learned it's a place of power. You've got me in the palm of Your hand! The enemy would love for me to go through life worried and upset, but I am protected, loved, and cared for. I can have a confident expectation of good! That's why I'm going to make the most of this day. I'm going to give You praise and be a blessing to somebody today. That's what's going to help me see Your goodness and favor in a greater way. In Jesus' Name, Amen.

"Commit your way to the LORD;
trust in Him, and He will act."

PSALM 37:5, ESV

I give You praise, not because
everything is perfect in my life, but
because You are in control. I'm coming
back to that place of faith, that place
of gratefulness, that place of peace. I've
learned it's a place of power.

3

SET YOUR EYES ON GOD

Dear God,

You know that sometimes I can be doing one thing while I am thinking about something else. But right now, I am lifting my eyes to You, the One that my help comes from. I shift my eyes away from my problems, away from my distractions, away from negativity, and I turn them toward You. When my attention is on You, Your attention is on me. And if I have Your attention, then I have everything You have for me: Resources, blessing, and favor are being drawn into my life right now. I will set my eyes on You, the One Who helps me, Who saves me, Who sets me free, Who provides all the resources I need. I'm not looking to my job or to other people. I am going to keep my eyes on You. Fill me with Your goodness, Lord. Fill me with Your mercy as I set You on the throne of my heart. In Jesus' Name, Amen.

*"I lift up my eyes to the mountains
— where does my help come from?
My help comes from the LORD, the
Maker of heaven and earth."*

PSALM 121:1–2, NIV

. . . if I have Your attention,
then I have everything You have
for me: Resources, blessing,
and favor are being drawn into
my life right now.

GOD'S REFRESHING BELONGS TO YOU

Dear Lord,

Thank You for this opportunity to refresh my soul in prayer. You said in Isaiah 44 that You are the refresher — that You will pour streams of living water out on me and my descendants. So right now, I open my heart to You and shake off any stress or negative thoughts. I know that nothing is impossible with You. Thank You for today. I don't take it for granted that I got up this morning, that I can breathe, that I can live another day in Your presence. God, don't allow me to let the little irritants and annoyances of life hinder me from keeping You first place. Thank You that I can put my focus on You, knowing You are my highest aim. I want to align myself with You and the power, the wisdom, the goodness You have for me. Thank You, Father, for all You've done in my life and for all that You're going to do. In Jesus' Name, Amen!

"For I will pour water on the thirsty land, and streams on the dry ground; I will pour My Spirit upon your offspring, and My blessing on your descendants. They shall spring up among the grass like willows by flowing streams."

ISAIAH 44:3–4, ESV

I open my heart to You, Father, and shake off any stress or negative thoughts. I know that nothing is impossible with You.

GIVE GOD YOUR BATTLES

Father,

You have called me "more than a conqueror." It doesn't matter what I feel like today. It matters what I know deep down on the inside — that You are fighting my battles. I trust You, and I rest in that trust. You are everything I need. Thank You for giving me the courage and wisdom to deal with things that You bring to light. I'm not going to keep responding to negative situations in ways that don't serve Your purposes for me. You are refining me, guiding me, directing my steps, so that I will take new ground and become all that You have created me to be. In Jesus' Name, Amen.

"Who shall separate us from the love of Christ? Shall trouble or hardship or persecution or famine or nakedness or danger or sword? No, in all these things we are more than conquerors through Him who loved us."

ROMANS 8:35,37, NIV

You are fighting my battles. I trust You, and I rest in that trust. You are everything I need.

LOOK TO GOD IN YOUR THOUGHTS

Father,

Everything we do involves You. You are there in every need, every joy, every sorrow. Thank You. Today, we remind ourselves to look to You in our thoughts, thanking You, asking for Your help, and developing the habit of acknowledging You. That's when You will show out in our lives to fight our battles and make crooked places straight.

Your Word says, *". . . in all your ways acknowledge Him, And He shall direct your paths,"* (Proverbs 3:6, NKJV). When we make acknowledging You our highest priority, You can make all the other details in our lives fall in line. We're not going to get upset or stressed out about what we have to do today or what's going on next week. We're going to stand on Your Word, knowing You have good plans for us, plans to prosper us and not to harm us, to give us a future and a hope! In Jesus' Name, Amen.

"And whatever you do, in word or deed, do everything in the name of the Lord Jesus, giving thanks to God the Father through Him."

COLOSSIANS 3:17, ESV

When we make acknowledging You our highest priority, You can make all the other details in our lives fall in line.

THE LORD LOVES YOU AS YOU ARE

Dear God,

Thank you for all You've done. Thank You that You receive us just the way we are. We don't walk in shame or condemnation. We walk in newness of life, that freshness in You. We throw our shoulders back and thank You for what You did for us. As we pray today, we ask that You clear away any distractions, any worry or complaining, anything that would try to hinder us from being able to absorb all that You are in us and through us. We will honor You by moving forward and by being a light in the world. We thank You, and give You glory and honor. In Jesus' Name, Amen.

"Therefore, if anyone is in Christ, he is a new creation. The old has passed away; behold, the new has come."

2 CORINTHIANS 5:17, ESV

Thank You that You receive us just the way we are. We don't walk in shame or condemnation. We walk in newness of life, that freshness in You.

HAVE COURAGE TO CHANGE

Father,

Help us to walk by the spirit and not by the flesh.
Help us to change in areas where we may have
gotten lazy. Show us where we have blind spots.
Give us the courage to commit to making the
changes You are calling us to make. Thank You
for giving us the grace to do what we need to do
and helping us to shine brighter for Your glory.
Equip and empower us to break strongholds that
have held our families back for years. Lord, we
will be the difference-makers. Thank You that
we are strong, anointed, favored, and well-able
to do what You have called us to do. In Jesus'
Name, Amen.

"For God has not given us a spirit of fear and timidity, but of power, love, and self-discipline."

2 TIMOTHY 1:7, NLT

Lord, we will be the difference-makers. Thank You that we are strong, anointed, favored, and well-able to do what You have called us to do.

MOVE FORWARD IN FAITH

Lord,

Thank You for opening the right doors and closing the wrong doors. I thank You that every force that's trying to stop me is broken right now in the Name of Jesus. I believe and declare that You are bringing the right people across my path and weeding out those who shouldn't be there. Help me to make decisions that honor You. Lord, You said if I need wisdom, I could ask and You'd freely give it. So, I am asking for Your wisdom today. Thank You for clear direction in my life, for making the path easy for me to see. Lord, for the mistakes I have made, I ask for Your forgiveness. I receive Your mercy and move forward in faith today. Lord, I know that Your mercy is bigger than any mistake, and You can still get me to where I'm supposed to be. In Jesus' Name, Amen.

"If any of you lacks wisdom, you should ask God, Who gives generously to all without finding fault, and it will be given to you."

JAMES 1:5, NIV

Lord, thank You for Your clear direction in my life, for making the path easy for me to see.

NOT IF, BUT WHEN!

Lord,

We're reminded that the Scripture says in Hebrews, "Hold fast your profession of faith, without wavering, for He who promised is faithful." We've got to hold fast to the promises and dreams You put in our hearts because we know that doubts can arise and try to talk us out of them. But You are faithful. That's what gives us the strength to hold on — we are not holding on for our own sakes. We're holding on because we know we serve a faithful God. That's what gives us the strength to hold fast, so today, we know that You love us with an everlasting love. You want to see those promises and those dreams come to pass. Sometimes, it takes longer than we think, and we have to say in the face of doubt, "No, my God is faithful." We have to say in the face of fear, "No, my God is faithful." No matter what we're facing, we know that our God is faithful, and that's what we're standing on! In Jesus' Name, Amen.

"He who calls you is faithful,
who also will do it."

1 THESSALONIANS 5:24, NKJV

When those "if-only" thoughts come —
"if only this happened, if only that
happens" — we have to say, "No,
not "if-only" it happens, but when it
happens" because our God is faithful,
and that's what we're standing on!

SEE YOUR WORLD WITH EYES OF FAITH

Lord,
Help me to believe and to become all that You've created me to be. Show me a fresh mindset that keeps coming back to You in every situation. I know You can take me where I can't go on my own. You can open doors that no person can shut. Thank You, Lord, for showing me Your goodness in new ways. By faith, I see You breaking chains of addiction off my life. I believe and declare chains of anxiety, depression, and sickness are being broken right now. You are doing a new thing. I see it through eyes of faith. I am breaking out of ruts that would hold me down. Thank You for helping me step into the fullness of my destiny and showing me Your goodness, mercy, and favor in new ways, In Jesus' Name, Amen.

"See, I am doing a new thing! Now it springs up; do you not perceive it? I am making a way in the wilderness and streams in the wasteland."

ISAIAH 43:19, NIV

Thank You for helping me step into the fullness of my destiny and showing me Your goodness, mercy, and favor in new ways, In Jesus' Name, Amen.

We serve an overflow God! Even in famine, the Scripture says that the righteous will have more than enough. That's my prayer for you today!

LEAN ON THE LORD

Father,

We thank You for always being with us and revealing Who You are through the gift of Your Word. Thank You for doing what only You can do because, in this moment, there are things too big for us to handle. Right now, Father, we give You our cares and worries. We cast them onto You right now, Lord. And we just walk today with a light load. We lean on You, knowing that You are taking care of us and meeting every need that we have. Instead of worrying, getting upset, living afraid, we are going to see the good, Lord. We pray, open our eyes. Help us to recognize all of the great things that You are doing, Lord. Thank You for protecting us, our families, and loved ones. In Jesus' Name, Amen.

"Cast all your anxiety on Him because He cares for you."

1 PETER 5:7, NIV

We lean on You, knowing that
You are taking care of us and
meeting every need that we have.
Instead of worrying, getting upset,
living afraid, we are going to see
the good, Lord.

HEALTH IS FLOWING YOUR WAY

Dear Lord,

I lift up my health today and all who are not feeling well or living with pain of any kind — physical, mental, or emotional. Lord, You said You would restore health back to Your people. So, thank You, Father, that healing and wholeness are flowing into our areas of need right now. We receive it by faith. You said with long life You would satisfy us. Lord, we believe that You can do what even medicine cannot do. You have the final say. Right now, I declare healing, wholeness, strength, and vitality, that we will run and not be weary. Lord, I thank You for it. In Jesus' Name, Amen.

"For I will restore health to you,
and your wounds I will heal,
declares the LORD . . .*"*

JEREMIAH 30:17, ESV

Thank You, Father, that healing
and wholeness are flowing into
our areas of need right now.
We receive it by faith.

RELEASE THE OLD. RECEIVE THE NEW.

Dear God,

Some things in my life are not working out as
I had hoped and prayed and planned. I'm going
to step into a new, fresh way of thinking today
because that's what new beginnings are about.
They are about wiping the slate clean, knowing
that Your mercies are fresh and new every
morning. God, I visualize new things happening,
turnarounds, things shifting. Thank You that in
Your presence there is fullness of whatever we
need: Joy, favor, wisdom, health, restoration. The
Bible says You want to help us fulfill our destiny,
help us walk in victory. That's why You came.
You are always redeeming us from anything in
our paths, so that we can walk in victory. Thank
You for creating in us new beginnings, new starts,
new ways of thinking. Lord, we give You all the
praise, all the honor, and all the glory. In Jesus'
Name, Amen.

"The faithful love of the LORD never ends! His mercies never cease. Great is His faithfulness; His mercies begin afresh each morning."

LAMENTATIONS 3:22–23, NLT

I aim to see myself the way God sees me. Today is a new day. I am a child of the Most High God! I will become all I was created to be. In Jesus' Name, Amen.

BELIEVE BIGGER, BECOME YOUR BEST

Lord,

The seed You put in our hearts is taking root. Thank You that we will believe bigger. We will dream bigger, Lord, and we will know, even in the silent seasons, that You are still in control. Even the things we don't understand, we believe it is all working for our good. Lord, help us to believe when that doubt comes, and help us to guard our minds. Lord, thank You that we will become all that You have created us to be. Thank You for protection, for favor, for wisdom, Lord, and for peace and creativity, in Jesus' Name, Amen.

*"And we know that in all things
God works for the good of those
who love Him, who have been called
according to His purpose."*

ROMANS 8:28, NIV

We will know, even in the silent seasons,
that You are still in control. Even the
things we don't understand, we believe it is
all working for our good. Lord, help us to
believe when that doubt comes, and help
us to guard our minds.

GOD HAND-PICKED YOU!

Father,

I've been letting other people determine how I see myself. I've been allowing my past or what I'm up against to determine my self-image. But now I see that it is a distorted image. That's not who I really am. I aim to see myself the way God sees me. Today is a new day. I believe and declare: I am blessed, prosperous, redeemed, forgiven, healthy, whole, talented, creative, confident, secure, disciplined, focused, prepared, qualified, motivated, valuable, free, determined, equipped, empowered, anointed, accepted, and approved — not average, not mediocre. I am a child of the Most High God! I will become all I was created to be. In Jesus' Name, Amen.

"Even before He made the world, God loved us and chose us in Christ to be holy and without fault in His eyes. God decided in advance to adopt us into His own family by bringing us to Himself through Jesus Christ. This is what He wanted to do, and it gave Him great pleasure."

EPHESIANS 1:4–5, NLT

I aim to see myself the way God sees me. Today is a new day. I am a child of the Most High God! I will become all I was created to be, in Jesus' Name, Amen.

GOD IS FOR YOU

Dear Lord,

Thank You that today is a breakthrough day, and You are doing what only You can do. You have done it in the past, and I believe You will do it again in the future. My spiritual ears and eyes are open, sensitive, responsive to Your voice. I can clearly hear what the Spirit is saying. Lord, I have made mistakes and taken wrong turns, so thank You that Your mercy is bigger than my mistakes, that You can still get me to where I'm supposed to be. I let go of guilt, condemnation, lies, and negativity. I believe You are for me, that I am redeemed and restored, and that I'm well able to do what You've called me to do, in Jesus' Name, Amen.

*". . . blessed are your eyes
because they see, and your ears
because they hear."*

MATTHEW 13:16, NIV

My spiritual ears and eyes are
open, sensitive, responsive to Your
voice. I can clearly hear what the
Spirit is saying.

BLESS AND BE BLESSED

Lord,

You know every hair on my head. You know what I need before I even ask. So, God, knowing that You know me and You are such a big God, I am going to turn my attention to others, just like Job did. I know as I pray for others and link my faith with them, You will restore health unto me. You will restore prosperity unto me. You will restore favor unto me. Father, thank You so much for this time with You. There is no distance in prayer, so I send out prayers to all those in need right now. Thank You that You are working now in our midst. You can do anything in our lives. We look to You for good, and we thank You that You are good. I stand in faith today, knowing that You can do the impossible. In Jesus' Name, Amen.

"For where two or three gather in my name, there am I with them."

MATTHEW 18:20, NIV

I know as I pray for others and link my faith with them, You will restore health unto me. You will restore prosperity unto me. You will restore favor unto me.

SURROUNDED BY GOD'S FAVOR

Dear God,

I come before You today with a heart full of gratitude and expectation, knowing that Your favor surrounds me. I thank You for the promises in Your Word that declare Your unending favor on my life. As I step into this new day, I pray that Your favor would go before me, opening doors of opportunity and divine connections. I declare Your favor is a shield that surrounds and protects me. Help me to walk in confidence, knowing that Your favor empowers me to overcome any obstacle that comes my way. I declare Your Word from Psalm 5:12, NKJV, *"Surely, O LORD, You bless the righteous; You surround them with Your favor as with a shield."* Thank You, Lord, for Your abundant favor in every area of my life. In Jesus' Name, Amen.

*"For the LORD God is a sun
and shield; the LORD bestows favor
and honor; no good thing does He
withhold from those whose walk
is blameless."*

PSALM 84:11, NIV

Thank You for the promises in Your
Word that declare Your unending favor
on my life. As I step into this new day,
I pray that Your favor would go before
me, opening doors of opportunity and
divine connections.

STEP OUT IN FAITH

Father,
Thank You for showing out in my life in ways
that could only be You. Lord, Your favor
transforms lives and brings light into the darkest
places. I stand in awe of Your power and grace.
Thank You for directing my steps and making
things happen that I could never make happen.
I pray that You fill me with Your love and peace
that passes all understanding, that I may glorify
You in all that I do. Help me to trust in Your plan
for my life and step out in faith, knowing that
You will never leave me. In Jesus' Name, Amen.

"So we have come to know and to believe the love that God has for us. God is love, and whoever abides in love abides in God, and God abides in him."

1 JOHN 4:16, ESV

I pray that You fill me with Your love and peace that passes all understanding, that I may glorify You in all that I do.

GOD'S UNLIMITED SUPPLY OF FAVOR

Heavenly Father,

We come to You today with grateful hearts, knowing that You are a God of favor and abundance. We ask for Your favor to be poured out over our homes, our jobs, our finances, and our health. We believe Your Word which says in Philippians 4:19 that You will supply all our needs according to Your glorious riches in Christ Jesus. We declare victory over any obstacles that may come our way, knowing that with You by our side, we are victors and never victims. In Jesus' Name, Amen.

"For the LORD *your God
is the One Who goes with you to
fight for you against your enemies
to give you victory."*

DEUTERONOMY 20:4, NIV

We declare victory over any
obstacles that may come our way,
knowing that with You by our side,
we are victors and never victims.
In Jesus' Name, Amen

'Call to me and I will answer you and tell you great and unsearchable things you do not know.'

GRATITUDE IS THE KEY TO GREATER BLESSINGS

Dear God,

We all have reasons to be grateful. The more we thank You for what's right in life, the more You will take care of what's wrong in life. When we're grateful, we can come back to a place of peace and say, "God, I know You're on the throne. I know You're bigger than what I'm facing." We expect You to do great things. We receive it by faith today and are refreshed in spirit. We set down our troubles and burdens at the feet of Jesus. As we stir up our faith, God's going to rain down favor, healing, strength, and peace. This day is going to go better because we took this time with You. In Jesus' Name, Amen

". . . give thanks in all circumstances; for this is God's will for you in Christ Jesus."

1 THESSALONIANS 5:18, NIV

Set down your troubles and burdens at the feet of Jesus. As you stir up your faith, God's going to rain down favor, healing, strength, and peace. Your day is going to go better because you took this time with Him. In Jesus' Name, Amen.

THAT BATTLE BEFORE YOU? IT'S GOD'S!

Dear Lord,

Your Word shows us the power of praise, like King Jehoshaphat standing in front of an army that was larger than him. Enemies surrounded him, but he looked to You. You told him to put the praisers out front *"for the battle is not yours, but God's"* (2 Chronicles 20:15, NKJV). So today we are putting our praises ahead of us. We believe and declare that our battles are Yours. Enemies that are trying to come against us, negative attitudes in our minds and hearts, walls that we've put up . . . Father, we give them all to You. We honor You for Who You are, in all Your holiness, in all Your majesty, and in all Your greatness. In Jesus' Name, Amen.

"With him is an arm of flesh; but with us is the LORD our God, to help us and to fight our battles."

2 CHRONICLES, 32:8, NKJV

We believe and declare that our battles are Yours. Enemies that are trying to come against us, negative attitudes in our minds and hearts, walls that we've put up . . . Father, we give them all to You.

GOD'S CLOSE TO YOU AND YOUR PAIN

Father,

I pray that I feel Your presence in my life. There are things I'm going through that I just can't manage on my own. They are too big: loss, hurt, disappointments. Lord, You said You're close to the broken-hearted. Thank You that what was meant for harm, You're turning to my advantage. Thank You that You're healing my broken heart. You're restoring what the enemy is trying to steal. You're taking me through the valley. I'm not staying here. Lord, I believe that I will see Your goodness, Your mercy, fresh anointing, fresh favor, new relationships, new beginnings! Your Word says that weeping endures for a night, but joy is coming in the morning. So, thank You that joy is on the way! I receive it by faith. In Jesus' Name, Amen.

"Weeping may endure for a night,
But joy comes in the morning."

PSALM 30:5, NKJV

You're taking me through
the valley. I'm not staying here.
Lord, I believe that I will see
Your goodness, Your mercy,
fresh anointing, fresh favor, new
relationships, new beginnings!

COME BOLDLY TO THE THRONE OF GRACE

Heavenly Father,

I'm putting You first place. I believe and declare that You are with me and for me, breathing in my direction right now. Lord, You have a great plan for my life. I believe as I have the right image of You, then I can do as the Scripture says: to come boldly before the throne of grace, receiving help in my time of need. As I align my thoughts with Your Word, I will become all that You created me to be: blessed, prosperous, favored, equipped, anointed, forgiven, and redeemed. In Jesus' Name, Amen.

"Let us then with confidence draw near to the throne of grace, that we may receive mercy and find grace to help in time of need."

HEBREWS 4:16, ESV

As I align my thoughts with
Your Word, I will become all that
You created me to be: blessed,
prosperous, favored, equipped,
anointed, forgiven, and redeemed.
In Jesus' Name, Amen.

BE A BELIEVER, NOT A DOUBTER

Lord,

The Scripture promises us that when we believe, all things become possible. We are standing on that promise today. We are believers and not doubters. By faith, we believe that we have not seen Your greatest victories yet! They are still in our future! You have said in Your Word that you take us *"from glory to glory"* (2 Corinthians 3:18). So even though we go through some challenges, some ups and downs, we believe that *"the path of the righteous . . . shines brighter and brighter"* (Proverbs 4:18, ESV). Today we are taking the limits off ourselves and letting go of what did not work out. Your favor is on us in a new way. You are going to show out in our lives! We're going to come to reach the end of this year and say, "Look what the Lord has done!" In Jesus' Name, Amen.

*"Jesus looked at them and said,
'With man this is impossible, but
with God all things are possible.'"*

MATTHEW 19:26, NIV

Today we are taking the limits off
ourselves and letting go of what did
not work out. Your favor is on us in
a new way. You are going to show
out in our lives!

POUR OUT GOD'S BLESSINGS AND BE FILLED

Dear God,

What a joy it is to give . . . to be part of someone's life, whether I know them or not. God, I believe You have blessed me to be a blessing. Your Word gives me hope in this promise, *"Whoever brings blessing will be enriched . . ."* I'm so thankful to bless others in Your precious Name, Lord. That can never be taken away from me. These are not only earthly blessings, but they are also eternal blessings. Thank You, Father, for using my life to bless others, to praise You by lifting up others . . . I am blessed! In Jesus' Name, Amen.

"Whoever brings blessing will be enriched, and one who waters will himself be watered."

PROVERBS 11:25, ESV

Thank You, Father, for using my life to bless others, to praise You by lifting up others . . . I am blessed! In Jesus' Name, Amen.

LIVING REFRESHED AND RENEWED

Dear Lord,

Thank You for having good things in store for me and thank You, Father, for having me in the palm of Your Hand. As I stir up my faith and expectancy, I believe You are going to show out in my life in an unusual way. You being for me is more than the world being against me. In this time with You, Lord, I'm shaking off all the worry, all the doubt, what somebody said, the mistakes I've made. I will live today refreshed and renewed. Like a computer, I'm rebooting my thoughts and attitudes. I'm clearing out negativity and coming back to a place of peace. Praise precedes the victory! In Jesus' Name, Amen.

"Do not be conformed to this world, but be transformed by the renewal of your mind, that by testing you may discern what is the will of God, what is good and acceptable and perfect."

ROMANS 12:2, NIV

As I stir up my faith and expectancy, I believe You are going to show out in my life in an unusual way. You being for me is more than the world being against me.

"YES AND SO BE IT" TODAY

Lord,
Thank You for being a faithful God. I know that You are working behind the scenes in my life. And You have a promise of everything that I am in need of today. The Scripture says that Your promises are all "yes" and "amen" in Christ Jesus! *Amen* means "so be it." Lord, may it be so today as I get in agreement with Your promises. You are my waymaker and my promise keeper, Father God. I'm believing that You can do the impossible. Thank You for all that You are doing in my life, and for all of the times You said yes to every good thing. So be it today. In Jesus' Name, Amen.

"For no matter how many promises God has made, they are 'Yes' in Christ. And so through Him the 'Amen' is spoken by us to the glory of God."

2 CORINTHIANS 1:20, NIV

The Scripture says that Your promises are all "yes" and "amen" in Christ Jesus! *Amen* means "so be it." Lord, may it be so today as I get in agreement with Your promises.

RECEIVE ALL THAT GOD HAS FOR YOU

Father,

You have blessed me and "crowned me with favor and honor." Thank You, Lord! I am so grateful to be Your child — equipped, anointed, and empowered to accomplish all that You have created me to be. Your Word says You have good things in front of me. They are already prepared. I just need to walk in them. So today, I am putting on the helmet of salvation . . . that right way of thinking. And I'm putting on the breastplate of righteousness, and Father, by faith, I'm running boldly into Your presence today and receiving everything You have for me. In Jesus' Name, Amen.

"Praise the LORD, my soul, and forget not all His benefits — Who forgives all your sins and heals all your diseases, Who redeems your life from the pit and crowns you with love and compassion, Who satisfies your desires with good things so that your youth is renewed like the eagle's."

PSALM 103:2–5, NIV

I am so grateful to be Your child — equipped, anointed, and empowered to accomplish all that You have created me to be.

PRAISE PRECEDES THE VICTORY

Heavenly Father,

I come before You today with a heart full of gratitude and praise. Thank You for Your love and for arming me with strength for every battle I face. As I put You first in my life, I trust that You will guide me to where I need to be. Lord, help me to take hold of that strength today and always. In Romans 8, I'm reminded that You are mindful of me and that You care about every aspect of my life. Help me to remember this truth, even when circumstances may tell me otherwise. Encourage me to run toward You, not away, knowing that You are my loving Father, ready to turn things around for my good. In Jesus' Name, Amen.

*"And we know that in all things
God works for the good of those
who love Him, who have been called
according to His purpose."*

ROMANS 8:28, NIV

Thank You for Your love and for
arming me with strength for every
battle I face. As I put You first in my
life, I trust that You will guide me to
where I need to be.

JOEL OSTEEN

You're not reading this by accident. God has you in the palm of His hand. Stir your faith up today. My prayer is that you're going to receive more strength, more joy, more victory. Be grateful for what God has done in your life!

NO PROBLEM IS GREATER THAN GOD

Lord,

Today, I could focus on how big my problems are, but instead, I'm focusing on how big You are. Thank You for all that You have done for me in the past and all that You are going to do in the future. You haven't brought me this far to leave me. So even though I've got problems, Lord — things that I'm worried about — I'm going to get in the right frame of mind, knowing that You being for me is more than the world being against me. I believe and declare that You have the answers, the resolution, the healing I'm believing for. In Your presence, there is an abundance of joy, an abundance of faith, an abundance of victory. In Jesus' Name, Amen.

"The thief comes only to steal and kill and destroy; I have come that they may have life, and have it to the full."

JOHN 10:10, NIV

I'm going to get in the right frame of mind, knowing that You being for me is more than the world being against me. I believe and declare that You have the answers, the resolution, the healing I'm believing for.

YOU'RE MARKED FOR GOOD THINGS

Dear God,

I acknowledge that I'm not doing life on my own: You are protecting me and guiding me. I'm humbled to know You handpicked me to be Your child, marking my life for favor, for blessings, for promotion, good breaks, and opportunities. I know it's not because of who I am but because of Who You are, Lord. Thank You. I know my skills and talents can only take me so far, and what You have planned is bigger than anything I can do on my own. Lord, You can show out in my life in a way that there will be no doubt that it wasn't my abilities but Your favor that made it all possible. Thank You, Father. In Jesus' Name, Amen.

"Every good gift and every perfect gift is from above, and comes down from the Father of lights, with Whom there is no variation or shadow of turning."

JAMES 1:17, NKJV

I'm humbled to know You handpicked me to be Your child, marking my life for favor, for blessings, for promotion, good breaks, and opportunities.

STRONGHOLDS ARE BROKEN IN THE UNSEEN REALM

Father,

I take hold of divine wisdom and courage today, Lord, believing that a new mindset — a mindset of healing and wholeness — is rising up on the inside, even now. I thank You that every stronghold in my mind is being broken. Chains are being broken in the name of Jesus . . . chains of depression, of anxiety, of fear, of lack, addictions, sicknesses, trouble at work, trouble at home. Lord, I thank You that every force that is trying to stop me is being broken off my life — that it has already happened in the unseen realm. My trust and confidence are in You. Thank You that today is a breakthrough day. In Jesus' Name, Amen.

"For though we walk in the flesh, we are not waging war according to the flesh. For the weapons of our warfare are not of the flesh but have divine power to destroy strongholds. We destroy arguments and every lofty opinion raised against the knowledge of God, and take every thought captive to obey Christ."

2 CORINTHIANS 10:3–5, ESV

Lord, I thank You that every force that is trying to stop me is being broken off my life — that it has already happened in the unseen realm.

THE POWER OF "NOW" FAITH

Lord,

I love the thought of stirring up my faith to believe for right now. Sometimes, I can get so set on the future that I'm not releasing my faith for today. God, I believe Your promise in Jeremiah 32:17, that *". . . nothing is too hard for You"* — not tomorrow, not today, not right now or ever. God, I believe You are turning my problems for good. Right now, You are freeing me from what's hindering me. Right now, healing is flowing into my body. Right now, new doors of opportunity are beginning to open. The Scripture says, *"Now faith is . . ."* I don't want to always live in the future. I believe, Lord, it's happening now. In Jesus' Name, Amen.

"Now faith is the assurance of things hoped for, the conviction of things not seen."

HEBREWS 11:1, ESV

Right now, You are freeing me from what's hindering me.

STAND ON GOD'S RESURRECTION POWER

Lord,

Thank You that the same power that raised Jesus from the dead lives on the inside of me. Lord, You know how to resurrect dead things. All You ask me to do is not figure it out and to just believe. So Lord, I believe the promises You've put in my heart — some dreams and promises that I have even let go of. God, You're still going to bring them to pass. Those dreams that look dead . . . You are going to do a resurrection in my life. You've done it in the past, and You can do it again in the future. I'm ready for You to do unusual things, amazing things — not tomorrow or when I get past this tough season, but right now. Thank You, Father. In Jesus' Name, Amen.

"He restores my soul; He leads me in the paths of righteousness for His name's sake."

PSALM 23:3, NKJV

Lord, I believe the promises You've put in my heart — some dreams and promises that I have even let go of. God, You're still going to bring them to pass.

GOD WANTS YOUR EVERY CARE AND WORRY

Dear God,

Your Word says that You will never leave or forsake me, and You inhabit my praises. Right now, Lord, I give You all the praise and all the glory, as I invite You into my circumstances. You are not a God that shies away from what is trying to hinder me. You say, "Bring it all to Me. Give Me your cares. Give Me your concerns. Give Me your worries." You didn't design me to take on every problem, every struggle, everything that the enemy wants to put on me. In faith, I say, "God, I'm giving you my problems right now. In the face of everything, I am going to trust You. I turn it all over to You, knowing that You will invade any situation that I'm in right now." Thank You, Father, for showing out in my life in a greater way. In Jesus' Name, Amen.

"Trust in the LORD with all your heart and lean not on your own understanding; in all your ways submit to Him, and He will make your paths straight."

PROVERBS 3:5–6, NIV

In faith, I say, "God, I'm giving you my problems right now. In the face of everything, I am going to trust You. I turn it all over to You, knowing that You will invade any situation that I'm in right now."

HE IS YOUR STRENGTH IN TOUGH TIMES

Lord,

You said the number of our days You would fulfill. So, I thank You even now, healing, wholeness, strength, and energy are flowing into me and every person who has a need. I thank You for what You said, Lord, that we would run and not be weary. We would walk and not be fearful. We're not fainting. And Lord, not just physically, but also for those of us who have been through loss, those who are in heartache right now, You said You're close to the broken-hearted. Comfort our hearts, Lord. I ask for strength in those times when we don't think we can go on. Thank You that You're at work in our lives right now, breathing in our direction, hope, fresh vision, new beginnings. In Jesus Name, Amen.

"But they who wait for the LORD shall renew their strength; they shall mount up with wings like eagles; they shall run and not be weary; they shall walk and not faint."

ISAIAH 40:31, ESV

Lord, I ask for strength in those times when we don't think we can go on. Thank You that You're at work in our lives right now, breathing in our direction, hope, fresh vision, new beginnings. In Jesus Name, Amen.

GOD DOESN'T CONDEMN YOU

Dear Lord,

I declare to You today that I am done living under guilt and condemnation. I know that You are the Father of mercies and that You gladly welcome me. Thank You that I am coming out of hiding. I don't have to live afraid, upset, worried. Help me to see You for Who You really are. You are not mad at me. You are madly in love with me! I ask for Your blessing today over my life and the lives of all those I love, protecting them, watching over them, favoring them, honoring them. You are breathing in our direction, each new day filled with Your love and goodness and mercy. In Jesus' Name, Amen.

"The LORD your God in your midst, the Mighty One, will save; He will rejoice over you with gladness, He will quiet you with His love, He will rejoice over you with singing."

ZEPHANIAH 3:17, NKJV

Help me to see You for Who You really are. You are not mad at me. You are madly in love with me! I ask for Your blessing today over my life and the lives of all those I love, protecting them, watching over them, favoring them, honoring them.

THANK YOU FOR EVERYTHING, GOD

Lord,

I look back over my life and see the times You made a way where I did not see a way. You opened doors I couldn't open. You healed me when I was sick. You lifted me when I was down. You restored me when I was broken. Lord, You've been good to me. I recognize I didn't get to where I am on my own, without Your blessing, Your favor, Your wisdom, Your guidance. Lord, I thank You for all that You've done. And Lord, I thank You that You didn't bring me this far to leave me where I am, that You have greater things in store. Thank You for helping me make decisions that move me toward my God-given destiny. In Jesus' Name, Amen.

*"Now to Him who is able to do far
more abundantly than all that we
ask or think, according to the power
at work within us."*

EPHESIANS 3:20, ESV

Lord, I thank You that You
didn't bring me this far to leave me
where I am, that You have greater
things in store.

HAVE FAITH WHEN NOTHING MAKES SENSE

Dear God,

You are the waymaker and promise keeper. You are sovereign, and I know that You will get me and my loved ones to where we are supposed to be. We're going to trust You even in the things that don't make sense, in things that we don't understand right now. Lord, we trust You enough to believe that You're in control. It's not random. Your plans for us are good. Help us to believe. Help us to have faith to reach our destiny. Thank You for watching over us, giving us wisdom, protection, and favor. Our lives are in Your hands. We trust You. In Jesus' Name, Amen.

"For My thoughts are not your thoughts, neither are your ways My ways," declares the LORD. "As the heavens are higher than the earth, so are My ways higher than your ways, and My thoughts than your thoughts."

ISAIAH 55:8–9, NIV

We're going to trust You even in the things that don't make sense, in things that we don't understand right now. Lord, we trust You enough to believe that You're in control. It's not random. Your plans for us are good.

PSALM 121:1–2, NIV

I lift up my eyes to the mountains — where does my help come from? My help comes from the LORD, the Maker of heaven and earth.

FEELING SURROUNDED? GOD'S GOT YOU

Heavenly Father,

Thank You that You're surrounding what surrounds me. Thank You that You're greater, not by my might, but in the power of Your Spirit. These things I declare that my loved ones and I are walking boldly in victory into a new, unprecedented era of freedom, in Jesus' Name. We declare that we will flourish underneath the abundance of Your overflow. We declare protections, safety, and great health over all children. Help parents to walk, not in a spirit of fear, but in the power, love, and sound mind You have given us. In Jesus' Name, Amen.

"For God gave us a spirit not of fear but of power and love and self-control."

2 TIMOTHY 1:7, ESV

I declare that my loved ones and I are walking boldly in victory into a new, unprecedented era of freedom, in Jesus' Name. I declare that we will flourish underneath the abundance of Your overflow.

HAND YOUR HURTS TO THE VINDICATOR

Dear God,

I've gone through some unfair situations, gotten some bad breaks. I don't want to live angry, bitter. I'm going to encourage myself in You and the promises of Your Word. Lord, You are a just God. You know every person who has hurt me. Nobody else may know, but God, You saw it, and You knew it wasn't right. Thank You for Your promise in the book of Isaiah — that You would pay me back double for every unfair thing that has happened. Thank You, God, for not just bringing me out the same, but better than before. I can hold my head up high because I am Yours. Lord, help me to let it go and let You be my Vindicator. In Jesus' Name, Amen.

"Instead of your shame there shall be a double portion; instead of dishonor they shall rejoice in their lot; therefore in their land they shall possess a double portion; they shall have everlasting joy."

ISAIAH 61:7, ESV

I can hold my head up high because I am Yours. Lord, help me to let it go and let You be my Vindicator. In Jesus' Name, Amen.

REACH FOR NEW LEVELS OF YOUR DESTINY

Dear Lord,

Thank You that my spiritual ears and eyes are open, sensitive, and responsive to Your voice. Lord, thank You that I will not be at this same place next year as I am right now, but I am moving forward, stepping into new levels of my destiny — closer in my walk with You, better off in my health, better off in how I treat people, kinder, more considerate, quicker to forgive. Lord, let my gifts and talents come out to the full — stronger, bolder, with more confidence, being a bigger blessing. I thank You that I will not get stuck, that You are taking me from glory to glory. In Jesus' Name, Amen.

"Forgetting what is behind and straining toward what is ahead, I press on toward the goal to win the prize for which God has called me heavenward in Christ Jesus."

PHILIPPIANS 3:13–14, NIV

Thank You that my spiritual ears and eyes are open, sensitive, and responsive to Your voice.

GOD WILL MAKE YOUR WRONGS RIGHT

God,

Thank You for showing me what it means to be merciful like You are merciful, that the people who hurt me, who caused me pain have problems of their own. That doesn't excuse their behavior. It shows that somebody hurt them, didn't give them what they needed. I'm turning to You, acknowledging that, yes, what they did to me was wrong. But God, I'm not going to try to pay them back. God, I'm asking You to heal them of their hurts. Give them what they need. I believe the more I can pray for my enemies, when I can bless those that have done me wrong, like the Scripture says, Lord, You are going to make my wrongs right. In Jesus' Name, Amen.

"Judge not, and you shall not be judged. Condemn not, and you shall not be condemned. Forgive, and you will be forgiven."

LUKE 6:37, NKJV

I believe the more I can pray for my enemies, when I can bless those that have done me wrong, like the Scripture says, Lord, You are going to make my wrongs, right. In Jesus' Name, Amen.

MAKE ROOM FOR GOD TODAY

Dear God,

I'm getting into agreement with Your Word that says, "Cast your cares upon the Lord because He cares for you." That tells me that You care about what I am concerned about. But You also have everything in the palm of Your hand. And if I give You my cares and concerns, that leaves room for what You can do in my life. I see that if I'm taking up all the space with worries, I'm not leaving room for You to work. Today, I'm making room for You, Lord. I'm not going to be so filled with my concerns, my cares, my what-ifs that I can't make room for You because what You can take care of is far better than what I can take care of. You can do a greater work than I ever could do in my life. So, thank You that You are aiding me in casting all of my cares and concerns on to You. Father, I give You all the praise and all the glory. In Jesus' Name, Amen.

". . . casting all your cares [all your anxieties, all your worries, and all your concerns, once and for all] on Him, for He cares about you [with deepest affection, and watches over you very carefully]."

1 PETER 5:7, AMP

Today, I'm making room for You, Lord. I'm not going to be so filled with my concerns, my cares, my what-ifs that I can't make room for You because what You can take care of is far better than what I can take care of.

YOUR RENEWING IS IN THE WAITING

Father,

I'm reminded of the verse in Isaiah 40:31 that says, *"They that wait upon the Lord shall renew their strength . . ."* I need strength today, Lord, as I wait on You for answers, for things to change. It's easy to become weary and discouraged. God, renew my spirit. Help me to wait well with an attitude of faith. I believe You are strengthening me, and You're going to do things that will make it absolutely clear Your hand is on my life. Father, thank You so much for being a God Who provides. You are Jehovah Jireh, the One Who meets every need I have. Father, I come into Your presence with a rendered heart, a surrendered heart, thanking You that You'll do what only You can do — that You'll fill me with Your strength, with Your wisdom, with Your purpose and that You'll bring miracles into my life even now. Father, thank You for it in Jesus' Name, I pray, Amen.

*"I remain confident of this: I will
see the goodness of the LORD in
the land of the living. Wait for the
LORD; be strong and take heart
and wait for the LORD."*

PSALM 27:13–14, NIV

I believe You are strengthening me, and
You're going to do things that will make
it absolutely clear Your hand is on my life.
Father, thank You so much for being a God
who provides. You are Jehovah Jireh, the
One Who meets every need I have.

GOD IS GOING BEFORE YOU

Lord,

I believe that the best is still out in front of me.
I'm enlarging my vision and stirring up my faith!
The coming days and months will be a bountiful
time, a productive time, a favor-filled time. As I
read this today, I'm committing my life afresh and
anew into Your hands. Thank You that You are
going before me, making crooked places straight.
You are opening the right doors and closing the
wrong doors. You are bringing the right people
across my path. Lord, right now, I let go of the
old, the disappointments, what didn't work out,
the mistakes I've made; and I let today be a new
beginning. I believe breakthroughs are coming,
favor is coming, healing is coming. In Jesus'
Name, Amen.

"For You, O LORD, will bless the righteous; with favor You will surround him as with a shield."

PSALM 5:12, NKJV

The coming days and months will be a bountiful time, a productive time, a favor-filled time. As I read this today, I'm committing my life afresh and anew into Your hands. I believe breakthroughs are coming, favor is coming, healing is coming. In Jesus' Name, Amen.

GOD CAN DO ANYTHING BUT FAIL YOU

Dear God,

You've given me some big dreams and promises, and I am absolutely convinced that they are coming to pass. There is no sign of it — yet. But, in my heart, there is this knowing that You are working behind the scenes, even now, to make things happen that I can't make happen. So, I lean into that today, overflowing with hope that my finances are more than enough. My health is good. My children will be strong in You. In other words, I'm going to hope on in faith. You've not failed me before, and I know You won't start now. Thank You, Father. In Jesus' Name, Amen.

"When everything was hopeless, Abraham believed anyway, deciding to live not on the basis of what he saw he couldn't do but on what God said He would do."

ROMANS 4:18, MSG

I'm going to hope on in faith. You've not failed me before, and I know You won't start now. Thank You, Father. In Jesus' Name, Amen.

SAY "YES" TO GOD'S GOOD PLANS

Father,

You have given me breath and life and strength for this journey. I declare that I am going to make the necessary changes, so I can stay in balance, Lord. Not worried, not stressed, but keeping my eyes on You. Lord, I thank You for bringing the healing, the direction, the favor, Lord, that You will help me become what I have been created to be. Show me areas where I am being drained. Show me areas in my life where I need courage to say no, Lord, so that I can say yes to Your plan for my life. And help me to reach the fullness of my destiny. In Jesus' Name, Amen.

"For we are God's masterpiece. He has created us anew in Christ Jesus, so we can do the good things He planned for us long ago."

EPHESIANS 2:10, NLT

I thank You for bringing the healing, the direction, the favor, Lord, that You will help me become what I have been created to be.

OPEN DOORS ARE YOURS WITH GOD

Dear Lord,

My hope is in You today. I thank You that faith
is rising in my spirit, that You are strengthening
me, filling me with Your wisdom, Your goodness,
Your mercy. Lord, I thank You, not for an
average year but for a bountiful year. Lord,
You are opening doors that no person can shut,
taking me where I can't go on my own. Father,
You said You would make streams in the desert,
that even in famine, the righteous will have more
than enough. I know that You are a supernatural
God. So, God, my eyes are upon You today. I just
thank You, Lord, for all You have done in the
past, and I believe the best is still in front of me.
In Jesus' Name, Amen.

"They will be like a tree planted by the water that sends out its roots by the stream. It does not fear when heat comes; its leaves are always green. It has no worries in a year of drought and never fails to bear fruit."

JEREMIAH 17:8, NIV

Father, You said You would make streams in the desert, that even in famine, the righteous will have more than enough. I know that You are a supernatural God. So, God, my eyes are upon You today.

JOEL OSTEEN

Jesus put it this way,
"According to your faith
it will be done unto you."
As you learn to pray bold
prayers and expect big
responses, God will do the
extraordinary in your life!

YOU'RE PROMISED MORE THAN YOU CAN IMAGINE

Lord,

Your mercy amazes me. I still feel some shame and guilt about past mistakes I've made, even though Your Word says in Isaiah 43:25 that "God remembers our sins no more." I have to ask myself, "If God forgets it, why don't I forget it? If the Creator of the universe lets it go, why don't I let it go?" I believe You are showing me this for a purpose and that it's time to quit remembering what You have forgotten! It's time to stop telling You how bad I am, how messed up I am, how I lost my temper. Lord, I see that You have forgiven me completely the very first time I asked. Now my heart is open to receiving Your mercy that covers every mistake, every failure, everything that once shamed me. Thank You, Lord. In Jesus' Name, Amen.

"I — yes, I alone — will blot out your sins for My own sake and will never think of them again."

ISAIAH 43:25, NLT

I have to ask myself, "If God forgets it, why don't I forget it? If the Creator of the universe lets it go, why don't I let it go?" I believe You are showing me this for a purpose and that it's time to quit remembering what You have forgotten!

TAKE OFF PEOPLE'S LABELS OF YOU

God,

Thank You for Your mercies that are new every morning. I grab hold of them today. Lord, I've got some people trying to come against me. They're trying to label me a certain way, make me feel condemned. But they can't stop what You have ordained for my life. They may put all kinds of labels on me, but I'm taking them right off because I'm not defined by my mistakes. I'm defined by what You say about me: I am forgiven, I am redeemed, my past is over, my mistakes are behind me, the failures are in my yesterdays, and I'm not bringing them into today. I receive Your mercy. In Jesus' Name, Amen.

"For you, O Lord, are good and forgiving, abounding in steadfast love to all who call upon You."

PSALM 86:5, ESV

I'm defined by what You say about me: I am forgiven, I am redeemed, my past is over, my mistakes are behind me, the failures are in my yesterdays, and I'm not bringing them into today.

COME INTO GOD'S PRESENCE AND REST

Father,

I am so thankful for this time with You, knowing that You are a good God. You will help me. You will crown my efforts with success. You're not mad at me. You are madly in love with me! I'm pausing right now and focusing on You. I say, world, you just stand still right now because I am in the presence of Almighty God. Lord, You are a personal and up-close God. You are as close as the very breath I breathe. You've never left me or forsaken me. And Lord, I'm so grateful how Your love always chases me down. In Jesus' Name I pray, Amen.

*"And we have believed,
and have come to know, that You
are the Holy One of God."*

JOHN 6:69, ESV

Father, You are as close as the
very breath I breathe. You've never
left me or forsaken me. And Lord,
I'm so grateful how Your love
always chases me down. In Jesus'
Name I pray, Amen.

BELIEVE, YES, BELIEVE GOD'S WORD!

Dear Lord,

I know You are a promise keeper, a miracle worker, a waymaker. I'm speaking faith into my future right now in this prayer time with You. Lord, You're still on the throne. I know You're fighting my battles, and I wouldn't be alive unless there were some great victories up in front of me. I'm stirring my faith up to believe bigger! I'm a believer, not a doubter. There are enough doubters in the world. Today I'm tuning all that out and saying what You say of me: I am healed. I am free. I am a masterpiece. In Jesus' Name, Amen.

"Jesus said to him, 'I am the way, and the truth, and the life. No one comes to the Father except through Me.'"

JOHN 14:6, ESV

There are enough doubters in the world. Today I'm tuning all that out and saying what You say of me: I am healed. I am free. I am a masterpiece. In Jesus' Name, Amen.

GOD CAN DO ANYTHING

Father God,
Your Word says in Ephesians 3:20 that You are
able to do exceedingly abundantly above all that
we ask or think. Lord, that is a favorite scripture
of many of Your children. Today, I pray for them
and for my own circumstances, believing that
You are making room for far-and-beyond favor
in our lives. You're positioning us under the open
windows of Heaven. You have new opportunities
for us, good breaks, blessings that will chase us
down. We don't see how this could happen, but
You have a thousand ways to increase us that
we have never thought of. You can bless us with
one good break, one promotion, one idea, one
inheritance, and we are thrust to new levels of
our destiny. Thank You, Lord, for making a way
where we don't see a way. In Jesus' Name, Amen.

"God can do anything, you know — far more than you could ever imagine or guess or request in your wildest dreams! He does it not by pushing us around but by working within us, His Spirit deeply and gently within us."

EPHESIANS 3:20, MSG

Lord, You're positioning us under the open windows of Heaven. You have new opportunities for us, good breaks, blessings that will chase us down. We don't see how this could happen, but You have a thousand ways to increase us that we have never thought of.

A PRAYER AND DECLARATION FOR HEALING

Lord,

I'm in need of healing — some might even say a miracle. God, You know the details. I'm here, Lord, to be filled with faith, to declare Your Word and to come into agreement with You. So, Father, I stand on the promise that I am Yours, a child of the Most High God. I have royalty in my blood. There is a crown of favor that belongs to me. I was not made to live defeated, depressed, addicted, unfulfilled. My mind may be in a fog, but I believe in my spirit something is coming alive. Strongholds that have held me back are being broken. Wrong mindsets, limited thinking, defeated mentality — those chains are being loosed. I'm equipped and empowered to receive Your healing and wholeness. In Jesus' Name, Amen.

"'He Himself bore our sins' in His body on the cross, so that we might die to sins and live for righteousness; 'by His wounds you have been healed.'"

1 PETER 2:24, NIV

Strongholds that have held me back are being broken. Wrong mindsets, limited thinking, defeated mentality — those chains are being loosed. I'm equipped and empowered to receive Your healing and wholeness. In Jesus' Name, Amen.

GOD IS CLOSE TO THE HURTING

Lord,

I am praying for myself and my loved ones who are in tough times, going through loss. You said You are close to those who are hurting. You said You're close to the brokenhearted. Today, I ask for Your comfort and protection, to help us know down in our spirits that there are new beginnings in store. Lord, I pray that we feel Your presence, the peace only You can give. Thank You that we will see good days still in front of us. You said weeping endures for a night, but joy is coming in the morning. I thank You for hope, fresh vision, fresh anointing, and new beginnings. In Jesus' Name, Amen.

"The thief does not come except to steal, and to kill, and to destroy. I have come that they may have life, and that they may have it more abundantly."

JOHN 10:10, NKJV

Today, I ask for Your comfort and protection, to help us know down in our spirits that there are new beginnings in store. Lord, I pray that we feel Your presence, the peace only You can give.

GOD IS MAKING YOUR PATH CLEAR

Father,

Today, I commit my dreams, my loved ones, my career, my health, my decisions all into Your hands. Lord, I put You first place and thank You for leading me, guiding me, directing my steps — that You're making the path clear. Lord, I let go of all the mistakes I've made, what I should've done better. I am not going to go another day with guilt, fear, doubt, or condemnation. I receive Your mercy today, and I am letting go of the old and receiving the new, Lord. I just thank You that I'm walking today with fresh vision, with fresh anointing, with fresh favor, and that You're taking me where I can't go on my own. In Jesus' Name, Amen.

"I have been crucified with Christ. It is no longer I who live, but Christ Who lives in me. And the life I now live in the flesh I live by faith in the Son of God, Who loved me and gave Himself for me."

GALATIANS 2:20, ESV

Lord. I just thank You that I'm walking today with fresh vision, with fresh anointing, with fresh favor, and that You're taking me where I can't go on my own. In Jesus' Name, Amen.

SEE MORE OF GOD IN YOUR LIFE

Lord God,

When I look out over my life, I don't want to just see what is happening, the problems, the circumstances that won't change. I want to see more of You, Father, and for You to show out in my life. Today, I'm believing that this life is more than just a journey, a daily walk. That's good, but I also believe that I'm going somewhere good with You, Lord. Give me a new, fresh vision for my life. And I thank You Father that You are good. You flung stars into the heavens. You created something out of nothing. Father, I thank You that I will see something good in my life today. In Jesus' Name, Amen.

"Beloved, we are God's children now, and what we will be has not yet appeared; but we know that when He appears we shall be like Him, because we shall see Him as He is."

1 JOHN 3:2, ESV

I want to see more of You, Father, and for You to show out in my life.

LET THE LORD HELP YOU BELIEVE

God,

Like David, I have some giants in my life today — things I'm up against that are so much bigger than myself. But Lord, I'm going to put my trust in You. I realize that it's all setting me up for You to show out in my life. Help me to believe, God. Help me to become all that You have created me to be. Lord, as I do my part, I thank You that You will breathe on my gifts and talents. Lord, You have done it in the past, but I'm asking You to do it again. Take me to a new level in my destiny, so that I see Your goodness in new ways. Thank You, Lord, that You are doing what only You can do, causing me to shine for Your glory. In Jesus' Name, Amen.

"So shall My word be that goes out from My mouth; it shall not return to Me empty, but it shall accomplish that which I purpose, and shall succeed in the thing for which I sent it."

ISAIAH 55:11, ESV

I have some giants in my life today — things I'm up against that are so much bigger than myself. But Lord, like David, I'm going to put my trust in You. I realize that it's all setting me up for You to show out in my life. Help me to believe, God. Help me to become all that You have created me to be.

1 JOHN 5:14–15, NIV

This is the confidence we
have in approaching God:
that if we ask anything
according to His will,
He hears us. And if we
know that He hears us —
whatever we ask — we
know that we have what
we asked of Him.

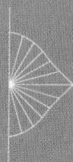

Giving the world the HOPE of Jesus Christ through our media outreaches!

SundayNight.tv

For a full listing, visit
JoelOsteen.com/How-To-Watch

NOTES:

NOTES: